Table of Contents

PHP & MySQL: Novice to Ninja, 6th Edition

by Tom Butler and Kevin Yank

Copyright © 2017 SitePoint Pty. Ltd.

Product Manager: Simon Mackie **Technical Editor:** Bruno Škvorc
English Editor: Ralph Mason **Cover Designer:** Alex Walker

Published by SitePoint Pty. Ltd.

48 Cambridge Street Collingwood
VIC Australia 3066
Web: www.sitepoint.com
Email: books@sitepoint.com

ISBN 978-0-9943469-8-8 (print)

ISBN 978-0-9953827-8-7 (ebook)
Printed and bound in the United States of America

About Tom Butler

Tom is a web developer, a Ph.D student researching software best practices, and university lecturer from the UK with an interest in programming best practices, separation of concerns and a "less is more" approach to code.

About Kevin Yank

Before joining Culture Amp in 2015, Kevin taught a generation of web developers during his time at SitePoint, starting with the first edition of the book that you now hold in your hands. While there, he helped to launch success stories like 99designs and Flippa. More recently, he quizzed web developers on HTML, CSS and JavaScript by leading the team behind Sit the Test, and has spoken at tech conferences around the world. On weekends he performs improvised theatre with Impro Melbourne, which is a lot more like building websites than you might expect.

About SitePoint

SitePoint specializes in publishing fun, practical, and easy-to-understand content for web professionals. Visit http://www.sitepoint.com/ to access our blogs, books, newsletters, articles, and community forums. You'll find a stack of information on JavaScript, PHP, Ruby, mobile development, design, and more.

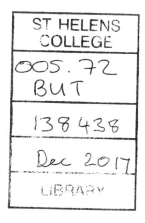

Chapter 5   **Relational Database Design** 183

Chapter 6   **Structured PHP Programming**.....208

Chapter 7   Improving the Insert and Update Functions 247

Chapter 8   Objects and Classes 294

Chapter 9   **Creating an Extensible**

Framework **353**

Chapter 12   MySQL Administration.................497

Chapter 14   Content Formatting with Regular Expressions 617

Preface

It was 1998, I was twelve, and my parents had just bought the family our first modern PC. It wasn't long before I had figured out how to change the code for one of my favorite first-person shooter games—little things like making the rocket launcher fire a hundred rockets a second instead of one, then having it fire a hundred rockets in every direction … and promptly crashing the game. I was hooked, and I've been programming ever since.

The game was multiplayer. Other people had also discovered how to change the code, and the arms race quickly escalated. Someone would fire a hundred rockets at me. I'd have a script ready that would instantly build a wall right in front of me to block them all.

My opponent would spawn a dozen land mines underneath me. I'd turn off the gravity, then jump, soaring away from the impending explosion. Everyone could fly. It got to the point where it was no longer fun. You'd enter a game and someone had written a script to teleport you to the other side of the map, kill you instantly and force you to respawn, repeating the process a dozen times a second. They'd freeze your controls too, of course.

We discovered ways to block all this, but by the end it was a stalemate. Whoever managed to enter the game first could take complete control of it, and no matter how good your scripts were, there was nothing you could do. It was fun while it lasted.

That's how I learned the basics of coding, and that the only limit is your own imagination and creativity. During that time, I'd also taught myself HTML, and had my own website where I shared some of my game hacking techniques and scripts. No, the website is not still up. Yes, it was terrible, full of bad grammar and cheesy animations (which was the style at the time, I promise!).

By 2000, I had taught myself the basics of PHP/MySQL and was running a website for a group of fellow gamers. I wrote some crude PHP scripts for posting news on the website, as well as polls, and even a script for handling our mini-tournament rankings and fixtures.

After that, I moved onto writing desktop applications in a horrible language called Delphi, writing tools that aided people in modding various games. I graduated from University in 2007 with a degree in Software Engineering, worked for various companies as a PHP developer, and these days I'm back at the University studying for a PhD and working as a lecturer, spreading my passion for programming.

I'm 31 now, and I've been programming for more of my life than not. It's fun, it's something I thoroughly enjoy doing. I'm writing this book to share my knowledge with you and help you steer clear of some traps that are easy to fall into.

Learning to code is very enjoyable and rewarding. You can watch your program come alive as you build it. However, it can also be an incredibly frustrating experience. In this book, I'm going to try to use my own experience to give you a smoother ride than I and a lot of developers have had. I can steer you in the right direction from the start.

Before I introduce you to any code, I'm going to give you some general advice about programming and learning to code which I give to all my students.

Who Should Read This Book

This book is aimed at intermediate and advanced web designers looking to make the leap into server-side programming. You'll be expected to be comfortable with simple HTML, as I'll make use of it without much in the way of explanation. No knowledge of Cascading Style Sheets (CSS) or JavaScript is assumed or required, but if you *do* know JavaScript, you'll find it will make learning PHP a breeze, since these languages are quite similar.

By the end of this book, you can expect to have a grasp of what's involved in building a modern PHP website, the basics of PHP, and tried and tested techniques that are used by developers today.

Programming Has Changed

As a novice developer starting now, there's a lot more you need to know before you can publish a website than someone who was building a website in 2001.

When I started, it was a much simpler time. For example, website security wasn't much of a consideration. Unless you were a bank or a company taking credit card payments, there was very little chance anyone would target your site.

These days, however, every single website is constantly bombarded by bots and scripts specifically looking to exploit even the smallest doors you may have left open.

The way PHP scripts are written has changed dramatically as well—certainly for the better. It's now much, much easier to download and use someone else's code in your own project. The downside to this is that you need a much broader understanding of programming concepts before you can do anything useful.

To keep up with the competition, and with the needs of more demanding projects, PHP and MySQL have also had to evolve. PHP is now a far more intricate and powerful language than it was back in 2001, and MySQL is a vastly more complex and capable database. Learning PHP and MySQL today opens up a lot of doors that would have remained closed to the PHP and MySQL experts of 2001.

That's the good news. The bad news is that, in the same way that a butter knife is easier to figure out than a Swiss army knife (and less likely to cause self-injury!), all these dazzling new features and improvements have indisputably made PHP and MySQL more difficult for beginners to learn.

It Takes 10,000 Hours to Become an Expert

The science behind this statement is questionable, but the sentiment is correct. Programming is a skill, and it's incredibly difficult to master. Don't expect to become proficient overnight. By the end of this book, you'll have a good understanding of PHP, but there's always more to learn, regardless of the level you're at.

Having said that, in programming a little knowledge can go a long way. You'll be surprised how much you can do with just a few tools at your disposal!

You'll find that, after you've learned the very basics, you can achieve almost anything you want. There'll be very little you can't do, even though you only know a fraction of the programming concepts that are out there. The more advanced concepts are about making your code more efficient, quicker and easier to write, and much simpler to build on top of.

Resist the Temptation to Skip Ahead

This is one I reiterate time and time again for my students who miss lectures. Programming concepts build on top of each other. For the most part, you need to learn the earlier concepts before you can move on to the next one. If you try to move too fast, you'll get needlessly confused and make it more difficult for yourself.

There aren't many programming concepts that exist in isolation, so if you get stuck, it's often a result of not fully understanding an earlier concept. Don't be afraid to go back and give yourself a refresher on what you think you already know from before. It's usually quicker overall than struggling and trying to press forward when you get stuck!

You're Not Learning PHP

Yes, you read that right. This book is focused entirely on PHP on MySQL, but don't fall into the trap of thinking you're *learning PHP*. Well, you are learning PHP, but I'm using PHP to teach you *to code.*

When you learn to drive, you don't learn to drive a Ford. You learn the concepts of driving, and you can apply them to any car you get in, even if a few of the controls are in a different place.

Concepts you'll learn here will apply to almost any other language you wish to learn in the future. Sure, there are some differences, but the underlying concepts are the same.

Once you can program proficiently in one language, you can get to a reasonable standard in another within a few days! So don't read this book thinking "I'm learning PHP," but instead think "I'm learning to code."

It's more important to remember the *concepts* than the *syntax*. You can always look up the correct syntax, but understanding the underlying concepts is more difficult. Which brings me to my next point…

Getting Braces and Semicolons in the Right Place Is the Easy Part

When you start out, you'll constantly put brackets, braces, semicolons, dots and pretty much everything else in the wrong place. You'll forget to put in a single character and your whole program won't work.

This can be incredibly frustrating at first! But once you get the hang of it, you soon realize that getting the syntax right is the easy part. It's easy because it's strict. It's either right or it's wrong. It works or it doesn't.

The hard part is actually writing the *logic*, breaking a problem down to its smallest parts so you can explain it to the computer. The computer will quickly tell you if the syntax is wrong, but there's no way for it to tell you whether you've given it the right instructions to solve the problem at hand.

You Won't Get Anything Done by Planning

You won't get anything done by planning. — Karl Pilkington

If you've done any reading about programming, you've probably heard that you need to spend lots of time designing your code—that you should carefully plan the logic of your program and how it will work before writing a single line of code. You'll come across books and articles that teach development methodologies, something called "requirements engineering", diagrams for visually representing code, and all sorts of tips on how to plan your code out before you write it.

I'm now going to say something that will make most programmers wince: ignore that advice entirely and get stuck into writing code.

When I say this in lectures, my students breathe a sigh of relief. They're there to learn to code, and the best way to learn to code is to start writing.

The fundamental problem with this advice is that it forgets a somewhat obvious fact: to design software, you need to know what tools are available and the problems they solve. Otherwise, any design you come up with will be meaningless if you don't know what tools are available.

Let's assume you know nothing about building a house. You don't know how to use a hammer, a saw, how strong a beam needs to be to support your roof, how deep your foundations need to be, how to plumb in the bathroom, what materials are suitable for which part of the house, etc.

You can spend as long on the design as you like and plan things as carefully as possible, but unless you know what your tools are capable of and their limitations, you'll end up with a design that doesn't fully utilize the tools, or a design that just isn't possible with the tools/materials available to you. Without knowing that you need a six-meter foundation for a three-story house, you can't design a three-story house.

Equally, you can't design a computer program if you don't know how to program!

To demonstrate my point, here's a story from a TED talk called *"Want to help someone? Shut up and listen"*, by Ernesto Strolli.

> It was a project where we Italians decided to teach Zambian people how to grow food. So we arrived there with Italian seeds in southern Zambia in this absolutely magnificent valley going down to the Zambezi River. And we were amazed that the local people in such a fertile valley would not have any agriculture. But instead of asking them how come they were not growing anything, we simply said, "Thank God we're here. Just in the nick of time to save the Zambian people from starvation."
>
> And of course, everything in Africa grew beautifully and we had these magnificent tomatoes. In Zambia, the tomatoes grew even larger than they did in Italy. And we were telling the Zambians, look how easy agriculture is. When the tomatoes were nice and ripe and red, overnight, some 200 hippos came up from the river and they ate everything. And we said to the Zambians, "My God, the hippos." And the Zambians said, "Yes, that's why we have no agriculture here."

Ernesto's team knew exactly what they were doing. They carefully planned everything out and managed to get the result they wanted. However, all that planning and designing was wasted because of something they didn't see coming.

Programmers don't encounter hippos, but there are lots of obstacles you won't be able to anticipate, and you'll inevitably run into them. Any time you spend designing is wasted when the equivalent of 200 hippos come and eat your code. You have to scrap the design and start again.

During this book, I'll warn you about the various hippos you might encounter, but it's a good idea to test it for yourself. Learn by doing. Rush in. Write some code. It almost certainly won't work the first time, but you'll have learned something in the process. Try again with a different approach and you'll come up with something that does work.

There's no way to design a program until you're aware of the problems you're likely to encounter and the limitations of the tools available to you.

Okay, Design Isn't All Bad

To prevent a wave of hate mail from other programmers, I'm going to conclude this section by saying that, for *professional programmers*, spending time up front designing the code before building it is *vital*. However, professionals are writing code they may need to work with for years or decades to come. The code they write needs to be written in such a way that it's extensible and easy for others to follow.

During this book, I'll get you to think about the structure of your code and how to write code that's reusable and extensible. But you're not here to write code that will be used in real projects and will need to be maintained for years to come. You're here to learn. Go and find all those hippos. You'll learn more from making mistakes than you will from code that works right away.

The time you spend planning your code should be proportional to your programming ability. If you're just starting out, as long as you have a broad understanding of what you want the program to do, jump in and start writing code until it does what you want. You can get stuck and try a different approach without feeling like you're *doing it wrong* because it's going against that design you spent hours working on. What I said above about the Concorde fallacy applies here as well.

For the first few chapters, at least, just dive in. Run your code, see if it works. Try solving some of the problems I set before I give you the solutions. You'll learn more by discovering the solutions yourself than blindly typing in the code I give you.

As your knowledge grows, you'll have a firmer understanding of what tools are available and the way problems need to be broken up. Once you reach that level, you can start planning things out in more detail before writing your code.

Code Samples

Code in this book is displayed using a fixed-width font, like so:

```
<h1>A Perfect Summer's Day</h1>
<p>It was a lovely day for a walk in the park.
The birds were singing.</p>
```

If the code is to be found in the book's code archive, the name of the example will appear at the top of the program listing, like this:

```
                                                    0-1. Layout

.footer {
    background-color: #CCC;
    border-top: 1px solid #333;
}
```

Some lines of code should be entered on one line, but we've had to wrap them because of page constraints. An ↪ indicates a line break that exists for formatting purposes only, and should be ignored:

```
URL.open("http://www.sitepoint.com/responsive-web-design-real
↪ -user-testing/?responsive1");
```

Conventions Used

You'll notice that we've used certain typographic and layout styles throughout this book to signify different types of information. Look out for the following items.

Tips, Notes, and Warnings

 Hey, You!

Tips provide helpful little pointers.

 Ahem, Excuse Me ...

Notes are useful asides that are related—but not critical—to the topic at hand. Think of them as extra tidbits of information.

 Watch Out!

Warnings highlight any gotchas that are likely to trip you up along the way.

Supplementary Materials

- The book's code archive, which contains the code files used throughout the book.[1]. Instructions on how to use the sample code are contained in <u>Appendix A</u>.
- <u>https://www.sitepoint.com/community/</u> are SitePoint's forums, for help on any tricky web problems.
- **books@sitepoint.com** is our email address, should you need to contact us to report a problem, or for any other reason.

[1.] https://github.com/spbooks/phpmysql6

Chapter **1**

Installation

In this book, I'll guide you as you take your first steps beyond the static world of building web pages with the purely client-side technologies of HTML, CSS, and JavaScript. Together, we'll explore the world of building websites, and discover the dizzying array of dynamic tools, concepts, and possibilities they open up. Whatever you do, don't look down!

Okay, maybe you *should* look down. After all, that's where the rest of this book is. But remember, you were warned!

Before you build your first dynamic website, you must gather together the tools you'll need for the job. Like baking a cake, you'll need the ingredients before you can start following the recipe. In this chapter, I'll show you how to download and set up the software packages required.

If you're used to building websites with HTML, CSS, and perhaps even a smattering of JavaScript, you're probably familiar with uploading the files that make up your site to a certain location. It might be a web hosting service you've paid for, web space provided by your Internet service provider (ISP), or maybe a web server set up by the IT department of the company you work for. In any case, once you copy your files to any of these destinations, a software program called a web server is able to find and serve up copies of those files whenever they're requested by a web browser like Microsoft Edge, Internet Explorer, Google Chrome, Safari, or Firefox. Common web server software programs you may have heard of include Apache HTTP Server (Apache), NGINX and Internet Information Services (IIS).

PHP is a server-side scripting language. You can think of it as a plugin for your web server that enables it to do more than just send exact copies of the files requested by web browsers. With PHP installed, your web server will be able to run little programs (called PHP scripts) that can do tasks like retrieve up-to-the-minute information from a database and use it to generate a web page on the fly, before sending it to the browser that requested it. Much of this book will focus on writing PHP scripts to do exactly that. PHP is completely free to download and use.

For your PHP scripts to retrieve information from a database, you must first *have* a database. That's where MySQL comes in. MySQL is a **relational database management system**, or RDBMS. We'll discuss the exact role it plays and how it works later, but briefly, it's a software program that's able to organize and manage many pieces of information efficiently while keeping track of how all those pieces of information are related to each other. MySQL also makes that information really easy to access with server-side scripting languages such as PHP. And, like PHP, it's completely free for most uses.

The goal of this first chapter is to set you up with a web server equipped with PHP and MySQL. I'll provide step-by-step instructions that work on recent versions of Windows, macOS and Linux, so no matter what flavor of computer you're using, the instructions you need should be right here.

Your Own Web Server

Chances are, your current web host's web server already has PHP and MySQL installed—which is one of the reasons PHP and MySQL are so popular. If your web host is so equipped, the good news is that you'll be able to publish your first website without having to shop for a web host that supports the right technologies.

When developing static websites, you can simply load your HTML files directly from your hard disk into your browser to see how they look. There's no web server software involved when you do this, which is fine, because web browsers can read and understand HTML code all by themselves.

However, when it comes to dynamic websites built using PHP and MySQL, your web browser needs some help. Web browsers are unable to understand PHP scripts. Instead, PHP scripts contain instructions for a PHP-savvy web server to execute in order to *generate* the HTML code that browsers can understand.

Even if you have an existing web host that supports PHP, you're still going to want to be able to run PHP scripts yourself without needing to use someone else's server. For this, you'll need to set up your own web server. The word "server" might make you think of a large, air-conditioned room filled with big computers in racks. But don't worry, you don't need any fancy new hardware. Your laptop or desktop will work just fine.

To run PHP scripts on your web host, you need to write them in your editor, open your FTP or SSH client and upload them to the server. Only then can you see the result in your browser by navigating to the URI of the file you created. If you made a mistake and there's an error, you'll need to change the code, go back into your FTP program, upload the file again and then reload the page. This is tedious, and uses up precious time that you could be using to write code. By running a server on your own PC, you'll be able to save a file in your editor and view the changes in your browser by simply refreshing the page—no file uploading required. This is a real time saver, and one of the biggest (although not only!) advantages of running a server on your PC—even if you have a perfectly good web host already.

So how do you get a web server running on your PC? There are three methods of achieving this, each with its own advantages and disadvantages.

Server Setup 1: Manually Installing All the Software Components

Apache is a web server, and like most software it comes with an installer that lets you easily set it up on your PC. Without much effort, you can have it *serve* web pages. However, there are hundreds of configuration options, and unless you know what you're doing, it can be time consuming and confusing to get it working for developing PHP websites.

For our purposes of running PHP scripts, a web server alone is not enough. For manual installation, you'll also need to install PHP—which doesn't have an installer—and configure it. As with Apache, there are lots of options, and the defaults are set up as if you're running a live website. For developing code, this is bad, as there are no errors shown. If you made a mistake, you'll get a blank page with no indication of what went wrong. Even a single character out of place—such as a missing brace or semicolon—will give you a blank page, with no indication of what caused the problem. To solve this, you'll need to manually configure the PHP installation and tweak the settings to show error messages and enable other tools that make development a more pleasant task.

You'll also need to configure Apache to talk with PHP, so that when someone connects to the server and requests a file with a .php extension, the file is first sent to PHP for processing.

For this book, you'll also want MySQL, which means manually installing and configuring that as well.

Apache, MySQL and PHP each have dozens of configuration options, and unless you know exactly what you're doing, they can be difficult to set up. Even if you're an expert, it will take at least an hour to get everything working!

Manual installation requires a significant amount of knowledge or research and is beyond the scope of this book. Although being able to configure a server is a useful skill, it doesn't help you learn how to program using PHP—which is what you're really interested in if you're reading this book.

This option is not for the faint hearted, and even for seasoned professionals it's very easy to miss some important settings. Luckily for us, we don't need to worry about setting up and configuring all the software individually.

Server Setup 2: Pre-packaged Installations

The problems with manual installations have been recognized by groups of developers over the years, and to overcome them they've built pre-packaged installations—a single installer that installs PHP, Apache, MySQL and other relevant software, all pre-configured with appropriate settings for developers like you. Some example packages are XAMPP (X, Apache, MySQL, PHP, Perl), WAMP (Windows, Apache, MySQL, PHP) and LAMP (Linux, Apache, MySQL, PHP).

This is obviously a lot simpler than manually installing each piece of software, and doesn't require learning how to configure your server. It's quick and easy and a lot better than a manual installation, though there are still a couple of problems you may encounter with this method:

1. Your web host is probably running Linux, but your PC probably isn't. Although Apache, MySQL and PHP work in Windows, Linux or macOS, there are some big differences between the way the operating systems work. On Windows, file names are not *case-sensitive*, meaning that `FILE.PHP` is the same as `file.php` and `fIlE.pHp`. On your web host, this will almost certainly not be the case! This causes frequent problems when a script working perfectly on your Windows development server doesn't work once it's uploaded, because files are being referenced in the code with the wrong case.

2. Apache and MySQL are *servers*, and they run in the background. Even when you're not developing software, they'll be running, using up your computer's RAM and processing power.

3. Pre-packaged software is always slightly out of date. Although security fixes aren't a priority for a development computer (you shouldn't be allowing people to access it across the web!), it's always useful for developers to stay on the most recent versions of software to check for problems that might be encountered when the software on your web host is updated. If your web host

is using a newer version of PHP than your development server, this can cause problems with features that have been changed or removed. Finally, developers like to play with new features as they're released. You won't be able to do this if you're not using the latest versions!

Although pre-packaged installations are much better than installations, these problems don't make them ideal. Luckily, there's an even better approach!

Server Setup 3: Virtual Servers

The third method of getting a server up and running is a **virtual server**. A virtual server acts like a web server on a different computer. This computer can be running any operating system, and you can connect to it from your PC as if it were somewhere else in the world.

Virtualization software such as VMWare and VirtualBox is common. As a web developer, you may be familiar with tools such as modern.ie[2], a helpful service provided by Microsoft that lets you download **virtual machines** running various versions of Windows, Microsoft Edge and Internet Explorer. If you want to see what your website looks like in Internet Explorer 8 on Windows XP, you can download the relevant virtual machine and run it in a Window on your Windows 10/macOS/Linux desktop without having to actually install and run Windows 7 with Internet Explorer 8 inside your existing Windows 10, Linux or MacOS installation.

---

[2] "http://modern.ie/

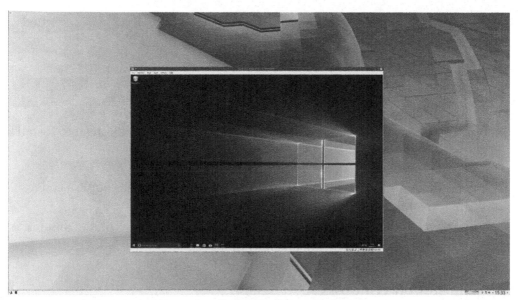

1-2. indows 10 running inside Arch Linux

Software like VirtualBox allows you to run an operating system inside another operating system. For testing Internet Explorer 8, you can run Windows 7 in a virtual machine. However, for our purposes of running PHP scripts, this allows us to do something a lot cooler: we can run a Linux web server with PHP, Apache and MySQL installed on our Windows or macOS PC.

This can be used to allow you to run the exact same versions of PHP, MySQL and Apache that are being used on your web host, on the exact same operating system, which prevents any issues that may exist due to version differences or differences in the operating systems being used.

One of the biggest advantages is that you can download pre-configured virtual machines, like the Windows XP and Internet Explorer 8 virtual machine provided by Microsoft, or a virtual machine that has PHP, Apache and MySQL installed and configured to work together. This is like the pre-configured package but runs on Linux as if it's a real web server on your network.

The downside to all this is that you have to download an entire operating system in order to run your code. That means more downloading, but in the era of 10 Mbit/s+ internet connections and terabyte hard drives, this isn't really an issue worth worrying about! Because this is a best-of-both-worlds approach, and has advantages over the other two methods, I'll be showing you how to get a virtual server up and running. It's a lot easier than you might think!

Your Own Virtual Server

Before writing any PHP code and developing your website, you'll need to install several pieces of software to run a virtual server:

- Git, which allows you to quickly and easily download other people's code.
- VirtualBox, the software that runs the virtual machines.
- Vagrant, a tool that allows quick and easy configuration of virtual machines. This works with VirtualBox to create your server.

Installation on Windows

Firstly, download and install the latest versions of the following software:

1. Git[3]
2. VirtualBox[4]
3. Vagrant[5]

Once you've installed all the software, use your Start menu to open a newly installed program called "Git Bash" and proceed to the *Getting Started with Vagrant* section below. All the commands given should be typed into the Git Bash program, not Windows Command Prompt.

Installation on macOS

Firstly, download and install the latest versions of the following software:

1. Git[6]
2. VirtualBox[7]

[3.] http://www.git-scm.org/
[4.] https://www.virtualbox.org/
[5.] http://www.vagrantup.com/
[6.] http://www.git-scm.org/
[7.] https://www.virtualbox.org/

3. Vagrant[8]

Once you've installed all the software, open up the Terminal program and proceed to the *Getting Started with Vagrant* section below.

Installation on Linux

Linux makes installing software very simple. On most distributions, this can be done via your package manager.

Debian/Ubuntu:

```
sudo apt-get install git dkms virtualbox virtualbox-dkms
↪ vagrant
```

Fedora/Red Hat:

```
sudo dnf install git VirtualBox vagrant vagrant-libvirt
```

Arch Linux:

```
sudo pacman -S git virtualbox vagrant
```

Once you've installed all the software, open up your favorite terminal program and proceed with the following steps below.

Getting Started with Vagrant

Now that you have all the software installed, it's time to download a virtual server. From here on, the instructions are the same whether you're using Windows, macOS or Linux. For a full tutorial on doing this, see the SitePoint article "Quick Tip: Get a Homestead Vagrant VM Up and Running"[9].

[8.] http://www.vagrantup.com/

We'll be using a pre-built virtual machine (or "box") called Homestead Improved. This contains PHP, MySQL and NGINX already configured for development purposes. To download it, from your terminal prompt firstly navigate into the directory you wish to store your website's files in, and then run these commands:

```
git clone https://github.com/swader/homestead_improved
↪ my_project
cd my_project; mkdir -p Project/public
bin/folderfix.sh
```

 Using the Command Prompt to Navigate

If you don't know how to navigate around using the command prompt, you use the `cd` command (short for *change directory*). Git Bash uses Unix style paths, so `C:\Users\Tom\Desktop` becomes `/c/Users/Tom/Desktop`. If you want to store your files inside your **Documents** directory, e.g. **Documents**/**Website**, you can navigate to it using `cd /c/Users/[Account Name]/Documents/Website`.

If you have any spaces in the directory names, simply surround the entire path with quotation marks, e.g. `cd "/c/Users/[Account Name]/Documents/My Website"`.

After you've run the commands, several files will be created inside your project directory. These files contain instructions for creating and configuring the virtual server. Finally, you just need to start the server using this single command:

```
vagrant up
```

 Running the Command in the Right Place

You *must* run the `vagrant up` command from the directory that stores the files that were downloaded via the `git clone` command earlier. If you type `ls`, you should see `Vagrantfile` listed. If you don't see it, you'll need to navigate to the correct directory using the `cd` command.

---

9. http://www.sitepoint.com/quick-tip-get-homestead-vagrant-vm-running/

The server will start and you'll see something like this:

1-3. Running `vagrant up`

If the `vagrant up` Command Hangs

If the `vagrant up` command hangs on the line `Connection timed out.`
`Retrying…` for more than a few minutes, it's likely your PC isn't configured for
virtualization, which it needs to be for running virtual machines. To fix this, you'll
need to boot into your PC's BIOS and enable a technology called VT-x (if you have
an Intel processor) or AMD-V (for AMD processors). To do this, refer to your
computer's manual, or use Google to find instructions for getting into the BIOS on
your PC. This setting is sometimes called **virtualization technology**, **VT-x**, **SVM** or
hardware virtualization, depending on the make of your PC.

The first time vagrant runs, it will take a few minutes to load, as it requires
downloading quite a large file. Don't worry, it won't take this long each time you
want to start your server. In future, all the downloading and initial configuration
is done.

Unlike using a manual NGINX/PHP/MySQL installation directly on your PC, the server is only started when you want it to be, by running `vagrant up`. You can stop the server at any time, by running `vagrant halt`, and boot it again using `vagrant up` when you need it.

You can also use `vagrant suspend`, which is like shutting the lid on your laptop. It pauses the virtual machine so it doesn't need to reboot next time you run `vagrant up`. Unless you're low on disk space, `suspend` is preferable, as the virtual machine will start up considerably faster.

One of the directories that was created is called `Project`. Open this directory and the `public` directory inside it. This is where you'll store your PHP scripts, HMTL files, CSS files and images. Any files placed inside the `public` directory will be accessible on your virtual server.

Using your favorite text editor, create a file called `index.html` that contains the following code:

```html
<!DOCTYPE html>
<html>
    <body>
        <h1>Hello World!</h1>
    </body>
</html>
```

You can now view your web page on the server. The server acts like a computer on your local network and uses the IP address `192.168.10.10`. If you open your browser and navigate to `http://192.168.10.10/`, you should see your `Hello World` test page. If you can see the page, it means your server is running and you've written your file to the right directory.

The numeric IP address may look at little strange. Usually, when you access to a website, you connect to something like `http://www.sitepoint.com/` or `http://www.google.com`. However, behind the scenes all websites use an IP address. If you type `http://216.58.201.46/` into your browser, you'll see the Google home page.

It would be very hard to remember the IP address of every website you wanted to visit. (I struggle with my PIN!) So we typically buy a domain name and associate it with an IP address. When you type `sitepoint.com` into your web browser, the browser looks up the corresponding IP address and actually connects to that behind the scenes. You can think of it a bit like a phone book. Rather than remembering someone's phone number, you can look through a contact list and find them by a more easily recognizable name. This process happens for every website you visit, and every website has an IP address similar to 129.168.10.10.[10]

It would be possible to buy a domain name and associate it with `192.168.10.10`, but for the purpose of this book we'll just stick to the IP address, as we won't need to type it often.

 Linux Issues

If you're using Linux and either the `vagrant up` command isn't working or you're unable to connect to the web server on `http://192.168.10.10/`, see Appendix B.

 Text Editors

Text editors provided by your operating system, such as Notepad or TextEdit, aren't really suitable for editing HTML and PHP scripts. However, there are a number of solid text editors with rich support for editing PHP scripts that you can download for free. Here are a few that work on Windows, macOS, and Linux:

- Atom[11]
- Sublime Text[12]
- Brackets[13]

These are all very similar, and for the purposes of this book, any of them is a good choice and will make your life as a developer a lot simpler than Notepad or TextEdit.

[10.] Now, or in the near future (depending on your ISP), you might start seeing IP addresses in the format `2001:0db8:85a3:0000:0000:8a2e:0370:7334`. This is an *IPv6* address, which works in the exact same way as the notation shown in this chapter. The problem with IP addresses in the format 0.0.0.0 (IPv4) is that there are *only* around 4 billion possible addresses. That sounds like a lot, but every single website, phone or computer connected to the Internet needs a unique IP address ... and we've pretty much run out of them! The new IPv6 addresses will keep us going for quite a while longer.

In this chapter, you've learned how to set up a web server with Homestead Improved, and how to host an HTML file on the server. I've only covered the basics in order to quickly get to the meat and bones of this book: actually programming in PHP. However, having a good development workflow as a PHP developer is a skill in its own right. For more information on Homestead Improved and PHP workflows, see *Jump Start PHP Environment*[14], by Bruno Škvorc. For our purposes, however, the server is up and running, and you're ready to write your first PHP script.

---

11. "http://atom.io/
12. http://www.sublimetext.com/
13. http://brackets.io/
14. https://www.sitepoint.com/premium/books/jump-start-php-environment

Chapter

2

Introducing PHP

Now that you have your virtual server up and running, it's time to write your first PHP script. PHP is a server-side language. This concept may be a little difficult to grasp, especially if you've only ever designed websites using client-side languages like HTML, CSS, and JavaScript.

A server-side language is similar to JavaScript in that it allows you to embed little programs (scripts) into the HTML code of a web page. When executed, these programs give you greater control over what appears in the browser window than HTML alone can provide. The key difference between JavaScript and PHP is the stage of loading the web page at which these embedded programs are executed.

Client-side languages like JavaScript are read and executed by the web browser after downloading the web page (embedded programs and all) from the web server. In contrast, server-side languages like PHP are run by the web *server*, before sending the web page to the browser. Whereas client-side languages give you control over how a page behaves once it's displayed by the browser, server-side languages let you generate customized pages on the fly before they're even sent to the browser.

Once the web server has executed the PHP code embedded in a web page, the result takes the place of the PHP code in the page. All the browser sees is standard HTML code when it receives the page, hence the name "server-side language." Let's look at simple example of some PHP that generates a random number between 1 and 10 and then displays it on the screen:

2-1. PHP-RandomNumber

```
<!DOCTYPE html>
<html lang="en">
    <head>
        <meta charset="utf-8">
        <title>Random Number</title>
    </head>
    <body>
        <p>Generating a random number between 1 and 10:
            <?php

            echo rand(1, 10);

            ?>
        </p>
    </body>
</html>
```

Most of this is plain HTML. Only the line between <?php and ?> is PHP code. <?php marks the start of an embedded PHP script and ?> marks its end. The web server is asked to interpret everything between these two delimiters and convert it to regular HTML code before it sends the web page to the requesting browser. If you right-click inside your browser and choose **View Source** (the text may be different depending on the browser you're using) you can see that the browser is presented with the following:

```
<!DOCTYPE html>
<html lang="en">
    <head>
        <meta charset="utf-8">
        <title>Random Number</title>
    </head>
    <body>
        <p>Generating a random number between 1 and 10:
            5
        </p>
    </body>
</html>
```

Notice that all signs of the PHP code have disappeared. In its place the output of the script has appeared, and it looks just like standard HTML. This example demonstrates several advantages of server-side scripting …

■ **No browser compatibility issues**. PHP scripts are interpreted by the web server alone, so there's no need to worry about whether the language features you're using are supported by the visitor's browser.

■ **Access to server-side resources**. In the example above, we placed a random number generated by the web server into the web page. If we had inserted the number using JavaScript, the number would be generated in the browser and someone could potentially amend the code to insert a specific number. Granted, there are more impressive examples of the exploitation of server-side resources, such as inserting content pulled out of a MySQL database.

■ **Reduced load on the client**. JavaScript can delay the display of a web page significantly (especially on mobile devices!) as the browser must run the script before it can display the web page. With server-side code, this burden is passed to the web server, which you can make as beefy as your application requires (and your wallet can afford).

■ **Choice**. When writing code that's run in the browser, the browser has to understand how to run the code given to it. All modern browsers understand HTML, CSS and JavaScript. To write some code that's run in the browser, you must use one of these languages. By running code on the server that generates HTML, you have a choice of many languages—one of which is PHP.

Basic Syntax and Statements

PHP syntax will be very familiar to anyone with an understanding of JavaScript, C, C++, C#, Objective-C, Java, Perl, or any other C-derived language. But if these languages are unfamiliar to you, or if you're new to programming in general, there's no need to worry about it.

A PHP script consists of a series of **commands**, or statements. Each statement is an instruction that must be followed by the web server before it can proceed to the next instruction. PHP statements, like those in the aforementioned languages, are always terminated by a semicolon (;).

This is a typical PHP statement:

```
echo 'This is a <strong>test</strong>!';
```

This is an echo statement, which is used to generate content (usually HTML code) to send to the browser. An echo statement simply takes the text it's given and inserts it into the page's HTML code at the position of the PHP script where it was contained.

In this case, we've supplied a string of text to be output: This is a <strong>test</strong>!. Notice that the string of text contains HTML tags (<strong> and </strong>), which is perfectly acceptable.

So, if we take this statement and put it into a complete web page, here's the resulting code:

2-2. PHP-Echo

```
<!DOCTYPE html>
<html lang="en">
    <head>
        <meta charset="utf-8">
        <title>Test page</title>
    </head>
    <body>
 <p><?php echo 'This is a
↪ <strong>test</strong>!'; ?></p>
    </body>
</html>
```

If you place this file on your web server and then request it using a web browser, your browser will receive this HTML code:

```
<!DOCTYPE html>
<html lang="en">
    <head>
        <meta charset="utf-8">
        <title>Test page</title>
    </head>
    <body>
 <p>This is a
↪ <strong>test</strong>!</p>
    </body>
</html>
```

The random.php example we looked at earlier contained a slightly more complex echo statement:

```
echo rand(1, 10);
```

You'll notice that, in the first example, PHP is given some text to print directly, and in the second, PHP is given an instruction to follow. PHP tries to read anything that exists outside quotes as an instruction it must follow. Anything inside quotes is treated as a **string**, which means PHP doesn't process it at all but just passes it to the command you called. So the following code will pass the string This is a test! directly to the echo command:

```
echo 'This is a <strong>test</strong>!';
```

A string is signified using a start quote and an end quote. PHP will see the first ' as the start of the string and find the next ' and use that as the end of the string.

In contrast, the following code will first run the built-in function rand to generate a random number and then pass the result to the echo command:

```
echo rand(1, 10);
```

You can think of built-in functions as tasks that PHP knows how to do without you needing to spell out the details. PHP has many built-in functions that let you do everything, from sending email to working with information stored in various types of databases.

PHP won't try to run anything that's inside a string. The following code won't have the result you may be expecting:

```
echo 'rand(1, 10)';
```

Instead of running the inbuilt function rand, PHP will see it as a string, and rather than printing out a random number, it will actually send the text rand(1, 10) to the browser, which probably isn't what you wanted to do. It's important to understand the difference between a string and *code*. PHP will see any text outside quotes as a series of commands it should follow. Anything inside quotes is a string and is *data* that PHP will work with.

PHP doesn't try to understand strings. They can contain any characters in any order. But code—which is essentially a series of *instructions*—must follow a rigid structure for a computer to understand it.

Syntax Highlighting

Using an editor with syntax highlighting makes it easy to quickly see if something is a string or code. Strings will be shown in a different color from code that needs to be processed.

Quotes

PHP supports both single quotes ' and double quotes " to encase strings. For most purposes, they're interchangeable. PHP developers tend to favor single quotes, because we deal with HTML code a lot, which tends to contain a lot of double quotes. For example:

```
echo '<a href="http://www.sitepoint.com">Click
↳ here</a>';
```

If double quotes were used here, we'd need to tell PHP that the quote after `href=` is not the end of the string by placing a \ before it (known as an **escape character**) and do the same with any quotes we actually want to send to the browser as part of the HTML:

```
echo "<a href=\"http://www.sitepoint.com\">Click
↳ here</a>";
```

For this reason, PHP developers use single quotes, although there are some differences between the two quotes. For our purposes, they are effectively interchangeable.

When you **invoke** a function in PHP—that is, ask it to do its job—you're said to be **calling** that function. Most functions return a value when they're called; PHP then behaves as if you'd actually just typed that returned value in your code instead. In the `echo 'rand(1, 10)';` example, our `echo` statement contains a call to the `rand` function, which returns a random number as a string of text. The `echo` statement then outputs the value returned by the function call.

Every function in PHP can have one or more **arguments** that allow you to make the function behave in a slightly different way. The `rand` function takes two arguments: the minimum random number and the maximum. By changing the values that are passed to the function, you're able to change the way it works. For example, if you wanted a random number between 1 and 50, you could use the code:

```
echo rand(1, 50);
```

You may wonder why we need to surround the arguments with parentheses (`(1, 50)`). The parentheses serve two purposes. First, they indicate that `rand` is a function that you want to call. Second, they mark the beginning and end of a list of arguments—PHP statements that you wish to provide—in order to tell the function what you want it to do. In the case of the `rand` function, you need to provide a minimum and a maximum value. Those values are separated by a comma.

Later on, we'll look at functions that take different kinds of arguments. We'll also consider functions that take no arguments at all. These functions will still need the parentheses, even though there will be nothing to type between them.

Variables, Operators, and Comments

Variables

Variables in PHP are identical to variables in most other programming languages. For the uninitiated, a **variable** can be thought of as a name given to an imaginary box into which any value may be placed. The following statement creates a variable called `$testVariable` (all variable names in PHP begin with a dollar sign) and assigns it a value of `3`:

```
$testVariable = 3;
```

PHP is a **loosely typed** language. This means that a single variable may contain any type of data—be it a number, a string of text, or some other kind of value—and may store different types of values over its lifetime. The following statement—if you were to type it after the aforementioned statement—assigns a new value to the existing $testVariable. Where it used to contain a number, it now contains a string of text:

```
$testVariable = 'Three';
```

Operators

The equals sign we used in the last two statements is called the **assignment operator**, as it's used to assign values to variables. Other operators may be used to perform various mathematical operations on values:

```
$testVariable = 1 + 1;   // assigns a value of 2
$testVariable = 1 - 1;   // assigns a value of 0
$testVariable = 2 * 2;   // assigns a value of 4
$testVariable = 2 / 2;   // assigns a value of 1
```

From these examples, you can probably tell that + is the **addition operator**, - is the **subtraction operator**, * is the **multiplication operator** and / is the **division operator**. These are all called **arithmetic operators**, because they perform arithmetic on numbers.

Comments

Each of the arithmetic lines above ends with a **comment**. Comments enable you to describe what your code is doing. They insert explanatory text into your code—text that the PHP interpreter will ignore. Comments begin with // and they finish at the end of the same line. If you want a comment to span several lines, start it with /*, and end it with */. The PHP interpreter will ignore everything between these two delimiters. I'll be using comments throughout the rest of this book to help explain some of the code I present.

Returning to the operators, one that sticks strings of text together is called the **string concatenation operator**:

```
$testVariable = 'Hi ' . 'there!';   // Assigns a value of 'Hi
↳ there!'
```

Variables may be used almost anywhere that you use a value. Consider this series of statements:

```
$var1 = 'PHP';          // assigns a value of 'PHP' to $var1
$var2 = 5;              // assigns a value of 5 to $var2
$var3 = $var2 + 1;      // assigns a value of 6 to $var3
$var2 = $var1;          // assigns a value of 'PHP' to $var2
 $var4 = rand(1, 12);    // assigns a value to $var4 using
↳ the rand() function
echo $var1;             // outputs 'PHP'
echo $var2;             // outputs 'PHP'
echo $var3;             // outputs '6'
 echo $var4;             // outputs the random number
↳ generated above
echo $var1 . ' rules!'; // outputs 'PHP rules!'
echo '$var1 rules!';    // outputs '$var1 rules!'
echo "$var1 rules!"     // outputs 'PHP rules!'
```

Note the last two lines in particular: if you place a variable inside *single* quotes, it will print the name rather than the contents of the variable. In contrast, when using double quotes, the variable in the string is replaced with the variable's contents.

Placing variables inside double quotes works in simple situations, but for most of this book it won't be usable, as we won't be using such simple code. So it's a good idea to get used to the practice of concatenation (shown in the third from last line).

Control Structures

The examples of PHP code we've seen so far have been either one-statement scripts that output a string of text to the web page, or a series of statements that were to be executed one after the other in order. If you've ever written programs in other languages (such as JavaScript, Objective-C, Ruby, or Python), you already know that practical programs are rarely so simple.

PHP, just like any other programming language, provides facilities that enable you to affect the flow of control. That is, the language contains special statements that you can use to deviate from the one-after-another execution order that has dominated our examples so far. Such statements are called **control structures**. Don't understand? Don't worry! A few examples will illustrate it perfectly.

If Statements

The most basic, and most often used, control structure is the `if` statement. The flow of a program through an `if` statement can be visualized like this:

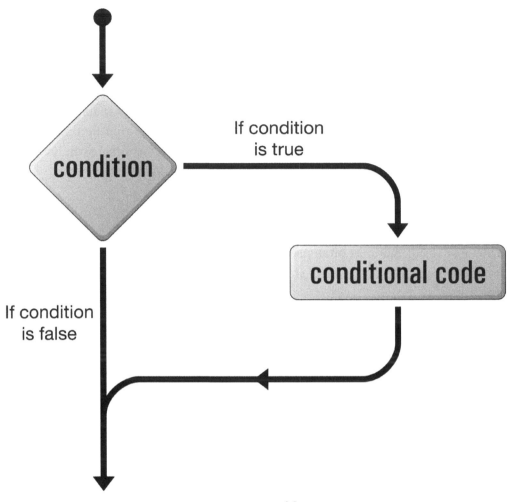

2-3. The logical flow of an **if** statement

Here's what an **if** statement looks like in PHP code:

```
if (condition) {
    ⋮ conditional code to be executed if condition is true
}
```

This control structure lets us tell PHP to execute a set of statements only if some condition is met.

For example, we might want to create a game that mimics a dice roll and in which you have to roll a six to win. The dice roll can be modeled using the rand() function we used earlier and setting the minimum and maximum from 1 to 6:

```php
$roll = rand(1, 6);

echo 'You rolled a ' . $roll;
```

To print out a message if the player rolls a six and wins, you can use an **if** statement:

2-4. PHP-DiceRoll

```php
$roll = rand(1, 6);

echo 'You rolled a ' . $roll;

if ($roll == 6) {
    echo 'You win!';
}
```

The == used in the condition above is the **equals operator**, which is used to compare two values to see whether they're equal. A single equals = is used for *assignment* and cannot be used for comparison.

The **if** statement uses braces { and } to surround the code you want to run when the condition is met. You can place as many lines of code as you like between the braces and the code will only be run when the condition is met. Any code placed after the closing brace (}) will be run all the time:

```php
$roll = rand(1, 6);

echo 'You rolled a ' . $roll;

if ($roll == 6) {
 echo 'You win!'; // This line will only be printed if they
↪ rolled a 6
```

```
}

  echo 'Thanks for playing'; // This line will always be
↳ printed
```

 Use the Double-Equals

Remember to type the double-equals (==). A common mistake among beginning
PHP programmers is to type a condition like this with a single equals sign:

```
if ($roll = 6)      // Missing equals sign!
```

This condition is using the assignment operator (=) instead of the equal operator
(==). Consequently, instead of comparing the value of $roll to the number 6, it
will actually *set* the value of $roll to 6. Oops!

To make matters worse, the if statement will use this assignment operation as a
condition, which it will consider to be true, so the conditional code within the if
statement will always be executed, regardless of what the original value of $roll
happened to be.

If you run diceroll.php, you'll see the random number being generated, and if
you run it until you win, you'll see this in the browser:

```
You rolled a 6You win!Thanks for playing
```

This isn't very pretty, but because PHP outputs HTML you can add some
paragraph tags in order to format the output:

```
$roll = rand(1, 6);

echo '<p>You rolled a ' . $roll . '</p>';

if ($roll == 6) {
    echo '<p>You win!</p>';
}

echo '<p>Thanks for playing</p>';
```

If you run the updated `diceroll-html.php` page, you'll see that it now prints this in the browser:

```
You rolled a 6

You win!

Thanks for playing
```

This is much more user friendly. To make the game itself more user friendly, you might want to display a different message to people who didn't roll a 6 and didn't win. This can be done with an **else** statement. The **else** statement must follow an **if**, and will be run if the condition is not met:

```php
$roll = rand(1, 6);

echo '<p>You rolled a ' . $roll . '</p>';

if ($roll == 6) {
    echo '<p>You win!</p>';
}
else {
  echo '<p>Sorry, you didn\'t win, better luck next
↪ time!</p>';
}

echo '<p>Thanks for playing</p>';
```

 Escaping the Quote

Because the word `didn't` contains a single quote, it needs to be *escaped*. By preceding the single quote with a backslash (\), it tells PHP not to treat the ' in `didn't` as the end of the string.

With an else statement one (and only one!) of the two blocks of code is guaranteed to run. Either the code in the `if` block will run if the condition is met, or the code in the `else` block will run if it isn't.

Conditions can be more complex than a single check for equality. An `if` statement can contain more than one condition. For example, imagine if the game was adjusted so that both 5 and 6 were winning numbers. The `if` statement could be changed to the following:

```
if ($roll == 6 || $roll == 5) {
    echo '<p>You win!</p>';
}
else {
 echo '<p>Sorry, you didn\'t win, better luck next
↳ time!</p>';
}
```

The double pipe (||) operator means "or". The condition above is now met if either expression evaluates to true. This can be read as "If they rolled a 6 or they rolled a 5".

However, this can be expressed in an even better way. if statements aren't limited to using the equals (==) operator. They can also utilize the mathematical greater than (>) and less than (<) operators. The if statement above could also be done with a single expression:

```
if ($roll > 4) {
    echo '<p>You win!</p>';
}
else {
 echo '<p>Sorry, you didn\'t win, better luck next
↳ time!</p>';
}
```

$roll > 4 will evaluate to true if the value stored in the $roll variable is greater than 4, allowing us to have 5 and 6 as winning numbers with a single condition. If we wanted 4, 5 and 6 as winning numbers, the condition could be changed to $roll > 3.

Like the or expression (||), there's another expression called and that's is only met when both conditions evaluate to true. We could expand the game to include two dice and require players to roll two sixes to win:

2-9. PHP-DiceRoll-TwoDice

```php
$roll1 = rand(1, 6);
$roll2 = rand(1, 6);

echo '<p>You rolled a ' . $roll1 . ' and a ' . $roll2
  . '</p>';

if ($roll1 == 6 && $roll2 == 6) {
    echo '<p>You win!</p>';
}
else {
    echo '<p>Sorry, you didn\'t win, better luck next
    time!</p>';
}

echo '<p>Thanks for playing</p>';
```

The expression if ($roll1 == 6 && $roll2 == 6) will only evaluate to true if $roll1 == 6 is true *and* $roll2 == 6. This means that the player has to roll a 6 on both dice to win the game. If we changed the and (&&) to an or (||)—that is, if ($roll1 == 6 || $roll2 == 6)—the player would win if they rolled a 6 on either dice.

We'll look at more complicated conditions as the need arises. For the time being, a general familiarity with if … else statements is sufficient.

 or **and** and

PHP also allows the use of the or in place of || and **and** in place of &&. For example:

```php
if ($roll == 6 or $roll == 5) { … }
```

There are some minor differences between the way or and || work that can lead to unexpected behavior. Generally speaking, avoiding the "spelled out" operators and sticking to the double pipe (||) and double ampersand (&&) will help prevent confusing bugs.

Loops

Another type of control structure that's very useful is a **loop**. Loops allow repeating the same lines of code over and over. Two important kind of loops are `for` loops and `while` loops. Let's look at how they work.

For Loops

The `for` loop is used when you know up front how many times you need to run the same code. The image below shows the flow of a `for` loop:

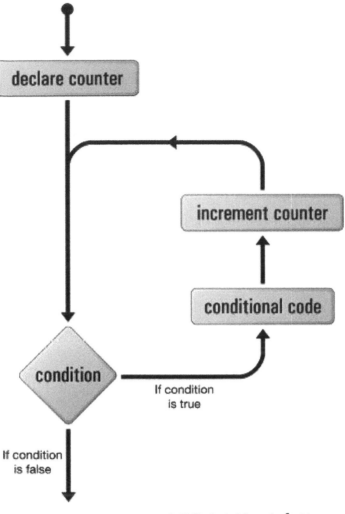

2-10. The logical flow of a *for* loop

Here's what it looks like in code:

```
for (declare counter; condition; increment counter) {
  ⋮ statement(s) to execute repeatedly as long as condition is
  ↪ true
}
```

The `declare counter`declare counter statement is executed once at the start of the loop. The condition statement is checked each time through the loop before the statements in the body are executed. The increment counter statement is executed each time through the loop after the statements in the body.

To count to 10 using a `for` loop, you can use the following code:

```
for ($count = 1; $count <= 10; $count++) {
    echo $count . ' ';
}
```

This looks quite scary, as there's a lot going on, but let me break it down for you:

- `$count = 1;`: this sets the counters initial value to 1.
- `$count <= 10;`: this is the condition. It can be read of as "keep looping while $count is less than or equal to 10".
- `$count++`: this says "add 1 to the counter each time". It's identical to `$count = $count + 1`.
- `echo $count . ' ';`: this prints the value of the counter followed by a space.

The condition in this example uses the operator `<=`. This acts similarly to the `<` less than operator, but evaluates to true if the number being compared is less than *or equal to* the second. Other available operators include `>=` (greater than or equal) and `!=` (not equal).

As you can see, the statements that initialize and increment the `$count` variable are placed with the condition on the first line of the `for` loop. Although, at first glance, the code seems a little more difficult to read, putting all the code that deals with controlling the loop in the same place actually makes it easier to understand once you're used to the syntax. Many of the examples in this book will use `for` loops, so you'll have plenty of opportunities to practice reading them.

You can change each part of the `for` loop to have different results. For example, here's how to add 3 each time you can change the `for` loop:

```php
for ($count = 1; $count <= 10; $count = $count + 3) {
    echo $count . ' ';
}
```

This will result in the following:

```
1 4 7 10
```

for loops can be combined with other statements such as if statements to perform specific tasks on each iteration. For example, rather than refreshing the page on our dice game each time, we might want to roll the dice 10 times and print the results:

```php
for ($count = 1; $count <= 10; $count++) {
    $roll = rand(1, 6);
    echo '<p>You rolled a ' . $roll . '</p>';

    if ($roll == 6) {
        echo '<p>You win!</p>';
    }
    else {
        echo '<p>Sorry, you didn\'t win, better
        luck next time!</p>';
    }
}

echo '<p>Thanks for playing</p>';
```

This lets us roll the dice 10 times without needing to refresh the page each time. Using a loop is functionally identical to copy/pasting the code 10 times, and will produce the exact same outcome as the following:

```
$roll = rand(1, 6);
echo '<p>You rolled a ' . $roll . '</p>';

if ($roll == 6) {
    echo '<p>You win!</p>';
}
else {
    echo '<p>Sorry, you didn't win, better luck
    next time!</p>';
}

$roll = rand(1, 6);
echo '<p>You rolled a ' . $roll . '</p>';

if ($roll == 6) {
    echo '<p>You win!</p>';
}
else {
    echo '<p>Sorry, you didn't win, better luck next
    time!</p>';
}

$roll = rand(1, 6);
echo '<p>You rolled a ' . $roll . '</p>';

if ($roll == 6) {
    echo '<p>You win!</p>';
}
else {
 echo '<p>Sorry, you didn't win, better luck next
↪ time!</p>';
}

// and so on …
```

The computer doesn't care which method you use, whether you copy/paste or use a loop. It will just run the code. However, as a developer, you'll quickly realize that a loop is the better choice. If you wanted to update the code to also allow 5 as a winning number, you'd need to update the condition in 10 different places. Using a loop, you can change the code in one place and it will affect each iteration of the loop. If you ever find yourself copy/pasting code, there's always a better way of achieving what you're trying to do.

While Loops

Another often-used PHP control structure is the `while` loop. Where the `if … else` statement allows us to choose whether or not to execute a set of statements depending on some condition, the `while` loop allows us to use a condition to determine how many *times* we'll execute a set of statements repeatedly.

The following image shows how a `while` loop operates:

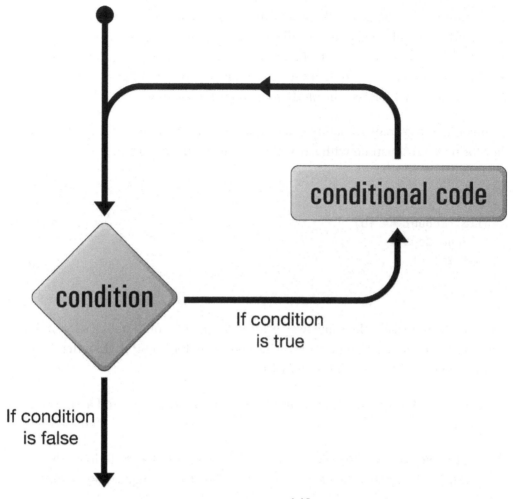

2-13. The logical flow of a while loop

Here's what a while loop looks like in code:

```
while (condition) {
  ⋮ statement(s) to execute repeatedly as long as condition is
  ↳ true
}
```

The while loop works very similarly to an if statement. The difference arises when the condition is true and the statement(s) are executed. Instead of continuing the execution with the statement that follows the closing brace (}), the condition is checked again. If the condition is still true, the statement(s) are executed a second time, and a third, and will continue to be executed as long as the condition remains true. The first time the condition evaluates false (whether it's the first time it's checked, or the 101st), the execution jumps immediately to the statement that follows the `while` loop, after the closing brace.

Loops like these come in handy whenever you're working with long lists of items, but for now I'll illustrate with a trivial example, counting to ten:

2-14. PHP-WhileCount

```php
while ($count <= 10) {
    echo $count . ' ';
    ++$count;
}
```

This works in exactly the same way as a `for` loop, and you'll notice a lot of the same statements in different places. This code may look a bit frightening, I know, but let me talk you through it line by line:

- `$count = 1;`. The first line creates a variable called `$count` and assigns it a value of 1.

- `while ($count <= 10)`. The second line is the start of a `while` loop, the condition being that the value of `$count` is less than or equal (`<=`) to 10.

- `{`. The opening brace marks the beginning of the block of conditional code for the `while` loop. This conditional code is often called the **body** of the loop, and is executed over and over again, as long as the condition holds true.

- `echo $count . ' ';`. This line simply outputs the value of `$count`, followed by a space.

- `++$count;`. The fourth line adds one to the value of `$count`. `++$count` is a shortcut for `$count = $count + 1`. `$count++` will also work here! The position of the `++` can be important, but in this case it doesn't matter. If the `++` is before the variable name, the counter is incremented before the value is read. When `$count` is zero, the code `echo ++$count;` will print 1, whereas `echo $count++;` will print 0. Be careful when using `++`, as putting it in the wrong place can cause bugs.

▪ `}`. The closing brace marks the end of the `while` loop's body.

So here's what happens when this code is executed. The first time the condition is checked, the value of `$count` is 1, so the condition is definitely true. The value of `$count` (1) is output, and `$count` is given a new value of 2. The condition is still true the second time it's checked, so the value (2) is output and a new value (3) is assigned. This process continues, outputting the values 3, 4, 5, 6, 7, 8, 9, and 10. Finally, `$count` is given a value of 11, and the condition is found to be false, which ends the loop.

The net result of the code is shown in the following image:

1 2 3 4 5 6 7 8 9 10

2-15. The net result of the `while` loop code

While loops aren't generally used for simple counters like this, which is normally the job of the `for` loop. Although you can create a counter with a `while` loop, usually they're used to keep running code until something happens. For example, we might want to keep rolling the dice until we get a six. There's no way to know how many dice rolls will be needed when we write the code: it could take one roll or hundreds to get a six. So you can place the dice roll in a `while` loop:

```
$roll = 0;
while ($roll != 6) {
    $roll = rand(1, 6);
    echo '<p>You rolled a ' . $roll . '</p>';

    if ($roll == 6) {
        echo '<p>You win!</p>';
    }
    else {
        echo '<p>Sorry, you didn\'t win, better luck
        next time!</p>';
    }
}
```

This will keep rolling the dice until a 6 is rolled. Each time you run the code it will take a different number of rolls before you win.

The while statement uses the condition $roll != 6. In order for the while loop to be run the first time, the $roll variable must be set to a value for the initial comparison. That's the purpose of the $roll = 0; line above the while loop. By setting the value to zero initially, when the while loop runs the first time, while ($roll != 6) will evaluate to true (because $roll is equal to zero, not 6!) and the loop will start. Without this line, you'd get an error, because the $roll variable hadn't been set to anything before it was used.

There's a variant of the while loop called do … while, which is useful in these kinds of cases. It allows you to run some code without a condition and then run it again if the code isn't set. This takes the following structure:

```
do {
 statement(s) to execute and then repeat if the condition is
 ↳ true
}
while (condition);
```

For the dice roll example above, this allows you to ignore the first line:

```php
do {
    $roll = rand(1, 6);
    echo '<p>You rolled a ' . $roll . '</p>';

    if ($roll == 6) {
        echo '<p>You win!</p>';
    }
    else {
 echo '<p>Sorry, you didn\'t win, better luck next
↪ time!</p>';
    }
}
while ($roll != 6);
```

This time, because the condition is at the bottom, by the time the `while` statement is run, the `$roll` variable has been given a value, so you don't need to give it an initial value of zero to force the loop to run the first time.

PSR-2

PHP doesn't mind how you format your code and whitespace is ignored. You could express the previous example as:

```php
do {
    $roll = rand(
    1,
    6);

    echo '
You rolled a ' .
    $roll . '
';

if (
    $roll == 6
    )
    {
        echo '
You win!
';
    }
    else
    {
        echo '
Sorry, you didn\'t win, better luck next
                time!
';
    }
}
while ($roll != 6);
```

The script will execute in the exact same way. Different programmers have different preferred styles, such as using tabs or spaces for indentation, or placing the opening brace on the same line as the statement or after it. Throughout this book I'll be using a convention known as PSR-2[1] but use whatever style you feel most comfortable with.

Arrays

An **array** is a special kind of variable that contains multiple values. If you think of a variable as a box that contains a value, an array can be thought of as a box with compartments where each compartment is able to store an individual value.

To create an array in PHP, use square brackets [and] containing the values you want to store, separated by commas:

```
$myArray = ['one', 2, '3'];
```

The array Keyword

Arrays in PHP can also be defined using the **array** keyword. The following code is equivalent to the square bracket notation above:

```
$myArray = array('one', 2, 3);
```

The square bracket notation was introduced in PHP 5.4 and is preferred by PHP developers, as it's less to type, and square brackets are more easily visible among round brackets in control structures like **if** statements and **while** loops. /p>

This code creates an array called $myArray that contains three values: 'one', 2, and '3'. Just like an ordinary variable, each space in an array can contain any type of value. In this case, the first and third spaces contain strings, while the second contains a number.

To access a value stored in an array, you need to know its **index**. Typically, arrays use numbers as indices to point to the values they contain, starting with zero. That is, the first value (or element) of an array has index 0, the second has index 1, the third has index 2, and so on. Therefore, the index of the nth element of an array is n–1. Once you know the index of the value you're interested in, you can retrieve that value by placing that index in square brackets after the array variable

---

1. https://github.com/php-fig/fig-standards/blob/master/accepted/PSR-2-coding-style-guide.md

name:

```
echo $myArray[0];    // outputs 'one'
echo $myArray[1];    // outputs '2'
echo $myArray[2];    // outputs '3'
```

Each value stored in an array is called an **element**. You can use a key in square brackets to add new elements, or assign new values to existing array elements:

```
$myArray[1] = 'two';    // assign a new value
$myArray[3] = 'four';   // create a new element
```

You can also add elements to the end of an array using the assignment operator as usual, but leaving empty the square brackets that follow the variable name:

```
$myArray[] = 'five';
echo $myArray[4];    // outputs 'five'
```

Array elements can be used like any other variable, and in a lot of cases choosing to use an array or multiple variables will depend on the programmer's preference. However, arrays can be used to solve problems that normal variables can't!

Remember the dice game from the last section? It would be more user-friendly if it showed the English word rather than the numeral for the result. For example, instead of "You rolled a 3" or "You rolled a 6", it might be nicer to read "You rolled a three" or "You rolled a six".

To do this, we need some way of converting from a numeral to the English word for that number. This is possible with a series of if statements:

```php
$roll = rand(1, 6);

if ($roll == 1) {
    $english = 'one';
}
else if ($roll == 2) {
    $english = 'two';
}
else if ($roll == 3) {
    $english = 'three';
}
else if ($roll == 4) {
    $english = 'four';
}
else if ($roll == 5) {
    $english = 'five';
}
else if ($roll == 6) {
    $english = 'six';
}

echo '<p>You rolled a ' . $english . '</p>';

if ($roll == 6) {
    echo '<p>You win!</p>';
}
else {
 echo '<p>Sorry, you didn\'t win, better luck next
↪ time!</p>';
}
```

This solution works, but it's very inefficient, as you need to write an `if` statement for each possible dice roll. Instead, you can use an array to store each roll value:

```php
$english = [
    1 => 'one',
    2 => 'two',
```

```
    3 => 'three',
    4 => 'four',
    5 => 'five',
    6 => 'six'
];
```

The => notation allows you to define both the keys and the values when creating the array. This is equivalent to:

```
$english = [];
$english[1] = 'one';
$english[2] = 'two';
$english[3] = 'three';
$english[4] = 'four';
$english[5] = 'five';
$english[6] = 'six';
```

Although these are equivalent, the code required to use the shorthand notation is a lot quicker to type, is arguably easier to read, and easier to understand.

Now that the array is created, it's possible to read each English word from it:

```
echo $english[3];     //Prints "three"
echo $english[5];     //Prints "five"
```

In PHP, a number like 3 it can be replaced with a variable that contains that value. This is also possible with array keys. For example:

```
$var1 = 3;
$var2 = 5;

echo $english[$var1];     //Prints "three"
echo $english[$var2];     //Prints "five"
```

Knowing this, we can piece it all together and adjust the dice game to display the English word of the dice roll by reading the relevant value from the array using the $roll variable:

```php
$english = [
    1 => 'one',
    2 => 'two',
    3 => 'three',
    4 => 'four',
    5 => 'five',
    6 => 'six'
];

$roll = rand(1, 6);

echo '<p>You rolled a ' . $english[$roll]
  . '</p>';

if ($roll == 6) {
    echo '<p>You win!</p>';
}
else {
    echo '<p>Sorry, you didn\'t win, better luck
    next time!</p>';
}
```

As you can see, this is a lot cleaner and tidier than a long list of if statements. There are two big advantages here:

1. If you wanted to represent a 10-sided dice, it's a lot easier to add to the array than add an extra if statement for each number.
2. The array is reusable. For the version with two dice, you can just reuse the $english array rather than repeating all the if statements for each dice roll:

```php
$roll1 = rand(1, 6);
$roll2 = rand(1, 6);

if ($roll1 == 1) {
    $english = 'one';
}
else if ($roll1 == 2) {
    $english = 'two';
}
else if ($roll1 == 3) {
    $english = 'three';
}
else if ($roll1 == 4) {
    $english = 'four';
}
else if ($roll1 == 5) {
    $english = 'five';
}
else if ($roll1 == 6) {
    $english = 'six';
}

if ($roll2 == 1) {
    $englishRoll2 = 'one';
}
else if ($roll2 == 2) {
    $englishRoll2 = 'two';
}
else if ($roll2 == 3) {
    $englishRoll2 = 'three';
}
else if ($roll2 == 4) {
    $englishRoll2 = 'four';
}
else if ($roll2 == 5) {
    $englishRoll2 = 'five';
}
else if ($roll2 == 6) {
    $englishRoll2 = 'six';
```

```
}

echo '<p>You rolled a ' . $english . ' and a '
 . $englishRoll2 . '</p>';
```

Instead, the array can be used for both rolls:

2-21. PHP-DiceRoll-English-Array-TwoDice

```
$english = [
    1 => 'one',
    2 => 'two',
    3 => 'three',
    4 => 'four',
    5 => 'five',
    6 => 'six'
];

$roll1 = rand(1, 6);
$roll2 = rand(1, 6);

echo '<p>You rolled a ' . $english[$roll1] . ' and
 a ' . $english[$roll2] . '</p>';
```

While numbers are the most common choice for array indices, there's another possibility. You can also use strings as indices to create what's called an **associative array**. It's called this because it *associates* values with meaningful indices. In this example, we associate a date (in the form of a string) with each of three names:

```
$birthdays['Kevin'] = '1978-04-12';
$birthdays['Stephanie'] = '1980-05-16';
$birthdays['David'] = '1983-09-09';
```

Like the numerical indexes, you can use the shorthand notation for associative arrays as well:

```php
$birthdays = [
    'Kevin' => '1978-04-12',
    'Stephanie' => '1980-05-16',
    'David' => '1983-09-09'
];
```

Now, if we want to know Kevin's birthday, we look it up using the name as the index:

```php
echo 'Kevin\'s birthday is: ' . $birthdays['Kevin'];
```

This type of array is especially important when it comes to user interaction in PHP, as we'll see in the next section. I'll demonstrate other uses of arrays throughout this book.

 Escaping Quotes

> Because `Kevin's` contains an apostrophe (single quote) and PHP would see this as the end of the string, it must be escaped with a \ so that PHP treats it as part of the string, rather than marking the end.

User Interaction and Forms

For most database-driven websites these days, you need to do more than dynamically generate pages based on database data. You also need to provide some degree of interactivity, even if it's just a search box.

Veterans of JavaScript tend to think of interactivity in terms of event listeners, which let you react directly to the actions of the user—for example, the movement of the cursor over a link on the page. Server-side scripting languages such as PHP have a more limited scope when it comes to support for user interaction. As PHP code is only activated when a request is made to the server, user interaction occurs solely in a back-and-forth fashion: the user sends requests to the server, and the server replies with dynamically generated pages.[2]

The key to creating interactivity with PHP is to understand the techniques we can employ to send information about a user's interaction, along with a request for a new web page. As it turns out, PHP makes this quite easy.

Passing Variables in Links

The simplest way to send information along with a page request is to use the URL query string. If you've ever noticed a URL containing a question mark that follows the filename, you've seen this technique in use. For example, if you search for "SitePoint" on Google, it will take you to a search result page with a URL like this:

```
http://www.google.com/search?hl=en&q=SitePoint
```

See the question mark in the URL? The text that follows the question mark contains your search query (`SitePoint`). That information is being sent along with the request for `http://www.google.com/search`.

Let's code up an easy example of our own. Create a regular HTML file called `name.html` (no `.php` filename extension is required, since there won't be any PHP code in this file) and insert this link:

```
<a href="name.php?name=Kevin">Hi, I&rsquo;m
↪ Kevin!</a>
```

This is a link to a file called `name.php`, but as well as linking to the file, you're also passing a variable along with the page request. The variable is passed as part of the query string, which is the portion of the URL that follows the question mark. The variable is called `name`, and its value is `Kevin`. So, you've created a link

---

2. To some extent, the rise of Ajax techniques in the JavaScript world in recent years has changed this. It's now possible for JavaScript code—responding to a user action such as mouse movement—to send a request to the web server, invoking a PHP script. For the purposes of this book, however, we'll stick to non-Ajax applications. If you'd like to learn all about Ajax, check out JavaScript: Novice to Ninja by Darren Jones: http://www.sitepoint.com/books/jsninja2/.

that loads name.php, and informs the PHP code contained in that file that name equals Kevin.

To really understand the effect of this link, we need to look at name.php. Create it as a new HTML file, but this time, note the .php filename extension: this tells the web server that it can expect to interpret some PHP code in the file. In the body of this new web page, type the following:

```
                                                          2-22. PHP-GET

$name = $_GET['name'];
echo 'Welcome to our website, ' . $name . '!';
?>
```

Now, put these two files (name.html and name.php) in the Project folder, and load the first file in your browser (the URL should be http://192.168.10.10/name.html). Click the link in that first page to request the PHP script. The resulting page should say "Welcome to our website, Kevin!", as shown in the following image:

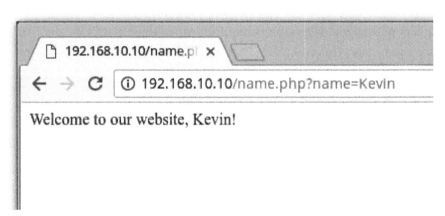

2-23. The welcome message, seen in the browser

Let's take a closer look at the code that made this possible. This is the most important line:

```
$name = $_GET['name'];
```

Using what you learned from the Arrays section above, you may be able to figure out what this line does. It assigns the value stored in the 'name' element of the array called $_GET to a new variable called $name. But where does the $_GET array come from?

It turns out that $_GET is one of a number of variables that PHP automatically creates when it receives a request from a browser. PHP creates $_GET as an array variable that contains any values passed in the URL query string. $_GET is an associative array, so the value of the name variable passed in the query string can be accessed as $_GET['name']. Your name.php script assigns this value to an ordinary PHP variable ($name), then displays it as part of a text string using an echo statement:

```
echo 'Welcome to our website, ' . $name . '!';
```

The value of the $name variable is inserted into the output string using the string concatenation operator (.) that we looked at in the Variables, Operators, and Comments section.

But watch out! There's a security hole lurking in this code! Although PHP is an easy programming language to learn, it turns out it's also especially easy to introduce security issues into websites using PHP if you're unaware of what precautions to take. Before we go any further with the language, I want to make sure you're able to spot and fix this particular security issue, since it's probably the most common one on the Web today.

The security issue here stems from the fact that the name.php script is generating a page containing content that's under the control of the user—in this case, the $name variable. Although the $name variable will normally receive its value from the URL query string in the link on the name.html page, a malicious user could edit the URL to send a different value for the name variable.

To see how this would work, click the link in name.html again. When you see the resulting page (with the welcome message containing the name "Kevin"), take a look at the URL in the address bar of your browser. It should look similar to this:

```
http://192.168.10.10/name.php?name=Kevin
```

Edit the URL to insert a `<b>` tag before the name and a `</b>` tag following the name:

```
http://192.168.10.10/name.php?name=<b>Kevin</b>
```

Hit Enter to load this new URL, and note that the name in the page is now bold, as shown in the following image:[3]

2-24. The name shown in bold

See what's happening here? The user can type any HTML code into the URL, and your PHP script includes it in the code of the generated page without question. If the code is as innocuous as a `<b>` tag, there's no problem, but a malicious user could include sophisticated JavaScript code that performs some low action like stealing the user's password. All the attacker would have to do is publish the modified link on some other site under the attacker's control, and then entice one of your users to click it. The attacker could even embed the link in an email and send it to your users. If one of your users clicked the link, the attacker's code would be included in your page and the trap would be sprung!

[3.] You might notice that some browsers will automatically convert the < and > characters into URL escape sequences (%3C and %3E respectively), but either way, PHP will receive the same value.

I hate to scare you with this talk of malicious hackers attacking your users by turning your own PHP code against you, particularly when you're only just learning the language. The fact is that PHP's biggest weakness as a language is how easy it is to introduce security issues like this. Some might say that much of the energy you spend learning to write PHP to a professional standard is spent on avoiding security issues. The sooner you're exposed to these issues, however, the sooner you become accustomed to avoiding them, and the less of a stumbling block they'll be for you in future.

So, how can we generate a page containing the user's name without opening it up to abuse by attackers? The solution is to treat the value supplied for the $name variable as plain text to be displayed on your page, rather than as HTML to be included in the page's code. This is a subtle distinction, so let me show you what I mean.

Open up your name.php file again and edit the PHP code it contains so that it looks like this:

2-25. PHP-GET-Sanitized

```php
<?php
$name = $_GET['name'];
echo 'Welcome to our website, ' .
    htmlspecialchars($name, ENT_QUOTES, 'UTF-8') . '!';
?>
```

There's a lot going on in this code, so let me break it down for you. The first line is the same as it was previously, assigning to $name the value of the 'name' element from the $_GET array. But the echo statement that follows it is drastically different. Whereas previously we simply dumped the $name variable, naked, into the echo statement, this version of the code uses the built-in PHP function htmlspecialchars to perform a critical conversion.

Remember, the security hole occurs because, in name.php, HTML code in the $name variable is dumped directly into the code of the generated page, and can therefore do anything that HTML code can do. What htmlspecialchars does is convert "special HTML characters" like < and > into HTML character entities like < and >, which prevents them from being interpreted as HTML code by the browser. I'll demonstrate this for you in a moment.

First, let's take a closer look at this new code. The call to the `htmlspecialchars` function is the first example in this book of a PHP function that takes more than one argument. Here's the function call all by itself:

```
htmlspecialchars($name, ENT_QUOTES, 'UTF-8')
```

The first argument is the `$name` variable (the text to be converted). The second argument is the PHP **constant**.[4]

---

[4] A PHP constant is like a variable whose value you're unable to change. Unlike variables, constants don't start with a dollar sign. PHP comes with a number of built-in constants like `ENT_QUOTES` that are used to control built-in functions like `htmlspecialchars`./span> `ENT_QUOTES`, which tells `htmlspecialchars` to convert single and double quotes in addition to other special characters. The third parameter is the string `'UTF-8'`, which tells PHP what character encoding to use to interpret the text you give it.

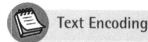

Text Encoding

You may have discerned that all the example HTML pages in this book contain the following meta tag near the top:

```
<meta charset="utf-8">
```

This tag tells the browser receiving this page that the HTML code of the page is encoded as UTF-8 text.[5]

UTF-8 is one of many standards for representing text as a series of ones and zeros in computer memory, called character encodings. If you're curious to learn all about character encodings, check out http://www.sitepoint.com/article/guide-web-character-encoding/.

In a few pages, we'll reach the section on "Passing Variables in Forms". By encoding your pages as UTF-8, your users can submit text containing thousands of foreign characters that your site would otherwise be unable to handle.

Unfortunately, many of PHP's built-in functions, such as `htmlspecialchars`, assume you're using the much simpler ISO-8859-1 (or Latin-1) character encoding by default. Therefore, you need to let them know you're using UTF-8 when utilizing these functions.

If you can, you should also tell your text editor to save your HTML and PHP files as UTF-8 encoded text. This is only required if you want to type advanced characters (such as curly quotes or dashes) or foreign characters (like "ó") into your HTML or PHP code. The code in this book plays it safe and uses HTML entity references (for example, `&rsquo;` for a curly right quote), which will work regardless.

Open up `name.html` in your browser and click the link that now points to your updated `name.php`. Once again, you'll see the message "Welcome to our website, Kevin!" As you did before, modify the URL to include `<b>` and `</b>` tags surrounding the name:

```
http://192.168.10.10/name.php?name=<b>Kevin</b>
```

When you hit *Enter* this time, instead of the name turning bold in the page, you

---

5.

should see the actual text that you typed as shown in the following image:

2-26. It sure is ugly, but it's secure!

If you view the source code of the page, you can confirm that the `htmlspecialchars` function did its job and converted the < and > characters into the `&lt;` and `&gt;` entity references respectively. This prevents malicious users from injecting unwanted code into your site. If they try anything like that, the code is harmlessly displayed as plain text on the page.

We'll make extensive use of the `htmlspecialchars` function throughout this book to guard against this sort of security hole. No need to worry too much if you're having trouble grasping the details of how to use it just at the minute. Before long, you'll find its use becomes second nature. For now, let's look at some more advanced ways of passing values to PHP scripts when we request them.

Passing a single variable in the query string was nice, but it turns out you can pass *more* than one value if you want to! Let's look at a slightly more complex version of the previous example. Open up your `name.html` file again, and change the link to point to `name.php` with this more complicated query string:

```
<a
↪ href="name.php?firstname=Kevin&amp;lastname=Yank">
Hi, I&rsquo;m Kevin Yank!</a>
```

This time, our link passes two variables: `firstname` and `lastname`. The variables are separated in the query string by an ampersand (&, which should be written as `&amp;` in HTML—yes, even in a link URL! ... although, if you do wrongly use &,

browsers will *mostly* fix it for you). You can pass even more variables by separating each `name=value` pair from the next with an ampersand.

As before, we can use the two variable values in our `name.php` file:

2-27. PHP-GET-TwoVars

```
$firstName = $_GET['firstname'];
$lastName = $_GET['lastname'];
echo 'Welcome to our website, ' .
    htmlspecialchars($firstName, ENT_QUOTES, 'UTF-8') . ' ' .
    htmlspecialchars($lastName, ENT_QUOTES, 'UTF-8') . '!';
?>
```

The `echo` statement is becoming quite sizable now, but it should still make sense to you. Using a series of string concatenations (.), it outputs "Welcome to our website," followed by the value of `$firstName` (made safe for display using `htmlspecialchars`), a space, the value of `$lastName` (again, treated with `htmlspecialchars`), and finally an exclamation mark.

The result looks like this:

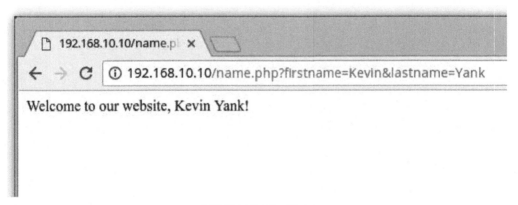

2-28. The echoed welcome

This is all well and good, but we're still yet to achieve our goal of true user interaction, where the user can enter arbitrary information and have it processed by PHP. To continue with our example of a personalized welcome message, we'd like to invite the user to type their name and have it appear in the resulting page.

To enable the user to type in a value, we'll need to use an HTML form.

Passing Variables in Forms

Rip the link out of `name.html` and replace it with this HTML code to create the form:

2-29. PHP-GET-Form

```
<form action="name.php" method="get">
    <label for="firstname">First name:</label>
    <input type="text" name="firstname" id="firstname">

    <label for="lastname">Last name:</label>
    <input type="text" name="lastname" id="lastname">

    <input type="submit" value="GO">
</form>
```

This is how the browser displays the form produced from this code:

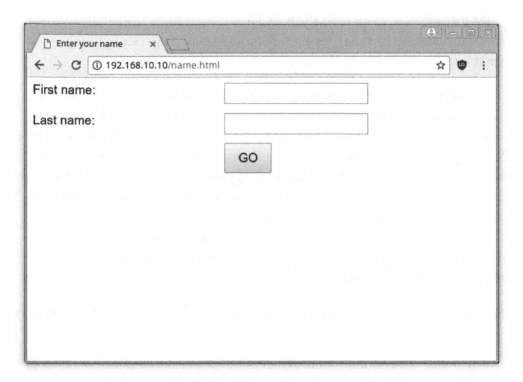

2-30. The form as it appears in a browser

 Adding Some CSS

I've added some CSS to the form (available in `form.css` in the sample code) to make it look a little prettier. The CSS I've used is very generic, and can be used to display any form in the format label-input-line break. I'll be including this CSS file on any page that contains a form.

Since this is a book about PHP and MySQL, however, I won't go into detail about how the CSS works. Check out SitePoint's The CSS3 Anthology[6] for advice on styling your forms with CSS.

This form has the exact same effect as the second link we looked at in the "Passing Variables in Links" section above (with `firstname=Kevin&amp;lastname=Yank` in the query string), except that you can now enter whichever names you like. When you click the submit button (labeled GO), the browser will load `name.php` and add the variables and their values to the

---

6. http://www.sitepoint.com/books/cssant4/

query string for you automatically. It retrieves the names of the variables from the name attributes of the `type="text"` inputs, and obtains the values from the text typed into the text fields by the user.

The `method` attribute of the form tag is used to tell the browser how to send the variables and their values along with the request. A value of `get` (as used in `name.html` above) causes them to be passed via the query string (and appear in PHP's `$_GET` array), but there is an alternative. It can be undesirable—or even technically unfeasible—to have the values appear in the query string. What if we included a textarea element in the form, to let the user enter a large amount of text? A URL whose query string contained several paragraphs of text would be ridiculously long, and would possibly exceed the maximum length for a URL in today's browsers. The alternative is for the browser to pass the information invisibly, behind the scenes.

Edit your `name.html` file once more. Modify the form method by setting it to `post`:

```
<form action="name.php" method="post">
    <label for="firstname">First name:</label>
    <input type="text" name="firstname" id="firstname">

    <label for="lastname">Last name:</label>
    <input type="text" name="lastname" id="lastname">

    <input type="submit" value="GO">
</form>
```

This new value for the method attribute instructs the browser to send the form variables invisibly as part of the page request, rather than embedding them in the query string of the URL.

As we're no longer sending the variables as part of the query string, they stop appearing in PHP's `$_GET` array. Instead, they're placed in another array reserved especially for "posted" form variables: `$_POST`. We must therefore modify `name.php` to retrieve the values from this new array:

2-31. PHP-POST-Form

```php
<?php
$firstname = $_POST['firstname'];
$lastname = $_POST['lastname'];
echo 'Welcome to our website, ' .
    htmlspecialchars($firstname, ENT_QUOTES, 'UTF-8') . ' ' .
    htmlspecialchars($lastname, ENT_QUOTES, 'UTF-8') . '!';
?>
```

Here's what the resulting page looks like once this new form is submitted:

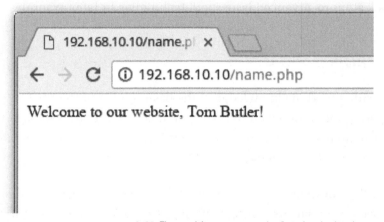

2-32. The resulting page once the form is submitted

The form is functionally identical to the previous one. The only difference is that the URL of the page that's loaded when the user clicks the GO button will be without a query string. On the one hand, this lets you include large values (or sensitive values such as passwords and credit card numbers) in the data that's submitted by the form without them appearing in the query string. On the other hand, if the user bookmarks the page that results from the form's submission, that bookmark will be useless, as it lacks the submitted values. This, incidentally, is the main reason why search engines use the query string to submit search terms. If you bookmark a search results page on Google, you can use that bookmark to perform the same search again later, because the search terms are contained in the URL.

GET or POST?

As a rule of thumb, you should only use GET forms if, when the form is submitted, nothing on the server *changes*—such as when you're requesting a list of search results. Because the search terms are in the URL, the user can bookmark the search results page and get back to it without having to type in the search term again. But if, after submitting the form, a file is deleted, or a database is updated, or a record is inserted, you should use POST. The primary reason for this is that if a user bookmarks the page (or presses back in their browser) it won't trigger the form submission again and potentially create a duplicate record.

That covers the basics of using forms to produce rudimentary user interaction with PHP. We'll look at more advanced issues and techniques in later examples.

Hiding the Seams

You're now armed with a working knowledge of the basic syntax of the PHP programming language. You understand that you can take any HTML web page, rename it with a .php file name extension, and inject PHP code into it to generate page content on the fly. Not bad for a day's work!

Before we go any further, however, I want to stop and cast a critical eye over the examples we've discussed so far. Assuming your objective is to create database-driven websites that hold up to professional standards, there are a few unsightly blemishes we need to clean up.

The techniques in the rest of this chapter will help advance your programming skills beyond the beginner level, giving them a certain professional polish. I'll rely on these techniques throughout the rest of this book to ensure that, no matter how simple the example, you can feel confident in the quality of the product you're delivering.

PHP Templates

In the simple examples we've seen so far, inserting PHP code directly into your HTML pages has been a reasonable approach. As the amount of PHP code that goes into generating your average page grows, however, maintaining this mixture of HTML and PHP code can become unmanageable.

Particularly if you work in a team of not-so-savvy web designers, PHP-wise, having large blocks of cryptic PHP code intermingled with the HTML is a recipe for disaster. It's far too easy for designers to accidentally modify the PHP code, causing errors they'll be unable to fix.

A much more robust approach is to separate out the bulk of your PHP code so that it resides in its own file, leaving the HTML largely unpolluted by PHP code.

The key to doing this is the PHP `include` statement. With an `include` statement, you can insert the contents of another file into your PHP code at the point of the statement. To show you how this works, let's rebuild the "count to ten" `for` loop example we looked at earlier.

Start by creating a new file, `count.php`, in this directory. Open the file for editing and type in this code:

```php
<?php
$output = '';
for ($count = 1; $count <= 10; $count++) {
    $output .= $count . ' ';
}

include 'count.html.php';
```

Yes, that's the *complete* code for this file. It contains no HTML code whatsoever. The `for` loop should be familiar to you by now, but let me point out the interesting parts of this code:

- Instead of `echo`ing out the numbers 1 to 10, this script will add these numbers to a variable named `$output`. At the start of this script, therefore, we set this variable to contain an empty string.
- The line `$output .= $count . ' ';` adds each number (followed by a space) to the end of the `$output` variable. The `.=` operator you see here is a shorthand way of adding a value to the end of an existing string variable, by combining the assignment and string concatenation operators into one. The longhand

version of this line is $output = $output . $count . ' ';, but the .= operator saves you some typing.

- The include statement instructs PHP to execute the contents of the count.html.php file at this location.[7] You can think of the include statement as a kind of *copy and paste*. You would get the same result by opening up count.html.php, copying the contents and pasting them into count.php, overwriting the include line.
- Finally, you might have noticed that the file doesn't end with a ?> to match the opening <?php. You can put it in if you really want to, but it's unnecessary. If a PHP file ends with PHP code, there's no need to indicate where that code ends; the end of the file does it for you. The big brains of the PHP world generally prefer to leave it off the end of files like this one that contain only PHP code.

Since the final line of this file includes the count.html.php file, you should create this next:

2-33. PHP-Count-Template

```
<!DOCTYPE html>
<html lang="en">
    <head>
        <meta charset="utf-8">
        <title>Counting to Ten</title>
    </head>
    <body>
        <p>
            <?php echo $output; ?>
        </p>
    </body>
</html>
```

This file is almost entirely plain HTML, except for the one line that outputs the

---

[7.] Outside of this book, you'll often see includes coded with parentheses surrounding the filename, as if include were a function like date or htmlspecialchars, which is far from the case. These parentheses, when used, only serve to complicate the filename expression, and are therefore avoided in this book. The same goes for echo, another popular one-liner.

value of the $output variable. This is the same $output variable that was created by the index.php file.

What we've created here is a PHP template: an HTML page with only very small snippets of PHP code that insert dynamically generated values into an otherwise static HTML page. Rather than embedding the complex PHP code that generates those values in the page, we put the code to generate the values in a separate PHP script—index.php in this case.

Using PHP templates like this enables you to hand over your templates to HTML-savvy designers without worrying about what they might do to your PHP code. It also lets you focus on your PHP code without being distracted by the surrounding HTML code.

I like to name my PHP template files so that they end with .html.php. As far as your web server is concerned, though, these are still .php files; the .html.php suffix serves as a useful reminder that these files contain both HTML and PHP code.

Security Concerns

One problem with separating out the HTML and PHP code into different files is that someone could potentially run the .html.php code without having had it included from a corresponding PHP file. This isn't a big problem, but anyone could visit count.html.php directly. If you type http://192.168.10.10/count.html.php into your web browser, instead of seeing the count from one to ten, you'll see an error message: Notice: Undefined variable: output in /home/vagrant/Code/Project/public/count.html.php on line 9.

It's better not to let people run code in a manner you're not expecting. Depending on what the page is doing, this might let them bypass security checks you have in place and view content they shouldn't have access to. For example, consider the following code:

```
if ($_POST['password'] == 'secret') {
    include 'protected.html.php';
}
```

Looking at this code, it appears that you need to submit a form and type `secret` in the password box to see the protected content in `protected.html.php`. However, if someone can navigate directly to `protected.html.php` and see the contents of the page, it makes the security check redundant. There are other potential security issues introduced by making all your files accessible via a URL. Avoiding security problems like these is easy. You can actually include files from a directory other than the `public` directory.

You may have wondered earlier why we created a `Project` directory and then wrote all our files to the `public` directory inside `Project`. Well, this issue of security is the reason why. None of the files outside the `public` directory are accessible via a URL (by someone typing the file name into their web browser).

The `include` command can be tweaked to include files from *another directory*. In our case, that directory is going to the `Project` directory, which contains the files we've been working on so far.

So the question is, when the include file is in a *different* directory, how does a PHP script find it? The most obvious method is to specify the location of the include file as an absolute path. Here's how this would look on a Windows server:

```php
<?php include 'C:/Program Files/Apache Software
↪ Foundation/Apache2.2/protected.html.php'; ?>
```

And here's how it would look using the Homestead Improved box:

```php
<?php include
↪ '/home/vagrant/Code/Project/protected.html.php'; ?>
```

While this method will work, it's undesirable because it ties your site's code to your web server configuration. Ideally, you should be able to drop your PHP-based website onto any PHP-enabled web server and just watch it run. This is particularly important because many developers will build a site on one server, then deploy it publicly on a different server. That's impractical if your code refers to drives and directories that are specific to one particular server. Even if you *do* have the luxury of working on a single server, you'll be kicking yourself if you ever need to move your website to another drive/directory on that server.

A better method is to use a *relative* path. That is, the location of a file relative to the current file. When you use include 'count.html.php' this is actually a *relative path*, count.html.php is being included from the same directory as the script that was executed.

To include a file from the *directory above*, you can use the following code:

```
include '../count.html.php';
```

../ tells PHP to look for the file in the directory *above* the directory of the current script. It will look for count.html.php in the Project directory instead of the public directory.

Go ahead and move count.html.php up a level into the Project directory and amend count.php to reference the new location:

2-34. PHP-Count-Template-Secured

```
<?php
$output = '';
for ($count = 1; $count <= 10; $count++) {
    $output .= $count . ' ';
}

include '../count.html.php';
```

If you run the code above, it will work. But there's a potential problem when you include files in this way. Relative paths are relative to the script that was run, not to each file.

That is, if you open up Project/count.html.php and add the line include 'count2.html.php'; you would expect count2.html.php to be included from the `Project` directory. However, the path is relative to something called the *current working directory*, which, when you run a PHP script, is initially set to the directory that script is stored in. So running `include 'count2.html.php';` from `count.html.php` will actually try to load `count2.html.php` from the `public` directory!

The current working directory is set at the start of the script and applies to all the `include` statements, regardless of what file they are in. To make things even more confusing, it's possible to change the current working directory using the `chdir()` function.

Because of this, we can't rely on this:

```
include '../count.html.php';
```

It will work, but if the directory is changed, or `count.php` itself is an include file, it may not have the result we're expecting.

To overcome this, we do actually need to use relative paths. Luckily, PHP provides a constant called __DIR__ (that's *two* underscores, before and after the word *DIR*) which will always contain the path that contains the *current file*.

For example, you could create a file called `dir.php` inside the `public` directory with the following code:

```
echo __DIR__;
```

This will display `/home/vagrant/Code/Project/public`, which is the full path to the directory containing `dir.php`. To read `count.html.php` from the directory above `public`, it's possible to combine the `/../` operator and the __DIR__ constant:

```
include __DIR__ . '/../count.html.php';
```

This will now include the file `/home/vagrant/Code/Project/public/../count.html`. That is, PHP will look in the `public` directory, then go up one level into `Project` and include `count.html.php`.

This approach will work on any server, because `__DIR__` will differ depending on where the file is stored, and it doesn't depend on the changing *current working directory*. I'll be using this approach for including files throughout this book.

From now on, we'll only write files to the `public` directory that we actually want users to be able to access directly from their web browser. The `public` directory will contain any PHP scripts the user needs to access directly along with any images, JavaScript and CSS files required by the browser. Any files only referenced by an `include` statement will be placed outside the `public` directory so users can't access them directly.

As the book goes on, I'm going to introduce you to several different types of *include files*. To keep things organized, it's sensible to store different types of include file in different directories. We'll store template files (with a `.html.php` extension) inside a directory called `templates` inside the `Project` folder. We can then reference them in an `include` statement using `include __DIR__ . '../templates/file.html.php';`.

Many Templates, One Controller

What's nice about using `include` statements to load your PHP template files is that you can have *multiple* `include` statements in a single PHP script, as well as have it display different templates under various circumstances!

A PHP script that responds to a browser request by selecting one of several PHP templates to fill in and send back is commonly called a *controller*. A controller contains the logic that controls which template is sent to the browser.

Let's revisit one more example from earlier in this chapter: the welcome form that prompts a visitor for a first and last name.

We'll start with the PHP template for the form. For this, we can just reuse the `name.html` file we created earlier. Create a directory `templates` inside `Project` if you haven't already, and save a copy of `name.html` called `form.html.php` into this directory. The only code you need to change in this file is the action attribute of the form tag:

```
                                                    2-35. PHP-Form-Controller

<html>
    <head>
        <title>Enter your name</title>
        <link rel="stylesheet" href="form.css" />
        <meta charset="utf-8">
    </head>
    <body>
        <form action="" method="post">
            <label for="firstname">First name:</label>
            <input type="text" name="firstname" id="firstname">

            <label for="lastname">Last name:</label>
            <input type="text" name="lastname" id="lastname">

            <input type="submit" value="GO">
        </form>
    </body>
</html>
```

As you can see, we're leaving the action attribute blank. This tells the browser to submit the form back to the same URL it received it from—in this case, the URL of the controller that included this template file.

Let's take a look at the controller for this example. Create an index.php inside the public directory containing the following code:

```
<?php
if (!isset($_POST['firstname'])) {
    include __DIR__ . '/../templates/form.html.php';
} else {
    $firstName = $_POST['firstname'];
    $lastName = $_POST['lastname'];

    if ($firstName == 'Kevin' && $lastName == 'Yank') {
```

```
        $output = 'Welcome, oh glorious leader!';
    } else {
        $output = 'Welcome to our website, ' .
        htmlspecialchars($firstName, ENT_QUOTES, 'UTF-8') . ' ' .
        htmlspecialchars($lastName, ENT_QUOTES, 'UTF-8') . '!';
    }

    include __DIR__ . '/../templates/welcome.html.php';
}
```

This code should look quite familiar at first glance. It's a lot like the `name.php` script we wrote earlier. Let me explain the differences:

- The controller's first task is to decide whether the current request is a submission of the form in `form.html.php` or not. You can do this by checking if the request contains a `firstname` variable. If it does, PHP will have stored the value in `$_POST['firstname']`.

  `isset` is a built-in PHP function that will tell you if a particular variable (or array element) has been assigned a value or not. If `$_POST['firstname']` has a value, `isset($_POST['firstname'])` will be true. If `$_POST['firstname']` is unset, `isset($_POST['firstname'])` will be false.

  For the sake of readability, I like to put the code that sends the form in my controller first. We need this `if` statement to check if `$_POST['firstname']` is *not* set. To do this, we use the not operator (`!`). By putting this operator before the name of a function, you reverse the value that function returns—from true to false, or from false to true.

  Thus, if the request does *not* contain a `firstname` variable, then `!isset($_POST['firstname'])` will return true, and the body of the `if` statement will be executed.

- If the request is not a form submission, the controller includes the `form.html.php` file to display the form.

- If the request *is* a form submission, the body of the `else` statement is executed instead.

This code pulls the `firstname` and `lastname` variables out of the `$_POST` array, and then generates the appropriate welcome message for the name submitted.

▪ Instead of `echo`ing the welcome message, the controller stores the welcome message in a variable named `$output`.

▪ After generating the appropriate welcome message, the controller includes the `welcome.html.php` template, which will display that welcome message.

All that's left is to write the `welcome.html.php` into the `templates` directory. Here it is:

```
<!DOCTYPE html>
<html lang="en">
    <head>
        <meta charset="utf-8">
        <title>Form Example</title>
    </head>
    <body>
        <p>
            <?php echo $output; ?>
        </p>
    </body>
</html>
```

That's it! Fire up your browser and point it at `http://192.168.10.10/index.php`. You'll be prompted for your name, and when you submit the form, you'll see the appropriate welcome message. The URL should stay the same throughout this process.

You'll have noticed I asked you to name the file `index.php` instead of `name.php` or similar. The reason I used `index.php` is because it has a special meaning. `index.php` is known as a **directory index**. If you don't specify a filename when you visit the URL in your browser, the server will look for a file named `index.php` and display that. Try typing just `http://192.169.10.10` into your browser and you'll see the index page.

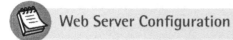

Web Server Configuration

Web servers can have different configurations and specify a different file to be the directory index. However, on most web servers index.php will work without any further configuration.

One of the benefits of maintaining the same URL throughout this process of prompting the user for a name and displaying the welcome message is that the user can bookmark the page at any time during this process and gain a sensible result. Whether it's the form page or the welcome message that's bookmarked, when the user returns, the form will be present once again. In the previous version of this example, where the welcome message had its own URL, returning to that URL without submitting the form would have generated a broken welcome message ("Welcome to our website, !"), or a PHP error message if, like Homestead Improved, the server is running with error reporting enabled.

Bring on the Database

In this chapter, we've seen the PHP server-side scripting language in action as we've explored all the basic language features: statements, variables, operators, comments, and control structures. The sample applications we've seen have been reasonably simple, but we've still taken the time to ensure they have attractive URLs, and that the HTML templates for the pages they generate are uncluttered by the PHP code that controls them.

As you may have begun to suspect, the real power of PHP is in its hundreds (even thousands) of built-in functions that let you access data in a MySQL database, send email, dynamically generate images, and even create Adobe Acrobat PDF files on the fly.

In Chapter 3, we'll delve into the MySQL functions built into PHP, and then create a database of jokes. Then in Chapter 4, we'll see how to publish the joke database we created to the Web. These tasks will set the scene for the ultimate goal of this book: to create a complete content management system for your website in PHP and MySQL.

Chapter

3

Introducing MySQL

In Chapter 1, we booted the Homestead Improved virtual machine. The virtual machine contains all the software we need, including a MySQL server.

As I explained in that chapter, PHP is a server-side scripting language that lets you insert instructions into your web pages that your web server software will execute before it sends those pages to browsers that request them. We've looked at a few basic examples including generating random numbers and using forms to capture input from a user.

Now, that's all well and good, but it *really* gets interesting when a database is added to the mix. In this chapter, we'll learn what a database is, and how to work with your own MySQL databases using Structured Query Language (SQL).

An Introduction to Databases

A database server (in our case, MySQL) is a program that can store large amounts of information in an organized format that's easily accessible through programming languages like PHP. For example, you could tell PHP to look in the database for a list of jokes that you'd like to appear on your website.

In this example, the jokes would be stored entirely in the database. The advantage of this approach is twofold. First, instead of writing an HTML page for each joke, you could write a single PHP script that was designed to fetch any joke from the database and display it by generating an HTML page for it on the fly. Second, adding a joke to your website would be a simple matter of inserting the joke into the database. The PHP code would take care of the rest, automatically displaying the new joke along with the others when it fetched the list from the database.

Let's run with this example as we look at how data is stored in a database. A database is composed of one or more **tables**, each of which contains a list of **items**, or *things*. For our joke database, we'd probably start with a table called joke that would contain a list of jokes. Each table in a database has one or more **columns**, or **fields**. Each column holds a certain piece of information about each item in the table. In our example, our joke table might have one column for the text of the jokes, and another for the dates on which the jokes were added to the database. Each joke stored in this way would be said to be a **row** or **entry** in the table. These rows and columns form a table that looks like this:

id	joketext	jokedate
1	Why did the chicken ...	2012-04-01
2	Knock-knock! Who's ...	2012-04-01

3-1. A typical database table containing a list of jokes

Notice that, in addition to columns for the joke text (`joketext`) and the date of the joke (`jokedate`), there's included a column named `id`. As a matter of good design, a database table should always provide a means by which each row can be identified uniquely. Since it's possible that two identical jokes could be entered on the same date, we can't rely on the `joketext` and `jokedate` columns to tell all the jokes apart. The function of the `id` column, therefore, is to assign a unique number to each joke, so that we have an easy way to refer to them and to keep track of which joke is which. We'll take a closer look at database design issues like this in Chapter 5.

To review, the table in the figure above is a three-column table with two rows (or entries). Each row in the table contains three fields, one for each column in the table: the joke's ID, its text, and the date of the joke. With this basic terminology under your belt, you're ready to dive into using MySQL.

Using MySQL Workbench to Run SQL Queries

Just as a web server is designed to respond to requests from a client (a web browser), the MySQL database server responds to requests from **client programs**. Later in this book, we'll write our own MySQL client programs in the form of PHP scripts, but for now we can use a client program written by the same people who write MySQL: MySQL Workbench. You can download MySQL Workbench[1] for free.

There are many different MySQL clients available to use, and earlier editions of this book used phpMyAdmin, a web-based MySQL client that has many of the same features. However, it's not as easy to use as MySQL Workbench, and can often be very slow.

Once you've downloaded and installed MySQL Workbench, open it up, and you should see a screen that looks like this:

[1.] https://www.mysql.com/products/workbench/

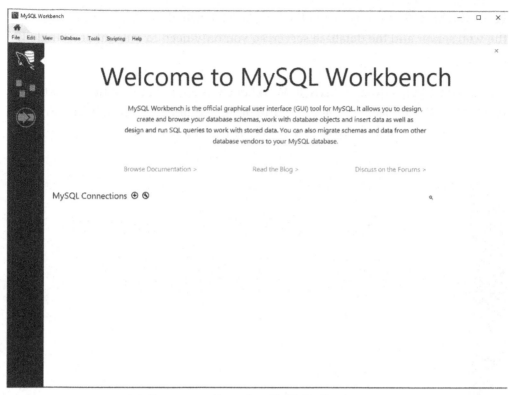

3-2. If you can see this, you have MySQL Workbench running

Before you can add any data to your database, you need to connect to it. MySQL is a server running in the Vagrant box you downloaded in Chapter 1, and you can connect to it using a MySQL client such as MySQL Workbench.

Connecting to the database requires three pieces of information:

- a server address
- a username
- a password

For the Homestead Improved Vagrant box, the information is:

- **Server:** 192.168.10.10
- **Username:** homestead
- **Password:** secret

You'll notice that the server IP is identical to the IP you've been connecting to in your web browser to view your PHP scripts. The virtual machine is running both the web server and the database server, so you only need to remember a single IP address.

To connect to a database in MySQL Workbench, press the plus button next to the label "MySQL Connections" in the centre of the window. (Admittedly, it isn't very clearly labeled, and its purpose isn's very clear, but never mind!)

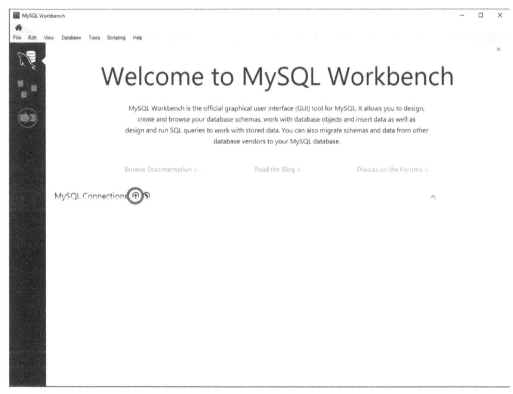

3-3. Add a connection

When you press the plus button, you'll see a new window that looks like this:

3-4. Add a connection

Enter the server address and username. You'll also need to give your connection a name. I've called it "Homestead", but you can call it whatever you like. This is just a name that it's listed as for future reference in MySQL Workbench.

Once you've entered the username and server, you can try connecting to the database by pressing the "Test Connection" button at the bottom of the window.

You should get a password prompt box that looks like this:

3-5. Password prompt

If you don't, follow these steps:

1. Double check that your Vagrant box is running. (If you've rebooted your PC since setting it up, you may need to run `vagrant up` again in the project's folder to get it running!)
2. Make sure the username and server address are correct.

 Case Sensitivity

> Usernames and passwords are case-sensitive, so make sure you type them both in lowercase!

Enter the password `secret` into the box and tick the box that says "Save password". By checking the box, you won't have to enter the password each time you connect. Then press **OK** .

If the password was entered correctly, you'll see a message telling you the connection was successful. Press **OK** in the "Set up new connection" window and you'll see a box appear in the main MySQL window with some of the information you entered:

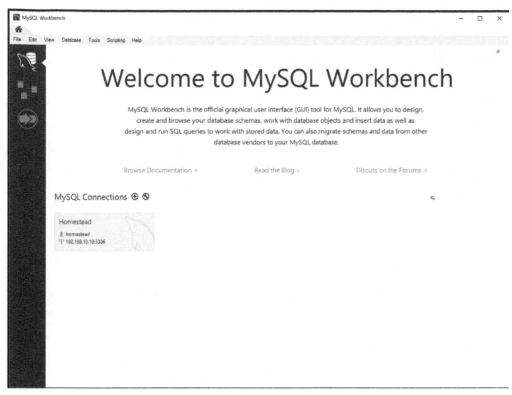

3-6. The main MySQL window showing information that was entered

Now that the connection is set up, it will be there each time you open MySQL workbench, you won't need to add the connection each time.

You're finally ready to actually connect to the database. To do this, simply double-click on the newly created box representing your connection and you'll be presented with a different screen:

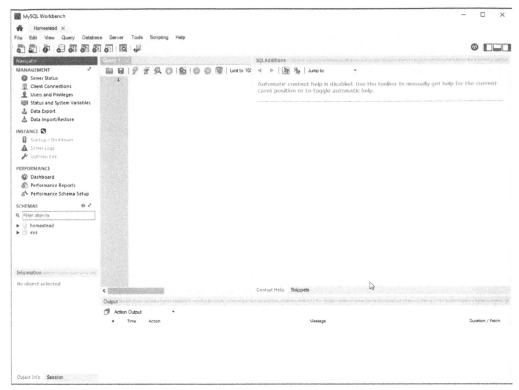

3-7. Initial screen

This looks a little daunting at first, as there are a lot of different buttons and panels all representing different things. Down the left-hand side is a menu with lots of different options. The only one you need to worry about is the bottom section titled "Schemas".

Schema is just a fancy word for "database". MySQL is a **database server**. In practical terms, this means that it can host lots of different databases, similarly to how a web server can host lots of different websites.

Creating a Database

Before you can add any information to a database, you need to create one. There are already two entries in the Schemas panel, `homestead` and `sys`. These come with Homestead, and although you could use them, for our purposes it would be better to create a database with a more suitable name.

To create a database, right-click in the Schemas panel and select "Create schema". This gives you a window with several options, but you only need to enter one: the schema name.

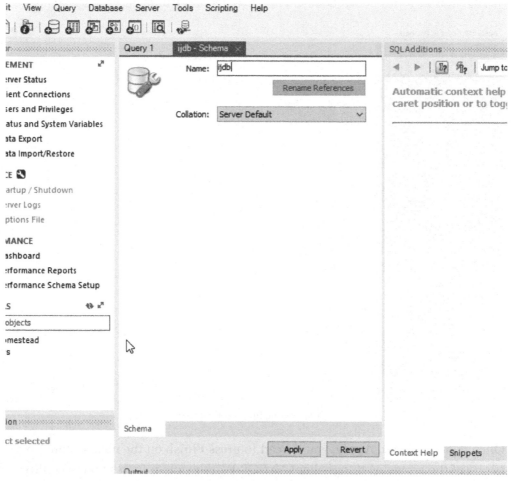

3-8. Creating a schema

I chose to name the database **ijdb**, for Internet Joke Database[2], because that fits with the example I gave at the beginning of this chapter: a website that displays a database of jokes. Feel free to give the database any name you like, though. (You'll need to type it out frequently as you progress through this book, so don't pick anything too complicated!)

---

[2] With a tip of the hat to the Internet Movie Database.

Once you've typed a name, you can safely leave the other options at their default values and press **Apply**. When you do this, MySQL Workbench will ask you to confirm your action. (Get used to these dialogs. MySQL Workbench insists on confirmation for almost everything you do!) Press **Apply** again on this screen:

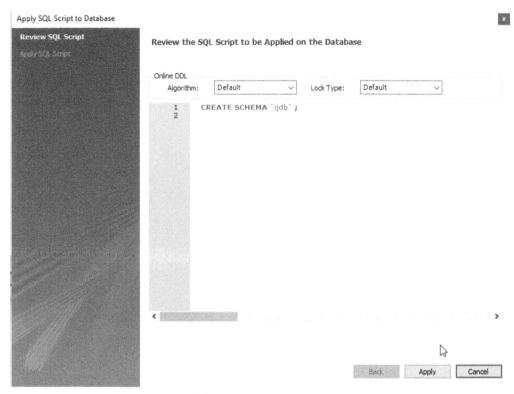

3-9. Confirming the schema creation

Once you've pressed **Apply**, you'll need to press **Finish** on the next screen. This is one of the annoying things about MySQL Workbench: it forces you to confirm and then **Finish** every action. However, it's better than the alternative, as we'll see shortly!

In the screenshot above, you'll see a white panel with the words CREATE SCHEMA ijdb. This is an SQL Query, and you'll see a lot more of these throughout this book. You could have typed out this command yourself and run it, avoiding the GUI and saving yourself going through MySQL Workbench's confirmation dialogs. And for a command as simple as CREATE SCHEMA ijdb, the GUI is probably overkill. However, as you'll see shortly, not all of the commands are this simple, and it's a lot easier to use MySQL Workbench's GUI for some of the more complex queries.

If you want to be able to delete databases (and this is probably a good ability to have, given the amount of experimentation I'm going to encourage you to do in this book), MySQL Workbench makes this easy. In the Schemas panel in the main window, right-click on the schema you want to delete and select **DROP Schema**. MySQL uses the word DROP for deleting things. (Somewhat inconsistently, **Delete** is also used for some things!)

Structured Query Language

Like the CREATE SCHEMA command we just saw, the commands we'll use to direct MySQL throughout the rest of this book are part of a standard called **Structured Query Language**, or **SQL** (pronounced as either "sequel" or "ess-cue-ell"—take your pick). Commands in SQL are also referred to as **queries**; I'll use these two terms interchangeably.

SQL is the standard language for interacting with most databases, so, even if you move from MySQL to a database like Microsoft SQL Server in the future, you'll find that the majority of commands are identical. It's important that you understand the distinction between SQL and MySQL. MySQL is the database server software that you're using. SQL is the language that you use to interact with that database.

Most of these commands can be generated by MySQL Workbench, and that's what we'll use to create the structure of our database. However, you'll need to learn some commands, as you'll be executing them from your PHP scripts rather than MySQL Workbench!

 Dive Deeper Into SQL

In this book, I'll teach you the essentials of SQL that every PHP developer needs to know. If you decide to make a career out of building database-driven websites, it pays to know some of the more advanced details of SQL, especially when it comes to making your sites run as quickly and smoothly as possible. To dive deeper into SQL, I highly recommend the book *Simply SQL*[3], by Rudy Limeback.

Case Sensitivity and Convention

Most MySQL commands are not case-sensitive, which means you can type CREATE DATABASE, create database, or even CrEaTe DaTaBaSe, and it will know what you mean. Database names and table names, however, are case-sensitive when the MySQL server is running on an operating system with a case-sensitive file system (such as Linux or macOS, depending on your system configuration).

Additionally, table, column, and other names must be spelled exactly the same when they're used more than once in the same query.

For consistency, this book will respect the accepted convention of typing database commands in all capitals, and database entities (databases, tables, columns, and so on) in all lowercase.

This also makes it easier for people (like you!) to read the queries. MySQL doesn't care, but you'll be able to identify a command quickly and easily because it's in capitals, and a reference to a table, column or database because it's in lowercase.

Once your database has been created, it will appear in the Schemas list on the left-hand side:

---

3. http://www.sitepoint.com/books/sql1/

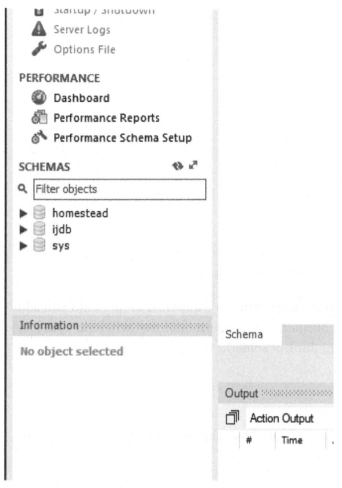

3-10. The Internet Joke Database schema

Now that you have a database, you need to tell MySQL Workbench that you want to use it. To do this, simply double-click the newly created schema and its name will go bold. You can only have one schema selected at a time, and you need to tell MySQL Workbench which you'd like to use:

3-11. The ijdb schema selected

You're now ready to use your database. Since a database is empty until you add tables to it, our first order of business is to create a table that will hold your jokes. (Now might be a good time to think of some!)

Creating a Table

If you expand your newly created `ijdb` schema by pressing the arrow next to the name, you'll see a few entries:

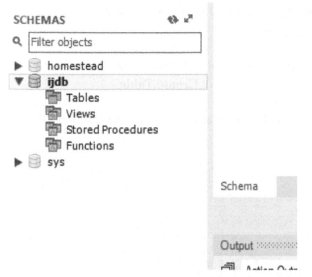

3-12. The ijdb schema expanded

The only one we're concerned with for the purposes of this book is the **Tables** entry. Because your schema has just been created, it doesn't have any tables.

A table describes the format of your data. You'll need to know the *structure* of the data you'd like to store. Before creating a table, you need to think about exactly what you want to store. For the jokes example, we want to store these pieces of information:

- the text of the joke
- the date it was added

Along with the text and date, we'll also need some way to identify each joke. To do this, we'll give each joke a unique ID.

Each piece of information is placed in a field in the table, and each field has a **type**. Types can be used to store data in different formats like numbers, text and dates.

There are three main kinds of types that you'll encounter:

- numbers, for storing numeric values
- text, for storing strings
- dates/times for storing timestamps

There are lots of column types in MySQL, but you only really need an understanding of three for most purposes!

To create a table using MySQL Workbench, expand the database in the Schemas list, then right-click on the Tables entry and select **Create Table**.

The middle panel of the window will change to show you something like this:

3-13. MySQL Workbench's New Table window

Every table is given a name to identify it and a series of columns. Firstly, enter the table's name as "joke" and add the following columns in the column list:

- id, which will act as a unique identifier for each joke so we can retrieve it later
- joketext, which will store the text of the joke
- jokedate, which will store the date the joke was added

3-14. Creating the joke table

You'll notice there's a second column called **Datatype**. Each column in a database table must be assigned a type. The three types we will need are:

- INT, meaning "integer" for the numeric `jokeid`
- TEXT, to store some text for the joke
- DATE, to store the date the joke was published

This helps to keep your data organized, and allows you to compare the values within a column in powerful ways, as we'll see later.

If we were to stop setting up the table at this point, you could start adding records to the table (and I'll show you how to do that very shortly!). However, you would have to provide all three pieces of information: the joke ID, the joke text and the joke date. This means that, to add the next joke, you'd need to keep track of how many were in there in order to assign the next ID.

This sounds like extra work, but fortunately MySQL Workbench provides a convenient way of avoiding it. Along with the name of the column and data type it stores, you'll notice there's a series of checkboxes for each field in the table.

There are three we're interested in here for our ID field:

- PK. This means "primary key". Ticking this box specifies that this column is to act as a unique identifier for the entries in the table, so all values in this column must be unique, ensuring that no two jokes will share the same ID.
- NN. This stands for "Not Null", and means that when a record is added, a value must be placed in the field. For our ID column, ticking this box tells MySQL not to accept jokes that don't have an ID.
- AI. This is the clever bit that will save us work. No, "AI" is not "Artificial Intelligence", some kind of computer-brain doing our work for us. In this case, it stands for "Auto Increment", and by checking this box (and it's only allowed on INT fields!), whenever a record (in our case, a joke) is added to the table, it will automatically be assigned the next available ID. This is a real time saver and a feature worth remembering.

Your table should now look like this:

3-15. The joke table complete

Press the **Apply** button and the joke table will be created. You'll see the following query appear in the window:

```
CREATE TABLE `ijdb`.`joke` (
`id` INT NOT NULL AUTO_INCREMENT,
`joketext` TEXT NULL,
```

```
`jokedate` DATE NULL,
PRIMARY KEY (`id`));
```

You'll notice a lot of the same information has been repeated that we entered into the GUI. The GUI just generates this code for us, which is a much quicker and easier way of creating tables than remembering all of the syntax and vocabulary needed to write the query yourself.

As a developer, you don't need to create tables often. You will need to interact with them, though—adding and removing records and retrieving them from the database—so it's worth spending time learning how to write queries to do this. But for creating tables, it's usually a lot quicker and easier to use the MySQL Workbench GUI, because once a table has been created, you won't need to write another create table statement.

We need to look at just one more task: deleting a table. This task is frighteningly easy, so be careful! If you delete a table, you can't get it back.

In the Schemas list, right-click on the table you you want to delete and select **Drop Table**. **Don't** run this command with your joke table, unless you actually do want to be rid of it. If you really want to try it, be prepared to re-create your joke table from scratch. When you delete a table, the table is removed permanently, along with any data stored inside it. *There is no way to recover the data after the table has been dropped*, so be very careful when using this command!

Adding Data

Now that the table has been created, it's time to add some data to it. Although this can be done using MySQL Workbench's GUI, this time we're going to write the query ourselves. Eventually, we'll need to be able to write our own database queries directly from PHP, so it's good to get some practice writing them.

To run a query, you need to open up a query window. The simplest way to do this is to expand your database in the Schema list. Expand the Tables entry, and you'll see the `joke` table that you just created. Right-click on the table and click on the topmost option "Select Rows - Limit 1000".

This will give you a slightly different screen that's split into two panels:

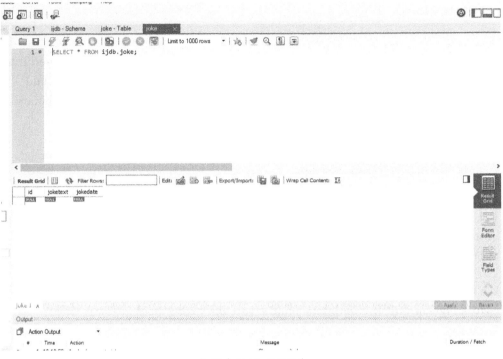

3-16. A new query panel

The top half is a text box into which you can type commands to ask your database server questions or make it perform tasks. The bottom half is the result of that query. You'll see there's already a query in the top panel:

```
SELECT * FROM `ijdb`.`joke`;
```

We'll come back to what this means shortly. Along with this query in the top panel, there's a list of rows in the bottom panel—or rather there would be, if there were anything in the table! Because the table was just created, it's currently empty. Before you can view the contents of the table, you need to add some records.

All that's left is to put some jokes into the database. The command that inserts data into a database is called, appropriately enough, INSERT. This command can take two basic forms:

```
INSERT INTO tableName SET
column1Name = column1Value,
column2Name = column2Value,
…
```

```
INSERT INTO tableName
(column1Name, column2Name, …)
VALUES (column1Value, column2Value, …)
```

So, to add a joke to our table, we can use either of these commands:

```
INSERT INTO joke SET
 joketext = "A programmer was found dead in the shower. The
↪ instructions read: lather, rinse, repeat.",
jokedate = "2017-06-01"
```

```
INSERT INTO joke
(joketext, jokedate) VALUES (
 "A programmer was found dead in the shower. The instructions
↪ read: lather, rinse, repeat.",
"2017-06-01")
```

Note that the order of the column/value pairs isn't important, but pairing the right values with the right columns, position-wise, is. If the first column mentioned in the first set of parentheses is joketext, then the first entry in the VALUES list must be the text that's going to be placed in the joketext column. The second column name in the first parentheses gets its values from the same position in the VALUES list. Otherwise, the order of the columns isn't important. Go ahead and swap the order of the column and value pairs and try the query.

As you typed the query, you'll have noticed that we used double quotes (") to mark where the text of the joke started and ended. A piece of text enclosed in quotes this way is called a **text string**, and this is how you represent most data

values in SQL. For instance, the dates are typed as text strings, too, in the form
`"YYYY-MM-DD"`.

If you prefer, you can type text strings surrounded with single quotes (`'`) instead
of double quotes:

```
INSERT INTO joke SET
joketext = '',
jokedate = '2017-06-01'
```

You might be wondering what happens when there are quotes used within the
joke's text. Well, if the text contains single quotes, you would surround it with
double quotes. Conversely, if the text contains double quotes, surround it with
single quotes.

If the text you want to include in your query contains both single *and* double
quotes, you'll have to escape the conflicting characters within your text string.
You escape a character in SQL by adding a backslash (\) immediately before it.
This tells MySQL to ignore any "special meaning" this character might have. In
the case of single or double quotes, it tells MySQL not to interpret the character
as the end of the text string.

To make this as clear as possible, here's an example of an `INSERT` command for a
joke containing single quotes, even though single quotes have been used to mark
the string:

```
INSERT INTO joke
(joketext, jokedate) VALUES (
'!false - it\'s funny because it\'s true',
"2017-06-01")
```

As you can see, I've marked the start and end of the text string for the joke text
using single quotes. I've therefore had to escape the two single quotes (the
apostrophes) within the string by putting backslashes before them. MySQL would
see these backslashes and know to treat the single quotes as characters within the
string, rather than end-of-string markers.

If you're especially clever, you might now be wondering how to include actual backslashes in SQL text strings. The answer is to type a double-backslash (\\), which MySQL will treat as a single backslash in the string of text.

Write your insert query into the top text box in MySQL Workbench and press the yellow lightning bolt icon above it to execute the query.

3-17. Executing a query using MySQL Workbench

When the query executes, a panel will appear at the bottom of the screen telling you if the query was executed successfully:

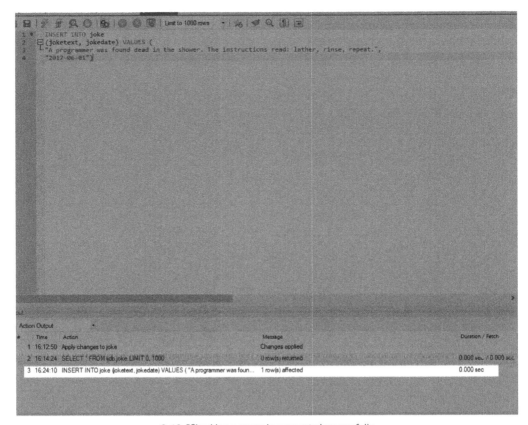

3-18. "Checking a query has executed successfully

If you get an error and the query isn't successful, take a look at the error message and it should give you a hint where to look. Double-check your syntax, and check your quotes and parentheses are in the right place.

 Displaying the Bottom Panel on Low-Res Screens

If you have a lower screen resolution than it's expecting, MySQL Workbench hides the bottom panel. To display it, hover your mouse just below the scroll bar at the bottom of the window and you'll get a resize cursor. You can then drag the panel into view.

Add both the jokes (and any others you can think of!) to the database using INSERT queries. Now that you know how to add entries to a table, let's see how we can view those entries.

A Word of Warning

You'll have noticed something slightly peculiar about the queries that have been generated by MySQL Workbench. Instead of a query that looks like this:

```
SELECT * FROM joke
```

The query generated will be:

```
SELECT * FROM `joke`
```

With those strange quotes around `joke`. Those aren't actually quotes, or even apostrophes like we've been using to designate strings. They're **backticks**.

This is a safety precaution. There are lots of words in SQL that have meaning to the language. You've seen a few already: `SELECT`, `FROM` and `INSERT`, but there are hundreds of others, known as **reserved words**. Imagine if you called your table `SELECT`. The query you would need to run would look like this:

```
SELECT * FROM SELECT
```

Unfortunately, this can cause MySQL to get a little confused. It may see `SELECT` as a command rather than as a table name. What's worse, `date` is one of these words, and it's not improbable that you might think to create a column in one of your tables called `date`. What would you expect to happen when the following query runs?

```
INSERT INTO joke
(joketext, date) VALUES (
'!false - it\'s funny because it\'s true',
"2012-04-01")
```

Because the word `date` already has meaning in SQL, it may not be seen as a column name but as part of the query, like VALUES or INTO.

MySQL is *usually* good at guessing whether you're referring to a table/column name or a command it needs to follow, but there are times when it isn't able to make that distinction. To avoid this kind of confusion, it's good practice to surround all table and column names with backticks. The backticks tell MySQL to treat the string as a *name* rather than an *instruction*. It's good to get into the habit of doing this from the very start, as it avoids issues later on that often aren't immediately obvious.

From now on, I'll surround all table, schema and column names with backticks. This will also help you—as a programmer—to distinguish between commands and column names. For instance, the INSERT query above would be written like this:

```
INSERT INTO `joke`
(`joketext`, `date`) VALUES (
'!false - it\'s funny because it\'s true',
"2012-04-01")
```

 ### Where's the Darned Backtick Key?

On many English keyboard layouts, the backtick key is the one to the immediate left of the numeric 1 key and below **Esc**. On Macs, it's often located to the left of the Z key. Its location may differ on non-English keyboards and/or on various devices such as laptops and tablets.

Viewing Stored Data

The command that we use to view data stored in database tables is SELECT. You saw an example SELECT query generated for you by MySQL Workbench earlier. The SELECT query is the most complicated command in SQL. The reason for this complexity is that the chief strength of a database is its flexibility in data retrieval. At this early point in our experience with databases, we need only focus on fairly simple lists of results, so let's consider the simpler forms of the SELECT command here.

This command will list everything that's stored in the joke table:

```
SELECT * FROM `joke`
```

This command says "select everything from joke", with the * meaning "all columns". By default, a SELECT query will return every record in the table. If you try this command, your results will resemble this:

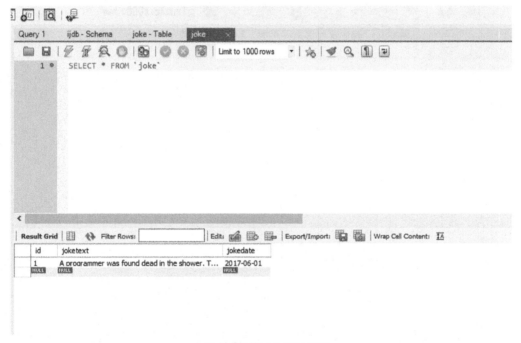

3-19. MySQL Workbench results

Notice that there are some values in the id column, even though you didn't specify them in the INSERT queries you ran earlier. MySQL has automatically assigned an ID to the joke. This is because you checked the "AI" (Auto Increment) checkbox when you created the table. If you hadn't checked the box, you'd have needed to specify the ID for each joke you inserted.

If you were doing serious work on such a database, you might be tempted to stop and read all the hilarious jokes in the database at this point. To save yourself the distraction, you might want to tell MySQL to omit the `joketext` column. The command for doing this is as follows:

```
SELECT `id`, `jokedate` FROM joke
```

This time, instead of telling it to "select everything," we told it precisely which columns we wanted to see. The result should look like this:

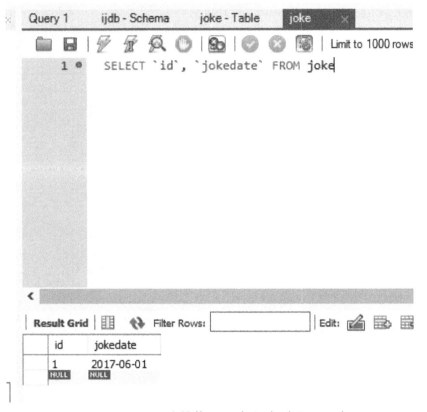

3-20. You can select only what you need

What if we'd like to see *some* of the joke text? As well as being able to name specific columns that we want the SELECT command to show us, we can use functions to modify each column's display. One function, called LEFT, enables us to tell MySQL to display a column's contents up to a specified number of characters. For example, let's say we wanted to see only the first 20 characters of the `joketext` column. Here's the command we'd use:

```
SELECT `id`, LEFT(`joketext`, 20), `jokedate` FROM `joke`
```

3-21. The LEFT function trims the text to a specified length

See how that worked? Another useful function is COUNT, which lets us count the number of results returned. If, for example, you wanted to find out how many jokes were stored in your table, you could use the following command:

```
SELECT COUNT(`id`) FROM `joke`
```

As you can see in the image below, you have just two jokes in your table:

3-22. The **COUNT** function counts the rows

 Using * Instead

You can use COUNT(*) for the same result, but this is slower, as all the columns will be selected from the table. By using the primary key, only one column needs to be retrieved.

So far, the examples we've looked at have fetched all the entries in the table. However, you can limit your results to only those database entries that have the specific attributes you want. You set these restrictions by adding what's called a WHERE clause to the SELECT command. Consider this example:

```
SELECT COUNT(*) FROM `joke` WHERE `jokedate` >=
↪ "2017-01-01"
```

This query will count the number of jokes that have dates greater than or equal to January 1, 2017. In the case of dates, "greater than or equal to" means "on or after". Another variation on this theme lets you search for entries that contain a certain piece of text. Check out this query:

```
SELECT `joketext` FROM `joke` WHERE `joketext` LIKE
↪ "%programmer%"
```

This query displays the full text of all jokes containing the text "programmer" in their `joketext` column. The `LIKE` keyword tells MySQL that the named column must match the given pattern.[4] In this case, the pattern we've used is `"%programer%"`. The `%` signs (called **wildcards**) indicate that the text "programmer" may be preceded and/or followed by any string of text.

Conditions may also be combined in the `WHERE` clause to further restrict results. For example, to display knock-knock jokes from April 2017 only, you could use the following query:

```
SELECT `joketext` FROM `joke` WHERE
`joketext` LIKE "%knock%" AND
`jokedate` >= "2017-04-01" AND
`jokedate` < "2017-05-01"
```

Enter a few more jokes into the table. (For example, "Why did the programmer quit his job? He didn't get arrays.") Then experiment with `SELECT` queries (For ideas, see Chapter 4.)

You can do a lot with the `SELECT` command, so I'd encourage you to become quite familiar with it. We'll look at some of its more advanced features later, when we need them.

Modifying Stored Data

Having entered data into a database table, you might find that you'd like to change it. Whether you're correcting a spelling mistake, or changing the date attached to a joke, such alterations are made using the `UPDATE` command. This command contains elements of the `SELECT` and `INSERT` commands, since the

---

[4] In case you were curious, `LIKE` is case-insensitive, so this pattern will also match a joke that contains "Programmer", or even "FuNkYProGRammeR".

command both picks out entries for modification and sets column values. The general form of the UPDATE command is as follows:

```
UPDATE `tableName` SET
    `colName` = newValue, …
WHERE conditions
```

So, for example, if we wanted to change the date on the joke we entered earlier, we'd use the following command:

```
UPDATE `joke` SET `jokedate` = "2018-04-01" WHERE id = "1"
```

Here's where that id column comes in handy, enabling you to easily single out a joke for changes. The WHERE clause used here works just as it did in the SELECT command. This next command, for example, changes the date of all entries that contain the word "programmer":

```
UPDATE `joke` SET `jokedate` = "2018-04-01"
WHERE `joketext` LIKE "%programmer%"
```

 WHERE is Optional

Believe it or not, the WHERE clause in the UPDATE command is optional. Consequently, you should be very careful when typing this command! If you leave the WHERE clause out, the UPDATE command will then apply to *all entries in the table*.

The following command will set the date for all the records in the table!

```
UPDATE `joke` SET `jokedate` = "2018-04-01"
```

Deleting Stored Data

Deleting entries in SQL is dangerously easy, which you've probably noticed is a recurring theme. Here's the command syntax:

```
DELETE FROM `tableName` WHERE conditions
```

To delete all programmer jokes from your table, you'd use the following query:

```
DELETE FROM `joke` WHERE `joketext` LIKE "%programmer%"
```

 Again, WHERE is Optional

As with UPDATE, the WHERE clause in the DELETE command is optional. Consequently, you should be very careful when using it. If you leave the WHERE clause out, the DELETE command will then apply to *all entries in the table*.

The following command will empty the joke table in one fell swoop:

```
DELETE FROM `joke`
```

Scary, huh?

Let PHP Do the Typing

There's a lot more to the MySQL database server software and SQL than the handful of basic commands I've presented here, but these commands are by far the most commonly used and useful!

At this stage, you might be thinking that databases seem a little cumbersome. SQL can be tricky to type, as its commands tend to be long and verbose compared with those of other computer languages. You're probably dreading the thought of typing in a complete library of jokes in the form of INSERT commands.

Don't sweat it! As we proceed through this book, you'll be surprised at how few SQL queries you actually type by hand. Generally, you'll be writing PHP scripts that type your SQL for you. For example, if you want to be able to insert a bunch of jokes into your database, you'll typically create a PHP script for adding jokes that includes the necessary INSERT query, with a placeholder for the joke text. You can then run that PHP script whenever you have jokes to add. The PHP script prompts you to enter your joke, then issues the appropriate INSERT query to your MySQL server.

For now, however, it's important to gain a good feel for typing SQL by hand. It will give you a strong sense of the inner workings of MySQL databases, and will make you appreciate all the more the work that PHP will save you!

To date, we've only worked with a single table, but to realize the true power of a relational database, you'll need to learn how to use multiple tables together to represent potentially complex relationships between the items stored in your database. I'll cover all this and more in Chapter 5, in which I'll discuss database design principles and show off some more advanced examples.

In the meantime, we've accomplished our objective, and you can comfortably interact with MySQL using the MySQL Workbench query window. In Chapter 4, the fun continues as we delve into the PHP language, and use it to create several dynamically generated web pages.

If you like, you can practice with MySQL a little before you move on, by creating a decent-sized joke table (for our purposes, five should be enough). This library of jokes will come in handy later.

Chapter

4

Publishing MySQL Data on the Web

This is it—the stuff you signed up for! In this chapter, you'll learn how to take information stored in a MySQL database and display it on a web page for all to see.

So far, you've written your first PHP code and learned the basics of MySQL, a relational database engine, and PHP, a server-side scripting language.

Now you're ready to learn how to use these tools together to create a website where users can view data from the database and even add their own.

The Big Picture

Before we leap forward, it's worth taking a step back for a clear picture of our

ultimate goal. We have two powerful tools at our disposal: the PHP scripting
language and the MySQL database engine. It's important to understand how these
will fit together.

The purpose of using MySQL for our website is to allow the content to be pulled
dynamically from the database to create web pages for viewing in a regular
browser. So, at one end of the system you have a visitor to your site using a web
browser to request a page. That browser expects to receive a standard HTML
document in return. At the other end you have the content of your site, which sits
in one or more tables in a MySQL database that only understands how to respond
to SQL queries (commands).

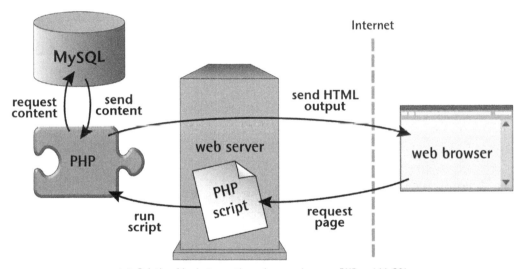

4-1. Relationships between the web server, browser, PHP and MySQL

As shown in the image above, the PHP scripting language is the go-between that
speaks both languages. It processes the page request and fetches the data from the
MySQL database (using SQL queries just like those you used to create a table of
jokes in Chapter 3. It then spits it out dynamically as the nicely formatted HTML
page that the browser expects.

Just so it's clear and fresh in your mind, this is what happens when there's a
visitor to a page on your website:

1. The visitor's web browser requests the web page from your web server.

2. The web server software (typically Apache or NGINX) recognizes that the

requested file is a PHP script, so the server fires up the PHP interpreter to execute the code contained in the file.

3. Certain PHP commands (which will be the focus of this chapter) connect to the MySQL database and request the content that belongs in the web page.

4. The MySQL database responds by sending the requested content to the PHP script.

5. The PHP script stores the content into one or more PHP variables, then uses echo statements to output the content as part of the web page.

6. The PHP interpreter finishes up by handing a copy of the HTML it has created to the web server.

7. The web server sends the HTML to the web browser as it would a plain HTML file, except that instead of coming directly from an HTML file, the page is the output provided by the PHP interpreter. The browser has no way of knowing this, however. As far as the browser is concerned, it's requesting and receiving a web page like any other.

Creating a MySQL User Account

In order for PHP to connect to your MySQL database server, it will need to use a username and password. So far, all that your joke database contains is a number of pithy *bon mots*, but before long it may contain sensitive information like email addresses and other private details about the users of your website. For this reason, MySQL is designed to be very secure, giving you tight control over what connections it will accept and what those connections are allowed to do.

The Homestead Improved[1] box already contains a MySQL user in Chapter 3, which you've already used to log in to the MySQL server.

You *could* connect to the database from your PHP script using the same username (homestead) and password (secret), but it's useful to create a new account—because if you have a web server, you may want to use it to host more

---

[1.] http://www.sitepoint.com/quick-tip-get-homestead-vagrant-vm-running/

than one website. By giving each website its own user account, you'll have more control over who has access to the data for any given site. If you're working with other developers, you can give them access to the sites they're working on, but no more.

You should create a new user account with only the specific privileges it needs to work on the `ijdb` database that your website depends upon. Let's do that now:

1. To create a user, open up MySQL Workbench and connect to your server.

   ■ In the panel on the left-hand side of the window, there's an option labeled **Users and Privileges**.

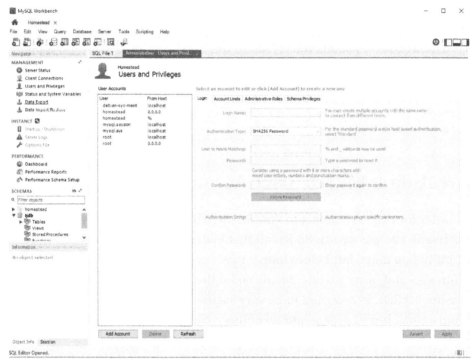

4-2. User management

   ■ After clicking on the link, you're able to add a user. There's already a few listed in the middle panel, including the `homestead` user you used to log in.

   ■ To add a new user, click the **Add Account** button near the bottom of the window. This will enable the fields that were visible on the right-hand side. You'll notice there are four tabs, offering quite a few options. Luckily, you can leave almost all of them with their defaults values.

- The main thing you need to add are the username and password you want to use to log in. Fill in the first form using the following information, leaving everything else at its defaults:

```
Login name | ijdbuser
---------- | ---------- |
```

If you prefer, you can just name the user `ijdb`. It's common to give an account restricted to accessing a single database the name of that database. I've chosen to name it `ijdbuser` in this book to help clarify the distinction between the name of the database (`ijdb`) and the user account that's allowed to access it (`ijdbuser`).

```
Limit to Hosts Matching | localhost
---------- | ---------- |
```

This option allows you to add extra security by only allowing connections from a specific location, instead of allowing anyone to connect to your database from anywhere on the internet. By entering `localhost` into this box, you'll only be able to connect from the computer running MySQL. Even if someone did manage to get hold of your database username and password, they wouldn't be able to log in without access to the server it's running from.

```
Password | mypassword
---------- | ---------- |
```

This is just the password I'm going to use in this book. You should probably have your own unique password, and remember it for later use in the PHP scripts you're going to write.

```
Confirm Password | mypassword
---------- | ---------- |
```

Enter your password again, just to verify that you typed it correctly the first time.

- Press **Apply**, and your new user will appear in the central panel. Click on the user and then select the **Schema Privileges**. By default, a user doesn't have access to read or write to any schemas. All they'll be able to do is log in. In order to allow your new user to access the `jokes` database, you need to click **Add Entry**, which opens a new window. Select **Selected Schema** and choose the `ijdb` schema from this list. This will give your new user access to the `ijdb` schema and no others. If someone did manage to gain access to the database with the `ijdbuser` account, they wouldn't be able to see data from any other website that you might have running on the server.

- When you click **OK**, you'll see a lot of checkboxes. Some of these are SQL commands you saw in the last chapter. Give your user full access by clicking **Select All** and finally press **Apply** again.

Your user is now set up, and you'll see the privileges in the box above the checkboxes:

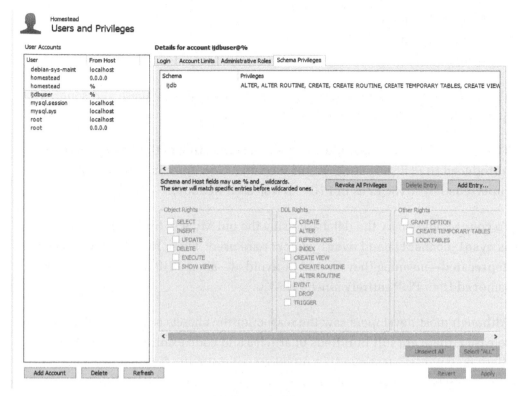

4-3. Users and privileges

Now that the user ijdbuser has been created, we can use it to connect to the database. It's possible to set up a connection in MySQL Workbench with this user, but since the permissions are limited, it's better to keep MySQL Workbench using the homestead account. Instead, we're going to use the new user when connecting from a PHP script.

Connecting to MySQL with PHP

Before you can retrieve content from your MySQL database for inclusion in a web page, you must know how to establish a connection to MySQL from inside a PHP script. So far, you've used an application called MySQL Workbench to connect to your database. Just as the MySQL Workbench can connect directly to a running MySQL server, so too can your own PHP scripts.

There are three methods of connecting to a MySQL Server from PHP:

- the MySQL library
- the MySQLi library
- the PDO library

These all essentially do the same job, connecting to the database and sending queries to it, but they use different code to achieve it.

The MySQL library is the oldest method of connecting to the database and was introduced in PHP 2.0. The features it contains are minimal, and it was superseded by MySQLi as of PHP 5.0 (released in 2004).

To connect and query the database using the old MySQL library, functions such as `mysql_connect()` and `mysql_query()` are used. These functions have been **deprecated**—meaning they should be avoided—since PHP 5.5, and have been removed from PHP entirely since PHP 7.0.

Although most developers saw the reason for the change as soon as PHP 5.0 was released, there are still hundreds of articles and code examples on the Web using these now non-existent `mysql_*` functions—despite the fact that MySQLi has effectively been the preferred library for over ten years.

If you come across a code example that contains the line `mysql_connect()`, check the date of the article. It's probably from the early 2000s, and in programming, you should never trust anything that old. Things change all the time—which is why this book is on its 6th edition!

In PHP 5.0, the MySQLi library, standing for "MySQL Improved", was released to address some of the limitations in the original MySQL library. You can identify the use of MySQLi, because the code will use functions such as `mysqli_connect()` and `mysqli_query()`.

Shortly after the release of the MySQLi library in PHP 5.0, PHP 5.1 was released, with a significant number of changes that helped shape the way we write PHP today (mostly to do with object-oriented programming, which you'll see plenty of later in this book). One of the major changes in PHP 5.1 was that it introduced a third library, PDO (PHP Data Objects) for connecting to MySQL databases.

There are a few differences between PDO and MySQLi, but the main one is that you can use the PDO library to connect to almost any database server—such as an

Oracle server, or a Microsoft SQL Server. For developers, the biggest advantage of this generic approach is that once you've learned how to use the library to interact with a MySQL database, it's very simple to interact with another database server.

Arguably, it's simpler to write code for PDO, and there are some nuances that can make PDO code more readable—named parameters in prepared statements being the main benefit. (Don't worry, I'll explain what that means later on.)

For these reasons, most recent PHP projects use the PDO library, and it's the library I'm going to show you how to use in this book. For more information on the differences, take a look at the SitePoint article "Re-introducing PDO – the Right Way to Access Databases in PHP"[2].

After that little history lesson, you're probably eager to get back to writing code. Here's how you use PDO to establish a connection to a MySQL server:

```
new PDO('mysql:host=hostname;dbname=database', 'username',
    'password')
```

For now, think of new PDO as a built-in function, just like the rand function we used in Chapter 2. If you're thinking "Hey, functions can't have *spaces* in their names!", you're smarter than the average bear, and I'll explain exactly what's going on here in a moment. In any case, it takes three arguments:

1. a string specifying the type of database (mysql:), the hostname of the server (host=hostname;), and the name of the database (dbname=database)

2. the MySQL username you want PHP to use

3. the MySQL password for that username

You may remember from Chapter 2 that PHP functions usually return a value when they're called. This new PDO "function" returns a value called a PDO object that identifies the connection that's been established. Since we intend to make

---

[2]. https://www.sitepoint.com/re-introducing-pdo-the-right-way-to-access-databases-in-php/

use of the connection, we should hold onto this value by storing it in a variable. Here's how that looks, with the necessary values filled in to connect to your database:

```
$pdo = new PDO('mysql:host=localhost;dbname=ijdb',
    'ijdbuser',
    'mypassword');
```

As described, the exact values of the three function parameters may differ for your MySQL server. At the very least, you'll need to substitute in the password you set for your ijdbuser user (assuming you used a password other than mypassword, the one I chose). What's important to see here is that the value returned by new PDO is stored in a variable named $pdo.

The MySQL server is a completely separate piece of software from the web server. Therefore, we must consider the possibility that the server may be unavailable or inaccessible due to a network outage, or because the username/password combination you provided is rejected by the server, or because you just forgot to start your MySQL server! In such cases, new PDO won't run, and will throw a PHP exception.

If you're wondering what it means to "throw a PHP exception," brace yourself! You're about to discover some more features of the PHP language.

A PHP exception is what happens when you tell PHP to perform a task and it's unable to do it. PHP will try to do what it's told, but will fail; and in order to tell you about the failure, it will throw an exception at you. An exception is little more than PHP just crashing with a specific error message. When an exception is thrown, PHP stops. No lines of code after the error will be executed.

As a responsible developer, it's your job to catch that exception and do something about it so the program can continue.

Uncaught Exceptions

If you don't catch an exception, PHP will stop running your PHP script and display a spectacularly ugly error message. That error message will even reveal the code of your script that threw the error. In this case, that code contains your MySQL username and password, so it's especially important to avoid the error message being seen by users!

To catch an exception, you should surround the code that might throw an exception with a `try` … `catch` statement:

```
try {
    ┊ do something risky
}
catch (ExceptionType $e) {
    ┊ handle the exception
}
```

You can think of a `try` … `catch` statement like an `if` … `else` statement, except that the second block of code is what happens if the first block of code fails to run.

Confused yet? I know I'm throwing (no pun intended) a lot of new concepts at you, but it will make more sense if I put it all together and show you what we have:

```
try {
    $pdo = new PDO('mysql:host=localhost;dbname=ijdb',
        'idjbuser', 'mypassword');
    $output = 'Database connection established.';
}
catch (PDOException $e) {
    $output = 'Unable to connect to the database server.';
}

include __DIR__ . '/../templates/output.html.php';
```

As you can see, this code is a `try` … `catch` statement. In the `try` block at the top, we attempt to connect to the database using `new PDO`. If this succeeds, we store the resulting PDO object in `$pdo` so that we can work with our new database connection. If the connection is successful, the `$output` variable is set to a message that will be displayed later.

Importantly, inside a `try` … `catch` statement, any code after an exception has been thrown will not get executed. In this case, if connecting to the database throws an exception (maybe the password is wrong or the server isn't responding), the `$output` variable will never get set to "Database connection established".

If our database connection attempt fails, PHP will throw a `PDOException`, which is the type of exception that `new PDO` throws. Our `catch` block, therefore, says that it will catch a PDOException (and store it in a variable named `$e`). Inside that block, we set the variable `$output` to contain a message about what went wrong.

However, this error message isn't particularly useful. All it tells us is that PDO could not connect to the database server. It would be better to have some information about why that was—for example, because the username and password were invalid.

The `$e` variable contains details about the exception that occurred, including an error message describing the problem. We can add this to the output variable using concatenation:

```php
try {
    $pdo = new PDO('mysql:host=localhost;dbname=ijdb',
        'idjbuser', 'mypassword');
    $output = 'Database connection established.';
}
catch (PDOException $e) {
    $output = 'Unable to connect to the database server: ' . $e;
}

include __DIR__ . '/../templates/output.html.php';
```

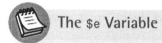

The $e Variable

The **$e** variable isn't actually a string, but an *object*. We'll come onto what that means shortly. For now, though, all you need to know is that it's possible to treat the **$e** variable as a string and use it to print a more descriptive error message.

Like an **if … else** statement, one of the two branches of a **try … catch** statement is guaranteed to run. Either the code in the **try** block will execute successfully or the code in the **catch** block will run. Regardless of whether the database connection was successful, there will be a message in the **$output** variable—either the error message, or the message saying the connection was successful.

Finally, regardless of whether the **try** block was successful, or the **catch** block runs, the template **output.html.php** is included. This is a generic template that just displays some text to the page:

```
<!doctype html>
<html>
    <head>
        <meta charset="utf-8">
        <title>Script Output</title>
    </head>
    <body>
        <?php echo $output; ?>
    </body>
</html>
```

The complete code can be found in *Example: PHPMySQL-Connect*.

When the template is included, it will display either the error message or the "Database connection established" message.

I hope the aforementioned code is now making some sense to you. Feel free to go back to the start of this section and read it all again if you're lost, as there were some tricky concepts in there. Once you have a firm grip on the code, however, you'll probably realize that I've still left one mystery unexplained: PDOs. Just what exactly is new PDO, and when I said it returns a "PDO object", just what exactly is an object?

 Schemas

All downloaded sample code includes a schema called `ijdb_sample` and a user called `ijdb_sample`, so that you're able to run it regardless of what you called your schema and user. A file containing the database is provided as `database.sql`, which you can import.

If you use the web-based sample code viewer provided, the `idbj_sample` database will be created as you load a sample, but any changes to this schema will be lost when you view another sample. (You can mess things up, and switching to another sample and back will reset it, but if you want to keep any changes you make, make them in the schema which you created.)

If you want to load the sample data into your schema using MySQL Workbench, import `database.sql` from the `project` directory by selecting **Data Import/ Restore**, select **Import from self-contained file**, browse to `database.sql` and select your schema name in **default** target schema. If you have created any tables with the same name, they'll be overwritten and all records lost.

A Crash Course in Object-oriented Programming

You may have noticed the word "object" beginning to creep into my vocabulary in the previous section. PDO is the PHP Data *Objects* extension, and new PDO returns a PDO *object*. In this section, I'd like to explain what objects are all about.

Perhaps you've come across the term **object-oriented programming (OOP)** in your own explorations of PHP or of programming in general. OOP is an advanced style of programming that's especially suited to building really complex programs with a lot of parts. Most programming languages in active use today support OOP. Some of them even *require* you to work in an OOP style. PHP is a little more easygoing about it, and leaves it up to the developer to decide whether or not to write their scripts in the OOP style.

So far, we've written our PHP code in a simpler style called **procedural programming**, and we'll continue to do so for now, with a more detailed look at objects later on. Procedural style is well suited to the relatively simple projects we'll tackle at the moment. However, almost all complex projects you'll come across use OOP, and I'll cover it in more detail later in this book.

That said, the PDO extension that we'll use to connect to and work with a MySQL database is designed in the object-oriented programming style. What this means is that, rather than simply calling a function to connect to MySQL and then calling other functions that use that connection, we must first create a PDO *object* that will represent our database connection, and then use the features of that object to work with the database.

Creating an object is a lot like calling a function. In fact, you've already seen how to do it:

```
$pdo = new PDO('mysql:host=localhost;dbname=ijdb',
    'ijdbuser', 'mypassword');
```

The `new` keyword tells PHP that you want to create a new object. You then leave a space and specify a **class name**, which tells PHP what type of object you want to create. A **class** is a set of instructions that PHP will follow to create an object. You can think of a class as being a recipe, such as for a cake, and an object being the actual cake that's produced from following the recipe. Different classes can produce different objects, just as different recipes can produce different dishes.

Just as PHP comes with a bunch of built-in functions that you can call, PHP comes with a library of classes that you can create objects from. `new PDO`, therefore, tells PHP to create a new `PDO` object—that is, a new object of the built-in `PDO` class.

In PHP, an object is a value, just like a string, number, or array. You can store an object in a variable or pass it to a function as an argument—all the same stuff you can do with other PHP values. Objects, however, have some useful additional features.

First of all, an object behaves a lot like an array, in that it acts as a container for other values. As we saw in Chapter 2, you can access a value inside an array by specifying its index (for example, `$birthdays['Kevin']`). When it comes to objects, the concepts are similar but the names and code are different. Rather than

accessing the value stored in an array index, we say that we're accessing a
property of the object. Instead of using square brackets to specify the name of the
property we want to access, we use **arrow notation** (`->`)—for instance,
`$myObject->someProperty`:

```
$myObject = new SomeClass();     // create an object
$myObject->someProperty = 123;   // set a property's value
echo $myObject->someProperty;    // get a property's value
```

Whereas arrays are normally used to store a list of *similar* values (such as an array
of birthdays), objects are used to store a list of *related* values (for example, the
properties of a database connection). Still, if that's all objects did, there wouldn't
be much point to them: we might just as well use an array to store these values,
right? Of course, objects do more.

In addition to storing a collection of properties and their values, objects can
contain a group of functions designed to bring us more useful features. A function
stored in an object is called a **method** (one of the more confusing names in the
programming world, if you ask me). A method is just a function inside a class.
More confusingly, when we get onto writing our own classes, methods are
defined using the `function` keyword! Even experienced developers often wrongly
use *function* and *method* interchangeably.

To call a method, we again use arrow notation—`$myObject->someMethod()`:

```
$myObject = new SomeClass();     // create an object
$myObject->someMethod();         // call a method
```

Just like standalone functions, methods can take arguments and return values.

At this stage, this is probably all sounding a little complicated and pointless, but
trust me: pulling together collections of variables (properties) and functions
(methods) into little bundles called objects results in much tidier and easier-to-
read code for certain tasks—working with a database being just one of them. One
day, you may even want to develop custom classes that you can use to create
objects of your own devising.

For now, however, we'll stick with the classes that come included with PHP. Let's keep working with the PDO object we've created, and see what we can do by calling one of its methods.

Configuring the Connection

So far, I've shown you how to create a PDO object to establish a connection with your MySQL database, and how to display a meaningful error message when something goes wrong:

```php
<?php
try {
    $pdo = new PDO('mysql:host=localhost;dbname=ijdb',
     'ijdbuser', 'mypassword');
    $output = 'Database connection established.';
} catch (PDOException $e) {
    $output = 'Unable to connect to the database server: ' . $e;
}

include __DIR__ . '/../templates/output.html.php';
```

Assuming the connection succeeds, though, you need to configure it before use. You can configure your connection by calling some methods of your new PDO object.

Our first task is to configure how our PDO object handles errors. You've already learned how to use a try … catch statement to handle any problems PHP might run into when connecting to your database. However, by default, PDO switches to a "silent failure" mode after establishing a successful connection[3].

This "silent failure" mode makes it more difficult for us to find out when something goes wrong and handle it gracefully. Most of the time, we'd just see a blank page with no indication that anything was wrong (other than the information we're expecting to see on the page not appearing).

[3.] You can read about the details of PDO's error-handling modes in http://php.net/manual/en/pdo.error-handling.php

We'd like our PDO object to throw a `PDOException` any time it fails to do what we ask. We can configure it do to so by calling the PDO object's `setAttribute` method:

```
$pdo->setAttribute(PDO::ATTR_ERRMODE,
↳ PDO::ERRMODE_EXCEPTION);
```

The two values we're passing as arguments are constants, just like the `ENT_QUOTES` constant that you learned to pass to the `htmlspecialchars` function in Chapter Chapter 2. Don't be thrown by the `PDO::` at the start of their names; that just indicates that these constants are part of the `PDO` class that we're using, rather than constants built into the PHP language itself. Essentially, what we're saying with this line is that we want to set the PDO attribute that controls the error mode (`PDO::ATTR_ERRMODE`) to the mode that throws exceptions (`PDO::ERRMODE_EXCEPTION`).

Next, we need to configure the character encoding of our database connection. As I mentioned briefly in Chapter 2, you should use UTF-8 encoded text in your websites to maximize the range of characters users have at their disposal when filling in forms on your site. By default, when PHP connects to MySQL, it uses the simpler ISO-8859-1 (or Latin-1) encoding instead of UTF-8. If we left it as is, we wouldn't easily be able to insert Chinese, Arabic or most non-English characters.

Even if you're 100% sure that your website will only be used by English speakers, there are other problems caused by not setting the character set. If your web page is not set to UTF-8 you'll run into problems when people write certain characters such as curly quotes " into a text box, because they'll appear in the database as a different character.

Therefore, we now need to set our new `PDO` object to use the UTF-8 encoding.

We can instruct PHP to use UTF-8 when querying the database by appending `;charset=utf8` to the connection string. There are no downsides to doing this, provided your PHP script is also being sent to the browser as `utf8` (which is the default in recent PHP versions).

```
$pdo = new PDO('mysql:host=localhost;dbname=ijdb;
  charset=utf8', 'ijdbuser', 'mypassword');
```

Other Ways to Set the Charset

If you go searching, you'll find different ways to set the charset, and earlier editions of this book instructed you to use this code:

```
$pdo->exec('SET NAMES "utf8"');
```

This is because until PHP 5.3.6, the charset option was not correctly applied by PHP. Since this is fixed in any PHP version you're actually going to be using, setting the charset as part of the connection string is the preferred option.

The complete code we use to connect to MySQL and then configure that connection, therefore, is this:

4-4. MySQL-Connect-Complete

```
<?php
try {
    $pdo = new PDO('mysql:host=localhost;dbname=ijdb;
    charset=utf8', 'ijdbuser', 'mypassword');
    $pdo->setAttribute(PDO::ATTR_ERRMODE,
      PDO::ERRMODE_EXCEPTION);
    $output = 'Database connection established.';
} catch (PDOException $e) {
    $output = 'Unable to connect to the database server: ' . $e;
}

include __DIR__ . '/../templates/output.html.php';
```

Fire up this example in your browser. (If you've placed your database code in index.php inside the public directory and the output.html.php file in the templates directory, the URL for the page will be http://192.168.10.10/.)

If your server is up and running, and everything is working properly, you should see a message indicating success like this:

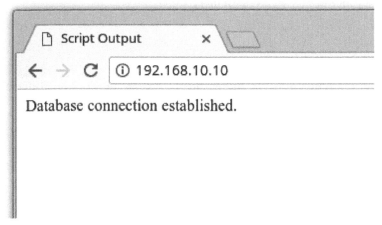

4-5. A successful connection

If PHP is unable to connect to your MySQL server, or if the username and password you provided are incorrect, you'll instead see a similar screen to that shown below. To make sure your error-handling code is working properly, you might want to misspell your password intentionally to test it out.

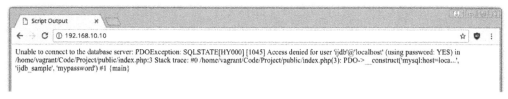

4-6. A connection failure

Thanks to our `catch` block, the error message from the database has been included on the page:

```
catch (PDOException $e) {
    $output = 'Unable to connect to the database server: ' . $e;
}
```

Remember I said that $e is actually an object? Some objects can be *converted* to a string. That is, if they're included in an `echo` statement, the object will provide a string. Not all objects support this behavior (in fact, most don't!). The

PDOException class also has a getMessage() method that contains the error message. If you'd like to be more explicit, you can change the catch block to this:

```
catch (PDOException $e) {
    $output = 'Unable to connect to the database server: ' .
     $e->getMessage();
}
```

There are some other methods—including getFile() and getLine()—for returning the file name and line number that the exception was thrown on. You can generate a very detailed error message like this:

```
catch (PDOException $e) {
    $output = 'Unable to connect to the database server: ' .
    $e->getMessage() . ' in ' .
    $e->getFile() . ':' . $e->getLine();
}
```

This is incredibly useful if you have a large website with dozens of include files. The error message will tell you exactly which file to look in and which line the error occurred on.

If you're curious, try inserting some other mistakes in your database connection code (for example, a misspelled database name) and observe the detailed error messages that result. When you're done, and your database connection is working correctly, go back to the simple error message. This way your visitors won't be bombarded with technical gobbledygook if a genuine problem emerges with your database server.

With a connection established and a database selected, you're ready to begin using the data stored in the database.

What Happens After the Script Has Finished?

You might be wondering what happens to the connection with the MySQL server after the script has finished executing. If you really want to, you can force PHP to disconnect from the server by discarding the **PDO** object that represents your connection. You do this by setting the variable containing the object to **null**:

```
$pdo = null;  // disconnect from the database server
```

That said, PHP will automatically close any open database connections when it finishes running your script, so you can usually just let PHP clean up after you.

Sending SQL Queries with PHP

In Chapter 3 we connected to the MySQL database server using MySQL Workbench, which allowed us to type SQL queries (commands) and view the results of those queries immediately. The **PDO** object offers a similar mechanism—the exec method:

```
$pdo->exec($query)
```

Here, **$query** is a string containing whatever SQL query you want to execute.

As you know, if there's a problem executing the query (for instance, if you made a typing mistake in your SQL query), this method will throw a **PDOException** for you to catch.

Consider the following example, which attempts to produce the joke table we created in Chapter 3:

```
try {
    $pdo = new PDO('mysql:host=localhost;dbname=ijdb;
    charset=utf8', 'ijdbuser', 'mypassword');
    $pdo->setAttribute(PDO::ATTR_ERRMODE,
     PDO::ERRMODE_EXCEPTION);

    $sql = 'CREATE TABLE joke (
    id INT NOT NULL AUTO_INCREMENT PRIMARY KEY,
    joketext TEXT,
    jokedate DATE NOT NULL
    ) DEFAULT CHARACTER SET utf8 ENGINE=InnoDB';

    $pdo->exec($sql);

    $output = 'Joke table successfully created.';
}
catch (PDOException $e) {
    $output = 'Database error:' . $e->getMessage() . ' in ' .
    $e->getFile() . ':' . $e->getLine();
}

include __DIR__ . '/../templates/output.html.php';
```

Note once again that we use the same try … catch statement technique to handle possible errors produced by the query. It would be possible to use multiple try … catch blocks to display different error messages, one for the connection and one for the query, but this can result in a considerable amount of extra code.

Instead, I've opted to use the same try statement to contain both the connection and the query. The try … catch block will stop executing code once an error occurs, so if an error occurs during the database connection, the $pdo->exec($run) line will never run, ensuring that if a query is sent to the database a connection must have been established.

This approach gives us a little less control over the error message that is displayed, but saves typing a try … catch statement for each database operation. Later in this book, we'll break these up into different blocks, but for now, keep all the database operations in the same `try` block.

This example also uses the `getMessage` method to retrieve a detailed error message from the MySQL server. The following image shows the error that's displayed when, for example, the joke table already exists:

4-8. The **CREATE TABLE** query fails because the table already exists

For `DELETE`, `INSERT`, and `UPDATE` queries (which serve to modify stored data), the `exec` method returns the number of table rows (entries) that were affected by the query. Consider the following SQL command, which we used in <u>Chapter 3</u> to set the dates of all jokes that contained the word "chicken":

```
try {
    $pdo = new PDO('mysql:host=localhost;dbname=ijdb;
    charset=utf8', 'ijdbuser', 'mypassword');
    $pdo->setAttribute(PDO::ATTR_ERRMODE,
     PDO::ERRMODE_EXCEPTION);

    $sql = 'UPDATE joke SET jokedate="2012-04-01"
        WHERE joketext LIKE "%programmer%"';

    $affectedRows = $pdo->exec($sql);

    $output = 'Updated ' . $affectedRows .' rows.';
}
catch (PDOException $e) {
    $output = 'Database error: ' . $e->getMessage() . '
     in ' .$e->getFile() . ':' . $e->getLine();
}

include __DIR__ . '/../templates/output.html.php';
```

By storing the value returned from the exec method in $affectedRows, we can use the variable in the $output variable for printing in the template.

The image below shows the output of this example, assuming there's only one "programmer" joke in your database.

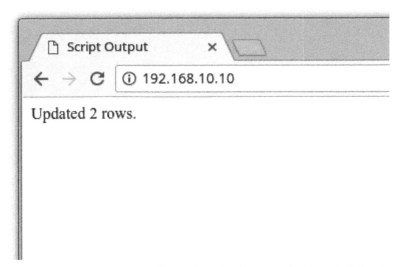

4-10. The number of database records updated is displayed

If you refresh the page to run the same query again, you should see the message change as shown in the following image. It indicates that no rows were updated, since the new date being applied to the jokes is the same as the existing date:

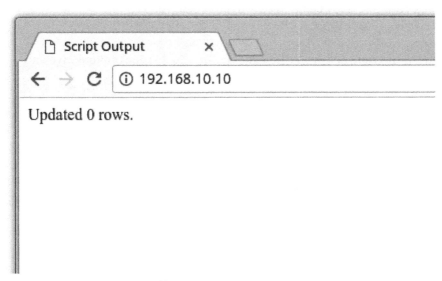

4-11. MySQL lets you know when you're wasting its time

SELECT queries are treated a little differently, as they can retrieve a lot of data, and PHP provides ways to handle that information.

Handling SELECT Result Sets

For most SQL queries, the exec method works just fine. The query does something to your database, and you get the number of affected rows (if any) from the method's return value. SELECT queries, however, require something a little fancier than exec. You'll recall that SELECT queries are used to view stored data in the database. Instead of only affecting the database, SELECT queries have results—and we need a method to return them.

The query method looks just like exec in that it accepts an SQL query as an argument to be sent to the database server. What it returns, however, is a PDOStatement object, which represents a **result set** containing a list of all the rows (entries) returned from the query.

```php
<?php
try {
    $pdo = new PDO('mysql:host=localhost;dbname=ijdb;
    charset=utf8', 'ijdbuser', 'mypassword');
    $pdo->setAttribute(PDO::ATTR_ERRMODE,
     PDO::ERRMODE_EXCEPTION);

    $sql = 'SELECT `joketext` FROM `joke`';
    $result = $pdo->query($sql);
} catch (PDOException $e) {
    $output = 'Unable to connect to the database server: '
    . $e->getMessage() . ' in ' .
    $e->getFile() . ':' . $e->getLine();
}
```

Provided that no error was encountered in processing the query, this code will store a result set (in the form of a PDOStatement object) into the variable $result. This result set contains the text of all the jokes stored in the joke table. As there's no practical limit on the number of jokes in the database, the result set can be quite big.

I mentioned back in Chapter 2 that the while loop is a useful control structure when we need to loop but don't know how many times. We can't use a `for` loop because we don't know how many records the query returned. Indeed, you could use a `while` loop here to process the rows in the result set one at a time:

```
while ($row = $result->fetch()) {
    : process the row
}
```

The condition for the `while` loop is probably different from the conditions you're used to, so let me explain how it works. Consider the condition as a statement all by itself:

```
$row = $result->fetch();
```

The `fetch` method of the `PDOStatement` object returns the next row in the result set as an array (we discussed arrays in Chapter 2). When there are no more rows in the result set, `fetch` returns `false` instead.[4]

Now, the above statement assigns a value to the `$row` variable, but, at the same time, the statement as a whole takes on that same value. This is what lets you use the statement as a condition in the `while` loop. Since a `while` loop will keep looping until its condition evaluates to `false`, this loop will occur as many times as there are rows in the result set, with `$row` taking on the value of the next row each time the loop executes. All that's left to figure out is how to retrieve the values out of the `$row` variable each time the loop runs.

Rows of a result set returned by `fetch` are represented as associative arrays, with the indices named after the table columns in the result set. If `$row` is a row in our result set, `$row['joketext']` is the value in the `joketext` column of that row.

Our goal in this code is to store away the text of all the jokes so that we can

---

[4.] This is one case where asking a PDO object to do something it cannot do (as `fetch` cannot return the next row when there are no rows left in the result set) will *not* throw a `PDOException`. If it did, we'd be unable to use the `fetch` method in a `while` loop condition the way we do here.

display them in a PHP template. The best way to do this is to store each joke as a new item in an array, $jokes:

```php
while ($row = $result->fetch()) {
    $jokes[] = $row['joketext'];
}
```

With the jokes pulled out of the database, we can now pass them along to a PHP template jokes.html.php.

To summarize, here's the code of the controller for this example so far:

```php
<?php

try {
    $pdo = new PDO('mysql:host=localhost;dbname=ijdb;
    charset=utf8', 'ijdbuser', 'mypassword');
    $pdo->setAttribute(PDO::ATTR_ERRMODE,
     PDO::ERRMODE_EXCEPTION);

    $sql = 'SELECT `joketext` FROM `joke`';
    $result = $pdo->query($sql);

    while ($row = $result->fetch()) {
        $jokes[] = $row['joketext'];
    }
} catch (PDOException $e) {
    $output = 'Unable to connect to the database server: ' .
    $e->getMessage() . ' in ' .
    $e->getFile() . ':' . $e->getLine();
}

include __DIR__ . '/../templates/jokes.html.php';
```

The $jokes variable is an array that stores a list of jokes. If you wrote out the contents of the array in PHP it would look something like this:

```
$jokes = [];
 $jokes[0] = 'A programmer was found dead in the shower. The
↪ instructions read: lather, rinse, repeat.';
$jokes[1] = '!false - it\'s funny because it\'s true';
 $jokes[2] = 'A programmer\'s wife tells him to go to the
↪ store and "get a gallon of milk, and if they have eggs, get a
↪ dozen." He returns with 13 gallons of milk.';
```

However, the data has been retrieved from the database rather than being typed out manually in the code.

You'll have noticed that there are two different variables being set, $jokes and $error, depending on whether the try block executed successfully.

In the jokes.html.php template, we need to display the contents of the $jokes array or the error message contained in the $error variable.

To check whether a variable has been assigned a value, we can use the isset function that we used earlier for checking if a form has been submitted. The template can include an if statement to determine whether to display the error or the list of jokes.

```
if (isset($error)) {
    ?>
    <p>
    <?php
    echo $error;
    ?>
    </p>
}
else {
    : display the jokes
}
```

There's nothing new here, but to display the jokes, we need to display the contents of the $jokes array. Unlike other variables we've used up to this point, the `$jokes` array contains more than just a single value.

The most common way to process an array in PHP is to use a loop. We've already seen `while` loops and `for` loops. The `foreach` loop is particularly helpful for processing arrays:

```
foreach (array as $item) {
    ⋮ process each $item
}
```

Instead of a condition, the parentheses at the top of a `foreach` loop contain an array, followed by the keyword `as`, and then the name of a new variable that will be used to store each item of the array in turn. The body of the loop is then executed once for each item in the array. Each time that item is stored in the specified variable, so that the code can access it directly.

It's common to use a `foreach` loop in a PHP template to display each item of an array in turn. Here's how this might look for our `$jokes` array:

```
<?php
foreach ($jokes as $joke) {
    ?>
    ⋮ HTML code to output each $joke
<?php
}
?>
```

With this blend of PHP code to describe the loop and HTML code to display it, the code looks rather untidy. Because of this, it's common to use an alternative way of writing the `foreach` loop when it's used in a template:

```
foreach (array as $item):
    ⋮ process each $item
endforeach;
```

The two pieces of code are functionally identical, but the latter looks more friendly when mixed with HTML code. Here's how this form of the code looks in a template:

```php
<?php foreach ($jokes as $joke): ?>
    : HTML code to output each $joke
<?php endforeach; ?>
```

The same thing can be done with the `if` statement, making it nicer to look at inside HTML templates by avoiding the braces:

```php
<?php if (isset($error)): ?>
    <p>
    <?php echo $error; ?>
    </p>
<?php else: ?>
    : display the jokes
<?php endif; ?>
```

With these new tools in hand, we can write our template to display the list of jokes:

```
<!doctype html>
<html>
    <head>
        <meta charset="utf-8">
        <title>List of jokes</title>
    </head>
    <body>
        <?php if (isset($error)): ?>
        <p>
            <?php echo $error; ?>
        </p>
        <?php else: ?>
        <?php foreach ($jokes as $joke): ?>
        <blockquote>
            <p>
            <?php echo htmlspecialchars($joke,
            ENT_QUOTES, 'UTF-8') ?>
            </p>
        </blockquote>
        <?php endforeach; ?>
        <?php endif; ?>
    </body>
</html>
```

Either the $error text is displayed on the page or each joke is displayed in a
paragraph (<p>) contained within a block quote (<blockquote>), since we're
effectively quoting the author of each joke in this page.

Because jokes might conceivably contain characters that could be interpreted as
HTML code (for example, <, >, or &), we must use htmlspecialchars to ensure
they're translated into HTML character entities (that is, <, >, and &) so
that they'll be displayed correctly.

The following image shows what this page looks like once you've added a couple
of jokes to the database.

How many programmers does it take to screw in a lightbulb? None, it's a hardware problem.

Why did the programmer quit his job? He didn't get arrays

Why was the empty array stuck outside? It didn't have any keys

4-13. A list of jokes from the database

 Using `foreach`

Remember how we used a `while` loop in our controller to fetch the rows out of the **PDOStatement** result set one at a time?

```
while ($row = $result->fetch()) {
    $jokes[] = $row['joketext'];
}
```

It turns out **PDOStatement** objects are designed to behave just like arrays when you pass them to a `foreach` loop. You can therefore slightly simplify your database processing code using a `foreach` loop instead of a `while` loop:

```
foreach ($result as $row) {
    $jokes[] = $row['joketext'];
}
```

I'll be using this tidier `foreach` form in the rest of this book.

Another neat tool PHP offers is a shorthand way to call the `echo` command—which, as you've already seen, we need to use frequently. Our `echo` statements look like this:

```
<?php echo $variable; ?>
```

Instead, you can use this:

```
<?=$variable?>
```

This does exactly the same thing. `<?=` means **echo** and gives you a slightly shorter way to print variables. There's a limitation to this, though: if you use `<?=`, you can only print; you can't include **if** statements, **for** statements, etc., although you can use concatenation, and it can be followed by a function call.

Here's an updated template using the shorthand echo:

```
<!doctype html>
<html>
    <head>
        <meta charset="utf-8">
        <title>List of jokes</title>
    </head>
    <body>
        <?php if (isset($error)): ?>
        <p>
            <?=$error?>
        </p>
        <?php else: ?>
        <?php foreach ($jokes as $joke): ?>
        <blockquote>
            <p>
            <?=htmlspecialchars($joke, ENT_QUOTES, 'UTF-8')?>
            </p>
        </blockquote>
        <?php endforeach; ?>
        <?php endif; ?>
    </body>
</html>
```

I'll be using the shorthand notation when it's applicable from this point on.

 ## Using the Shorthand

In versions of PHP prior to 5.4, this shorthand notation required a fairly uncommon PHP setting to be enabled, so it was discouraged for compatibility reasons. Using the shorthand notation may have caused your code to stop working when moving from a server that had it enabled to one that didn't.

As of PHP 5.4 (so any version you're realistically going to encounter these days), the shorthand echo works regardless of PHP settings, so you can safely use it without worrying that it might not work on all servers.

Thinking Ahead

In the example we just looked at, we created a template, `jokes.html.php`, which contains all the HTML required to display the page. However, as our website grows, we'll add more pages. We'll certainly want a page for people to be able to add jokes to the website, and we'll also need a home page with some introductory text, a page with the owner's contact details, and, as the site grows, perhaps even a page where people can *log in* to the website.

I'm jumping ahead a quite a bit here, but it's always worth considering how a project will grow. If we apply the approach we just used for `jokes.html.php` to the rest of the templates—`addjoke.html.php`, `home.html.php`, `contact.html.php`, `login.html.php` and so on—we'll end up with a lot of repeated code.

Every template will look something like this:

```
<!doctype html>
<html>
    <head>
        <meta charset="utf-8">
        <title>IJDB - Internet Joke Database</title>
        </head>
    <body>
        <?php if (isset($error)): ?>
        <p>
            <?=$error?>
        </p>
        <?php else: ?>
            : do whatever is required for this page: show text,
            : show a form, list records from the database, etc.
        <?php endif; ?>
    </body>
</html>
```

As a programmer, repeating code is one of the worst things you can do. In fact, programmers often refer to the **DRY** principle, which stands for "Don't repeat yourself". If you find yourself repeating sections of code, there is almost certainly a better solution.

All the best programmers are lazy, and repeating code means repeating work. Using this copy/paste approach for templates makes the website very difficult to maintain. Let's imagine there's a footer and a navigation section that we want to appear on each page. Our templates would now look like this:

```
<!doctype html>
<html>
    <head>
        <meta charset="utf-8">
        <title>IJDB - Internet Joke Database</title>
    </head>
    <body>
        <nav>
            <ul>
 <li><a
 ↪ href="index.php">Home</a></li>
 <li><a href="jokes.php">Jokes
 ↪ List</a></li>
            </ul>
        </nav>

        <main>
            <?php if (isset($error)): ?>
            <p>
                <?=$error?>
            </p>
            <?php else: ?>
                : do whatever is required for this page: show text,
                : show a form, list jokes, etc.
            <?php endif; ?>

        </main>

        <footer>
            &copy; IJDB 2017
        </footer>
    </body>
```

```
</html>
```

We'll run into a problem in 2018! If the templates for all the pages on the website—for example, `jokes.html.php` `addjoke.html.php`, `home.html.php`, `contact.html.php` and `login.html.php`—contain code in the structure above, to update the year in the copyright notice to "2018" you'd need to open each of the templates and change the date.

We could be clever and have the date dynamically read from the server's clock (`echo date('Y');` if you're curious!) to avoid this issue, but what if we wanted to add a `<script>` tag that was included on every page? Or add a new link to the menu? We'd still need to open every template file and change it!

Changing five or six templates may be slightly annoying, but it's not going to pose much of a problem. However, what if the website grows to dozens or hundreds of pages? Each time you wanted to add a link to the menu you'd have to open every single template and change it.

This problem *could* be solved with a series of `include` statements. For example:

```html
<!doctype html>
<html>
    <head>
        <meta charset="utf-8">
        <title>IJDB - Internet Joke Database</title>
    </head>
    <body>
        <nav>
            <?php include 'nav.html.php'; ?>
        </nav>

        <main>
            <?php if (isset($error)): ?>
            <p>
                <?=$error?>
            </p>
            <?php else: ?>
```

```
                    : do whatever is required for this page: show text,
                    : show a form, list jokes, etc.
             <?php endif; ?>

        </main>

        <footer>
            <?php include 'footer.html.php'; ?>
        </footer>
    </body>
</html>
```

But this method requires clairvoyance: we need to anticipate exactly what changes might need to be made in the future and use relevant `include` statements in the places we foresee changes will happen.

In the example above, for example, it's easy to add new menu entries by adding them to `nav.html.php`, but adding a `<script>` tag to every page, or even something as trivial as adding a CSS class to the `nav` element, still means opening every template to make the change.

There's no way to accurately predict all the changes that might be needed over the lifetime of the website, so instead the approach I showed you at the beginning of this chapter is actually better:

```
<!doctype html>
<html>
    <head>
        <meta charset="utf-8">
        <link rel="stylesheet" href="jokes.css">
        <title><?=$title?></title>
    </head>
    <body>

        <header>
            <h1>Internet Joke Database</h1>
        </header>
        <nav>
```

```
            <ul>
 <li><a
 ↪ href="index.php">Home</a></li>
 <li><a href="jokes.php">Jokes
 ↪ List</a></li>
            </ul>
        </nav>

        <main>
            <?=$output?>
        </main>

        <footer>
            &copy; IJDB 2017
        </footer>
    </body>
</html>
```

If we always include this template, which we'll call `layout.html.php`, it's possible to set the `$output` variable to some *HTML code* and have it appear on the page with the navigation and footer.

I've also snuck in a `$title` variable so each controller can define a value that appears between the `<title>` and `</title>` tag along with some CSS (available as `jokes.css` in the sample code) to make the page a little prettier.

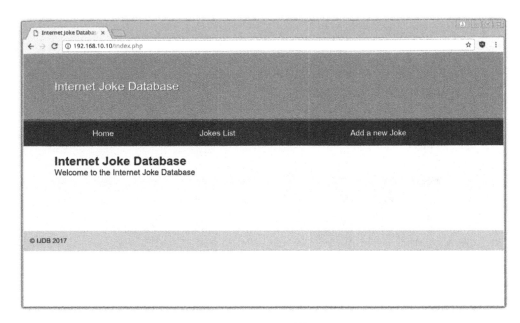

4-15. IJDB – Now with CSS styles

Any controller can now use `include   __DIR__ . '/../templates/layout.html.php';` and provide values for `$output` and `$title`.

Our `jokes.php` using `layout.html.php` looks like this:

```php
<?php

try {
    $pdo = new PDO('mysql:host=localhost;dbname=ijdb;
    charset=utf8', 'ijdbuser', 'mypassword');
    $pdo->setAttribute(PDO::ATTR_ERRMODE,
        PDO::ERRMODE_EXCEPTION);

    $sql = 'SELECT `joketext` FROM `joke`';
    $result = $pdo->query($sql);

    while ($row = $result->fetch()) {
        $jokes[] = $row['joketext'];
    }

    $title = 'Joke list';

    $output = '';

    foreach ($jokes as $joke) {
        $output .= '<blockquote>';
        $output .= '<p>';
        $output .= $joke;
        $output .= '</p>';
        $output .= '</blockquote>';
    }
} catch (PDOException $e) {
    $title = 'An error has occurred';

    $output = 'Database error: ' . $e->getMessage() . '
     in ' .$e->getFile() . ':' . $e->getLine();
}

include __DIR__ . '/../templates/layout.html.php';
```

But wait! What's going on with `$output` in the `try` block? The `$output` variable actually contains some HTML code: the loop builds a string containing the HTML code for the jokes list.

In principle, this is what we want to happen: the $output variable contains the HTML code that's going to be inserted between the navigation and the footer in layout.html.php, but I think you'll agree the code is incredibly ugly.

I already showed you how to avoid mixing HTML and PHP code via the include statement. Like we did earlier, it would be good to move the HTML for displaying the jokes to its own file, but this time, only the HTML code that is unique to the joke list page.

jokes.html.php in the templates directory should contain this code:

```php
<?php foreach ($jokes as $joke): ?>
<blockquote>
    <p>
    <?=htmlspecialchars($joke, ENT_QUOTES, 'UTF-8')?>
    </p>
</blockquote>
<?php endforeach; ?>
```

Importantly, this is only the code for displaying the jokes. It doesn't contain the navigation, footer, <head> tag or anything we want repeated on every page; it's only the HTML code that's unique to the joke list page.

To use this template, you might try the following:

```php
    while ($row = $result->fetch()) {
        $jokes[] = $row['joketext'];
    }

    $title = 'Joke list';

    include 'jokes.html.php';
}
```

Or if you're very clever:

```
    while ($row = $result->fetch()) {
        $jokes[] = $row['joketext'];
    }

    $title = 'Joke list';

    $output = include 'jokes.html.php';
}
```

With this approach, your logic would be entirely sound. We need to include the jokes.html.php. Unfortunately, the include statement just executes the code from the included file at the point it's called. If you run the code above, the output will actually be something like this:

```
<blockquote>
    <p>
 A programmer was found dead in the shower. The instructions
↳ read: lather, rinse, repeat.
    </p>
</blockquote>
<blockquote>
    <p>
    !false - it's funny because it's true
    </p>
</blockquote>
<!doctype html>
<html>
    <head>
        <meta charset="utf-8">
        <title>Joke List</title>
    </head>
    <body>
        ...
```

Because jokes.html.php is included first, it's sent to the browser first. What we need to do is load jokes.html.php, but instead of sending the output straight to the browser, we need to capture it and store it in the $output variable so that it can be used later by `layout.html.php`.

The `include` statement doesn't return a value, so `$output = include 'jokes.html.php';` does not have the desired effect, and PHP doesn't have an alternative statement to do that. However, that doesn't mean that it's not possible.

PHP does have a useful feature called "output buffering". It might sound complicated, but the concept is actually very simple: when you use `echo` to print something, or `include` to include a file that contains HTML, usually it's sent directly to the browser. By making use of output buffering, instead of having the output being sent straight to the browser, the HTML code is stored on the server in a "buffer", which is basically just a string containing everything that's been printed so far.

Even better, PHP lets you turn on the buffer and read its contents at any time.

There are two functions we need:

- `ob_start()`, which starts the output buffer. After calling this function, anything printed via `echo` or HTML printed via `include` will be stored in a buffer rather than sent to the browser.
- `ob_get_clean()`, which returns the contents of the buffer and clears it.

As you've probably guessed, "ob" in the function names stands for "output buffer".

To capture the contents of an included file, we just need to make use of these two functions:

```
while ($row = $result->fetch()) {
    $jokes[] = $row['joketext'];
}

$title = 'Joke list';

// Start the buffer

ob_start();
```

```
// Include the template. The PHP code will be executed,
// but the resulting HTML will be stored in the buffer
// rather than sent to the browser.

include __DIR__ . '/../templates/jokes.html.php';

// Read the contents of the output buffer and store them
// in the $output variable for use in layout.html.php

$output = ob_get_clean();
}
```

When this code runs, the $output variable will contain the HTML that was generated in the jokes.html.php template.

We'll use this approach from now on. Each page will be made up of two templates:

- layout.html.php, which contains all of the common HTML needed by every page
- a unique template that contains only the HTML code that's unique to that particular page

The complete jokes.php looks like this:

```
try {
    $pdo = new PDO('mysql:host=localhost;dbname=ijdb;
    charset=utf8', 'ijdbuser', 'mypassword');
    $pdo->setAttribute(PDO::ATTR_ERRMODE,
        PDO::ERRMODE_EXCEPTION);

    $sql = 'SELECT `joketext` FROM `joke`';
    $result = $pdo->query($sql);

    while ($row = $result->fetch()) {
        $jokes[] = $row['joketext'];
    }
```

```php
    $title = 'Joke list';

    ob_start();

    include __DIR__ . '/../templates/jokes.html.php';

    $output = ob_get_clean();
}
catch (PDOException $e) {
    $title = 'An error has occurred';

    $output = 'Database error: ' . $e->getMessage() . ' in '
    . $e->getFile() . ':' . $e->getLine();
}

include __DIR__ . '/../templates/layout.html.php';
```

Let's make the "Home" link work by adding an `index.php`. We could put anything on this page: the latest jokes, the best joke of the month or whatever we like. For now, though, we'll keep it simple and just have a message that says "Welcome to the Internet Joke Database".

Create a file called `home.html.php` in the `templates` folder:

```php
<h2>Internet Joke Database</h2>

<p>Welcome to the Internet Joke Database</p>
```

Our `index.php` is considerably simpler than `jokes.html.php`. It doesn't get any information from the database, so it doesn't need a database connection and we don't need a `try … catch` statement, so we'll just load the two templates and set the `$title` and `$output` variables:

4-17. MySQL-ListJokes-Layout-3

```php
<?php

$title = 'Internet Joke Database';

ob_start();

include __DIR__ . '/../templates/home.html.php';

$output = ob_get_clean();

include __DIR__ . '/../templates/layout.html.php';
```

 Only Connect to the Database Where Necessary

It's good practice to only connect to the database if you need to. Databases are the most common performance bottleneck on most websites, so making as few connections as possible is preferred.

Test that both pages work in your browser. You should have a list of jokes visible when you visit http://192.168.10.10/jokes.php and the welcome message on http://192.168.10.10. Both pages should contain the navigation and the footer.

Try amending layout.html.php. The changes you make will appear on both pages. If the site had dozens of pages, changes to the layout would affect every page.

Inserting Data into the Database

In this section, I'll demonstrate how to use the tools at your disposal to enable site visitors to add their own jokes to the database.

If you want to let your site visitors enter new jokes, you'll obviously need a form. Here's a template for a form that will fit the bill:

```html
<form action="" method="post">
```

```
    <label for="joketext">Type your joke here:
    </label>
    <textarea id="joketext" name="joketext"
        rows="3" cols="40">
    </textarea>
    <input type="submit" name="submit" value="Add">
</form>
```

Save this as `addjoke.html.php` in the `templates` directory.

The most important part of the `<form>` element is the `action` attribute. The `action` attribute tells the browser where to send the data once the form is submitted. This can be the name of a file, such as `"addjoke.php"`.

However, if you leave the attribute empty by setting it to `""`, the data provided by the user will be sent back to the page you're currently viewing. If the browser's URL shows the page as `addjoke.php`, that's were the data will be sent when the user presses the submit button.

Let's tie this form into the preceding example, which displayed the list of jokes in the database. Open up `layout.html.php` and add a link to **Add a new Joke** which goes to `addjoke.php`:

```
<!doctype html>
<html>
    <head>
        <meta charset="utf-8">
        <link rel="stylesheet" href="jokes.css">
        <title><?=$title?></title>
    </head>
    <body>
        <nav>
            <header>
                <h1>Internet Joke Database</h1>
            </header>
            <ul>
 <li><a
↪ href="index.php">Home</a></li>
```

```
 <li><a href="jokes.php">Jokes
↳ List</a></li>
 <li><a href="addjoke.php">Add a new
↳ Joke</a></li>
            </ul>
        </nav>

        <main>
            <?=$output?>
        </main>

        <footer>
            &copy; IJDB 2017
        </footer>
    </body>
</html>
```

While you have `layout.html.php` open, include the `form.css` stylesheet from Chapter 2 as I have above. Now, any form displayed inside the layout will have the styles we used before.

When this form is submitted, the request will include a variable, `joketext`, that contains the text of the joke as typed into the text area. This variable will then appear in the `$_POST` array created by PHP.

Let's create `addjoke.php` in the `public` directory. The basic logic for this controller is:

▨ If no `joketext` POST variable is set, display a form.
▨ Otherwise, insert the supplied joke into the database.

Create this skeleton `addjoke.php`:

```php
<?php
if (isset($_POST['joketext'])) {
    try {
        $pdo = new PDO('mysql:host=localhost;dbname=ijdb;
        charset=utf8', 'ijdbuser', 'mypassword');
```

```
        $pdo->setAttribute(PDO::ATTR_ERRMODE,
            PDO::ERRMODE_EXCEPTION);
    } catch (PDOException $e) {
        $title = 'An error has occurred';

        $output = 'Database error: ' . $e->getMessage() . ' in '
        . $e->getFile() . ':' . $e->getLine();
    }
} else {
    $title = 'Add a new joke';

    ob_start();

    include __DIR__ . '/../templates/addjoke.html.php';

    $output = ob_get_clean();
}
include __DIR__ . '/../templates/layout.html.php';
```

This opening `if` statement checks if the `$_POST` array contains a variable called `joketext`. If it's set, the form has been submitted; otherwise, the form from `addjoke.html.php` is loaded into the `$output` variable for displaying in the browser.

If you do open `addjoke.php` in your browser at this point, you'll see the form, but typing in a joke and pressing submit won't work, because we haven't yet done anything with the data contained in `$_POST['joketext']`.

To insert the submitted joke into the database, we must execute an `INSERT` query using the value stored in `$_POST['joketext']` to fill in the `joketext` column of the `joke` table. This might lead you to write some code like this:

```
$sql = 'INSERT INTO `joke` SET
    `joketext` ="' . $_POST['joketext'] . '",
    `jokedate` ="2017-02-04"';

$pdo->exec($sql);
```

There is a serious problem with this code, however: the contents of
`$_POST['joketext']` are entirely under the control of the user who submitted the
form. If a malicious user were to type some nasty SQL code into the form, this
script would feed it to your MySQL server without question. This type of attack is
called an **SQL injection attack**, and in the early days of PHP it was one of the
most common security holes that hackers found and exploited in PHP-based
websites.

If the user types `How many programmers does it take to screw in a`
`lightbulb? None, it's a hardware problem.` into the text box, the query sent
to the database will be:

```
INSERT INTO `joke` SET
    `joketext` ="How many programmers does it take to screw
    in a lightbulb? None, it's a hardware problem.",
    `jokedate` ="2017-02-04
```

But what if the user types in the joke: `A programmer's wife tells him to go`
`to the store and "get a gallon of milk, and if they have eggs, get a`
`dozen." He returns with 13 gallons of milk.`

In this case, the query sent to the database will be:

```
INSERT INTO `joke` SET
    `joketext`="A programmer's wife tells him to go to the store
    and "get a gallon of milk, and if they have eggs, get
    a dozen."
    He returns with 13 gallons of milk.",
    `jokedate`="2017-02-04
```

Because the joke contains a quote character, MySQL will return an error, as it will
see the quote before `get` as the end of the string.

To make this a valid query, we need to escape all quotes in the text so that the
query sent to the database becomes:

```
INSERT INTO `joke` SET
    `joketext`="A programmer's wife tells him to go to the store
 and \"get a gallon of milk, and if they have eggs, get a
↳ dozen.\"
    He returns with 13 gallons of milk.",
    `jokedate`="2017-02-04
```

Data not being inserted if it contains a quote is an annoying problem for users. They'll lose whatever they typed in. But malicious users are able to abuse this. In older versions of PHP, it was possible to run multiple queries from PHP by separating them with a semicolon (;).

Imagine if the user typed this into the box:

```
"; DELETE FROM `joke`; --
```

This would send the following queries to the database:

```
INSERT INTO `joke` SET
        `joketext`="";

DELETE FROM `joke`;

--`jokedate`="2017-02-04
```

-- is a single line comment in MySQL, so the last line would be ignored, and the INSERT query would run, followed by the DELETE query the user had typed into the box. In fact, the user could type any query they like into the box and it will be run on the database!

In the early days of PHP, these attacks were so feared that the team behind PHP added some built-in protections against SQL injections to the language. Firstly, they disabled the ability to send multiple queries at once. Secondly, they added something called **magic quotes**. This protective feature of PHP automatically analyzed all values submitted by the browser and inserted backslashes (\) in front of any "dangerous" characters like apostrophes—which can cause problems if they're included in an SQL query inadvertently.

The problem with the magic quotes feature is that it causes as many problems as it prevents. First of all, the characters that it detects and the method it uses to sanitize them (prefixing them with a backslash) are only valid in some circumstances. Depending on the character encoding of your site and the database server you're using, these measures may be completely ineffective.

Second, when a submitted value is used for some purpose *other* than creating an SQL query, those backslashes can be really bothersome. I mentioned this briefly in Chapter 2 when, in the welcome message example, the magic quotes feature would insert a spurious backslash into the user's last name if it contained an apostrophe.

In short, the magic quotes feature was a bad idea, so much so that it's been removed from PHP since version 5.4. However, due to PHP's age and the amount of code out there, you might come across some references to it, so it's worth having a basic understanding of what it was supposed to do.

Once magic quotes was identified as a bad idea, the advice from PHP developers was to turn it off. However, this meant that there were some web servers with it turned off and others with it turned on. This was a headache for developers: they either had to instruct everyone who was ever going to use their code to turn it off—which wasn't possible on some shared servers—or write extra code to account for it.

Most developers chose the latter, and you may come across some code like this:

```
if (get_magic_quotes_gpc()) {
    // code here
}
```

If you see an `if` statement like this in legacy code you've been given to work with, you can safely delete the entire block, as no code inside the `if` statement will ever be executed on recent PHP versions.

If you do see code like this, it means the original developer understood the problems with magic quotes and was doing their best to prevent it. As of PHP 5.4 (which you should never come across, as it's no longer supported) `get_magic_quotes_gpc()` will always return `false` and the code will never be executed.

All you really need to know about magic quotes is that it was a bad solution to the problem at hand. Of course, without magic quotes, you need to find a different solution to the problem. Luckily, the PDO class can do all the hard work for you using something called *prepared statements*.

A **prepared statement** is a special kind of SQL query that you've sent to your database server ahead of time, giving the server a chance to prepare it for execution—but not actually execute it. Think of it like writing a `.php` script. The code is there, but doesn't actually get run until you visit the page in your web browser. The SQL code in prepared statements can contain placeholders that you'll supply the values for later, when the query *is* to be executed. When filling in those placeholders, PDO is smart enough to guard against "dangerous" characters automatically.

Here's how to prepare an `INSERT` query and then execute it safely with `$_POST['joketext']` as the text of the joke:

```
$sql = 'INSERT INTO `joke` SET
    `joketext` = :joketext,
    `jokedate` = "today's date"';

$stmt = $pdo->prepare($sql);

$stmt->bindValue(':joketext', $_POST['joketext']);
$stmt->execute();
```

Let's break this down one statement at a time. First, we write our SQL query as a PHP string and store it in a variable (`$sql`) as usual. What's unusual about this `INSERT` query, however, is that no value is specified for the `joketext` column. Instead, it contains a placeholder for this value (`:joketext`). Don't worry about the `jokedate` field just now—we'll circle back to it in a moment.

Next, we call the prepare method of our PDO object ($pdo), passing it our SQL query as an argument. This sends the query to the MySQL server, asking it to *prepare* to run the query. MySQL can't run it yet—there's no value for the joketext column. The prepare method returns a PDOStatement object (yes, the same kind of object that gives us the results from a SELECT query), which we store in $stmt.

Now that MySQL has prepared our statement for execution, we can send it the missing value(s) by calling the bindValue method of our PDOStatement object ($stmt). We call this method once for each value to be supplied (in this case, we only need to supply one value—the joke text), passing as arguments the placeholder that we want to fill in (':joketext') and the value we want to fill it with ($_POST['joketext']). Because MySQL knows we're sending it a discrete value, rather than SQL code that needs to be parsed, there's no risk of characters in the value being interpreted as SQL code. Using prepared statements, SQL injection vulnerabilities simply aren't possible!

Finally, we call the PDOStatement object's execute method to tell MySQL to execute the query with the value(s) we've supplied.[5]

One interesting thing you'll notice about this code is that we never placed quotes around the joke text. :joketext exists inside the query without any quotes, and when we called bindValue we passed it the plain joke text from the $_POST array. When using prepared statements, you don't need quotes because the database (in our case, MySQL) is smart enough to know that the text is a string and it will be treated as such when the query is executed.

The lingering question in this code is how to assign today's date to the jokedate field. We *could* write some fancy PHP code to generate today's date in the YYYY-MM-DD format that MySQL requires, but it turns out that MySQL itself has a function to do this: CURDATE:

```
$sql = 'INSERT INTO `joke` SET
    `joketext` = :joketext,
    `jokedate` = CURDATE()';
```

[5.] Yes, this PDOStatement method is called execute, unlike the similar method of PDO objects, which is called exec. PHP has many strengths, but consistency isn't one of them.

```
$stmt = $pdo->prepare($sql);
$stmt->bindValue(':joketext', $_POST['joketext']);
$stmt->execute();
```

The MySQL CURDATE function is used here to assign the current date as the value of the jokedate column. MySQL actually has dozens of these functions, but I'll introduce them only as required.

Now that we have our query, we can complete the if statement we started earlier to handle submissions of the "Add Joke" form:

```
if (isset($_POST['joketext'])) {
    try {
    $pdo = new PDO('mysql:host=localhost;dbname=ijdb;
    charset=utf8', 'ijdbuser', 'mypassword');
    $pdo->setAttribute(PDO::ATTR_ERRMODE,
        PDO::ERRMODE_EXCEPTION);

    $sql = 'INSERT INTO `joke` SET
        `joketext` = :joketext,
        `jokedate` = CURDATE()';

    $stmt = $pdo->prepare($sql);

    $stmt->bindValue(':joketext', $_POST['joketext']);

    $stmt->execute();
    }
    catch (PDOException $e) {
    $title = 'An error has occurred';

    $output = 'Database error: ' . $e->getMessage() . ' in '
    . $e->getFile() . ':' . $e->getLine();
    }
}
```

But wait! This `if` statement has one more trick up its sleeve. Once we've added the new joke to the database, instead of displaying the PHP template as previously, we want to redirect the user's browser back to the list of jokes. That way they're able to see the newly added joke among them. That's what the two lines at the end of the `if` statement above do.

In order to achieve the desired result, your first instinct might be to allow the controller to simply fetch the list of jokes from the database after adding the new joke and displaying the list using the `jokes.html.php` template as usual. The problem with doing this is that the list of jokes, from the browser's perspective, would be the result of having submitted the "Add Joke" form. If the user were then to refresh the page, the browser would resubmit that form, causing another copy of the new joke to be added to the database! This is rarely the desired behavior.

Instead, we want the browser to treat the updated list of jokes as a normal web page that's able to be reloaded without resubmitting the form. The way to do this is to answer the browser's form submission with an HTTP redirect[6]—a special response that tells the browser to navigate to a different page.

The PHP `header` function provides the means of sending special server responses like this one, by letting you insert specific headers into the response sent to the browser. In order to signal a redirect, you must send a `Location` header with the URL of the page to which you wish to direct the browser:

```
header('Location: URL');
```

In this case, we want to send the browser to `jokes.php`. Here are the two lines that redirect the browser back to our controller after adding the new joke to the database:

```
header('Location: jokes.php');
```

[6.] HTTP stands for HyperText Transfer Protocol, and is the language that describes the request/response communications that are exchanged between the visitor's web browser and your web server.

Here's the complete code of the addjoke.php controller:

4-18. MySQL-AddJoke

```php
<?php
if (isset($_POST['joketext'])) {
    try {
        $pdo = new PDO('mysql:host=localhost;dbname=ijdb;
        charset=utf8', 'ijdbuser', 'mypassword');
        $pdo->setAttribute(PDO::ATTR_ERRMODE,
            PDO::ERRMODE_EXCEPTION);

        $sql = 'INSERT INTO `joke` SET
        `joketext` = :joketext,
        `jokedate` = CURDATE()';

        $stmt = $pdo->prepare($sql);

        $stmt->bindValue(':joketext', $_POST['joketext']);

        $stmt->execute();

        header('location: jokes.php');
    } catch (PDOException $e) {
        $title = 'An error has occurred';

        $output = 'Database error: ' . $e->getMessage() . ' in '
        . $e->getFile() . ':' . $e->getLine();
    }
} else {
    $title = 'Add a new joke';

    ob_start();

    include __DIR__ . '/../templates/addjoke.html.php';

    $output = ob_get_clean();
}
include __DIR__ . '/../templates/layout.html.php';
```

As you review this to ensure it all makes sense to you, note that the code that connects to the database by creating a `new` `PDO` object must come before any of the code that runs database queries. But a database connection isn't required for displaying the "Add Joke" form. The connection is only made when the form has been submitted.

Load this up and add a new joke or two to the database via your browser.

There you have it: you're able to view existing jokes in—and add new jokes to—your MySQL database.

Deleting Data from the Database

In this section, we'll make one final enhancement to our joke database site. Next to each joke on the jokes page (`jokes.php`), we'll place a button labeled **Delete**. When clicked, it will remove that joke from the database and display the updated joke list.

If you like a challenge, you might want to take a stab at writing this feature yourself before you read on to see my solution. Although we're implementing a brand new feature, we'll mainly be using the same tools as employed in the previous examples in this chapter. Here are a few hints to start you off:

▧ You'll need a new controller (`deletejoke.php`).

▧ The SQL `DELETE` command will be required, which I introduced in <u>Chapter 3</u>

▧ To delete a particular joke in your controller, you'll need to identify it uniquely. The `id` column in the `joke` table was created to serve this purpose. You're going to have to pass the ID of the joke to be deleted with the request to delete a joke. The easiest way to do this is to use a hidden form field.

At the very least, take a few moments to think about how you'd approach this. When you're ready to see the solution, read on!

To begin with, we need to modify the `SELECT` query that fetches the list of jokes from the database. In addition to the `joketext` column, we must also fetch the `id` column so that we can identify each joke uniquely:

```
try {
    $pdo = new PDO('mysql:host=localhost;dbname=ijdb;
    charset=utf8',  'ijdbuser', 'mypassword');
    $pdo->setAttribute(PDO::ATTR_ERRMODE,
        PDO::ERRMODE_EXCEPTION);


    $sql = 'SELECT `id`, `joketext` FROM `joke`';
    $result = $pdo->query($sql);
    // …
```

We also have to modify the `while` loop that stores the database results into the `$jokes` array. Instead of simply storing the text of each joke as an item in the array, we store both the ID and text of each joke. One way to do this is to make each item in the `$jokes` array an array in its own right:

```
while ($row = $result->fetch()) {
    $jokes[] = ['id' => $row['id'], 'joketext' =>
    $row['joketext']];
}
```

 Using a `foreach` Loop Instead

If you've already switched to using a **foreach** loop to process your database result rows, that will work just fine too:

```
foreach ($result as $row) {
    $jokes[] = array('id' => $row['id'], 'joketext' =>
    $row['joketext']);
}
```

Once this loop runs its course, we'll have the `$jokes` array, each item of which is an associative array with two items: the ID of the joke and its text. For each joke (`$jokes[n]`), we can therefore retrieve its ID (`$jokes[n]['id']`) and its text (`$jokes[n]['text']`).

Our next step is to update the `jokes.html.php` template to retrieve each joke's text from this new array structure, as well as provide a **Delete** button for each joke:

```php
<?php foreach ($jokes as $joke): ?>
<blockquote>
    <p>
    <?=htmlspecialchars($joke['joketext'],
        ENT_QUOTES, 'UTF-8')?>
    <form action="deletejoke.php" method="post">
 <input type="hidden" name="id"
↪ value="<?=$joke['id']?>">
        <input type="submit" value="Delete">
    </form>
    </p>
</blockquote>
<?php endforeach; ?>
```

Here are the highlights of this updated code:

▪ Each joke will be displayed with a form, which, if submitted, will delete that joke. We signal this to a new controller, `deletejoke.php`, using the form's `action` attribute.

▪ Since each joke in the `$jokes` array is now represented by a two-item array instead of a simple string, we must update this line to retrieve the text of the joke. We do this using `$joke['text']` instead of just `$joke`.

▪ When we submit the form to delete this joke, we send along the ID of the joke to be deleted. To do this, we need a form field containing the joke's ID, but we'd prefer to keep this field hidden from the user; that's why we use a hidden form field (`input type="hidden"`). The name of this field is `id`, and its value is the ID of the joke to be deleted (`$joke['id']`).

Unlike the text of the joke, the ID is not a user-submitted value, so there's no need to worry about making it HTML-safe with `htmlspecialchars`. We can rest assured it will be a number, since it's automatically generated by MySQL for the `id` column when the joke is added to the database.

■ The submit button (`input type="submit"`) submits the form when clicked. Its value attribute gives it a label of **Delete**.

■ Finally, we close the form for this joke.

 Why Aren't the Form and Input Tags Outside the Blockquote?

If you know your HTML, you're probably thinking the form and input tags belong outside of the blockquote element, since they aren't a part of the quoted text (the joke).

Strictly speaking, that's true: the form and its inputs should really be either before or after the blockquote. Unfortunately, making that tag structure display clearly requires a little CSS code that's really beyond the scope of this book.

Rather than teach you CSS layout techniques in a book about PHP and MySQL, I've decided to go with this imperfect markup. If you plan to use this code in the real world, you should invest some time into learning CSS (or at least secure the services of a CSS guru). That way, you can take complete control of your HTML markup without worrying about the CSS required to make it look nice.

Add the following CSS to `jokes.css` to make the buttons appear to the right of the jokes and draw a line between them:

```
blockquote {display: table; margin-bottom: 1em;
↪ border-bottom: 1px solid #ccc; padding: 0.5em;}
blockquote p {display: table-cell; width: 90%;
↪ vertical-align: top;}
blockquote form {display: table-cell; width: 10%;}
```

The following image shows what the joke list looks like with the **Delete** buttons added:

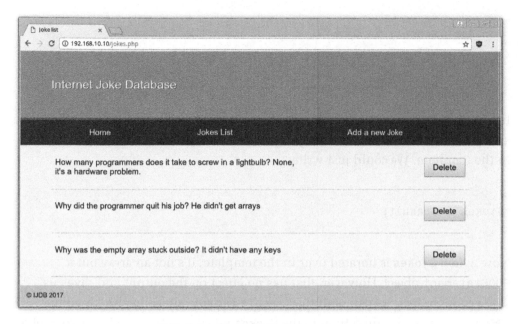

4-19. Each button can delete its respective joke

But wait! Before we move on to making the **Delete** button work, let's briefly step back and take a careful look at this line:

```
$jokes[] = ['id' => $row['id'], 'joketext' =>
$row['joketext']];
```

Here we're looping over the PDOStatement object, which gives us a $row variable containing the keys id and joketext along with corresponding values, and we're using that to build another array with the same keys and values.

You may have already realized this is terribly inefficient. We could achieve the same thing using this code:

```
while ($row = $result->fetch()) {
    $jokes[] = $row;
}
```

But as we know, this can also be achieved with a foreach loop:

```
foreach ($result as $row) {
    $jokes[] = $row;
}
```

In this instance, we're using `foreach` to iterate over the records from the database and build an array. We're then looping over the array with another `foreach` loop in the template. We could just write:

```
$jokes = $result;
```

Now, when `$jokes` is iterated over in the template, it's not an array but a `PDOStatement` object. However, that has no effect on the output and saves us some code. In fact, we can omit the `$result` variable altogether and load the `PDOStatement` object directly into the `$jokes` variable. The complete `jokes.php` controller now looks like this:

```
try {
    $pdo = new PDO('mysql:host=localhost;dbname=ijdb;
    charset=utf8', 'ijdbuser', 'mypassword');
    $pdo->setAttribute(PDO::ATTR_ERRMODE,
    PDO::ERRMODE_EXCEPTION);

    $sql = 'SELECT `joketext`, `id` FROM joke';

    $jokes = $pdo->query($sql);

    $title = 'Joke list';

    ob_start();

    include __DIR__ . '/../templates/jokes.html.php';

    $output = ob_get_clean();
}
catch (PDOException $e) {
    $title = 'An error has occurred';
```

```
    $output = 'Database error: ' . $e->getMessage() . ' in '
    . $e->getFile() . ':' . $e->getLine();
}


include __DIR__ . '/../templates/layout.html.php';
```

Now we don't even have a `while` loop iterating over the records in the controller, but just iterate over the records directly in the template, saving some code and making the page execute slightly faster, as it now only loops over the records once.

Back to our new **Delete** button: all that remains to make this new feature work is to add a relevant `deletejoke.php` to issue a `DELETE` query to the database:

```
try {
 $pdo = new
↪ PDO('mysql:host=localhost;dbname=ijdb;charset=utf8',
    'ijdbuser', 'mypassword');
    $pdo->setAttribute(PDO::ATTR_ERRMODE,
    PDO::ERRMODE_EXCEPTION);

    $sql = 'DELETE FROM `joke` WHERE `id` = :id';

    $stmt = $pdo->prepare($sql);

    $stmt->bindValue(':id', $_POST['id']);
    $stmt->execute();

    header('location: jokes.php');
}
catch (PDOException $e) {
    $title = 'An error has occurred';

 $output = 'Unable to connect to the database server: ' .
↪ $e->getMessage() . ' in '
    . $e->getFile() . ':' . $e->getLine();
}
```

```
include __DIR__ . '/../templates/layout.html.php';
```

The complete code for the updated `jokes.php` and `deletejoke.php` is available as *MySQL-DeleteJoke*.

This chunk of code works exactly like the one we added to process the "Add Joke" code earlier in the chapter. We start by preparing a `DELETE` query with a placeholder for the joke ID that we wish to delete.[7] We then bind the submitted value of `$_POST['id']` to that placeholder and execute the query. Once that query is achieved, we use the PHP `header` function to ask the browser to send a new request to view the updated list of jokes.

[7.] You might think that a prepared statement is unnecessary in this instance to protect our database from SQL injection attacks, since the joke ID is provided by a hidden form field invisible to the user. In fact, *all* form fields—even hidden ones—are ultimately under the user's control. There are widely distributed browser add-ons, for example, that will make hidden form fields visible and available for editing by the user. Remember: any value submitted by the browser is ultimately suspect when it comes to protecting your site's security.

Don't Use Hyperlinks to Perform Actions

If you tackled this example yourself, your first instinct might have been to provide a **Delete** hyperlink for each joke, instead of going to the trouble of writing an entire HTML form containing a **Delete** button for each joke on the page. Indeed, the code for such a link would be much simpler:

```php
<?php foreach ($jokes as $joke): ?>
    <blockquote>
    <p>
        <?=htmlspecialchars($joke['joketext'],
            ENT_QUOTES, 'UTF-8')?>
        <a href="deletejoke.php&amp;
        id=<?=$joke['id']?>">Delete</a>
    </p>
    </blockquote>
<?php endforeach; ?>
```

In short, hyperlinks should never be used to perform *actions* (such as deleting a joke); they must only be used to provide a link to some related content. The same goes for forms with `method="get"`, which should only be used to perform queries of existing data. Actions must only ever be performed as a result of a form with `method="post"` being submitted.

The reason why is that forms with `method="post"` are treated differently by browsers and related software. If you were to submit a form with `method="post"` and then click the **Refresh** button in your browser, for example, the browser would ask if you're certain you wish to resubmit the form. Browsers have no similar protection against resubmission when it comes to links and forms with `method="get"`.

Similarly, web accelerator software (and some modern browsers) will automatically follow hyperlinks present on a page in the background, so that the target pages will be available for immediate display if the user clicks one of those links. Search engines will also follow all the links on your site in order to work out when to show your site's pages in search results.

If your site deleted a joke as a result of a hyperlink being followed, you could find your jokes being deleted automatically.

Mission Accomplished

In this chapter, you learned all about PHP Data Objects (PDO), a collection of built-in PHP classes (`PDO`, `PDOException`, and `PDOStatement`) that allow you to interface with a MySQL database server by creating objects and then calling the methods they provide. While you were at it, you also picked up the basics of object-oriented programming (OOP), no mean feat for a PHP beginner!

Using PDO objects, you built your first database-driven website, which published the `ijdb` database online and allowed visitors to add and delete jokes.

In a way, you could say this chapter achieved the stated mission of this book: to teach you how to build a database-driven website. Of course, the example in this chapter contained only the bare essentials. In the rest of the book, I'll show you how to flesh out the skeleton you learned to build in this chapter.

In the next chapter, we return to the SQL Query window in MySQL Workbench. We'll learn how to use relational database principles and advanced SQL queries to represent more complex types of information, and give our visitors credit for the jokes they add!

Chapter **5**

Relational Database Design

Since <u>Chapter 3</u>, we've worked with a very simple database of jokes, composed of a single table named (appropriately enough) joke. While this database has served us well as an introduction to MySQL databases, there's more to relational database design than can be understood from this simple example. In this chapter, we'll expand on this database and learn a few new features of MySQL, in an effort to realize and appreciate the real power that relational databases have to offer.

Be forewarned that I'll cover several topics only in an informal, non-rigorous sort of way. As any computer science major will tell you, database design is a serious area of research, with tested and mathematically provable principles that, while useful, are beyond the scope of this text.

For more complete coverage of database design concepts and SQL in general, pick

up a copy of *Simply SQL*[1]. If you're *really* into learning the hard principles
behind relational databases, *Database in Depth*[2] (Sebastopol: O'Reilly, 2005) is a
worthwhile read

Giving Credit Where Credit Is Due

To start off, let's recall the structure of our `joke` table. It contains three columns:
`id`, `joketext`, and `jokedate`. Together, these columns allow us to identify jokes
(`id`), and keep track of their text (`joketext`) and the date they were entered
(`jokedate`). For your reference, here's the SQL code that creates this table and
inserts a couple of entries:[3]

```
# Code to create a simple joke table

CREATE TABLE `joke` (
    `id` INT NOT NULL AUTO_INCREMENT PRIMARY KEY,
    `joketext` TEXT,
    `jokedate` DATE NOT NULL
) DEFAULT CHARACTER SET utf8 ENGINE=InnoDB;

# Adding jokes to the table

INSERT INTO `joke` SET
 `joketext` = 'Why was the empty array stuck outside? It
↪ didn\'t have any keys',
`jokedate` = '2017-04-01';

INSERT INTO `joke`
(`joketext`, `jokedate`) VALUES (
'!false - It\'s funny because it\'s true',
```

[1.] http://www.sitepoint.com/books/sql1/"

[2.] http://oreilly.com/catalog/9780596100124/

[3.] If you ever need to re-create your database from scratch, you can use MySQL Workbench
to drop all the tables and then go to Data Import/Restore and select the **database.sql**
from the sample code. Note that the **database.sql** file will change depending on which
sample you're viewing. In this way, you can use the **.sql** files in this book's code archive
as database snapshots to load up whenever you need them.

```
"2017-04-01"
);
```

Now, let's say we wanted to track another piece of information about our jokes: the names of the people who submitted them. It would be natural to add a new column to our joke table for this. The SQL ALTER TABLE command (which we've yet to see) lets us do exactly that.

As I demonstrated earlier, you can either type out these queries yourself or have a tool such as MySQL Workbench do it for you. When you use the GUI of MySQL Workbench to interact with the database, it generates the queries for you. It even shows them to you before applying them to the database. If you're not quite sure how to write a query, you can always get MySQL Workbench to generate it for you and then amend it to suit your needs.

SQL Queries fall into two categories:

- **Data definition language (DDL) queries**. These are the queries that describe *how* the data will be stored. These are the CREATE TABLE and CREATE DATABASE queries that I showed you in <u>Chapter 3</u> along with the aforementioned ALTER TABLE query.
- **Data manipulation language (DML) queries**. These are the queries that you use to manipulate the data in the database. You've seen some of these already: INSERT, UPDATE, DELETE and SELECT.

It's worthwhile for a PHP developer to learn the syntax and different variations of the DML queries, as they regularly need to be typed out in PHP scripts. It's also useful to know what's going on behind the scenes. That said, it's not going to be detrimental to your progress as a developer to have MySQL Workbench generate your DDL queries rather than typing them out yourself. Having the queries generated for you can be a time saver, as it gives you a lot less syntax learn, and the DDL query format can be considerably more difficult to follow than most of the DML queries.

To add a new column to a database table, open up MySQL Workbench,, connect to your database, double-click on the schema we created in <u>Chapter 3</u> called ijdb, and expand the tables entry. You'll see the joke table.

May Need to Boot the Server

If you've logged out or rebooted your PC since the last chapter, you'll need to boot your server as you did in Chapter 1 using the `vagrant up` command.

To add a new column, right click on the table name and select "Alter Table". This will bring up the familiar table editing screen. From here you can add columns in the same way you did in Chapter 3.

Add a new column called `authorname`, which is going to store the name of the joke's author along with each joke. Set the type to `VARCHAR(255)`. The type declared is a **variable-length character string** of up to 255 characters, `VARCHAR(255)`—plenty of space for even very esoteric names. Let's also add a column for the authors' email addresses, set the column name to `authoremail` and the type to `VARCHAR(255)`.

Once you press **Apply**, you'll see a confirmation dialog appear with the following DDL queries:

```
ALTER TABLE `joke` ADD COLUMN `authorname` VARCHAR(255)
ALTER TABLE `joke` ADD COLUMN `authoremail` VARCHAR(255)
```

You could have typed these in yourself, but the GUI in MySQL Workbench provides some useful error checks, and it will always generate valid queries.

Just to make sure the two columns were added properly, right-click on the table name in the Schemas panel and select "Select Rows - Limit 1000". You should see the two extra columns listed. Of course, at the moment, none of your jokes have values for either of these fields.

This should give you a table of results like the one below:

id	joketext	jokedate	authorname	authoremail
1	Whv was the emptv arrav stuck outside? It didn...	2017-04-01	NULL	NULL
2	!false - It's funnv because it's true	2017-04-01	NULL	NULL
NULL		NULL	NULL	NULL

5-1. Our **joke** table now contains five columns

Looks good, right? Obviously, to accommodate this expanded table structure, we'd need to make changes to the HTML and PHP form code we wrote in <u>Chapter 4</u> that allowed us to add new jokes to the database. Using UPDATE queries, we could now add author details to all the jokes in the table. But before we spend too much time on such changes, we should stop and consider whether this new table design was the right choice here. In this case, it turns out it wasn't.

Rule of Thumb: Keep Entities Separate

As your knowledge of database-driven websites continues to grow, you may decide that a personal joke list is too limited. In fact, you might receive more submitted jokes than you have original jokes of your own. Let's say you decide to launch a website where people from all over the world can share jokes with each other. Adding the author's name and email address to each joke certainly makes a lot of sense, but the method we used above leads to potential problems:

- What if a frequent contributor to your site named Joan Smith changed her email address? She might begin to submit new jokes using the new address, but her old address would still be attached to the jokes she'd submitted in the past. Looking at your database, you might simply think there were two people named Joan Smith who had submitted jokes. She might inform you of the change of address, and you may try to update all the old jokes with the new address, but if you missed just one joke, your database would still contain incorrect information. Database design experts refer to this sort of problem as an **update anomaly**.

- It would be natural for you to rely on your database to provide a list of all the people who've ever submitted jokes to your site. In fact, you could easily obtain a mailing list using the following query:

```
SELECT DISTINCT `authorname`, `authoremail`
FROM `joke`
```

The word DISTINCT in the above query stops MySQL from outputting duplicate
result rows. For example, if Joan Smith submits 20 jokes to your site, using the
DISTINCT option would cause her name to only appear once in the list instead of
20 times.

Then, if for some reason, you decided to remove all the jokes that a particular
author had submitted to your site, you'd remove any record of this person from
the database in the process, and you'd no longer be able to email him or her with
information about your site! Database design experts call this a **delete anomaly**.

As your mailing list might be a major source of income for your site, it's unwise
to go throwing away an author's email address just because you disliked the jokes
that person submitted.

■ You have no guarantee that Joan Smith will enter her name the same way each
time. Consider the variations: Joan Smith, J. Smith, Smith, Joan—you catch
my drift. This makes keeping track of a particular author exceedingly difficult,
especially if Joan Smith also has several email addresses she likes to use.

These problems—and more—can be dealt with very easily using established
database design principles. Instead of storing the information for the authors in
the same table as the jokes, let's create an entirely new table for our list of
authors. Just as we have an id column in our joke table to identify each joke with
a unique number, we'll use an identically named column in our new table to
identify our authors. We can then use those author IDs in our joke table to
associate authors with their jokes. The complete database layout will look like
this:

joke

id	joketext	jokedate	authorid
1	Why did the chicken ...	2012-04-01	1
2	Knock-knock! Who's ...	2012-04-01	1
3	A man walks into a bar ...	2012-05-16	2

author

id	name	email
1	Kevin Yank	thatguy@kevinyank.com
2	Joan Smith	joan@example.com

5-2. The relationship between the joke and author tables

These tables show that there are three jokes and two authors. The `authorid` column of the `joke` table establishes a relationship between the two tables, indicating that Kevin Yank submitted jokes 1 and 2 and Joan Smith submitted joke 3. Notice that since each author now only appears once in the database, and independently of the jokes submitted, we've avoided all the potential problems just outlined.

What's really important to note about this database design is that we're storing information about two types of *things* (jokes and authors), so it's most appropriate to have two tables. This is a rule of thumb that you should always keep in mind when designing a database: *each type of entity (or "thing") about which you want to be able to store information should be given its own table.*

To set up the aforementioned database from scratch is fairly simple (involving just two `CREATE TABLE` queries), but since we'd like to make these changes in a nondestructive manner (that is, without losing any of our precious jokes), we'll use MySQL Workbench to remove the `authorname` and `authoremail` columns from the `joke` table. To do this, right-click on the `joke` table in the Schema list and select "Alter Table". Once again, it will give you an editable grid containing all the columns in the table. To delete the two columns, right-click on the column name and select **Delete Selected**. You'll need to do this for both columns. Once you click **Apply**, you'll see MySQL Workbench has generated this query for you:

```
ALTER TABLE `ijdb`.`joke`
DROP COLUMN `authoremail`,
DROP COLUMN `authorname`;
```

This is a DDL `ALTER TABLE` query for removing columns. As with all of these DDL queries, you could have typed this into the query panel manually and executed it, but we've used the GUI to avoid having to remember all the different commands.

Now, we need to create a new table to store the authors. To do this, follow the same procedure you used to create the `joke` table: right-click on the `Tables` entry in the Schemas panel and select "Create Table".

Set the table name to `author` and add the following fields:

1. `id`, and check the `PK`, `AI` and `NN` boxes
2. `name`, `VARCHAR(255)`
3. `email`, `VARCHAR(255)`

Click **Apply**, and MySQL Workbench will generate a `CREATE TABLE` query similar to this:

```
CREATE TABLE `author` (
    `id` INT NOT NULL AUTO_INCREMENT PRIMARY KEY,
    `name` VARCHAR(255),
    `email` VARCHAR(255)
) DEFAULT CHARACTER SET utf8 ENGINE=InnoDB
```

Finally, we add the `authorid` column to our `joke` table. Edit the `joke` table and add a column called `authorid` with the type `INT`.

If you prefer, here are the `CREATE TABLE` commands that will create the two tables from scratch:

```
# Code to create a simple joke table that stores an author
↳ ID

CREATE TABLE `joke` (
    `id` INT NOT NULL AUTO_INCREMENT PRIMARY KEY,
    `joketext` TEXT,
    `jokedate` DATE NOT NULL,
    `authorid` INT
) DEFAULT CHARACTER SET utf8 ENGINE=InnoDB;

# Code to create a simple author table

CREATE TABLE `author` (
    `id` INT NOT NULL AUTO_INCREMENT PRIMARY KEY,
    `name` VARCHAR(255),
    `email` VARCHAR(255)
) DEFAULT CHARACTER SET utf8 ENGINE=InnoDB;
```

All that's left to do is add some authors to the new table, and assign authors to all the existing jokes in the database by filling in the `authorid` column.[4] Go ahead and do this now if you like, as it will give you some practice with `INSERT` and `UPDATE` queries. If you're rebuilding the database from scratch, however, here's a series of `INSERT` queries that will do the trick:

```
# Adding authors to the database
# We specify the IDs so they're known when we add the jokes
↳ below.
```

[4.] For now, you'll have to do this manually. But rest assured, in Chapter 9 we'll see how PHP can insert entries with the correct IDs automatically, reflecting the relationships between them.

```
INSERT INTO `author` SET
    `id` = 1,
    `name` = 'Kevin Yank',
    `email` = 'thatguy@kevinyank.com';

INSERT INTO `author` (`id`, `name`, `email`)
VALUES (2, 'Tom Butler', 'tom@r.je');

# Adding jokes to the database

INSERT INTO `joke` SET
 `joketext` = 'How many programmers does it take to screw in
↪ a lightbulb? None, it\'s a hardware problem.',
    `jokedate` = '2017-04-01',
    `authorid` = 1;

INSERT INTO `joke` (`joketext`, `jokedate`, `authorid`)
VALUES (
 'Why did the programmer quit his job? He didn\'t get
↪ arrays',
    '2017-04-01',
    1
);

INSERT INTO `joke` (`joketext`, `jokedate`, `authorid`)
VALUES (
 'Why was the empty array stuck outside? It didn\'t have any
↪ keys',
    '2017-04-01',
    2
);
```

 Both Kinds of INSERT

I've used this opportunity to refresh your memory about both kinds of INSERT query syntax. They both do exactly the same job and have the same result, so it's up to you which you use, and boils down mainly to personal preference rather than any practical reason.

SELECT with Multiple Tables

With your data now separated into two tables, it may seem that you're complicating the process of data retrieval. Consider, for example, our original goal: to display a list of jokes with the name and email address of the author next to each joke. In the single-table solution, you could gain all the information needed to produce such a list using a single SELECT query in your PHP code:

```php
try {
    $pdo = new PDO('mysql:host=localhost;dbname=ijdb;
    charset=utf8', 'ijdb', 'mypassword');
    $pdo->setAttribute(PDO::ATTR_ERRMODE,
    PDO::ERRMODE_EXCEPTION);

    $sql = 'SELECT `id`, `joketext` FROM `joke`';

    $jokes = $pdo->query($sql);

    $title = 'Joke list';

    ob_start();

    include __DIR__ . '/../templates/jokes.html.php';

    $output = ob_get_clean();
}
catch (PDOException $e) {
    $title = 'An error has occurred';

    $output = 'Database error: ' . $e->getMessage() . ' in '
    . $e->getFile() . ':' . $e->getLine();
}

include __DIR__ . '/../templates/layout.html.php';
```

With our new database layout, this would, at first, no longer seem possible. As the author details of each joke are no longer stored in the joke table, you might think that you'd have to fetch those details separately for each joke you wanted to display. The code required would involve a call to the PDO query method for each and every joke to be displayed. This would be messy and involve a considerable amount of extra code.

Taking all this into account, it would seem that the "old way" was the better solution, despite its weaknesses. Fortunately, relational databases like MySQL are designed to make it easy to work with data stored in multiple tables! Using a new form of the SELECT statement, called a **join**, you can have the best of both worlds. Joins allow you to treat related data in multiple tables as if they were stored in a single table. Here's what the syntax of a simple join looks like:

```
SELECT columns
FROM `table1`
INNER JOIN `table2`
    ON condition(s) for data to be related
```

In your case, the columns we're interested in are id and joketext in the joke table, and name and email in the author table. The condition for an entry in the joke table to be related to an entry in the author table is that the value of the authorid column in the joke table is equal to the value of the id column in the author table.

Let's look at an example of a join. The first two queries show you what's contained in the two tables; they're unnecessary to perform the join. The third query is where the action's at:

```
SELECT `id`, LEFT(`joketext`, 20), `authorid` FROM `joke`
```

This query should now give the following results:

id	LEFT(`joketext`, 20)	authorid
1	How many programmers	1
2	Why did the programm	1
3	Why was the empty ar	2

5-3. Results of the `joke` table query

```
SELECT * FROM `author`
```

And this query, as you'd expect, will show all the authors:

id	name	email
1	Kevin Yank	thatauv@kevinyank.com
2	Tom Butler	tom@r.ie
NULL	NULL	NULL

5-4. "All of the authors from the **authors** table

It's possible to query data from both tables by using the SQL `JOIN` statement:

```
SELECT `joke`.`id`, LEFT(`joketext`, 20), `name`, `email`
FROM `joke` INNER JOIN `author`
    ON `authorid` = `author`.`id`
```

This will display all the data from both tables:

id	LEFT(`joketext`, 20)	name	email
1	How many programmers	Kevin Yank	thatauv@kevinyank.com
2	Why did the programm	Kevin Yank	thatauv@kevinyank.com
3	Why was the empty ar	Tom Butler	tom@r.ie

5-5. The results of your first join

See? The results of the third `SELECT`—a join—group the values stored in the two tables into a single table of results, with related data correctly appearing together. Even though the data is stored in two tables, you can still access all the information you need to produce the joke list on your web page with a single database query. Note in the query that, since there are columns named `id` in both tables, you must specify the name of the table when you refer to either `id` column. The joke table's ID is referred to as `joke.id`, while the author table's ID column is `author.id`. If the table name is unspecified, MySQL won't know which `id` you're referring to, and will produce the following error:

```
Error Code: 1052. Column 'id' in field list is ambiguous
```

Now that you know how to access the data stored in your two tables efficiently, you can rewrite the code for your joke list to take advantage of joins:

```php
try {
    $pdo = new PDO('mysql:host=localhost;dbname=ijdb;
    charset=utf8', 'ijdb', 'mypassword');
    $pdo->setAttribute(PDO::ATTR_ERRMODE,
    PDO::ERRMODE_EXCEPTION);

    $sql = 'SELECT `joke`.`id`, `joketext`, `name`, `email`
    FROM `joke` INNER JOIN `author`
        ON `authorid` = `author`.`id`';

    $jokes = $pdo->query($sql);

    $title = 'Joke list';

    ob_start();

    include __DIR__ . '/../templates/jokes.html.php';

    $output = ob_get_clean();
}
catch (PDOException $e) {
    $title = 'An error has occurred';
```

```
    $output = 'Database error: ' . $e->getMessage() . ' in '
      . $e->getFile() . ':' . $e->getLine();
}


include __DIR__ . '/../templates/layout.html.php';
```

You can then update your template `jokes.html.php` to display the author information for each joke:

```php
<?php foreach($jokes as $joke): ?>
<blockquote>
    <p>
    <?=htmlspecialchars($joke['joketext'],
        ENT_QUOTES, 'UTF-8')?>

    (by <a href="mailto:<?php
    echo htmlspecialchars($joke['email'], ENT_QUOTES,
        'UTF-8'); ?>"><?php
    echo htmlspecialchars($joke['name'], ENT_QUOTES,
        'UTF-8'); ?></a>)

    <form action="deletejoke.php" method="post">
        <input type="hidden" name="id"
        value="<?=$joke['id']?>">
        <input type="submit" value="Delete">
    </form>
    </p>
</blockquote>
<?php endforeach; ?>
```

If you run this script, you'll see the following result:

5-6. Jokes with authors

The more you work with databases, the more you'll come to realize the power of combining data from separate tables into a single table of results. Consider, for example, the following query, which displays a list of all jokes written by Tom Butler:

```
SELECT `joketext`
FROM `joke` INNER JOIN `author`
    ON `authorid` = `author`.`id`
WHERE `name` = "Tom Butler"
```

The results that are output from this query, shown below, come only from the joke table, but the query uses a join to let it search for jokes based on a value stored in the author table. There will be plenty more examples of clever queries like this throughout the book, but this example alone illustrates that the practical applications of joins are many and varied, and, in almost all cases, can save you a lot of work!

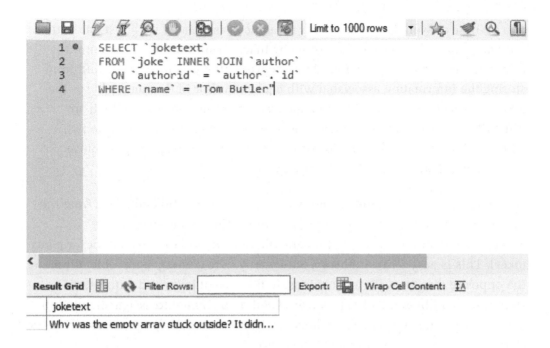

```
1 •   SELECT `joketext`
2     FROM `joke` INNER JOIN `author`
3       ON `authorid` = `author`.`id`
4     WHERE `name` = "Tom Butler"
```

Result Grid | Filter Rows: | Export: | Wrap Cell Content:

joketext
Why was the empty array stuck outside? It didn...

5-7. Tom Butler's jokes

Simple Relationships

The type of database layout for a given situation is usually dictated by the form of relationship that exists between the data that it needs to store. In this section, I'll examine the typical relationship types, and explain how best to represent them in a relational database.

In the case of a simple **one-to-one relationship**, a single table is all you'll need. An example of a one-to-one relationship is the email address of each author in our joke database. Since there will be one email address for each author, and one author for each email address, there's no reason to split the addresses into a separate table.[5]

A **many-to-one relationship** is a little more complicated, but you've already seen

---

[5.] There are exceptions to this rule. For example, if a single table grows very large with lots of columns, some of which are rarely used in SELECT queries, it can make sense to split those columns out into their own table. This can improve the performance of queries on the now-smaller table.

one of these as well. Each joke in our database is associated with just one author, but many jokes may have been written by that one author. This joke–author relationship is many-to-one. I've already covered the problems that result from storing the information associated with a joke's author in the same table as the joke itself. In brief, it can result in many copies of the same data, which are difficult to keep synchronized and waste space. If we split the data into two tables and use an ID column to link them together (making joins possible as shown before), all these problems disappear.

A **one-to-many relationship** is simply a many-to-one relationship seen from the opposite direction. As the joke–author relationship is many-to-one, the author–joke relationship is one-to-many (there is potentially one author for many jokes). This is easy to see in theory, but when you're coming at a problem from the opposite direction, it's less obvious. In the case of jokes and authors, we started with a library of jokes (the many) and then wanted to assign an author to each of them (the one). Let's now look at a hypothetical design problem where we start with the one and want to add the many.

Say we wanted to allow each of the authors in our database (the one) to have multiple email addresses (the many). When an inexperienced person in database design approaches a one-to-many relationship like this one, often the first thought is to try to store multiple values in a single database field like so:

author		
id	**name**	**email**
1	Kevin Yank	thatguy@kevinyank.com, kyank@example.com
2	Joan Smith	joan@example.com, jsmith@example.com

5-8. A table field overloaded with multiple values

This would work, but to retrieve a single email address from the database, we'd need to break up the string by searching for commas (or whatever special character you chose to use as a separator). It's a not-so-simple, potentially time-consuming operation. Try to imagine the PHP code necessary to remove one particular email address from a specific author! In addition, you'd need to allow for much longer values in the email column, which could result in wasted disk space, because the majority of authors would have just one email address.

Now take a step back, and realize that this one-to-many relationship is just the same as the many-to-one relationship we faced between jokes and authors. The solution, therefore, is also the same: split the new entities (in this case, email addresses) into their own table. The resulting database structure would be:

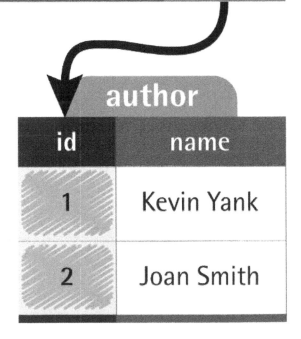

5-9. The `authorid` field associates each row of `email` with one row of `author`

Using a join with this structure, we can easily list the email addresses associated with a particular author:

```
SELECT `email`
FROM `author` INNER JOIN `email`
    ON `authorid` = `author`.`id`
WHERE `name` = "Kevin Yank"
```

Many-to-many Relationships

Okay, you now have a steadily growing database of jokes published on your website. It's growing so quickly, in fact, that the number of jokes has become unmanageable! Your site visitors are faced with a mammoth page that contains hundreds of jokes without any structure whatsoever. We need to make a change.

You decide to place your jokes into the following categories: knock-knock jokes, crossing-the-road jokes, lawyer jokes, light bulb jokes, and political jokes. Remembering our rule of thumb from earlier, you identify joke categories as a new entity, and create a table for them, either through MySQL Workbench or by issuing a CREATE TABLE query.

```
CREATE TABLE `category` (
    `id` INT NOT NULL AUTO_INCREMENT PRIMARY KEY,
    `name` VARCHAR(255)
) DEFAULT CHARACTER SET utf8 ENGINE=InnoDB
```

This table will store a name and an ID for each category in exactly the same way the joke table had an `authorid` column to attribute each joke to an author. We could add a `categoryid` table to the joke table to associate each joke with a category. It would even be possible to query all the jokes form a particular category using this:

```
SELECT `joketext`, `jokedate` FROM `joke` WHERE `categoryId`
↳ = 2
```

Now you come to the daunting task of assigning categories to your jokes. It occurs to you that a political joke might also be a crossing-the-road joke, and a knock-knock joke might also be a lawyer joke. A single joke might belong to many categories, and each category will contain many jokes. This is a many-to-many relationship.

Once again, many inexperienced developers begin to think of ways to store several values in a single column, because the obvious solution is to add a category column to the `joke` table and use it to list the IDs of those categories to which each joke belongs. A second rule of thumb would be useful here: *if you need to store multiple values in a single field, your design is probably flawed.*

The correct way to represent a many-to-many relationship is by using a **lookup table**. This is a table that contains no actual data, but lists pairs of entries that are related. The image below shows what the database design would look like for our joke categories:

5-10. Lookup table

The `jokecategory` table associates joke IDs (`jokeid`) with category IDs (`categoryid`). In this example, we can see that the joke that starts with "How many lawyers ..." belongs to both the lawyers and light bulb categories.

A lookup table is created in much the same way as is any other table. The difference lies in the choice of the primary key. Every table we've created so far has had a column named id that was designated to be the PRIMARY KEY when the table was created. Designating a column as a primary key tells MySQL to forbid two entries in that column from having the same value. It also speeds up join operations based on that column.

In the case of a lookup table, there's no single column that we want to force to have unique values. Each joke ID may appear more than once, as a joke may belong to more than one category, and each category ID may appear more than once, as a category may contain many jokes. What we want to prevent is the same *pair* of values appearing in the table twice. And, since the sole purpose of this table is to facilitate joins, the speed benefits offered by a primary key would come in very handy. For this reason, we usually create lookup tables with a multicolumn primary key as follows:

```
CREATE TABLE `jokecategory` (
    `jokeid` INT NOT NULL,
    `categoryid` INT NOT NULL,
    PRIMARY KEY (`jokeid`, `categoryid`)
) DEFAULT CHARACTER SET utf8 ENGINE=InnoDB
```

The same can be done in MySQL Workbench by checking the PK checkbox for both columns. This creates a table in which the jokeid and categoryid columns together form the primary key. This enforces the uniqueness that's appropriate to a lookup table, preventing a particular joke from being assigned to a specific category more than once, and speeds up joins that make use of this table.[6]

Now that your lookup table is in place and contains category assignments, you can use joins to create several interesting and practical queries. This query lists all jokes in the knock-knock category:

[6.] If you like, you can use the CREATE TABLE and INSERT commands to create the jokecategory table from scratch (and others, including the jokes within the tables) to follow along.

```
SELECT `joketext`
FROM `joke`
INNER JOIN `jokecategory`
    ON `joke`.`id` = `jokeid`
INNER JOIN `category`
    ON `categoryid` = `category`.`id`
WHERE name = "knock-knock"
```

As you can see, this query uses *two* joins. First, it takes the `joke` table and joins it to the `jokecategory` table. Then it takes that joined data and joins it to the category table. As your database structure becomes more complex, multijoin queries like this one become common.

The following query lists the categories that contain jokes beginning with "How many lawyers …":

```
SELECT `name`
FROM `joke`
INNER JOIN `jokecategory`
    ON `joke`.`id` = `jokeid`
INNER JOIN `category`
    ON `categoryid` = `category`.`id`
WHERE `joketext` LIKE "How many lawyers%"
```

And this query—which also makes use of our `author` table to join together the contents of *four tables*—lists the names of all authors who have written knock-knock jokes:

```
SELECT `author`.`name`
FROM `joke`
INNER JOIN `author`
    ON `authorid` = `author`.`id`
INNER JOIN `jokecategory`
    ON `joke`.`id` = `jokeid`
INNER JOIN `category`
    ON `categoryid` = `category`.`id`
```

```
WHERE `category`.`name` = "knock-knock"
```

This is starting to get complicated! Although JOINs can be used, later on in the book we'll see some different approaches that can help reduce this complexity—though sometimes at the expense of efficiency.

We won't add categories to the website just yet, but you now at least have a basic understanding of how the database could be structured to do so.

One for Many, and Many for One

In this chapter, I've explained the fundamentals of good database design, and covered how MySQL and, for that matter, all relational database management systems provide support for the representation of different types of relationships between entities. From your initial understanding of one-to-one relationships, you should now have expanded your knowledge to include many-to-one, one-to-many, and many-to-many relationships.

In the process, you've learned about some common SQL commands—in particular, how to use a SELECT query to join data spread across multiple tables into a single set of results.

With the increased expressiveness that multiple database tables bring, you're now equipped to extend the simple "joke list" site you assembled in Chapter 4 to include authors and categories, and that's exactly what Chapter 9 will be all about. Before you tackle this project, however, you should take some time to add to your PHP skills. Just as you spent this chapter learning some of the finer points of MySQL database design, Chapter 6 will teach you some of the subtleties of PHP programming—which will make the job of building a more complete joke database site much more fun.

Chapter **6**

Structured PHP Programming

Before we plow headlong into the next enhancements of our `joke` database, let's spend a little time honing your "PHP-fu." Specifically, I want to show you a few techniques to better structure your code.

Structured coding techniques are useful in all but the simplest of PHP projects. Already in Chapter 2, you've learned how to split your PHP code into multiple files: a controller and a set of associated templates. This lets you keep the server-side logic of your site separate from the HTML code used to display the dynamic content generated by that logic. In order to do this, you learned how to use the PHP `include` command.

The PHP language offers many such facilities to help you add structure to your code. The most powerful of these is undoubtedly its support for object-oriented programming (OOP), which we touched on briefly in Chapter 4. But there's no need to learn all the complexities of OOP to build complex (and well-structured) applications with PHP. Thankfully, there are also opportunities for structuring your code through the more basic features of PHP.

In this chapter, I'll explore some methods of keeping your PHP code manageable and maintainable. As projects grow in size, so does the code. When you want to make a change to something, you'll need to find the point in the code you want to change. This can be tricky, and sometimes requires editing code in more than one place.

Programmers are lazy, and we don't want to have to make the same change in multiple locations. By placing code in one place, and using it with the `include` statement, it allows us to avoid repetition. If you ever find yourself copying and pasting code, you're almost certainly better off moving that repeated code into its own file and using it in both locations with an `include` statement.

The computer doesn't care how you structure your code and will blindly follow any instructions you give it. Programmers structure the code, reduce repetition and break code into small chunks purely to make our own job easier. Code is a lot simpler to manage when broken up into small tasks. Trying to find an error in a 1000-line PHP script that does a dozen different things is a lot more difficult than finding the same error in a 30-line file that only performs a single task.

Include Files

Even very simple PHP-based websites often need the same piece of code in several places. You've already learned to use the PHP `include` command to load PHP templates from inside your controllers. It turns out you can use the same feature to save yourself from having to write the same code again and again, just like you did with `layout.html.php`: you wrote some HTML code and re-used it for every page.

Include files (also known just as **includes**) also contain snippets of PHP code that you can load into your other PHP scripts instead of having to retype them.

Including HTML Content

The concept of include files came long before PHP. If you're an old codger like me (which, in the Web world, means you're over 30), you may have experimented with server-side includes (SSIs). A feature of just about every web server out there, SSIs let you put commonly used snippets of HTML (and JavaScript, and CSS) into include files that you can then use in multiple pages.

In PHP, include files most commonly contain either pure PHP code or, in the case of PHP templates, a mixture of HTML and PHP code. But you don't *have* to put PHP code in your include files. If you like, an include file can contain strictly static HTML. This is most useful for sharing common design elements across your site, such as a copyright notice at the bottom of every page:

```
<footer>
    The contents of this web page are copyright &copy; 2017
    Example LLC. All Rights Reserved.
</footer>
```

This file is a **template partial**—an include file to be used by PHP templates. To distinguish this type of file from others in your project, I recommend giving it a name ending with .html.php, to differentiate from non-template pages. This naming convention is common in projects that use templates in this way.

You can then use this partial in any of your PHP templates:

```
<!DOCTYPE html>
<html lang="en">
    <head>
        <meta charset="utf-8">
        <title>A Sample Page</title>
    </head>
    <body>
        <main>
        This page uses a static include to display a standard
        copyright notice below.
        </main>
```

```
        <?php include 'footer.html.php'; ?>
    </body>
</html>
```

Finally, here's the controller that loads this template:

```php
<?php
include 'samplepage.tpl.php';
?>
```

6-1. The completed page

The screenshot above shows what the page looks like in the browser.

Now all you need to do to update your copyright notice is to edit `footer.html.php`. No more time-consuming, error-prone find-and-replace operations!

Of course, if you *really* want to make your life easier, you can just let PHP do the work for you:

```php
<p id="footer">
    The contents of this web page are copyright &copy;
    1998&ndash;<?php echo date('Y'); ?> Example LLC.
    All Rights Reserved.
</p>
```

Including PHP Code

On most websites with a database, almost every controller script must establish a database connection as its first order of business, and finally include the `layout.html.php` file. Our controllers all follow this pattern:

```php
<?php
try {
    $pdo = new PDO('mysql:host=localhost;dbname=ijdb;
    charset=utf8', 'ijdbuser', 'mypassword');
    $pdo->setAttribute(PDO::ATTR_ERRMODE,
    PDO::ERRMODE_EXCEPTION);

    // do something unique for this page
    // setting the $title and $output variables
} catch (PDOException $e) {
    $title = 'An error has occurred';

    $output = 'Unable to connect to the database server: '
    . $e->getMessage() . ' in '
    . $e->getFile() . ':' . $e->getLine();
}

include __DIR__ . '/../templates/layout.html.php';
```

At some 12 lines long, it's only a slightly cumbersome chunk of code, but having to repeat it in every controller script can quickly become annoying. Many new PHP developers will often omit essential error checking to save typing (for example, by leaving out the `try … catch` statement in this code), which can result in a lot of lost time looking for the cause when an error *does* occur. Others will make heavy use of the clipboard to copy pieces of code like this from existing scripts for use in new ones. Some even use features of their text editor software to store useful pieces of code as snippets for frequent use.

But what happens when the database password or some other detail of the code changes? Suddenly you're on a treasure hunt to find every occurrence of the code in your site to make the necessary change—a task that can be especially frustrating if you've used several variations of the code that you need to track down and update.

Files can help in this situation. Instead of repeating the code fragment in every file that needs it, write it just once in a separate file—known as the include file. That file can then be included in any other PHP files that need to use it.

Let's apply this technique to create the database connection in our joke list example to see how it works in detail.

Include files are just like normal PHP files, but typically they contain snippets of code that are only useful within the context of a larger script. As such, as with templates, we don't want people to be able to navigate directly to these files by typing the filename into their browser, as they only contain small snippets that won't produce any meaningful output on their own.

We'll solve problem the same way we did with templates: by creating a directory outside the `public` directory, so that any files placed in this new directory can only be accessed by other PHP scripts. We'll call this directory `includes`, and use it to store our code snippets.

Inside the new `includes` directory, create a file called `DatabaseConnection.php`[1] and place the database connection code inside it:

```php
<?php
$pdo = new PDO('mysql:host=localhost;dbname=ijdb;
charset=utf8', 'ijdbuser', 'mypassword');
$pdo->setAttribute(PDO::ATTR_ERRMODE,
PDO::ERRMODE_EXCEPTION);
```

---

[1] In previous versions of this book, the database connection was placed in a file named `db.inc.php`, which at the time was the convention: all include files were named with a `.inc.php` extension. This convention has lost popularity, and include files are generally created using camelCase. This is in part due to both the PSR-0 standard and heavy use of object-oriented programming in modern websites.

Now you can put this `DatabaseConnection.php` file to use in your controllers. Amend each of your controllers—`addjoke.php`, `deletejoke.php` and `jokes.php`—to include the new file.

The updated `jokes.php` looks like this:

```
                                                        6-2. Structure-Include

<?php

try {
    include __DIR__ . '/../includes/DatabaseConnection.php';

    $sql = 'SELECT `joke`.`id`, `joketext`, `name`, `email`
    FROM `joke` INNER JOIN `author`
        ON `authorid` = `author`.`id`';

    $jokes = $pdo->query($sql);

    $title = 'Joke list';

    ob_start();

    include __DIR__ . '/../templates/jokes.html.php';

    $output = ob_get_clean();
} catch (PDOException $e) {
    $title = 'An error has occurred';

    $output = 'Database error: ' . $e->getMessage() . ' in '
    . $e->getFile() . ':' . $e->getLine();
}

include __DIR__ . '/../templates/layout.html.php';
```

Make the same change to `addjoke.php` and `delete.php` so they use an `include` statement rather than repeating the database connection code.

As you can see, wherever our controller needs a database connection, we can obtain it simply by including the `DatabaseConnection.php` file with an include statement. And because the code to do this is a simple one-liner, we can make our code more readable by using a separate `include` statement just before each SQL query in our controller.

When PHP encounters an `include` statement, it puts the current script on hold and runs the specified PHP script. When it's finished, it returns to the original script and picks up where it left off.

Include files are the simplest way to structure PHP code. Because of their simplicity, they're also the most widely used method. Even very simple web applications can benefit greatly from using include files.

You've already seen how you can create a variable such as `$title` in the controller and that it's available in included files such as `layout.html.php`. Here, you can see the inverse is also true. The `$pdo` variable is created in `DatabaseConnection.php`, but can be used in the controller.

An `include` statement can be thought of as an automated copy-and-paste. When PHP encounters the line `include __DIR__ . '/../includes/DatabaseConnection.php';` it effectively reads the code from the file and copies/pastes it into the current code at the position of the `include` statement.

After you've amended all your controllers to have an `include` statement, if the database password gets updated, you only need to edit `DatabaseConnection.php`, rather than having to update the password in each of your controllers. Aren't you glad we made this change now instead of later when we've got more controllers?

Types of Includes

The `include` statement we've used so far is actually only one of four statements that can be used to include another PHP file in a currently running script:

- `include`
- `require`
- `include_once`
- `require_once`

The only difference between them is what happens when the specified file is unable to be included (that is, if it doesn't exist, or if the web server doesn't have permission to read it). With `include`, a warning is displayed and the script continues to run. With `require`, an error is displayed and the script stops.[2]

In general, you should use `require` whenever your application simply wouldn't work without the required code being successfully loaded. I do recommend using `include` whenever possible, however. Even if the `DatabaseConnection.php` file for your site is unable to load, for example, you might still want to let the script for your front page continue to load. None of the content from the database will display, but the user might be able to use the **Contact Us** link at the bottom of the page to let you know about the problem!

`include_once` and `require_once` work just like `include` and `require`, respectively—but if the specified file has already been included at least once for the current page request (using *any* of the four statements described here), the statement will be ignored. This is handy for include files performing a task that only needs to be done once, like connecting to the database.

`include_once` and `require_once` are also useful for loading function libraries, as we'll see in the following section.

Custom Functions and Function Libraries

By this point, you're probably quite comfortable with the idea of functions. A function is PHP code that you can invoke at will, where you'd usually provide one or more arguments for it to use, and often receive a return value as a result. You can use PHP's vast library of functions to do just about anything a PHP script could ever be asked to do, from retrieving the current date (`date`) to generating graphics on the fly (using `imagecreatetruecolor`[3]).

But what you may be unaware of is that you can create functions of your own!

---

[2] In production environments, warnings and errors are usually disabled in `php.ini`. In such environments, a failed `include` has no visible effect (aside from the lack of content that would normally have been generated by the include file), while a failed `require` causes the page to stop at the point of failure. When a failed `require` occurs before any content is sent to the browser, the unlucky user will see nothing but a blank page!

[3] http://www.php.net/imagecreatetruecolor

Custom functions, once defined, work just like PHP's built-in functions, and they can do anything a normal PHP script can do.

Let's start with a really simple example. Say you had a PHP script that needed to calculate the area of a rectangle given its width (3) and height (5). Thinking back to your basic geometry classes in school, you should recall that the area of a rectangle is its width multiplied by its height:

```php
$area = 3 * 5;
```

But it would be nicer to have a function called area that simply calculated the area of a rectangle given its dimensions:

```php
$area = area(3, 5);
```

As it happens, PHP has no built-in area function, but clever PHP programmers like you and me can just roll up our sleeves and write the function ourselves:

```php
<?php
function area($width, $height)
{
    return $width * $height;
}
```

This include file defines a single custom function: area. The <?php marker is probably the only line that looks familiar to you in this code. What we have here is a **function declaration**. Let me break it down for you one line at a time:

```php
function area($width, $height)
```

The keyword function tells PHP that we wish to declare a new function for use in the current script. Then, we supply the function with a name (in this case, area). Function names operate under the same rules as variable names—they must start with a letter or an underscore (_), and may contain letters, numbers, and underscores—except, of course, that there's no dollar sign prefix. Instead, function names are always followed by a set of parentheses (()), which may or may not be empty.

The parentheses that follow a function name enclose the list of arguments that the function will accept. You should already be familiar with this from your experience with PHP's built-in functions. For example, when you use `rand` to generate a random number, you can provide it with a minimum and maximum number within the parentheses.

When declaring a custom function, instead of giving a list of values for the arguments, you give a list of variable names. In this example, we list two variables: `$width` and `$height`. When the function is called, it will therefore expect to be given two arguments. The value of the first argument will be assigned to `$width`, while the value of the second will be assigned to `$height`. Those variables can then be used to perform the calculation within the function.

```
{
```

Speaking of calculations, the rest of the function declaration is the code that performs the calculation, or does whatever else the function is supposed to do. That code must be enclosed in a set of braces ({ … }), so here's the opening brace.

```
return $width * $height;
```

You can think of the code within those braces as a miniature PHP script. This function is a simple one, because it contains just a single statement: a `return` statement.

A `return` statement can be used in the code of a function to jump back into the main script immediately. When the PHP interpreter hits a `return` statement, it immediately stops running the code of this function and goes back to where the function was called. It's sort of an ejection seat for functions!

In addition to breaking out of the function, the `return` statement lets you specify a value for the function to *return* to the code that called it. In this case, the value we're returning is `$width * $height`—the result of multiplying the first parameter by the second.

```
}
```

The closing brace marks the end of the function declaration.

Writing a function on its own does nothing. No code inside the function is run until the function is called. Like the `rand` function we used at the start of this book, it just sits there waiting to be called.

You can think of writing a function like installing an app on your computer or phone. You need it there to use it, but once installed, it's dormant and available for use, but won't actually do anything until you run it.

In order to run the function, we must first include the file containing the function declaration:

```
include_once    __DIR__ .
'/../includes/area-function.inc.php';

$area = area(3, 5);

include 'output.html.php';
```

Technically, you could write the function declaration within the controller script itself, but by putting it in an include file, you can reuse the function in other scripts much more easily. It's tidier, too. To use the function in the include file, a PHP script need only include it with `include_once` (or `require_once` if the function is critical to the script).

Avoid using `include` or `require` to load include files that contain functions. As explained in the "Types of Includes" section earlier in this chapter, that would risk defining the functions in the library more than once and covering the user's screen with PHP warnings.

It's standard practice (but not required) to include your function libraries at the top of the script, so that you can quickly see which include files containing functions are used by any particular script.

What we have here are the beginnings of a **function library**—an include file that contains declarations for a group of related functions. If you wanted to, you could rename the include file to `geometry.inc.php`, add a whole bunch of functions to it, and perform various geometrical calculations.

Variable Scope

One big difference between custom functions and include files is the concept of **variable scope**. Any variable that exists in the main script will also be available and can be changed in the include file. While this is useful sometimes, more often it's a pain in the neck. Unintentionally overwriting one of the main script's variables in an include file is a common cause of error—and one that can take a long time to track down and fix! To avoid such problems, you need to remember the variable names in the script that you're working on, as well as any that exist in the include files your script uses.

Functions protect you from such problems. Variables created inside a function (including any argument variables) exist only within that function, and disappear when the function has run its course. In addition, variables created outside the function are completely inaccessible inside it. The only variables a function has access to are the ones provided to it as arguments.

In programmer-speak, the **scope** of these variables is the function; they're said to have **function scope**. In contrast, variables created in the main script outside of any function are unavailable inside functions. The scope of these variables is the main script, and they're said to have **global scope**.

Okay, but beyond the fancy names, what does this really *mean* for us? It means that you can have a variable called, say, $width in your main script, and another variable called $width in your function, and PHP will treat these as two entirely separate variables! Perhaps more usefully, you can have two different functions each using the same variable names, and they'll have no effect on each other, because their variables are kept separate by their scope.

On some occasions, you may actually *want* to use a global-scope variable (**global variable** for short) inside one of your functions. For example, the DatabaseConnection.php file creates a database connection for use by your script and stores it in the global variable $pdo. You might then want to use this variable in a function that needed to access the database.

Let's create a function that queries the database and returns to us the number of jokes that are currently held in the joke table. Disregarding variable scope, here's how you might expect such a function to work:

```
include_once __DIR__ .
'/../includes/DatabaseConnection.php';

function totalJokes() {
    $query = $pdo->prepare('SELECT COUNT(*) FROM `joke`');
    $query->execute();

    $row = $query->fetch();

    return $row[0];
}

echo totalJokes();
```

 Careful Where You Place Your Files

Note that the first line of this controller script uses a shared copy of the DatabaseConnection.php file in the **includes** directory. Make sure you've placed a copy of this file in the **includes** directory; otherwise, PHP will complain that it's unable to find the DatabaseConnection.php file.

The file DatabaseConnection.php creates the variable $pdo, which we're referencing inside the function.

The problem here is that the global variable $pdo is unavailable within the scope of the function. If you attempt to call this function as it is, you'll receive the errors shown in the following image:

6-3. The `totaljokes` function cannot access `$pdo`

The reason for this error is **scope**. The `$pdo` variable was created outside the function, so is not available for use inside it.

Although there *is* a way to make the same `$pdo` variable available in the function[4], it's a very bad idea. If, for example, the function changed the `$pdo` by accident to a string—`$pdo = 'select * from joke';`—the `$pdo` variable would now be a string everywhere else in the PHP script. Global variables are a *very* bad idea and lead to problems that are very difficult to track down and fix. You should avoid global variables at any cost.

To avoid this, you can use `$pdo` as an argument and pass in the required variables to your function:

```
function totalJokes($pdo) {
    $query = $pdo->prepare('SELECT COUNT(*) FROM `joke`');
    $query->execute();
```

[4.] See http://php.net/manual/en/reserved.variables.globals.php. Seriously, don't do this!

```
    $row = $query->fetch();

    return $row[0];
}
```

And then, when the function is called, you pass in the $pdo object created in DatabaseConnection.php:

```
include_once __DIR__ .
  '/../includes/DatabaseConnection.php';
echo totalJokes($pdo);
```

This makes the $pdo variable available in the totalJokes function by passing it in as an argument. It's worth taking a moment to understand exactly what's happening here. The $pdo variable is created in global scope by DatabaseConnection.php and then passed in to the function totalJokes. The object stored in the global $pdo variable is then copied to the local variable called $pdo inside the function. The $pdo variable needs to be passed in as an argument, because functions only have access to data they are given; they cannot access variables from the global scope.

Importantly, if there's a mistake in the function and the $pdo variable is overwritten with a string, it will only be a string inside the function, not throughout the rest of the script.

What this means is that there are actually two different variables called $pdo. We could rename the $pdo variable inside the function to $database and the script would still work:

```
function totalJokes($database) {
    $query = $database->prepare('SELECT COUNT(*)
    FROM `joke`');
    $query->execute();
```

```
    $row = $query->fetch();

    return $row[0];
}
```

Here, the `$database` variable stores the same PDO connection that is stored in the `$pdo` variable in global scope. Even though the function would still be called using `totalJokes($pdo)`, the content of the `$pdo` variable outside the function call is copied to the `$database` variable inside the function. Despite having different names, they reference the same database connection.

If you want to get technical, this process is called **dependency injection**, but all you need to know is that in practical terms, it's a method for making a single variable available in multiple locations.

It's a good idea to move functions into their own file. Place the `totalJokes` function inside a file called `DatabaseFunctions.php` in the `includes` directory, and you can then use the function like this:

6-4. Structure-TotalJokes

```
// Include the file that creates the $pdo variable and
↪ connects to the database
include_once __DIR__ .
'/../includes/DatabaseConnection.php';

// Include the file that provides the `totalJokes` function
include_once __DIR__ .
'/../includes/DatabaseConnection.php';

// Call the function
echo totalJokes($pdo);
```

Save this as `showtotaljokes.php` in the `public` directory and navigate to it in your browser. You should see a page that's mostly empty but displays the total number of jokes in your database.

You may have realized that if the program is broken up into functions like this, you'd need to pass the $pdo variable into each function you wanted to use. As you've probably suspected, this isn't the most efficient way of achieving this goal, as we'll see later on when we get to objects and classes.

Let's use our new function inside the website. At the top of the list of jokes we can print "[number] jokes have been submitted to the Internet Joke Database".

Open up jokes.php and change it to the following:

```php
<?php

try {
    include __DIR__ . '/../includes/DatabaseConnection.php';
    include __DIR__ . '/../includes/DatabaseFunctions.php';

    $sql = 'SELECT `joke`.`id`, `joketext`, `name`, `email`
    FROM `joke` INNER JOIN `author`
        ON `authorid` = `author`.`id`';

    $jokes = $pdo->query($sql);

    $title = 'Joke list';

    $totalJokes = totalJokes($pdo);

    ob_start();

    include __DIR__ . '/../templates/jokes.html.php';

    $output = ob_get_clean();
} catch (PDOException $e) {
    $title = 'An error has occurred';

    $output = 'Database error: ' . $e->getMessage()
    . ' in ' .$e->getFile() . ':' . $e->getLine();
}

include __DIR__ . '/../templates/layout.html.php';
```

This creates a `$totalJokes` variable that can be used in `jokes.html.php`:

```
                                              6-5. Structure-TotalJokeList

<p><?=$totalJokes?> jokes have been submitted to
↳ the Internet Joke Database.</p>

<?php foreach ($jokes as $joke): ?>
<blockquote>
    <p>
    <?=htmlspecialchars($joke['joketext'], ENT_QUOTES,
        'UTF-8')?>

    (by <a href="mailto:<?php
    echo htmlspecialchars(
    $joke['email'],
    ENT_QUOTES,
    'UTF-8'
); ?>"><?php
    echo htmlspecialchars(
            $joke['name'],
            ENT_QUOTES,
            'UTF-8'
        ); ?></a>)

    <form action="deletejoke.php" method="post">
        <input type="hidden" name="id"
            value="<?=$joke['id']?>">
        <input type="submit" value="Delete">
    </form>
    </p>
</blockquote>
<?php endforeach; ?>
```

You may be wondering what happens if the query inside the `totalJokes` function contains an error. We could put a `try … catch` statement inside the function, but because the function has been called inside the existing `try … catch` statement, we don't need to.

Exceptions *bubble up*. In practical terms, this means that, even if an exception is thrown inside a function, it will still be caught by a surrounding `try … catch` statement.

It's better to avoid handling errors inside functions. Imagine we have a `try … catch` statement inside the function like so:

```php
function totalJokes($database) {
    try {
        $query = $database->prepare('SELECT COUNT(*)
        FROM `joke`');
        $query->execute();

        $row = $query->fetch();

        return $row[0];
    }
    catch {
        $title = 'An error has occurred';

            $output = 'Database error: ' . $e->getMessage()
            . ' in ' . $e->getFile() . ':'
            . $e->getLine();

        include __DIR__ . '/../templates/layout.html.php';
        die();
    }
}
```

Not only do we have repeated code, but now regardless of where the `totalJokes` function is called from, the error will be handled in the same way. By keeping it out of the function, different error handling can be used in different places that the `totalJokes` function is used. For example, it's possible that we would want to use the website to generate a list of jokes as a PDF or an Excel file rather than as an HTML document. If this were the case, we certainly wouldn't want an error message displayed as HTML.

By just letting the error happen, we can handle the error in different ways under different circumstances.

Breaking Up Your Code Into Reusable Functions

Now that you're familiar with declaring your own functions, you can start writing functions to perform each task. For example, instead of writing out a SELECT query each time you want to read a specific joke from the database, you could write a reusable function to do that for you:

```
function getJoke($pdo, $id) {
    $query = $pdo->prepare('SELECT FROM `joke`
    WHERE `id` = :id');
    $query->bindValue(':id', $id);
    $query->execute();
    return $query->fetch();
}
```

This works in the same way as the totalJokes function from earlier. The only difference is that there's a second argument, $id, which is going to store the ID of the joke to be looked up.

This allows us to look up a joke very quickly by its ID:

```
include __DIR__ . '/../includes/DatabaseConnection.php';

$joke1 = getJoke($pdo, 1);

echo $joke1['joketext'];

$joke2 = getJoke($pdo, 2);

echo $joke2['joketext'];
```

You've probably already noticed a lot of similarity between the getJoke function and the totalJokes function. Both functions perform a prepare and execute, then fetch a given record.

Whenever you spot repeated code, it's usually a good idea to take the repeated code and place it in its own function. I mentioned earlier in the book that this is commonly referred to as the DRY (don't repeat yourself) principle. If you find yourself copying and pasting blocks of code, it's a good sign that the code belongs inside its own function.

Here's one of our functions:

```php
function totalJokes($pdo) {
    $query = $pdo->prepare('SELECT COUNT(*) FROM `joke`');
    $query->execute();

    $row = $query->fetch();

    return $row[0];
}
```

Here's the other:

```php
function getJoke($pdo, $id) {
    $query = $pdo->prepare('SELECT FROM `joke`
    WHERE `id` = :id');
    $query->bindValue(':id', $id);
    $query->execute();
    return $query->fetch();
}
```

You can see that these are doing very similar jobs. These lines are identical or almost the same in both functions:

```php
$query = $pdo->prepare('…');
$query->execute();
return $query->fetch();
```

Here's the code for executing a specific query. This code could easily be moved to its own function:

```php
function query($pdo, $sql) {
    $query = $pdo->prepare($sql);
    $query->execute();
    return $query;
}
```

The interesting part here is the line $query = $pdo->prepare($sql);. Instead of writing the query that's going to be executed as a string, we'll use a variable—the $sql argument.

This allows the totalJokes function to be simplified:

```php
function totalJokes($pdo) {
    $query = query($pdo, 'SELECT COUNT(*) FROM `joke`');
    $row = $query->fetch();
    return $row[0];
}
```

Something quite clever is happening here. The totalJokes function is calling the query function. In fact, you can call any function from any other function, allowing you to break up tasks into smaller and smaller reusable chunks.

It's now possible to do the same with the getJoke function, removing the repetition by using the new query function:

```php
function getJoke($pdo, $id) {
  $query = query($pdo, 'SELECT * FROM `joke` WHERE `id` =
↪ :id');
    return $query->fetch();
}
```

But wait! This isn't quite going to work as we intend. The original getJoke function contained this line:

```
$query->bindValue(':id', $id);
```

This binds the id SQL parameter to the variable $id, so the :id parameter is correctly set in the query SELECT FROM joke WHERE id = :id. The query function doesn't do this yet, so it must be altered somehow to bind parameters. It would be possible to write the query function like this:

```
function query($pdo, $sql, $id) {
    $query = $pdo->prepare($sql);
    $query->bindValue(':id', $id);
    $query->execute();
    return $query;
}
```

Then we could call it using this:

```
function getJoke($pdo, $id) {
    $query = query($pdo, 'SELECT * FROM `joke`
    WHERE `id` = :id', $id);
    return $query->fetch();
}
```

However, this is very inflexible; it will only work with queries that have an :id parameter. Instead, the query function should be able to take any number of parameters (including zero for the totalJokes function!). Luckily, there's a simple way of doing this. Remember back in Chapter 2 I showed you how to create arrays? Here, we can create an array of parameters that need to be bound, and pass them as an argument to the query function.

```
function getJoke($pdo, $id) {

  // Create the array of $parameters for use in the query
↳ function
    $parameters = [':id' => $id];
```

```
    // call the query function and provide the $parameters array
    $query = query($pdo, 'SELECT * FROM `joke`
WHERE `id` = :id', $parameters);

    return $query->fetch();
}
```

I've created a variable called $parameters to store the query parameters, and passed the entire array to the query function. Being able to pass arrays into functions is a nice trick when you don't always know how many arguments there will be.

Obviously the query function will need to be amended to use the new parameters:

```
function query($pdo, $sql, $parameters) {
    $query = $pdo->prepare($sql);

    foreach ($parameters as $name => $value ) {
        $query->bindValue($name, $value);
    }

    $query->execute();
    return $query;
}
```

The clever part here is the foreach loop:

```
foreach ($parameters as $name => $value ) {
    $query->bindValue($name, $value);
}
```

This loops over each of the supplied parameters, and binds them to the query.

One problem this is going to cause is that the totalJokes function doesn't send a list of parameters because there are none. The query doesn't need a WHERE statement or any parameters to be replaced:

```
function totalJokes($pdo) {
    $query = query($pdo, 'SELECT COUNT(*) FROM `joke`');
    $row =  $query->fetch();
    return $row[0];
}
```

Because the query function is expecting three arguments and only two are being sent, this will cause an error. One way of avoiding this is to re-write the totalJokes function to send an empty array of parameters to the query function:

```
function totalJokes($pdo) {
    // Create an empty array for sending to the query function
    $parameters = [];

    // Call the query function and pass it the
    // empty $parameters array
    $query = query($pdo, 'SELECT COUNT(*)
    FROM `joke`', $parameters);
    $row =  $query->fetch();
    return $row[0];
}
```

However, PHP has a nice, built-in way of handling this. Whenever you declare an argument, you can give it a "default value"—that is, a value that's used if none are supplied, like so:

```
function myFunction($argument1 = 1, $argument2 = 2) {
```

If the function is called without any arguments—for example, myFunction()—then the $argument1 variable is set to 1 and the $argument2 variable is set to 2.

This feature can be used with the query function to set the $parameters variable
to an empty array if no value is supplied:

```php
function query($pdo, $sql, $parameters = []) {
    $query = $pdo->prepare($sql);

    foreach ($parameters as $name => $value ) {
        $query->bindValue($name, $value);
    }

    $query->execute();
    return $query;
}
```

With a default value set on the $parameters argument, the function can be called
and provided with values for the $pdo and $sql arguments. If no third argument
is provided, $parameters will use the default value, which we defined to be an
empty array.

Now that $parameters has a default value, the totalJokes function can be left as
it was, and doesn't need to provide the third argument to the query function:

```php
function totalJokes($pdo) {
    $query = query($pdo, 'SELECT COUNT(*) FROM `joke`');
    $row = $query->fetch();
    return $row[0];
}
```

When the query function is called, the third parameter is missing and PHP will
automatically assign the value [] (an empty array) to it. When the function is run,
the foreach loop will still be executed. However, because the array is empty, it
will iterate zero times and bindValue will never be called:

```php
foreach ($parameters as $name => $value ) {
    $query->bindValue($name, $value);
}
```

Now that you know how this works, I'll show you a shortcut. This `foreach` statement that binds all the parameters can actually be removed. The `execute` method can optionally take an argument of parameters to be bound in exactly the same way, letting us reduce the code in the `query` function by passing the `$parameters` array directly to the `execute` method, rather than manually binding each, one by one:

```php
function query($pdo, $sql, $parameters = []) {
    $query = $pdo->prepare($sql);
    $query->execute($parameters);
    return $query;
}
```

Using Functions to Replace Queries

With the `query` function complete, you have the ability to query the database very quickly. The `totalJokes` function allows for easily querying the database for the number of jokes in the table. Let's take the same approach and apply it to adding jokes to the database with an `INSERT` query:

```php
function insertJoke($pdo, $joketext, $authorId) {
    $query = 'INSERT INTO `joke` (`joketext`, `jokedate`,
      `authorId`) VALUES (:joketext, CURDATE(), :authorId)';

    $parameters = [':joketext' => $joketext, ':authorId'
      => $authorId];

    query($pdo, $query, $parameters);
}
```

The `insertJoke` function lets us very quickly insert a record into the `joke` table with a single line of code by providing it the database connection (`$pdo`), the text of the joke (`$joketext`) and the ID of the author (`$authorId`):

```
insertJoke($pdo, 'Why did the programmer quit his job? He
↪ didn\'t get arrays', 1);
```

Each of the columns in the database is an argument for the function, which can now be called repeatedly to quickly issue the relevant INSERT query with far less code than we'd have needed previously:

```
insertJoke($pdo, 'Why was the empty array stuck outside? It
↪ didn\'t have any keys', 1);

insertJoke($pdo, 'An SQL query goes into a bar, walks up to
↪ two tables and asks "Can I join you?"', 2);
```

This approach is considerably quicker and easier than having to write all the code for running the query each time you insert a joke: preparing the query, binding the parameters and then finally executing the query.

Now, finally, you *could* use the following controller code for adding a joke:

```
if (isset($_POST['joketext'])) {
    try {
    include __DIR__ . '/../includes/DatabaseConnection.php';

    $sql = 'INSERT INTO `joke` SET
        `joketext` = :joketext,
        `jokedate` = CURDATE()';

    $stmt = $pdo->prepare($sql);

    $stmt->bindValue(':joketext', $_POST['joketext']);

    $stmt->execute();

    header('location: jokes.php');
    }
    catch (PDOException $e) {
```

```
    $title = 'An error has occurred';


    $output = 'Database error: ' . $e->getMessage() . '
in ' . $e->getFile() . ':' . $e->getLine();
    }
}
```

But instead of this, you can put the insertJoke and query functions in the
DatabaseFunctions.php file and then write this much simpler version:

6-6. Structure-AddJoke

```
if (isset($_POST['joketext'])) {
    try {
        include __DIR__ . '/../includes/DatabaseConnection.php';
        include __DIR__ . '/../includes/DatabaseFunctions.php';

        insertJoke($pdo, $_POST['joketext'], 1);

        header('location: jokes.php');
    }
    catch (PDOException $e) {
    $title = 'An error has occurred';

    $output = 'Database error: ' . $e->getMessage() . '
in ' . $e->getFile() . ':' . $e->getLine();
    }
}
```

You can see that I've put the query, totalJokes and insertJoke functions into a
file called DatabaseFunctions.php and included it as required.

For now, all jokes will have 1 set as the authorId. Later on, I'll show you how to
handle logins and associate the joke with the currently logged in user.

Updating Jokes

Along with inserting a joke, it's useful to be able to update a record. Perhaps there was a spelling error in one of the jokes and it needs to be changed.

An update function needs more information than the insert function. It needs to know the ID of the record being updated along with the new values for each column:

```
function updateJoke($pdo, $jokeId, $joketext, $authorId) {
    $parameters = [':joketext' => $joketext,
      ':authorId' => $authorId, ':id' => $jokeId];

    query($pdo, 'UPDATE `joke` SET `authorId` = :authorId,
      `joketext` = :joketext WHERE `id` = :id', $parameters);
}
```

The `updateJoke` function can be called anywhere a joke needs to be updated:

```
 updateJoke($pdo, 1, '!false - It\'s funny because it\'s
↪ true', 1);
```

The line above will update the joke with the id 1 with the supplied `authorId` and `jokeText`. The equivalent of running all the code:

```
$query = $pdo->prepare('UPDATE `joke`
SET `authorId` = :authorId, `joketext` = :joketext
WHERE id = :id');

$query->bindValue(':id', 1);
$query->bindValue(':authorId', 1);
 $query->bindValue(':joketext', '!false - It\'s funny
↪ because it\'s true');

$query->execute();
```

This is a significant advantage: anywhere in the code that a joke needs to be updated, the single function call can do it, saving a lot of time.

Editing Jokes on the Website

Let's make use of our new functions `getJoke` and `updateJoke` by adding a page that allows for editing the existing jokes. In essence, it's the same as `addjoke.php`. It will display a form, and when the form is submitted it will send the data to the database.

However, there are two main differences:

1. When the edit page loads, it needs to retrieve the current joke text from the database in order to pre-fill the `<textarea>` with the current joke. After all, if it's a simple typo, you don't want to make the user re-type the whole joke!

2. When the form is submitted, it needs to run an UPDATE query rather than an INSERT query.

In the `public` directory, create `editjoke.php` that looks like this:

```php
<?php
include __DIR__ . '/../includes/DatabaseConnection.php';
include __DIR__ . '/../includes/DatabaseFunctions.php';

try {
    if (isset($_POST['joketext'])) {
        updateJoke($pdo, $_POST['jokeid'], $_POST['joketext'], 1);

        header('location: jokes.php');
    } else {
        $joke = getJoke($pdo, $_GET['id']);

        $title = 'Edit joke';

        ob_start();

        include __DIR__ . '/../templates/editjoke.html.php';
```

```
        $output = ob_get_clean();
    }
} catch (PDOException $e) {
    $title = 'An error has occurred';

    $output = 'Database error: ' . $e->getMessage() . '
    in ' . $e->getFile() . ':' . $e->getLine();
}

include __DIR__ . '/../templates/layout.html.php';
```

There are a few main differences between this new editjoke.php page and the addjoke.php page.

Firstly, you may have noticed that the two include files have been included at the very top of the page. This is so the database functions are available whether or not the form has been submitted.

If the form hasn't been submitted, we need to query the database for the current joke text. If it has been submitted, we'll need to run the relevant update query.

Secondly, the try statement surrounds the if rather than having the if surround the try. The reason for this is simple: there may be an error in either the if or else block.

Speaking of the else block, that's the next change. Instead of just loading the form, the else block has this line of code:

```
$joke = getJoke($pdo, $_GET['id']);
```

This part of the code selects a joke from the database by its ID using the getJoke function from earlier. The ID of the joke being edited must be supplied using a GET variable—so that visiting editjoke.php?id=4, for example, will execute the query SELECT * FROMjokeWHEREid= 4 and store the resulting joke in the $joke array.

The `$joke` variable can now be used in the corresponding template file
`editjoke.html.php`:

```
<form action="" method="post">
    <input type="hidden" name="jokeid"
    value="<?=$joke['id'];?>">
    <label for="joketext">Type your joke here:
    </label>
    <textarea id="joketext" name="joketext" rows="3"
    cols="40"><?=$joke['joketext']?></textarea>
    <input type="submit" value="Save">
</form>
```

This template is slightly different from the template for adding jokes. The most
obvious change is that the current joke text, from the `$joke` variable, is loaded
into the `<textarea>` when the page loads. However, there's another change:
there's also a hidden input that sends the ID of the joke being edited back to the
page when the submit button is pressed.

In `editjoke.php`, there are now two `$_POST` variables available when the form
has been submitted—`$_POST['jokeid']`, representing the ID of the joke being
edited, and `$_POST['joketext']`, containing the new text for the joke.

These are then passed into our `updateJoke` function:

```
updateJoke($pdo, $_POST['jokeid'], $_POST['joketext'], 1);
```

Before you can test this example for yourself, you'll need to add a link next to
each joke in the joke list that gives us a link to the `editjoke.php` controller with
the ID of the joke being edited. If you go directly to `editjoke.php`, you'll see an
error, as `editjoke.php` needs the ID of the joke being edited in order for the
current value in the `joketext` column to be displayed in the `<textarea>`.

Open up `jokes.html.php` from the `templates` directory and add a link to
`editjoke.php` for each joke:

```php
 <p><?=$totalJokes?> jokes have been submitted to
↪ the Internet Joke Database.</p>

<?php foreach ($jokes as $joke): ?>
<blockquote>
    <p>
    <?=htmlspecialchars($joke['joketext'], ENT_QUOTES,
    'UTF-8')?>

    (by <a href="mailto:<?php
    echo htmlspecialchars(
    $joke['email'],
    ENT_QUOTES,
        'UTF-8'
); ?>"><?php
    echo htmlspecialchars(
            $joke['name'],
            ENT_QUOTES,
        'UTF-8'
        ); ?></a>)

    <a href="editjoke.php?id=<?=$joke['id']?>">
    Edit</a>

    <form action="deletejoke.php" method="post">
        <input type="hidden" name="id"
        value="<?=$joke['id']?>">
        <input type="submit" value="Delete">
    </form>
    </p>
</blockquote>
<?php endforeach; ?>
```

Each joke is linked to `editjoke.php?id=`, followed by the ID of the joke you wish to edit.

Try this example (*Structure-EditJoke*) and load up the jokes list. Each joke will have an **Edit** link after the author's name, and by clicking the link, the joke text will be loaded into the form. When you press **Save**, it will trigger the update query by calling the `updateJoke` function.

Delete Function

The same thing can now be done with **delete** to allow deletion of jokes in the same quick and easy way with a single line of code:

```php
function deleteJoke($pdo, $id) {
    $parameters = [':id' => $id];

    query($pdo, 'DELETE FROM `joke`
    WHERE `id` = :id', $parameters);
}
```

Then call the function to delete a joke with a specific ID from the database:

```php
// Delete a joke with the ID of 2
deleteJoke($pdo, 2);
```

Add the function to `DatabaseFunctions.php` and amend `deletejoke.php` to use the new function:

```php
<?php

try {
    include __DIR__ . '/../includes/DatabaseConnection.php';
    include __DIR__ . '/../includes/DatabaseFunctions.php';

    deleteJoke($pdo, $_POST['id']);

    header('location: jokes.php');
} catch (PDOException $e) {
    $title = 'An error has occurred';

    $output = 'Unable to connect to the database server: '
      . $e->getMessage() . ' in ' .
```

```
    $e->getFile() . ':' . $e->getLine();
}

include __DIR__ . '/../templates/layout.html.php';
```

Select Function

We can apply the same logic to fetching all the jokes from the `joke` table by adding an `allJokes` function to `DatabaseFunctions.php` and amending `jokes.php` accordingly:

```
function allJokes($pdo) {
    $jokes =  query($pdo, 'SELECT `joke`.`id`, `joketext`,
      `name`, `email`
            FROM `joke` INNER JOIN `author`
            ON `authorid` = `author`.`id`');

    return $jokes->fetchAll();
}
```

In this instance, the query is more complex than the one-liners used for `deleteJoke` and `updateJoke`. It's the same query we already had in `jokes.php` for selecting the jokes and the information about the author.

Here I've used PDO's `fetchAll` function. This returns an array of all records that were retrieved by the query. You can use the new `allJokes` function like this:

```
$jokes = allJokes($pdo);

echo '<ul>';
foreach ($jokes as $joke) {
    echo '<li>' . $joke . '</li>';
}
echo '</ul>';
```

This will print out all the jokes from the database in a list.

Update the `jokes.php` controller to use the new function:

```php
try {
    include __DIR__ . '/../includes/DatabaseConnection.php';
    include __DIR__ . '/../includes/DatabaseFunctions.php';

    $jokes = allJokes($pdo);

    $title = 'Joke list';

    $totalJokes = totalJokes($pdo);

    ob_start();

    include __DIR__ . '/../templates/jokes.html.php';

    $output = ob_get_clean();
}
catch (PDOException $e) {
    $title = 'An error has occurred';

    $output = 'Database error: ' . $e->getMessage() . '
    in ' . $e->getFile() . ':' . $e->getLine();
}

include __DIR__ . '/../templates/layout.html.php';
```

We've now got a set of reusable functions that can be used anywhere we need to interact with the database table. Whether it's finding all the jokes, a single joke or issuing an INSERT, UPDATE or DELETE query, it's possible to run the query without actually typing out all the code each time. Anywhere on the website we need to interact with the database table jokes, it's quick and easy using our new set of functions.

The Best Way

In this chapter, I've helped you to rise above the basic questions of what PHP can do for you, and begin to look for the *best* way to code a solution. Sure, you can approach many simple scripts as lists of actions you want PHP to do for you, but when you tackle site-wide issues such as database connections, shared navigation elements, visitor statistics, and access control systems, it really pays to be able to structure your code carefully.

We've now explored a couple of simple but effective devices for writing structured PHP code. Include files let you reuse a single piece of code across multiple pages of your site, greatly reducing the burden when you need to make changes. Writing your own functions to put in these include files lets you build powerful libraries of functions that can perform tasks as needed and return values to the scripts that call them. These new techniques will pay off in a big way in the rest of this book.

In the next chapter, you'll learn how to refine these functions further and make them even more reusable, using some new techniques that include writing your own objects and classes.

Chapter

7

Improving the Insert and Update Functions

In the last chapter, I showed you how to break the code up into easily reusable functions. This has several advantages:

- the code where the function is called is easier to read
- you can re-use the same function from anywhere

In this chapter, I'll take this a step further and show you how to make a function that could be used for *any* database table, and then show you how object-oriented programming can simplify this task even further.

Improving the Update Function

```
updateJoke($pdo, 1, 'Why did the programmer quit his job? He
↪ didn\'t get arrays', 1);
```

To run this function, all of the arguments for the function must be provided:

- joke ID
- joke text
- author ID

What if you just wanted to update the joke text, rather than the joke text and author ID? Or just update the joke's author? With the `updateJoke` function above, all the information needs to be provided each time.

A better way of doing this is to take the field values as an array, with the keys representing the field names and the array contents representing the data to be stored in the database. For example:

```
updateJoke($pdo, [
    'id' => 1,
    'joketext' => 'Why did the programmer quit his job?
    He didn\'t get arrays']
);
```

Another example:

```
updateJoke($pdo, [
    'id' => 1,
    'authorId' => 4
]);
```

This is a lot nicer, as only the information being updated (and the primary key) need to be sent to the function. It also has the advantage of being easier to read: you can read this code and see exactly what each field is being set to. With the earlier version, you have to know which parameter represents which field. If you applied that to a table with 10 or 20 fields, you'd have to get the order of the arguments exactly right and remember which field was at each position.

To make the function take an array, it needs to be updated. Currently it looks like this, and takes an argument for each field:

```
function updateJoke($pdo, $jokeId, $joketext, $authorId) {
    $parameters = [':joketext' => $joketext,
    ':authorId' => $authorId, ':id' => $jokeId];

    query($pdo, 'UPDATE `joke`
    SET `authorId` = :authorId, `joketext` = :joketext
    WHERE `id` = :id', $parameters);
}
```

Changing the function so that it can take an array as a second argument and run the query is less than straightforward, as the query above is expecting parameters for :authorid, :joketext and :primaryKey. What will happen if they're not all provided? If you try it, you'll get an error.

To work around this error, we need to dynamically generate the query so it only contains the relevant fields (only the ones we actually want to update).

The foreach loop (which we saw in Chapter 2) can loop over an array. Take the following code:

```
$array = [
    'id' => 1,
    'joketext' => 'Why was the empty array stuck outside?
    It didn\'t have any keys'
];

foreach ($array as $key => $value) {
    echo $key . ' = ' . $value . ',';
}
```

This will print the following:

```
 id = 1, joketext = Why was the empty array stuck outside? It
```

```
↳ didn't have any keys
```

It's possible to use a `foreach` loop to produce the UPDATE query:

```
$array = [
    'id' => 1,
    'joketext' => '!false - it\'s funny because it\'s true'
];

$query = ' UPDATE `joke` SET ';

foreach ($array as $key => $value) {
    $query .= '`' . $key . '` = :' . $key . ','
}

$query .= ' WHERE `id` = :primaryKey';

echo $query;
```

 ### The .= Operator

Note the use of the `.=` operator above. It adds to the end of the existing string, rather than overwriting it!

The code above will print this query:

```
UPDATE `joke` SET `id` = :id, `joketext` = :joketext,
                WHERE `id` = :primaryKey
```

The query is generated dynamically based on the contents of `$array`, and only the field names from the array will appear in the query.

You'll notice that the `id` field is included in the statement. This isn't needed, but having it here will simplify things later on.

The following code can be used to generate the query with just the `authorId`:

```
$array = [
    'id' => 1,
    'authorid' => 4
];

$query = 'UPDATE `joke` SET ';

foreach ($array as $key => $value) {
    $query .= '`' . $key . '` = :' . $key . ','
}

$query .= ' WHERE `id` = :primaryKey';

echo $query;
```

The code above will print the following query:

```
UPDATE `joke` SET `id` = :id, `authorId` = :authorId,
                WHERE `id` = :id
```

This lets us generate *almost* the exact query that's needed to update any field, or set of fields, in the `joke` table.

I say *almost*, because if you sent this query to the database you'd get an error. Unfortunately, there's a subtle problem with this generated query. You may have noticed that each time the loop runs, it adds a comma to each part of the SET clause, generating this:

```
SET `id` = :id, `authorId` = :authorId,
```

In the following section, I'll show what to do about this.

Stripping the Trailing Comma

The problem with this part of the query is that there's an extra comma at the end of the clause between `authorId` and `WHERE`:

```
UPDATE `joke` SET `id` = :id, `authorId` = :authorId,
                WHERE `id` = :id
```

To be a valid query, it should actually be this:

```
UPDATE `joke` SET `id` = :id, `authorId` = :authorId
                WHERE `id` = :id
```

This is a subtle, single character difference. However, it's the difference between a valid query and an invalid one! It would be possible to tweak the `foreach` loop to omit the comma on the last iteration, but it's simpler just to remove the comma after the string has been generated.

The `rtrim` function can be used to remove (or trim) specific characters from the end of a string. In our case, we want to remove the comma from the `$query` string before appending the `WHERE` clause:

```php
$array = [
    'id' => 1,
    'authorid' => 4
];

$query = 'UPDATE `joke` SET ';

foreach ($array as $key => $value) {
    $query .= '`' . $key . '` = :' . $key . ','
}

$query = rtrim($query, ',');

$query .= ' WHERE `id` = :primaryKey';
```

```
echo $query;
```

The line `$query = rtrim($query, ',');` will remove the trailing comma from the end of the `$query` string, giving us a valid SQL `UPDATE` query. This will display the entire query without the extra comma:

```
UPDATE `joke` SET `id` = :id, `joketext` = :joketext
                  WHERE `id` = :primaryKey
```

By placing this code into the function, the improved version of `updateJoke` can now be used:

```
function updateJoke($pdo, $fields) {

    $query = ' UPDATE `joke` SET ';

    foreach ($array as $key => $value) {
        $query .= '`' . $key . '` = :' . $key . ','
    }

    $query = rtrim($query, ',');

    $query .= ' WHERE `id` = :primaryKey';

    // Set the :primaryKey variable
    $fields['primaryKey'] = $fields['id'];

    query($pdo, $query, $fields);
}
```

You'll notice I set the `primaryKey` key manually with this line:

```
// Set the :primaryKey variable
$fields['primaryKey'] = $fields['id'];
```

This is so that the WHERE clause in the query is provided with the relevant ID to update. :id can't be used, because it has already been used in the query, and each parameter needs a unique name.

With this version of the updateJoke function, it's now possible to run it as we designed earlier:

```
updateJoke($pdo, [
    'id' => 1,
    'joketext' => '!false - it\'s funny because it\'s true']
);
```

Or we could do this:

```
updateJoke($pdo, [
    'id' => 1,
    'authorId' => 4]
);
```

 Writing Functions

When you write a function, it's usually easier to write some examples of how you think it should be called before writing the code inside the function itself. This gives you a target to work towards, and some code you can run to see whether it's working correctly or not.

Improving the Insert Function

Using this knowledge, we can do the same thing for the insertJoke function. The INSERT query can use a syntax different from UPDATE's, and it works like this:

```
$query = 'INSERT INTO `joke` (`joketext`, `jokedate`,
  `authorId`)
```

```
    VALUES (:joketext, CURDATE(), :authorId)';
```

There are two parts to this—the field names and the values. Firstly, let's handle the column names. As we did with the `updateJoke` function, we can use a loop and `rtrim` to create the list of fields for the first line of the query:

```
function insertJoke($pdo, $fields) {
    $query = 'INSERT INTO `joke` ('

    foreach ($fields as $key => $value) {
        $query .= '`' . $key . '`,';
    }

    $query = rtrim($query, ',');

    $query .= ') VALUES (';
}
```

This will generate the first part of the query, and `$query` will store the following:

```
INSERT INTO `joke` (`authorId`, `joketext`) VALUES (
```

... when called with this array:

```
[
    'authorId' => 4,
    'joketext' => '!false - it\'s funny because it\'s true'
]
```

The next part of the query should be the placeholders for the values:

```
VALUES (:authorId, :joketext)
```

These are the keys prefixed with a colon (:). Once again, we can use `foreach` to loop through the column names and add the placeholders before sending the query to the database:

```php
function insertJoke($pdo, $fields) {
    $query = 'INSERT INTO `joke` (';

    foreach ($fields as $key => $value) {
        $query .= '`' . $key . '`,';
    }

    $query = rtrim($query, ',');

    $query .= ') VALUES (';

    foreach ($fields as $key => $value) {
        $query .= ':' . $key . ',';
    }

    $query = rtrim($query, ',');

    $query .= ')';

    query($pdo, $query);
}
```

The `insertJoke` function can now be used to insert data into any of the fields:

```php
insertJoke($pdo, [
    'authorId' => 4,
    'joketext' => '!false - it\'s funny because it\'s true'
    ]
);
```

Of course, it will error if the wrong column names are used, but it's clearer to anyone seeing this code which data is being placed into each of the columns. As we'll see later, it also makes it easier to use the function with forms.

For now, amend your website to use the two new functions by replacing the existing ones in `DatabaseFunctions.php`:

```php
function insertJoke($pdo, $fields) {
    $query = 'INSERT INTO `joke` ('

    foreach ($fields as $key => $value) {
        $query .= '`' . $key . '`,';
    }

    $query = rtrim($query, ',');

    $query .= ') VALUES (';

    foreach ($fields as $key => $value) {
        $query .= ':' . $key . ',';
    }

    $query = rtrim($query, ',');

    $query .= ')';

    query($pdo, $query);
}

function updateJoke($pdo, $fields) {

    $query = ' UPDATE `joke` SET ';

    foreach ($fields as $key => $value) {
        $query .= '`' . $key . '` = :' . $key . ',';
    }

    $query = rtrim($query, ',');

    $query .= ' WHERE `id` = :primaryKey';

    // Set the :primaryKey variable
    $fields['primaryKey'] = $fields['id'];
```

```
    query($pdo, $query, $fields);
}
```

Amend `editjoke.php` to use the new `updateJoke` function:

```
updateJoke($pdo, [
    'id' => $_POST['jokeid'],
    'joketext' => $_POST['joketext'],
    'authorId' => 1
]);
```

You might try amending `addjoke.php` to use the new function:

```
 insertJoke($pdo, ['authorId' => 1, 'jokeText' =>
↳ $_POST['jokotext']]);
```

This example can be found in *Structure2-ArrayFunctions-Error*.

If you try this, you'll get an error:

```
 Database error: SQLSTATE[HY000]: General error: 1364 Field
↳ 'jokedate' doesn't have a default value in
↳ /home/vagrant/Code/Project/includes/DatabaseFunctions.php:5
```

The reason for the error is that we haven't supplied a value for the `jokedate` column.

Handling Dates

The cause of the above error is that we've lost the ability to supply a date when inserting a joke.

Previously, we used the `CURDATE()` function. Using the new `insertJoke` function, you may attempt to set the joke like so:

```
insertJoke($pdo, ['authorId' => 1,
    'jokeText' => $_POST['joketext'],
    'jokedate' => 'CURDATE()'
]);
```

Although the logic here is sound (we want to insert the current date into the
jokedate column), this approach won't work as intended. Just as whatever text is
stored in the $_POST['joketext'] variable will be inserted into the joketext
column, the above code would try to write the *value* CURDATE() into the jokedate
column, rather than executing the function and retrieving the date.

To solve this, we can read the current date using PHP—rather than from
MySQL—using the PHP DateTime class.

The PHP DateTime class can be used to represent dates in PHP and format them
in any way. For example:

```
$date = new DateTime();

echo $date->format('d/m/Y H:i:s');
```

By default, a new instance of a DateTime, without a provided argument, will
represent today's date. So if you were reading this on the 8th September 2019 at
around 7.00 p.m., this would print something like:

```
08/09/2019 19:12:34
```

You can give PHP a string to convert to a date and then format the date in any
way you like. For example:

```
$date = new DateTime('5th March 2019');
```

```
echo $date->format('d/m/Y');
```

The string d/m/Y here represents day/month/year, which would print 05/03/2019. The PHP DateTime class is very powerful and incredibly useful for handling dates in PHP. A full list of the available methods of formatting a data is available in the PHP manualhttp://php.net/manual/en/function.date.php

However, the only format we need to use is the format MySQL understands.

Dates and times in MySQL are always stored using the format YYYY-MM-DD HH:MM:SS. For example, MySQL would store the date of the 13th of July 2019 as 2019-07-13.

The DateTime class can be used to represent any date. Today's date could be induced in this format, like so:

```
// Don't give it a date so it uses the current date/time
$date = new DateTime();

echo $date->format('Y-m-d H:i:s');
```

The above will print something like this:

```
2019-09-08 19:16:34
```

This is the format that's needed when you insert into a DATETIME field in MySQL.

The insert function can already handle this. We can just pass the current date as one of the array keys to the function:

```
$date = new DateTime();

insertJoke($pdo, [
    'authorId' => 4,
```

```
    'joketext' => 'Why did the chicken cross the road? To get
↪ to the other side',
    'jokedate' => $date->format('Y-m-d H:i:s')
    ]
);
```

This will work fine. However, every time we want to use the function, we need to remember the date format used by MySQL. This can be a bit of a pain, as it requires repeating the code for formatting the date (and remembering the string Y-m-d H:i:s) each time a date needs to be inserted.

Instead, a better approach would be to have the function format the date for us, saving some work each time it's called:

```
function insertJoke($pdo, $fields) {
    $query = 'INSERT INTO `joke` (';

    foreach ($fields as $key => $value) {
        $query .= '`' . $key . '`,';
    }

    $query = rtrim($query, ',');

    $query .= ') VALUES (';

    foreach ($fields as $key => $value) {
        $query .= ':' . $key . ',';
    }

    $query = rtrim($query, ',');

    $query .= ')';

    foreach ($fields as $key => $value) {
        if ($value instanceof DateTime) {
            $fields[$key] = $value->format('Y-m-d');
        }
    }
```

```
        query($pdo, $query, $fields);
}
```

Using the above version of the function, a date *object* can be passed into the
function without formatting it:

```
insertJoke($pdo, [
    'authorId' => 4,
    'joketext' => '!false - it\'s funny because it\'s true',
    'jokedate' =>  new DateTime()
    ]
);
```

The function will look for any date objects it has been given and automatically
format them to the format needed by MySQL. When the function is called, you
don't need to remember the exact format needed by MySQL; it's done for you
inside the function. The function will automatically convert any `DateTime` object
it comes across into a string that MySQL can understand:

```
// Loop through the array of fields
foreach ($fields as $key => $value) {
    // If any of the values are a DateTime object
    if ($value instanceof DateTime) {
        // Then replace the value in the array with the date
        // in the format Y-m-d H:i:s
        $fields[$key] = $value->format('Y-m-d H:i:s');
    }
}
```

One operator you haven't come across yet is the `instanceof` operator. This is a
comparison operator like == or !=. However, instead of checking to see if the two
values are the *same*, it checks to see whether the variable on the left (`$value`) is
the same kind of object as the one on the right (`DateTime`). One important
distinction is that the *value* is not being checked, only the *type*. It's like saying "Is

it a car?" rather than "Is it an E-Type Jaguar?"

Wherever a `DateTime` object is found in the array, it's replaced with the equivalent date string in the format MySQL needs. This allows us to completely forget about the format MySQL actually needs and just supply `DateTime` objects to the `insertJoke` function.

Let's also add the automatic date formatting to the `updateJoke` function:

```
function updateJoke($pdo, $fields) {

    $query = ' UPDATE joke SET ';

    foreach ($fields as $key => $value) {
        $query .= '`' . $key . '` = :' . $key . ',';
    }

    $query = rtrim($query, ',');

    $query .= ' WHERE id = :primarykey';

    foreach ($fields as $key => $value) {
        if ($value instanceof DateTime) {
            $fields[$key] = $value->format('Y-m-d');
        }
    }

    // Set the :primaryKey variable
    $fields['primaryKey'] = $fields['id'];

    query($pdo, $query, $fields);
}
```

This will take the same approach we used in `insertJoke` and apply it to the update function. Any `DateTime` object that is passed to the function in the `$fields` array will be converted to a string that MySQL understands.

As we have copied/pasted code, it's good practice to move the duplicated code into its own function to save repetition and follow the DRY principle:

```php
function processDates($fields) {
    foreach ($fields as $key => $value) {
        if ($value instanceof DateTime) {
            $fields[$key] = $value->format('Y-m-d');
        }
    }

    return $fields;
}
```

Let's put the function in `DatabaseFunctions.php` and change the `updateJoke` and `insertJoke` functions to make use of it:

```php
function insertJoke($pdo, $fields) {
    $query = 'INSERT INTO `joke` (';

    foreach ($fields as $key => $value) {
        $query .= '`' . $key . '`,';
    }

    $query = rtrim($query, ',');

    $query .= ') VALUES (';

    foreach ($fields as $key => $value) {
        $query .= ':' . $key . ',';
    }

    $query = rtrim($query, ',');

    $query .= ')';

    $fields = processDates($fields);

    query($pdo, $query, $fields);
}
```

```php
function updateJoke($pdo, $fields) {

    $query = ' UPDATE `joke` SET ';

    foreach ($fields as $key => $value) {
        $query .= '`' . $key . '` = :' . $key . ',';
    }

    $query = rtrim($query, ',');

    $query .= ' WHERE `id` = :primaryKey';

    // Set the :primaryKey variable
    $fields['primaryKey'] = $fields['id'];

    $fields = processDates($fields);

    query($pdo, $query, $fields);
}
```

Finally, amend `addjoke.php` to provide the `DateTime()` object for the value of the `jokedate` column:

```php
insertJoke($pdo, ['authorId' => 1,
    'jokeText' => $_POST['joketext'],
    'jokedate' => new DateTime()
]);
```

This example can be found in *tructure2-ArrayFunctions-Dates*.

Displaying the Joke Date

While we're dealing with dates, let's display the date on which the joke was posted alongside the author's name in the template. The page will now display something like "By Tom Butler on 2019-08-04".

Firstly, we'll need to amend the `allJokes` function to retrieve the date from the database:

```php
function allJokes($pdo) {
    $jokes = query($pdo, 'SELECT `joke`.`id`, `joketext`,
     `jokedate`, `name`, `email`
        FROM `joke` INNER JOIN `author`
        ON `authorid` = `author`.`id`');

    return $jokes->fetchAll();
}
```

Now we can reference the date column in the template file `jokes.html.php`:

```php
 <p><?=$totalJokes?> jokes have been submitted to
↪ the Internet Joke Database.</p>

<?php foreach ($jokes as $joke): ?>
<blockquote>
    <p>
    <?=htmlspecialchars($joke['joketext'],
    ENT_QUOTES, 'UTF-8')?>

    (by <a href="mailto:<?=htmlspecialchars(
    $joke['email'],
    ENT_QUOTES,
        'UTF-8'
); ?>">
    <?=htmlspecialchars(
            $joke['name'],
            ENT_QUOTES,
        'UTF-8'
        ); ?></a> on <?=$joke['jokedate']; ?>)
    <a href="editjoke.php?id=<?=$joke['id']?>">
    Edit</a>

    <form action="deletejoke.php" method="post">
        <input type="hidden" name="id"
```

```
        value="<?=$joke['id']?>">
        <input type="submit" value="Delete">
    </form>

    </p>
</blockquote>
<?php endforeach; ?>
```

If you run the code above, you'll see the date printed on the page. Unfortunately, it will be printed in the format that MySQL uses—that is, 2019-08-04, rather than a nicer format that people who are viewing the website would prefer.

It's possible to use the DateTime class to do this for us by amending the template file to create an instance of the DateTime class and formatting the date in a nicer way:

```
(by <a href="mailto:<?=htmlspecialchars(
    $joke['email'],
    ENT_QUOTES,
        'UTF-8'
); ?>">
    <?=htmlspecialchars(
            $joke['name'],
            ENT_QUOTES,
        'UTF-8'
        ); ?></a> on
<?php
$date = new DateTime($joke['jokedate']);

echo $date->format('jS F Y');
?>)
    <a href="editjoke.php?id=<?=$joke['id']?>">
    Edit</a>
```

The DateTime class can take an argument of a date and, luckily for us, it understands the format MySQL uses—allowing us to quickly format the data in any way we like.

The line `echo $date->format('jS F Y');` formats the date in a much nicer way, and will display something like 4th August 2019.

This example can be found in *Structure2-ArrayFunctions-Dates2*.

Making Your Own Tools

> Blacksmiths are unique in that they make their own tools. Carpenters don't make their saws and hammers, tailors don't make their scissors and needles, and plumbers don't make their wrenches, but blacksmiths can make their hammers, tongs, anvils, and chisels — Daniel C. Dennet, *Intuition Pumps and Other Tools for Thinking*

This is an interesting observation—and I'll explain why I've included in in a moment-but it implies a small paradox. If a blacksmith is needed to make blacksmith's tools, where did the first blacksmith's tools come from? As it turns out, there's actually a simple explanation: the first tools were incredibly crude—just some rocks used to bash out some metal rods. But the blacksmith can fuse two of those rods together to make a basic hammer, and then use that hammer to make an even better hammer, gradually making newer and better equipment.

By improving the tools to be more precise and easier to use, the blacksmith can make products faster, create higher-quality items, produce a wider variety of products, make other specialist tools, and let lesser-skilled workers such as apprentices produce products beyond their skill level.

It does take time to create a tool, but once the tool is created, the blacksmith can use it to make thousands of products. Over the long term, the time spent making the tool quickly pays off.

You're probably wondering what any of this has to do with PHP programming. I'm going to amend Dennet's quote slightly and say that blacksmiths are *almost* unique in being able to make their own tools—because programmers also possess this ability.

Every opportunity I listed for blacksmiths to create their own tools exists for programmers as well. In fact, everything you use on your computer is a tool written by another programmer. Even the PHP programming language you're using is a tool originally written by a developer called Rasmus Lerdorf.

Programming languages don't just suddenly exist. Computers don't even understand PHP at all! They only understand binary code.

Like blacksmiths, programmers started with very crude tools: punch cards that had a hole or no hole to represent a one or a zero. These were then manually fed into the computer to program it. Writing and understanding the code took an incredible amount of skill. As computers developed, so did the way we program them.

Instead of representing everything as ones and zeros with punch cards, programmers invented tools that take human-readable and easier-to-understand code and convert it (or "compile" it, if you want to get technical) into the binary code that the computer understands. It's easy to forget that programming languages exist for humans, not for computers.

When you sit down in front of your computer with your favorite code editor, you can be forgiven for thinking you're using the most refined hammer that can be made and that you have all the tools available to pick from.

A programming language is just a tool, and you can use it to make your own tools. Every time you write a function, you're creating a new tool. You can either make tools that have many uses, which you can use over and over again, or tools with limited use that can only be used for one very specific job.

In your kitchen you have many tools. You probably need a knife to prepare nearly every meal, but how often do you use a garlic press?

A tool is more useful if it can be used for a variety of different tasks. In the kitchen, the more recipes the tool can help make, the more useful it is.

When writing a function in PHP (or any programming language), strive to write functions that are more like the knife than the garlic press. Write functions that can be used over and over again on any website, rather than functions that only apply to a very specific case on a single website.

So far in this chapter, we've taken functions that need an exact number of arguments in a very specific order and rewritten them as functions that allow arguments to be specified in (almost) any order, with values optionally omitted entirely if they don't need updating.

The problem with the function now is that it's more like the garlic press than the knife. Just as the garlic press is only useful for recipes that have garlic, the updateJoke function is only useful when we want to update a record in the joke table. We can't take this function and use it on another website, because the next website you build probably won't even have a table called joke.

The next step in refining our tools is to make our functions more like the knife, able to work with any database table. After all, a knife can be used to chop garlic anyway.

Generic Functions

Before we make any large-scale changes, let's expand the website and add a function for retrieving all the authors from the database in the same manner we used for the allJokes function:

```
function allAuthors($pdo) {
    $authors =  query($pdo, 'SELECT * FROM `author`');

    return $authors->fetchAll();
}
```

Let's also add functions for inserting and deleting authors from the author table:

```
function deleteAuthor($pdo, $id) {
    $parameters = [':id' => $id];

    query($pdo, 'DELETE FROM `author`
    WHERE `id` = :id', $parameters);
}
```

```php
function insertAuthor($pdo, $fields) {
    $query = 'INSERT INTO `author` (';

    foreach ($fields as $key => $value) {
        $query .= '`' . $key . '`,';
    }

    $query = rtrim($query, ',');

    $query .= ') VALUES (';

    foreach ($fields as $key => $value) {
        $query .= ':' . $key . ',';
    }

    $query = rtrim($query, ',');

    $query .= ')';

    $fields = processDates($fields);

    query($pdo, $query, $fields);
}
```

These `deleteAuthor` and `insertAuthor` functions are almost identical to the corresponding joke functions, `deleteJoke` and `insertJoke`. It would be better to create *generic* functions that could be used with any database table. That way, we can write the function *once* and use it for any database table. If we continued down the route of having five different functions for each database table, we'd very quickly end up with a lot of very similar code.

The differences between the functions are just the names of the tables. By replacing the table name with a variable, the function can be used to retrieve all the records from any database table. That way, it's no longer necessary to write a different function for each table:

```php
function findAll($pdo, $table) {
```

```
    $result = query($pdo, 'SELECT * FROM `' . $table . '`');

    return $result->fetchAll();
}
```

Once the function has been written, this new tool can be used to retrieve all the records from any database table:

```
// Select all the jokes from the database
$allJokes = findAll($pdo, 'joke');

// Select all the authors from the database
$allAuthors = findAll($pdo, 'author');
```

The same thing can be done with delete:

```
function delete($pdo, $table, $id) {
    $parameters = [':id' => $id];

    query($pdo, 'DELETE FROM `' . $table . '`
    WHERE `id` = :id', $parameters);
}
```

This allows deleting a record from any table based on its ID:

```
// Delete author with the ID of 2
delete($pdo, 'author', 2);

// Delete joke with the id of 5
delete($pdo, 'joke', 5);
```

This function works, but it's still a little inflexible: it assumes that the primary key field in the table is called id. This function can only work with tables that have a field named id for their primary key, which isn't always the case. A table that stored information about books, for example, might have `isbn` as the primary key. In order for our function to work with any database table structure, the primary key can also be replaced with a variable:

```
function delete($pdo, $table, $primaryKey, $id ) {
    $parameters = [':id' => $id];

    query($pdo, 'DELETE FROM `' . $table . '`
    WHERE `' . $primaryKey . '` = :id', $parameters);
}
```

Whenever the **delete** function is called, it's now supplied with four arguments:

- the `$pdo` database connection
- the name of the table to delete a record from
- the ID of the record to delete
- the field that acts as the primary key

And it can be called like this:

```
// Delete author with the ID of 2
delete($pdo, 'author', 'id', 2);

// Delete joke with the id of 5
delete($pdo, 'joke', 'id', 5);

// Delete the book with the ISBN 978-3-16-148410-0
delete($pdo, 'book', '978-3-16-148410-0', 'isbn');
```

Along with the delete and select functions, let's do the same thing with the **update** and **insert** functions by replacing the table name with a function argument:

```
function insert($pdo, $table, $fields) {
    $query = 'INSERT INTO `' . $table . '` (';
```

```
    foreach ($fields as $key => $value) {
        $query .= '`' . $key . '`,';
    }

    $query = rtrim($query, ',');

    $query .= ') VALUES (';

    foreach ($fields as $key => $value) {
        $query .= ':' . $key . ',';
    }

    $query = rtrim($query, ',');

    $query .= ')';

    $fields = processDates($fields);

    query($pdo, $query, $fields);
}

function update($pdo, $table, $primaryKey, $fields) {

    $query = ' UPDATE `' . $table .'` SET ';

    foreach ($fields as $key => $value) {
        $query .= '`' . $key . '` = :' . $key . ',';
    }

    $query = rtrim($query, ',');

    $query .= ' WHERE `' . $primaryKey . '` = :primaryKey';

    // Set the :primaryKey variable
    $fields['primaryKey'] = $fields['id'];

    $fields = processDates($fields);

    query($pdo, $query, $fields);
}
```

Notice that in the update function, I've also created a variable called primaryKey. That's because we can't assume that the primary key (used in the WHEREid= :primaryKey part of the query) will always be id.

In the last chapter we created a function called getJoke, which found a specific joke by its ID. That function, too, can be made to work with any database table. This findById function can be used to find a single record from any table using the primary key:

```
function findById($pdo, $table, $primaryKey, $value) {
    $query = 'SELECT * FROM `' . $table . '`
    WHERE `' . $primaryKey . '` = :value';

    $parameters = [
        'value' => $value
    ];

    $query = query($pdo, $query, $parameters);

    return $query->fetch();
}
```

We now have a set of functions that can be used to interact quickly and easily with *any* database table and use PHP's DateTime class for dates:

```
// Add a new record to the database
$record = [
    'joketext' => '!false - it\'s funny because it\'s true',
    'authorId' => 2,
    'jokedate' => new DateTime()
];

insert($pdo, 'joke', $record);

// Delete from the author table where `id` is `2`
```

```
delete($pdo, 'author', 'id', 2);

$jokes = findAll($pdo, $joke);
```

Finally, for the sake of completeness, let's also make the same change to the `totalJokes` function, allowing us to get the number of records in any table:

```
function total($pdo, $table) {
    $query = query($pdo, 'SELECT COUNT(*)
    FROM `' . $table . '`');
    $row = $query->fetch();
    return $row[0];
}
```

Using These Functions

Now that we've got the functions, let's put them into our controllers. Firstly, we'll change the the `addjoke.php` controller to use the new generic `insert` function. It currently looks like this:

```
<?php
if (isset($_POST['joketext'])) {
    try {
        include __DIR__ . '/../includes/DatabaseConnection.php';
        include __DIR__ . '/../includes/DatabaseFunctions.php';

        insertJoke($pdo, ['authorId' => 1,
        'jokeText' => $_POST['joketext'],
        'jokedate' => new DateTime()]);

        header('location: jokes.php');

        // …
```

To replace the `insertJoke` function with the generic `insert` function, we just need to change the name and supply the name of the table:

```php
<?php
if (isset($_POST['joketext'])) {
    try {
    include __DIR__ . '/../includes/DatabaseConnection.php';
    include __DIR__ . '/../includes/DatabaseFunctions.php';

 insert($pdo, 'joke', ['authorId' => 1, 'jokeText' =>
↪ $_POST['joketext'], 'jokedate' => new DateTime()]);

    header('location: jokes.php');

    // …
```

Now amend `editjoke.php` and `deletejoke.php` files in the same way. Firstly `editjoke.php`:

```php
<?php
include __DIR__ . '/../includes/DatabaseConnection.php';
include __DIR__ . '/../includes/DatabaseFunctions.php';

try {
    if (isset($_POST['joketext'])) {
        update($pdo, 'joke', 'id', ['id' => $_POST['jokeid'],
            'joketext' => $_POST['joketext'],
            'authorId' => 1]);

        header('location: jokes.php');
    } else {
        $joke = findById($pdo, 'joke', 'id', $_GET['id']);

        $title = 'Edit joke';

        ob_start();

        include __DIR__ . '/../templates/editjoke.html.php';
```

```
        $output = ob_get_clean();
    }
}
// …
```

And here's the updated `deletejoke.php`:

```php
<?php
try {
    include __DIR__ . '/../includes/DatabaseConnection.php';
    include __DIR__ . '/../includes/DatabaseFunctions.php';

    delete($pdo, 'joke', 'id', $_POST['id']);

    // …
```

The next part is the list of jokes. Currently, it uses the `allJokes` function, which also retrieves information about the author of each joke. There's no simple way to write a generic function that retrieves information from two tables. It would have to know which fields were used to join the tables and which tables were being joined. It would be possible to do this with a function with lots of arguments, but the function would be difficult to use and overly complex.

Instead, we can use the generic `findAll` and `findById` functions to achieve this:

```php
$result = findAll($pdo, 'joke');

$jokes = [];
foreach ($result as $joke) {

    $author = findById($pdo, 'author', 'id', $joke['authorId']);

    $jokes[] = [
        'id' => $joke['id'],
        'joketext' => $joke['joketext'],
```

```php
        'name' => $author['name'],
        'email' => $author['email']
    ];
}
```

The complete `jokes.php` looks like this:

```php
<?php

try {
    include __DIR__ . '/../includes/DatabaseConnection.php';
    include __DIR__ . '/../includes/DatabaseFunctions.php';

    $result = findAll($pdo, 'joke');

    $jokes = [];
    foreach ($result as $joke) {
        $author = findById($pdo, 'author', 'id',
            $joke['authorId']);

        $jokes[] = [
            'id' => $joke['id'],
            'joketext' => $joke['joketext'],
            'jokedate' => $joke['jokedate'],
            'name' => $author['name'],
            'email' => $author['email']
        ];
    }

    $title = 'Joke list';

    $totalJokes = total($pdo, 'joke');

    ob_start();

    include __DIR__ . '/../templates/jokes.html.php';

    $output = ob_get_clean();
```

```
    } catch (PDOException $e) {
        $title = 'An error has occurred';

        $output = 'Database error: ' . $e->getMessage() . '
        in ' . $e->getFile() . ':' . $e->getLine();
    }

    include __DIR__ . '/../templates/layout.html.php';
```

This example can be found in *Structure2-GenericFunctions*.

This works by fetching the list of jokes (without the author information), then looping over each joke and finding the corresponding author by their id, then writing the complete joke with the information from both tables into the $jokes array. This is essentially what an INNER JOIN does in MySQL.

Each joke is now made up of values from the $author variable, which is a record from the author table and values from the joke table.

You may have realized that this method is going to be slower, because more queries are sent to the database. This is a common issue with these kinds of generic functions, and it's called the **N+1 problem**[1] There are several methods for reducing this performance issue[2], but for smaller sites, where we're dealing with hundreds or thousands of records rather than millions, it's unlikely to cause any real problems. The difference will likely be in the region of milliseconds.

Repeated Code Is the Enemy

Whenever you're writing software, you need to be vigilant about repeated code. Any time you find yourself with two or more copies of identical or very similar code, it's always worth taking a step back and looking to see if there's a way of

---

[1] For more information on the N+1 problem, refer to the Microsoft article "Select N+1 Problem – How to Decrease Your ORM Performance": http://blogs.microsoft.co.il/gilf/ 2010/08/18/select-n1-problem-how-to-decrease-your-orm-performance/

[2] To see how the N+1 problem can be avoided entirely, refer to https://www.sitepoint.com/silver-bullet-n1-problem/

merging the code into one reusable block.

By creating the generic functions `insert`, `update`, `delete`, `findAll` and `findById`, it's now very quick and easy for us to create a website that deals with any kind of database operation. The functions can be used to interact very simply with any database table we might ever need.

But there's still room for improvement. The files `addjoke.php` and `editjoke.php` do very similar jobs: they display a form, and when the form is submitted, they send the submitted data off to the database.

Similarly, the template files `addjoke.html.php` and `editjoke.html.php` are almost identical. There's very little difference between them. The only real difference is that the edit page displays a pre-filled form where the add page presents an empty form.

The problem with repeated code is that, if something has to change, you have to make the same change in multiple locations. What if we wanted to add a category to a joke, so that when a joke was added or edited the user could choose *Knock knock jokes*, *Programming Jokes*, *Puns*, *One liners*, etc?

We could achieve this by adding a `<select>` box to the add joke page, but we'd also need to make the same change to the edit joke page. Each time we made a change to `addjoke.php`, we'd need to make the corresponding change in `editjoke.php`.

If you ever find yourself in a situation like this, where you have to make similar changes in multiple files, it's a good sign that you should combine both sets of code into one. Of course, the new code needs to handle both cases.

There are a couple of differences between `addjoke.php` and `editjoke.php`:

1. `addjoke.php` issues an INSERT query, while `editjoke.php` issues an UPDATE query.

2. `editjoke.php`'s template file has a hidden input that stores the ID of the joke being edited.

But everything else is almost the same.

Let's merge both pieces of code together, so that editjoke.php can handle both editing an existing joke and adding a new one. The script will be able to tell whether we're adding or editing based on whether or not an ID is supplied in the URI.

Visiting editjoke.php?id=12 will load the joke with the ID 12 from the database and allow us to edit it. When the form is submitted, it will issue the relevant UPDATE query, while just visiting editjoke.php—without an ID specified—will display an empty form and, when submitted, perform an INSERT query.

Creating a Page for Adding and Editing

Let's handle the form first—which either loads the joke into the fields or displays a blank form. Currently, editjoke.php assumes there's the id GETvariable set, and loads the joke accordingly before loading the template file:

```
else {
    $joke = findById($pdo, 'joke', 'id', $_GET['id']);

    $title = 'Edit joke';

    ob_start();

    include __DIR__ . '/../templates/editjoke.html.php';

    $output = ob_get_clean();
}
```

This can be replaced with an if statement to only load the joke from the database if an id has actually been provided:

```
else {
    if (isset($_GET['id'])) {
        $joke = findById($pdo, 'joke', 'id', $_GET['id']);
    }

    $title = 'Edit joke';
```

```
    ob_start();

    include __DIR__ . '/../templates/editjoke.html.php';

    $output = ob_get_clean();
}
```

If you try the above code and visit editjoke.php without supplying an ID as a GET variable, it won't quite work as intended. You'll actually see some strange errors appearing inside the <textarea>. That's because when editjoke.html.php is loaded, it references a variable called $joke which, because of the new if statement, is only created when the ID is supplied.

One solution would be to load the addjoke.html.php file if there's no ID set and editjoke.html.php if there is. Unfortunately, this doesn't solve the initial problem: to add a new field to the form using this approach, we'd still need to edit two files.

Instead, let's amend editjoke.html.php so it only tries to print the existing data into the textarea and hidden input if the joke variable is set:

```
<form action="" method="post">
    <input type="hidden" name="jokeid"
        value="<?php if (isset($joke)): ?>
            <?=$joke['id']?>
        <?php endif; ?>
    ?>">
    <label for="joketext">Type your joke here:
    </label>
    <textarea id="joketext" name="joketext" rows="3"
        cols="40"><?php if (isset($joke)): ?>
        <?=$joke['joketext']?>
    <?php endif; ?></textarea>
    <input type="submit" name="submit" value="Save">
</form>
```

Now the `joketext` and `id` will only be written to the page if the `$joke` variable has been set, and it's only set when we're editing an existing record.

Before continuing, let's tidy up the code a little. Previously, to print the ID of the joke into the hidden input, it required a simpler piece of code:

```
<input type="hidden" name="jokeid"
    value="<?=$joke[id]?>">
```

Now that we're using the `if` statement, we need the full `<?php` opening and several lines of code.

A nice feature introduced in PHP 7 is the **Null coalescing operator**. It's a very confusing name, but is actually just a shorthand for this:

```
if (isset($something)) {
    echo $something;
}
else {
    echo 'variable not set';
}
```

This can be expressed using the null coalescing operator (??) like so:

```
echo $something ?? 'variable not set';
```

On the left-hand side of the ?? operator is the variable being checked, and on the right is the output that's used if it's not set. In the case above, if the `$something` variable is set, it will print the contents of the variable. If the variable isn't set, it will print `variable not set`, and even better, it also works with arrays.

Let's make use of it in our templates, rather than having to write out the entire `if` statement for each field:

```
<form action="" method="post">
    <input type="hidden" name="jokeid"
        value="<?=$joke['id'] ?? ''?>">
    <label for="joketext">Type your joke here:
    </label>
    <textarea id="joketext" name="joketext" rows="3"
 cols="40"><?=$joke['joketext'] ??
↳ ''?></textarea>
    <input type="submit" name="submit" value="Save">
</form>
```

In this instance, the right-hand part is an empty string. Either the text of the loaded joke will be displayed in the text box, or if the $joke variable is not set, it will display an empty string '' in the box.

To complete this page, we need to change what happens when the form is submitted. Either an update or insert query will need to be run.

The simplest way would be to look to see if the ID field has been supplied:

```
if (isset($_POST['id']) && $_POST['id'] != '') {
    update(...);
}
else ;
    insert(...)
}
```

Although this would work, once again there's an opportunity to make this more generic. This logic for *if the ID is set, update, otherwise insert* is going to be the same for any form.

If we had a form for *authors*, the same logic would be useful: *if there's no ID, perform an insert; if there is, perform an update.* Indeed, this would apply anywhere we have a form that will be used for add or edit. The code above would need to be repeated for any form we implemented in this way.

Another problem with this approach is that it wouldn't work in cases where the primary key was a normal field on the form, such as ISBNs for books. Regardless of whether an UPDATE or INSERT query is required, the ISBN would be provided.

Instead, we can try to insert a record, and if it's unsuccessful, update instead using a try … catch statement:

```php
try {
    insert(…);

}
catch(PDOException $e) {
    update(…);
}
```

Now an INSERT will be sent to the database, but it *may* cause an error—"Duplicate key"—when a record with the supplied ID is already set. If an error does occur, an UPDATE query is issued instead to update the existing record.

To stop us needing to repeat this logic for every form, we could make another function, called save, which performs an insert or an update using the try … catch above:

```php
function save($pdo, $table, $primaryKey, $record) {
    try {
        if ($record[$primaryKey] == '') {
            $record[$primaryKey] = null;
        }
        insert($pdo, $table, $record);
    }
    catch (PDOException $e) {
        update($pdo, $table, $primaryKey, $record);
    }
}
```

This will work for any record in any table. If there's an error when trying to insert, it will issue the corresponding update query instead.

The `save` function here needs all the arguments required by both the `insert` and `update` functions in order to call them. There's no need to repeat any of the logic from those functions; they can just be called from within the relatively short `save` function.

The line `if ($record[$primaryKey] == '') {` is used here so that the `INSERT` function never tries to insert an empty string into the `ID` column. Most of the time, the primary key will be an `INT` column that only accepts numbers. By replacing the empty string with `NULL`, it will trigger MySQL's `auto_increment` feature and generate a new ID.

Now `editjoke.php` can be modified to use the new `save` function:

```
try {
    if (isset($_POST['joketext'])) {

        save($pdo, 'joke', 'id', ['id' => $_POST['jokeid'],
            'joketext' => $_POST['joketext'],
            'jokedate' => new DateTime(),
            'authorId' => 1]);

        header('location: jokes.php');
    }
```

Finally, you can delete the controller `addjoke.php` and the template `addjoke.html.php`, as they're no longer needed. Both add and edit are now handled by `editjoke.php`. Change the link in the menu in `layout.html.php` to go to `editjoke.php` instead of `addjoke.php`.

This example can be found in *Structure2-GenericFunction-Save*.

Further Polishing

The new `save` function can be used to add records to the database. It will automatically insert or update depending on whether the `id` field is set to an existing ID. For the add form, where the ID field isn't set, there's still an `id` key in the `$_POST` array, because the hidden input still exits on the form.

This allows us to treat add and edit identically, saving us a lot of work. Without this generic **save** function, we'd need different HTML forms and different controller logic for processing the submissions.

Using this approach, there's less code to write initially, and the lack of HTML or PHP code repetition is an extra bonus. To add a new field, all we need to do is add the field to the database, amend the template and supply the new value to the **save** function.

Adding new fields is a very simple process. Because the **save** function handles both **INSERT** and **UPDATE** queries, and the **insert** and **update** functions both dynamically generate the queries, adding a field to the query is now as easy as adding an entry to an array!

This updated code is incredibly easy to manage compared to the code we started with at the beginning of the last chapter. However—and you're probably anticipating me saying this by now—it's always worth asking whether it can be simplified further. Once again, the answer is yes.

There's a little repetition here:

```
[
    'id' => $_POST['jokeid'],
    'authorId' => 1,
    'jokedate' => new DateTime(),
    'joketext' => $_POST['joketext']
];
```

Each field in the `$_POST` array is mapped to a key in the `$joke` array with the same name.

Take a look at the line `'joketext' => $_POST['joketext'],`. All we're really doing here is creating a key in the `$joke` array with the name `joketext` and the value from the `$_POST` array's `joketext` element.

Really, we're just copying data from the `$_POST` array exactly into the `$joke` array. If the form had more fields, we'd need to copy those too.

It would be possible to do something similar using this code:

```php
$joke = $_POST;
$joke['authorId'] = 1;
$joke['jokedate'] = new DateTime();

save($pdo, 'joke', 'id', $joke);
```

This will automatically include all the fields from the form in the `$joke` array without needing to manually copy them.

Now, if we added a new field to the form, there are only two steps: add the column in the database and add the form. As long as the column name in the database is the same as the field name on the form, it's possible to add new fields to the form without ever opening up the controller!

As neat as that sounds, if you do try the code above, you'll find you get an error. That's because the `$_POST` array also contains the submit button. When the `INSERT` query is generated, it would actually generate this query:

```sql
INSERT INTO `joke` (`joketext`, `jokedate`, `authorid`,
↪ `submit`)
```

This is obviously a problem: there's no submit column in the database table `joke`. A quick and dirty way of fixing this is to remove the submit button from the array using `unset`:

```php
$joke = $_POST;

// Remove the submit element from the array
unset($joke['submit']);

$joke['authorId'] = 1;
$joke['jokedate'] = new DateTime();

save($pdo, 'joke', 'id', $joke);
```

Although this works, the problem with this approach is that you'd have to remove any form elements you don't want inserted into the database. For example, if you have a checkbox on the form that sends an email when checked, you'd also remove this checkbox from the $_POST array prior to calling the save function.

As usual, there's a better way. When using HTML forms, you can actually send an *array* as post data by changing the field names. Change editjoke.html.php to this:

```
<form action="" method="post">
    <input type="hidden" name="joke[id]"
        value="<?=$joke['id'] ?? ''?>">
    <label for="joketext">Type your joke here:
    </label>
    <textarea id="joketext" name="joke[joketext]" rows="3
 " cols="40"><?=$joke['joketext'] ??
↪ ''?></textarea>
    <input type="submit" name="submit" value="Save">
</form>
```

Each of the fields that represents some data for the joke has been changed slightly. The name attribute of each form field has been updated to represent an array: jokeid is now joke[id] and joketext is now joke[joketext].

This tells PHP to treat these fields like an array when the form is submitted.

If you submit the form, the $_POST array will store two values: submit and joke. $_POST['joke'] is itself an array from which you can read the id value using $_POST['joke']['id'].

For our purposes, we can read all of the information for the joke using $joke = $_POST['joke'] and it won't contain the submit button entry, or any other array keys/values that we don't want to send to the save function.

```
$joke = $_POST['joke'];
$joke['authorId'] = 1;
$joke['jokedate'] = new DateTime();
```

The `$joke` array will contain all the values from `$_POST['joke']` and any we want to add that don't come from the form—in this case, `authorId` and `jokedate`. Following this approach, however, it's important that the field names on the form directly match up to column names in the database, so I've used `joke[id]` instead of `joke[jokeid]`. The latter would try to write to a column in the database called `jokeid`, which doesn't exist.

Finally, you'll need to update the `if` statement that detects whether the form has been submitted to look for the new `joke` key, rather than `joketext` which no longer exits:

```
if (isset($_POST['joke'])) {
```

The complete controller code now looks like this:

```php
<?php
include __DIR__ . '/../includes/DatabaseConnection.php';
include __DIR__ . '/../includes/DatabaseFunctions.php';

try {
    if (isset($_POST['joke'])) {
        $joke = $_POST['joke'];
        $joke['jokedate'] = new DateTime();
        $joke['authorId'] = 1;

        save($pdo, 'joke', 'id', $joke);

        header('location: jokes.php');
    } else {
        if (isset($_GET['id'])) {
            $joke = findById($pdo, 'joke', 'id', $_GET['id']);
        }

        $title = 'Edit joke';

        ob_start();

        include __DIR__ . '/../templates/editjoke.html.php';

        $output = ob_get_clean();
    }
} catch (PDOException $e) {
    $title = 'An error has occurred';

    $output = 'Database error: ' . $e->getMessage() . ' in '
    . $e->getFile() . ':' . $e->getLine();
}

include __DIR__ . '/../templates/layout.html.php';
```

If we wanted add a field to the joke table and alter the form now, it would only require two changes: adding the field to the database and then editing the HTML form. A single update to editjoke.html.php will let us add a form field that works for both the edit and add pages.

Moving Forward

In this chapter, I've showed you how to reduce repeated code and write functions for use with any database table. We've moved from some very specific functions to functions that can be used in several different situations.

You now have a set of tools you can use to extend this website or even write a completely different one. None of the functions are tied to concepts like *jokes* or *authors*, which means we could use them on a website that dealt with entirely different concepts—for example, *books*, *products*, *blogs*, or anything you can think of. Now that you've written the tools, the hard part is done, and in your next project you can save a lot of time by reusing the tools you've created.

Chapter

8

Objects and Classes

In the last chapter, I showed you how to write generic, reusable functions that could be used to manipulate any database table. In this chapter, we'll move those functions into a class, to avoid some of the repetition that's needed when they're used.

One of the biggest problems with functions is that all the information they need to execute has to be sent to them in arguments. In the case of the `delete` function we wrote, there are four pieces of information:

- the `$pdo` database instance
- the name of the table to delete from
- the name of the primary key field
- the value to delete

The same is true of all the functions—findById, findAll, update, insert and save. Each of the functions we created needs to be passed at least the $pdo database instance and the name of the table. All of them except findAll and insert also need to know the name of the column that represents the primary key.

For example, the save function is used like this:

```
if (isset($_POST['joke'])) {

    $joke = $_POST['joke'];
    $joke['jokedate'] = new DateTime();
    $joke['authorId'] = 1;

    save($pdo, 'joke', 'id', $joke);
    // …
```

Each time one of the functions is called, it must be passed the $pdo instance. With up to four arguments for each function, it can be difficult to remember the order they need to be provided in.

A good method for avoiding this problem is putting the functions inside a class.

Time for Class

As each class needs a name, and ours will deal with functions that have something to do with database tables, we'll call ours DatabaseTable.

Like variables, classes can contain any sequence of alphanumeric characters. However, special characters like -, +, { or a space aren't allowed.

By convention, classes in PHP use **CamelCase**, starting with an uppercase letter followed by lowercase letters until the start of the next word. PHP allows for the class to be called databasetable, DATABASETABLE, or some other similar variation, but it's a good idea to follow the naming convention used by almost all PHP programmers.

You can think of a **class** as a collection of functions and data (variables). Each class will contain a set of functions and some data that the functions can access.

Our DatabaseTable class needs to contain all the functions we created for interacting with the database, along with any functions that those functions need to call.

As a first step, move all the database functions into a class wrapper:

```php
<?php
class DatabaseTable
{
    private function query($pdo, $sql, $parameters = [])
    {
        $query = $pdo->prepare($sql);
        $query->execute($parameters);
        return $query;
    }

    public function total($pdo, $table)
    {
        $query = $this->query($pdo, 'SELECT COUNT(*) FROM
            `' . $table . '`');
        $row = $query->fetch();
        return $row[0];
    }

    public function findById($pdo, $table, $primaryKey, $value)
    {
        $query = 'SELECT * FROM `' . $table . '` WHERE
            `' . $primaryKey . '` = :value';

        $parameters = [
            'value' => $value
        ];

        $query = $this->query($pdo, $query, $parameters);

        return $query->fetch();
    }
```

```php
private function insert($pdo, $table, $fields)
{
    $query = 'INSERT INTO `' . $table . '` (';

    foreach ($fields as $key => $value) {
        $query .= '`' . $key . '`,';
    }

    $query = rtrim($query, ',');

    $query .= ') VALUES (';

    foreach ($fields as $key => $value) {
        $query .= ':' . $key . ',';
    }

    $query = rtrim($query, ',');

    $query .= ')';

    $fields = $this->processDates($fields);

    $this->query($pdo, $query, $fields);
}

private function update($pdo, $table, $primaryKey, $fields)
{
    $query = ' UPDATE `' . $table .'` SET ';

    foreach ($fields as $key => $value) {
        $query .= '`' . $key . '` = :' . $key . ',';
    }

    $query = rtrim($query, ',');

    $query .= ' WHERE `' . $primaryKey . '` = :primaryKey';

    // Set the :primaryKey variable
    $fields['primaryKey'] = $fields['id'];
```

```php
        $fields = $this->processDates($fields);

        $this->query($pdo, $query, $fields);
    }

    public function delete($pdo, $table, $primaryKey, $id)
    {
        $parameters = [':id' => $id];

        $this->query($pdo, 'DELETE FROM `' . $table . '` WHERE
          `' . $primaryKey . '` = :id', $parameters);
    }

    public function findAll($pdo, $table)
    {
        $result = query($pdo, 'SELECT * FROM `' . $table . '`');

        return $result->fetchAll();
    }

    private function processDates($fields)
    {
        foreach ($fields as $key => $value) {
            if ($value instanceof DateTime) {
                $fields[$key] = $value->format('Y-m-d');
            }
        }

        return $fields;
    }

    public function save($pdo, $table, $primaryKey, $record)
    {
        try {
            if ($record[$primaryKey] == '') {
                $record[$primaryKey] = null;
            }
            $this->insert($pdo, $table, $record);
        } catch (PDOException $e) {
```

```
            $this->update($pdo, $table, $primaryKey, $record);
        }
    }
}
```

Like templates and include files, it's good practice to store classes outside the `public` directory. Create a new directory called `classes` inside your `Project` directory and save the code above as `DatabaseTable.php`.

 Naming Your Class Files

It's good practice to name your class files exactly the same as your classes. The class `DatabaseTable` would be placed in `DatabaseTable.php`, a class called `User` would be stored in `User.php` and so on. Although it doesn't matter at the moment, later on I'll introduce something called an *autoloader*, and it will be difficult to use without this convention.

 Methods

A function that exists inside a class is called a **method**. Although many developers—and the PHP language itself—use the word *function* to describe subroutines in classes, the correct term is *method*, which I'll be using throughout. However, the difference between a *function* and a *method* is that a *method* is inside a class, while a *function* isn't.

Anything you can do with a *function* (arguments, return values, calling other functions) can also be done with a *method*.

If you examine the code above, you'll see I've made two changes beyond just pasting the functions into the class. The first change I've made is that when functions from within the class are called, they're prefixed with `$this->`. Instead of `$result = query($pdo,…`, the updated code has `$result = $this->query($pdo,…`.

You can think of `this` as "this class". We can't just use `query()` anymore, because now that the `query()` function is inside the class, it can't be called like a *global* function, as it's outside of global scope. Any method inside a class can only be called on a *variable*. In the same way we use `$pdo->prepare()`, the `query()`

method is now called on an object. From within the class, the current object is referenced as $this. The $this variable is created automatically inside any method and will always exist without being declared.

Public vs Private

The second change I've made when converting functions to methods is that each is prefixed with either public or private. These are known as **visibility**, allowing the programmer to determine where the method can be called from.

Methods marked private can only be called from other methods inside the class, whereas methods marked public can be called from both inside and outside the class. You've already seen some public methods on the PDO instance we've been using throughout this book. When you call $pdo->prepare(), you're calling a *public* method called prepare. If the method was marked private, this wouldn't be possible.

What's the point of private methods then? Take a look at the methods I've marked as private in the DatabaseTable class: query and processDates. The reason these are private is that, on their own, they aren't very useful. Nobody using the DatabaseTable class should ever need to call the query method directly. The query method is only there to provide some shared functionality for the other methods in the class—save, findById, and so on. The same is true of the processDates function.

At first glance, it seems a little pointless. However, it's actually a very useful tool. Once a method such as query is private, you can completely rewrite the way it works, and you can guarantee the only place it's being called from is another method within the same class.

When you're working in large teams or sharing your code online, knowing exactly where a method is called from is useful. You can release a new version of the class without the query method, and you can be guaranteed it's not being used anywhere else. Someone else can use the new version and their code won't be broken.

If it was public and you changed the code, you'd have no idea if the query function was being called from anywhere else, and you'd need to be wary of changing the way it worked in case it broke someone else's code.

Objects

You can think of a class as a recipe. On its own, it's just a series of instructions. To make something from it that's actually useful—something you can eat—you need to follow the instructions.

A class on its own isn't very useful: it's just a series of instructions. There's no way to call a method from within the class without creating an **object**. An object is an *instance* of a class.

Creating an instance of the `DatabaseTable` class is done the same way as the `pdo` instance we've been using throughout this book: only the name of our class, `DatabaseTable`, is used:

```
$databaseTable = new DatabaseTable();
```

The `new` keyword creates an *object* from the defined class, which can then be used. Without this step, none of the functions defined in the class can be used.

At the moment, this feels like an extra step that doesn't achieve anything special. But as we'll see later on, this is a very powerful tool for programmers, allowing us to create different instances that represent different database tables.

Once the object is created, the methods can be called on the variable in the same way we call `$pdo->prepare()` on the `$pdo` object:

```
$databaseTable = new DatabaseTable();
$jokes = $databaseTable->findAll($pdo, 'joke');
```

Any of the `public` methods can be called in this way. However, if you try to call one of the `private` methods, you'll get an error.

Class Variables

At the start of this chapter, I mentioned that the goal of using objects and classes was to reduce repeated code. However, so far we've actually made the code longer. With the `DatabaseTable` class, each time we want to use one of the methods, we need to call it on an object:

```
$databaseTable = new DatabaseTable();

$jokes = $databaseTable->findAll($pdo, 'joke');

$databaseTable->save($pdo, 'joke', 'id', $_POST['joke']);
```

In this case, we've increased rather than reduced the amount of code that's required.

Each time one of the methods in the class is called, it needs the same information—at a minimum, the database connection and the name of the table that's being interacted with.

Rather than supply these values every time a method is called, it's possible to supply them once, to the class, and have the values used within the methods.

Every class can have variables that are available to be used within any method. To declare a variable that will be used inside the class, you need to declare the variable *within* the class. It's convention to define variables at the top of the class, before any methods.

To declare a variable, you must make it visible and give it a name. For example:

```
class MyClass {
    public $myVariable;
}
```

Once the variable has been declared, you can use it when you create an instance of the class. Like methods, variables can be written to and read from using the arrow (->) operator:

```
$myInstance = new MyClass();
$myInstance->myVariable = 'A value';

echo $myInstance->myVariable; // prints "A value"
```

An important distinction between **class variables** and normal variables is that they're bound to a specific *instance*. In practice, all this means is that each instance can have a different value for the same variable. For example:

```
$myInstance = new MyClass();
$myInstance->myVariable = 'A value';

$myInstance2 = new MyClass();
$myInstance2->myVariable = 'Another value';

echo $myInstance->myVariable;
echo $myInstance2->myVariable;
```

This will print "A value" and then "Another value", because each *instance* of the class has its own value for the myVariable variable. Later on, this will be very useful for our DatabaseTable class, but for now, let's just add the variables for the $pdo instance, the table name and the primary key to the class:

```
class DatabaseTable {
    public $pdo;
    public $table;
    public $primaryKey;

    // …
}
```

A class is more than just a collection of functions. You can think of it as a *blueprint* that can be used to create objects. Each object or *instance* of the class can store its own values for these variables.

For example, when you create the $pdo variable for your database connection, the $pdo variable stores the connection information—the database server address, username, password, etc. You don't need to send this information every time you call prepare or execute; the information is stored inside the $pdo object.

The same can be done with the DatabaseTable class. Once the variables have been declared, they can be written to on each instance:

```
$databaseTable = new DatabaseTable();
$databaseTable->pdo = $pdo;
$databaseTable->table = 'joke';
$databaseTable->prmaryKey = 'id';
```

Now that the variables are set, they can be used instead of the arguments inside any of the methods in the class. For example, the findAll and query methods can be rewritten to use the class variables, instead of having the database connection and table name passed in explicitly:

```
private function query($sql, $parameters = []) {
    $query = $this->pdo->prepare($sql);
    $query->execute($parameters);
    return $query;
}

public function findAll() {
    $result = $this->query('SELECT *
        FROM ' . $this->table);

    return $result->fetchAll();
}
```

The variables in the class are accessed the same way as the functions using the $this variable. Now, when the findAll() function is called, it doesn't need any arguments, because the $pdo connection and the name of the table are read from the class variables:

```php
$jokesTable = new DatabaseTable();
$jokesTable->pdo = $pdo;
$jokesTable->table = 'joke';

$jokes = $databaseTable->findAll();
```

Let's go ahead and make this change to all the methods. Anywhere $pdo, $table or $primaryKey was used as an argument, the argument can be removed and replaced with a reference to the class variable.

Here's what the total method looks like now:

```php
public function total() {
    $query = $this->query('SELECT COUNT(*)
        FROM `' . $this->table . '`');
    $row = $query->fetch();
    return $row[0];
}
```

The save method:

```php
public function save($record) {
    try {
        if ($record[$this->primaryKey] == '') {
            $record[$this->primaryKey] = null;
        }
        $this->insert($record);
    }
    catch (PDOException $e) {
        $this->update($record);
    }
}
```

The `update` method:

```php
private function update($fields) {
    $query = ' UPDATE `' . $this->table .'` SET ';

    foreach ($fields as $key => $value) {
        $query .= '`' . $key . '` = :' . $key . ',';
    }

    $query = rtrim($query, ',');

    $query .= ' WHERE `' . $this->primaryKey . '`
    = :primaryKey';

    // Set the :primaryKey variable
    $fields['primaryKey'] = $fields['id'];

    $fields = $this->processDates($fields);

    $this->query($query, $fields);
}
```

The `insert` method:

```php
private function insert($fields) {
    $query = 'INSERT INTO `' . $this->table . '` (';

    foreach ($fields as $key => $value) {
        $query .= '`' . $key . '`,';
    }

    $query = rtrim($query, ',');

    $query .= ') VALUES (';

    foreach ($fields as $key => $value) {
        $query .= ':' . $key . ',';
    }
```

```
    $query = rtrim($query, ',');

    $query .= ')';

    $fields = $this->processDates($fields);

    $this->query($query, $fields);
}
```

The findById method:

```
public function findById($value) {
    $query = 'SELECT * FROM `' . $this->table . '` WHERE
    `' . $this->primaryKey . '` = :value';

    $parameters = [
        'value' => $value
    ];

    $query = $this->query($query, $parameters);

    return $query->fetch();
}
```

The delete method:

```
public function delete($id ) {
    $parameters = [':id' => $id];

    $this->query('DELETE FROM `' . $this->table . '` WHERE
    `' . $this->primaryKey . '` = :id', $parameters);
}
```

The processDates method remains unchanged, as it doesn't require any of the class variables.

Now, to interact with the database, the common variables only need to be set once:

```php
$jokesTable = new DatabaseTable();
$jokesTable->pdo = $pdo;
$jokesTable->table = 'joke';
$jokesTable->primaryKey = 'id';
```

And then the methods can be used without repeating all the arguments:

```php
// Find the joke with the ID `123`
$joke123 = $jokesTable->findById(123);

// Find All the jokes
$jokes = $jokesTable->findAll();

foreach ($jokes as $joke) {
    // …
}

// Delete the joke with the ID `33`
$jokesTable->delete(33);

$newJoke = [
    'authorId' => 1,
    'jokedate' => new DateTime(),
  'joketext' => 'A man threw some cheese and milk at me.
↪ How dairy!'
];

$jokesTable->save($newJoke);
```

This reduces the number of arguments needed by each method, and makes it easier for someone using the methods to follow. They don't have to remember the order of all the arguments—for example, whether the table name is the first or second argument.

This is a huge improvement, but there are some potential problems. What happens if the variables aren't set before the `findAll()` method is called? What happens if the `$pdo` variable is set to a string rather than an object?

```
$jokesTable = new DatabaseTable();
$jokes = $databaseTable->findAll();
```

If you run this you'll get an error, because the `findAll` method is expecting the `$pdo` and `table` variables to be set to valid values. Luckily, there's a way of preventing this from happening.

Constructors

As the author of a class, you get to tell anyone who uses it how it works. (If you want to get technical, this is called the **Application Programming Interface** or **API**). You can make sure that any required variables are set before any functions are run.

There's a special function you can add to the class called a **constructor**. This is a function that is automatically run whenever an instance of the class is created. To add a constructor to a class, you simply add a function called `__construct()`.

 Magic Methods

That's *two* underscores in front of the word `construct`. If you use just one, it won't work!

In PHP, any method prefixed by two underscores is a **magic method**. These are generally called automatically in different cases. As the language evolves, more of these magic methods may be added, so it's a good idea to avoid giving your own methods names beginning with two underscores.

A complete list of the available magic methods can be found in the PHP manual[1].

This is a method like any other, but it's called automatically. For example:

[1.] http://php.net/manual/en/language.oop5.magic.php"

```
class MyClass {
    public function __construct() {
        echo 'construct called';
    }
}

$myclass1 = new MyClass();
$myclass2 = new MyClass();
```

Once a function with the name __construct() is created, each time you create a new instance of the class the function is called. The code above will output the following:

```
construct called
construct called
```

Even though we've never directly called the function using $myclass1->__construct(), you can see it's been called because the string construct called has been printed.

You'll also have noticed it's been called *twice*. This is because each time an *instance* of the class is created, the constructor is called.

Like any other function, the constructor can also take *arguments*. For example:

```
class MyClass {
    public function __construct($argument1) {
        echo $argument1;
    }
}
```

When you create an instance of the class, the arguments can be provided:

```
$myclass1 = new MyClass('one');
```

```
$myclass2 = new MyClass('two');
```

If you try to create an instance of the class that needs a constructor argument and doesn't have a default defined, but you fail to pass in an argument, you'll see an error.

Let's add a constructor to the DatabaseTable class that sets the $pdo, $table and $primaryKey variables:

```
class DatabaseTable {
    public $pdo;
    public $table;
    public $primaryKey;

    public function __construct($pdo, $table, $primaryKey) {
        $this->pdo = $pdo;
        $this->table = $table;
        $this->primaryKey = $primaryKey;
    }

    // ...
}
```

You'll come across constructors like this frequently if you start using objects and classes regularly, so it's important to understand what's happening here.

 Placing Your Constructor Methods

It's common practice to put the constructor at the top of the class, after variables but before any other methods.

There are two different variables with the same names, which can be confusing at first. The first version is the *argument*, which is defined in the line public function __construct($pdo, $table, $primaryKEy) {. When you create a function argument, the variable is only available inside that specific function and isn't available to be used in other functions in the class.

When the constructor is called, the $pdo instance is sent to it, but we want to make the $pdo instance available to *every* function in the class. The only way to make a variable available to every function inside the class is to make it a class variable like we did above. Instead of setting the class variable from outside the class—for example, $jokesTable->pdo = $pdo;—we want to set it from within the constructor inside the class.

Like before, the $this variable represents the current *instance*, and $this->pdo = $pdo; is doing the same thing as $jokesTable->pdo = $pdo;, only from inside the class. Both $jokesTable and $this reference the same *object*, and making changes to one will be reflected in the other.

You can think of this like the English language. Although you'll always refer to yourself as "I", your friends will use your name. Regardless of whether you're referring to yourself, or someone is referring to you by your name, it's always the same person—you—who's being referred to.

The same thing happens here. $this references the current instance from inside the class, like "I" in English. However, $jokesTable refers to the same instance using its name from outside the class.

Using either $jokesTable->pdo = $pdo from outside the class, or $this->pdo = $pdo; from inside the class, the $pdo class variable will be set and then be available inside any methods when they're called on that instance.

By using a constructor, when the instance is created, two variables *must* be supplied:

```
$jokesTable = new DatabaseTable($pdo, 'jokes', 'id');
```

If you tried to create an instance of the DatabaseTable class without passing it two arguments, it would give you an error, because the two arguments are required for the code to work.

This kind of check ensures the code is robust. It also helps anyone who uses the class, because they'll see an error as soon as they do something wrong.

Type Hinting

If we're trying to make the class foolproof, there's still a problem. What happens if the person using your `DatabaseTable` class gets the order of the arguments wrong? Consider these two examples:

```
$jokesTable = new DatabaseTable('jokes', $pdo, 'id');
```

```
$jokesTable = new DatabaseTable($pdo, 'jokes', 'id');
```

The first could easily be written instead of the second. This is an innocent mistake, and an easy one to make by accident. An error won't be seen until one of the functions in the class is called. For example:

```
$jokesTable = new DatabaseTable('jokes', $pdo, 'id');
$jokes = $jokes->findAll();
```

The code above will result in the error "Call to function prepare on non-object", because the `findAll` function contains the line `$result = $this->query('SELECT * FROM ' . $this->table);`, and the query function has the line `$query = $this->pdo->prepare($sql);`.

Because the order of the constructor arguments is wrong, the `$pdo` variable will actually be set to the string `joke`. The string `joke` does not have a function called `prepare`, which is what causes the error.

The error "Call to function prepare on non-object" doesn't make it clear what went wrong, and it would be difficult for the person who made the mistake to figure it out without looking in depth at your class and examining it line by line.

To help them out, it's better to ensure that the arguments are the correct **type**. PHP is **loosely typed**, meaning that a variable can be any type—such as a string, a number, an array, or an object. Even so, you can enforce types when you create a function. This is particularly useful for constructors, where getting the arguments in the wrong order appears to work. For example, take the following code:

```
$jokesTable = new DatabaseTable('jokes', $pdo);
```

This won't actually cause any errors. The person running this line of code won't know that it's wrong. It's possible to use `if` statements to check the type of each argument, but PHP also provides a nice feature called "type hinting".

Type hinting allows you to specify the type of an argument. The type can be a class name, or one of the basic types, such as string, array or integer.

 ## Type Hinting Compatibility

Type hinting for basic types (numbers strings, arrays—anything that isn't an object) was only introduced in PHP 7. It's possible your web host is still on PHP 5, so be careful when using this feature!

To provide a type hint for an argument, prefix the variable name with the type that the variable should be. For our database class this will be:

```
public function __construct(PDO $pdo, string $table, string
↪ $primaryKey) {
```

This tells PHP to check the types of each argument when they're provided. If the object is constructed with the wrong types now—as in `$jokesTable = new DatabaseTable('jokes', $pdo, 'id');`, for example—PHP will check to see whether the *type* of each argument matches the *hint*. If it doesn't, it will produce an error. The error that's printed in this case is this:

```
Uncaught TypeError: Argument 1 passed to
↪ DatabaseTable::__construct() must be an instance of PDO,
↪ string given
```

This error explains much more clearly what the problem is than "Call to function prepare on non-object", and it prevents the rest of the script from even running. As soon as a mistake is detected, the script is halted so you can fix it. This is a lot better than only getting a vague error message at the point you're trying to call one of the methods on the object!

By using type hinting on constructors like this, you can ensure that the class variables are set to the types you're expecting. This way, when the code `$this->pdo->prepare` is run inside one of the methods in the class, `$this->pdo` *must* be set to an instance of `$pdo` and have a `prepare` method. There's no way for the `$this->pdo` variable to be set to a string, a number, or even not set to anything.

This is known as **defensive programming**, and it's a very useful way of preventing bugs. By stopping variables being set to the wrong type, you can rule out the possibility of many potential bugs.

Private Variables

The class variables and constructor in the `DatabaseTable` class now look like this:

```php
class DatabaseTable {
    public $pdo;
    public $table;
    public $primaryKey;

    public function __construct(PDO $pdo, string $table,
      string $primaryKey) {
        $this->pdo = $pdo;
        $this->table = $table;
        $this->primaryKey = $primaryKey;
    }

    // ...
}
```

When an instance of the class is created, it *must* be passed three arguments, and those three arguments must be of specific types (a $pdo instance, a string and a string).

It's now impossible to construct the class without providing the correct parameters:

```
$jokesTable = new DatabaseTable($pdo, 'jokes', 'id');
```

Any other combination, such as new DatabaseTable($pdo, 'jokes');, or new DatabaseTable('jokes', $pdo, 'id'); or new DatabaseTable(); will display an error. Once one of the methods is called (for example, $jokesTable->findAll();), all of the class variables must have been set to the correct type, which should stop the $pdo variable being set to anything but a real database connection, a PDO instance.

However, the code still has a weak point. There's still a way of making it so the $pdo variable in the class is not a PDO instance.

That's because the variable $pdo is *public*. Like public functions, this means that the variables are accessible from outside the class, and it means the following code is possible:

```
// Correctly create the instance with a database connection
$jokesTable = new DatabaseTable($pdo, 'jokes', 'id');

$jokesTable->pdo = 'a string';

$jokes = $jokesTable->findAll();
```

Although the constructor is ensuring that a valid database connection is being set when the object is created, the code above has overwritten the $pdo class variable between the constructor being executed and the findAll method being called. The $pdo variable in the $jokesTable object has been set to "a string". When the findAll() method runs, $this->pdo->prepare() will throw an error, because $this->pdo is a string, not an object with a prepare method.

Public class variables like these cause problems because they allow the variable to be overwritten from anywhere. Instead, it's good practice to make class variables *private* to prevent these issues:

```php
class DatabaseTable {
    private $pdo;
    private $table;
    private $primaryKey;

    public function __construct(PDO $pdo, string $table, string
    $primaryKey) {
        $this->pdo = $pdo;
        $this->table = $table;
        $this->primaryKey = $primaryKey;
    }

    // …
}
```

When the variables are private, like private functions, they can't be accessed from outside the class (for either reading or writing).

By combining type hints, constructors and private properties, several conditions have been imposed on the class:

1. It's impossible to create an instance of the `DatabaseTable` class without passing it a `$pdo` instance.

2. The first argument must be a valid PDO instance.

3. There's no way to change the `$pdo` variable after it's been set.

As a result of these conditions, when any of the functions (such as `findAll()` or `save()`) are called, the `$pdo`, `$table` and `$primaryKey` variables must be set, and must be of the correct type. When `$this->pdo->prepare()` is called, it won't cause an error, because there's no way that `findAll()` can be called unless the variables are correctly set.

This type of defensive programming can take a little more thinking about—for example, what needs to be public and what needs to be private?—but in all but the most simple projects, it's worth it! By eliminating the conditions for a bug to exist, you can save yourself a lot of bug-tracking time later on.

Using the `DatabaseTable` Class

The final version of the `DatabaseTable` class looks like this:

```php
<?php
class DatabaseTable
{
    private $pdo;
    private $table;
    private $primaryKey;

    public function __construct(PDO $pdo, string $table,
     string $primaryKey)
    {
        $this->pdo = $pdo;
        $this->table = $table;
        $this->primaryKey = $primaryKey;
    }

    private function query($sql, $parameters = [])
    {
        $query = $this->pdo->prepare($sql);
        $query->execute($parameters);
        return $query;
    }

    public function total()
    {
        $query = $this->query('SELECT COUNT(*) FROM
        `' . $this->table . '`');
        $row = $query->fetch();
        return $row[0];
    }
```

```php
public function findById($value)
{
    $query = 'SELECT * FROM `' . $this->table . '` WHERE `' .
    $this->primaryKey . '` = :value';

    $parameters = [
        'value' => $value
    ];

    $query = $this->query($query, $parameters);

    return $query->fetch();
}

private function insert($fields)
{
    $query = 'INSERT INTO `' . $this->table . '` (';

    foreach ($fields as $key => $value) {
        $query .= '`' . $key . '`,';
    }

    $query = rtrim($query, ',');

    $query .= ') VALUES (';


    foreach ($fields as $key => $value) {
        $query .= ':' . $key . ',';
    }

    $query = rtrim($query, ',');

    $query .= ')';

    $fields = $this->processDates($fields);

    $this->query($query, $fields);
}
```

```php
private function update($fields)
{
    $query = ' UPDATE `' . $this->table .'` SET ';

    foreach ($fields as $key => $value) {
        $query .= '`' . $key . '` = :' . $key . ',';
    }

    $query = rtrim($query, ',');

    $query .= ' WHERE `' . $this->primaryKey . '` =
    :primaryKey';

    // Set the :primaryKey variable
    $fields['primaryKey'] = $fields['id'];

    $fields = $this->processDates($fields);

    $this->query($query, $fields);
}

public function delete($id)
{
    $parameters = [':id' => $id];

    $this->query('DELETE FROM `' . $this->table . '` WHERE
    `' . $this->primaryKey . '` = :id', $parameters);
}

public function findAll()
{
    $result = $this->query('SELECT * FROM ' .
    $this->table);

    return $result->fetchAll();
}

private function processDates($fields)
{
```

```php
        foreach ($fields as $key => $value) {
            if ($value instanceof DateTime) {
                $fields[$key] = $value->format('Y-m-d');
            }
        }

        return $fields;
    }

    public function save($record)
    {
        try {
            if ($record[$this->primaryKey] == '') {
                $record[$this->primaryKey] = null;
            }
            $this->insert($record);
        } catch (PDOException $e) {
            $this->update($record);
        }
    }
}
```

Let's save this in its own file, `DatabaseTable.php`. Remember to put the `<?php` tag at the top of the file.

 Omitting the Closing Tag from Your Files

Whenever you create a PHP file, you need to remember to put the PHP code inside PHP tags. However, the closing tag is optional, and it's actually better to omit it if the file only contains PHP code.

This is because, if there are any whitespace characters (blank lines, tabs or spaces) at the end of the file after the closing PHP tag `?>`, they'll be sent to the browser, which isn't what you want to happen. Instead, it's better to prevent this from happening by omitting the `?>` tag entirely. By leaving out the closing PHP tag, the whitespace will be interpreted on the server by PHP, and ignored, rather than being sent as part of the HTML code to the browser.

One of the most useful features of using classes is that, once a class has been written, it can be used as many times as you like. And each time you use it, by creating an *instance*, that instance can store different values of the class variables. For example, it's possible to use the `DatabaseTable` class to interact with the `joke` table and the `author` table.

Because each *instance* has its own version of the variables, we can have one version of the class where `$table` is set to `joke` and one version where `$table` is set to `author`:

```
$jokesTable = new DatabaseTable($pdo, 'joke', 'id');
$authorsTable = new DatabaseTable($pdo, 'author', id');

// Find the joke with the ID 123
$joke = $jokesTable->findById(123);

// Find the author with the ID 34
$author = $authorsTable->findById(34);
```

Because the class variable `$table` is different, a different table will be used for each of the instances.

When `$author = $authorsTable->findById(34)` is called, `$this->table` is equal to `author`, so the query that runs will be `SELECT * FROM author` …, whereas when `$joke = $jokesTable->findById(123);` is called, `$this->table` is set to `joke`, so the query that runs is `SELET * FROM joke` ….

This means the `DatabaseTable` class can now be used to insert, update or find records from any table in the database by constructing an instance with the table name in the constructor!

Updating the Controller to Use the Class

Now that we have the complete `DatabaseTable` class, let's use it in the controllers.

Firstly, delete `includes/DatabaseFunctions.php`. All our functions are now stored inside the class in `classes/DatabaseTable.php`.

Secondly, let's update `public/jokes.php` to use the new class:

```php
<?php

try {
    include __DIR__ . '/../includes/DatabaseConnection.php';
    include __DIR__ . '/../classes/DatabaseTable.php';

    $jokesTable = new DatabaseTable($pdo, 'joke', 'id');
    $authorsTable = new DatabaseTable($pdo, 'author', 'id');

    $result = $jokesTable->findAll();

    $jokes = [];
    foreach ($result as $joke) {
        $author = $authorsTable->findById($joke['authorId']);

        $jokes[] = [
            'id' => $joke['id'],
            'joketext' => $joke['joketext'],
            'jokedate' => $joke['jokedate'],
            'name' => $author['name'],
            'email' => $author['email']
        ];
    }

    $title = 'Joke list';

    $totalJokes = $jokesTable->total();

    ob_start();

    include __DIR__ . '/../templates/jokes.html.php';

    $output = ob_get_clean();
} catch (PDOException $e) {
    $title = 'An error has occurred';

    $output = 'Database error: ' . $e->getMessage() . ' in '
    . $e->getFile() . ':' . $e->getLine();
```

```
}

include  __DIR__ . '/../templates/layout.html.php';
```

This controller is better. We no longer have to provide the table name and $pdo instance to each of the functions—total, findById and findAll. The functions can each be called on either the $jokesTable variable or the $authorsTable variable to run the relevant query on either table.

Let's do the same thing with our other controllers.

Here's the updated deletejoke.php:

```php
<?php
try {
    include __DIR__ . '/../includes/DatabaseConnection.php';
    include __DIR__ . '/../classes/DatabaseTable.php';

    $jokesTable = new DatabaseTable($pdo, 'joke', 'id');

    $jokesTable->delete($_POST['id']);

    header('location: jokes.php');
} catch (PDOException $e) {
    $title = 'An error has occurred';

    $output = 'Unable to connect to the database server: ' .
     $e->getMessage() . ' in ' .
    $e->getFile() . ':' . $e->getLine();
}

include  __DIR__ . '/../templates/layout.html.php';
```

And editjoke.php:

```php
<?php
```

```php
try {
    include __DIR__ . '/../includes/DatabaseConnection.php';
    include __DIR__ . '/../classes/DatabaseTable.php';

    $jokesTable = new DatabaseTable($pdo, 'joke', 'id');

    if (isset($_POST['joke'])) {
        $joke = $_POST['joke'];
        $joke['jokedate'] = new DateTime();
        $joke['authorId'] = 1;

        $jokesTable->save($joke);

        header('location: jokes.php');
    } else {
        if (isset($_GET['id'])) {
            $joke = $jokesTable->findById($_GET['id']);
        }

        $title = 'Edit joke';

        ob_start();

        include __DIR__ . '/../templates/editjoke.html.php';

        $output = ob_get_clean();
    }
} catch (PDOException $e) {
    $title = 'An error has occurred';

    $output = 'Database error: ' . $e->getMessage() . ' in '
      . $e->getFile() . ':' . $e->getLine();
}

include __DIR__ . '/../templates/layout.html.php';
```

This example can befoound in *OOP-DatabaseTable*

Now that you're familiar with objects and classes, and you know that repeated code is a very bad thing for a programmer, it's time to start tidying up these controller scripts.

While making the last few changes, you would have found yourself making similar changes in multiple locations. As I mentioned earlier in this book, the DRY (Don't Repeat Yourself) principle states that it's bad practice to have repeated code.

DRY

Carefully examine the different controllers. What is actually different about them?

Each of the controllers follows this basic pattern:

```php
<?php
try {
    /*
        - include some required files
    */
    include __DIR__ . '/../includes/DatabaseConnection.php';
    include __DIR__ . '/../classes/DatabasetabaseTable.php';

    /*

        - create one or more database table instances
    */
    $jokesTable = new DatabaseTable($pdo, 'joke', 'id');

    /*
        - Do something that's unique to this particular page
            and create the $title and $output variables
    */
} catch (PDOException $e) {

    /*

        - Handle errors if they occur
    */
```

```
    $title = 'An error has occurred';

    $output = 'Database error: ' . $e->getMessage() . '
    in ' . $e->getFile() . ':' . $e->getLine();
}
    /*


        - Load the template file
    */
include __DIR__ . '/../templates/layout.html.php';
```

Using this approach, if you wanted to rename the `DatabaseConnection.php` file, you'd have to go through each controller to use the new name. Similarly, if you wanted to change the layout file, you'd need to edit each controller separately.

All that really changes for each controller is the middle section that creates the `$output` and `$title` variables for the layout to use.

Rather than having different files for each controller, it's possible to write a single controller that handles each *action* as a method. That way, we can have one file that handles all the parts that are common to each page, and methods in a class that handle the individual parts.

Creating a Controller Class

The first thing we could do is move the code for each controller into a method in a class. Firstly create a class called `JokeController`.

As this is a special type of class, we won't store it in the `classes` directory. Instead, create a new directory called `controllers` and save this as `JokeController`:

```
class JokeController {

}
```

Before moving the relevant code into methods, let's consider what variables this class needs. Any variables required by the various actions will need to be class variables so that they can be defined once and used in any of the methods.

In this case, there are only two variables that are common to the controllers: `$authorsTable` and `$jokesTable`. Add these two variables to the class:

```
class JokeController {
    private $authorsTable;
    private $jokesTable;
}
```

Like the `DatabaseTable` class, it's good practice to make these variables private so they can only be changed from within the class. Also, like the `DatabaseTable` class, you'll need a constructor so that the two variables can be set when the class is instantiated:

```
class JokeController {
    private $authorsTable;
    private $jokesTable;

    public function __construct(DatabaseTable $jokesTable,
     DatabaseTable $authorsTable) {
        $this->jokesTable = $jokesTable;
        $this->authorsTable = $authorsTable;
    }
}
```

Add the `listJokes` method first. Copy/paste the relevant section from `jokes.php`, but remember to use the class variables `$jokesTable` and `$authorsTable`, rather than including the existing code from `jokes.php` which creates them in the same block. We'll create the instances once and pass them into the controller:

```
public function list() {
    $result = $this->jokesTable->findAll();
```

```
$jokes = [];
foreach ($result as $joke) {
    $author =
    $this->authorsTable->findById($joke['authorId']);

    $jokes[] = [
        'id' => $joke['id'],
        'joketext' => $joke['joketext'],
        'jokedate' => $joke['jokedate'],
        'name' => $author['name'],
        'email' => $author['email']
    ];

}

$title = 'Joke list';

$totalJokes = $this->jokesTable->total();

ob_start();

include __DIR__ . '/../templates/jokes.html.php';

$output = ob_get_clean();

}
```

Before getting this working, let's add the other methods for the corresponding editjoke and deletejoke pages, along with the home page from index.php:

```
public function home() {
    $title = 'Internet Joke Database';

    ob_start();

    include __DIR__ . '/../templates/home.html.php';

    $output = ob_get_clean();
```

```php
}

public function delete() {
    $this->jokesTable->delete($_POST['id']);

    header('location: jokes.php');
}


public function edit() {
    if (isset($_POST['joke'])) {

        $joke = $_POST['joke'];
        $joke['jokedate'] = new DateTime();
        $joke['authorId'] = 1;

        $this->jokesTable->save($joke);

        header('location: jokes.php');

    }
    else {

        if (isset($_GET['id'])) {
            $joke = $this->jokesTable->findById($_GET['id']);
        }

        $title = 'Edit joke';

        ob_start();

        include __DIR__ . '/../templates/editjoke.html.php';

        $output = ob_get_clean();
    }
}
```

If you examine the controller code closely, you might notice that, regardless of how we eventually use this class, it's not going to be very useful. That's because the $title and $output variables can never be used in layout.html.php. Once either the home, edit or list methods are run, the $title and $output variables, along with their contents, are lost.

To make those variables available to the code that calls the methods, we'll use the return keyword. We already used return in the DatabaseTable class. Each time a method was run, it was able to send some data back to the place it was called from. The findAll method returns an array of all the records in the table.

It would be possible to return the $output variable using return $output, but when layout.html.php is loaded, it will need both the $output and the $title variables.

Like the findAll method, the individual controller methods can return arrays:

```php
public function home() {
    $title = 'Internet Joke Database';

    ob_start();

    include __DIR__ . '/../templates/home.html.php';

    $output = ob_get_clean();

    return ['output' => $output, 'title' => $title];
}

public function list() {
    $result = $this->jokesTable->findAll();

    $jokes = [];
    foreach ($result as $joke) {
        $author =
        $this->authorsTable->findById($joke['authorId']);

        $jokes[] = [
            'id' => $joke['id'],
            'joketext' => $joke['joketext'],
            'jokedate' => $joke['jokedate'],
```

```php
                'name' => $author['name'],
                'email' => $author['email']
            ];

        }

        $title = 'Joke list';

        $totalJokes = $this->jokesTable->total();

        ob_start();

        include __DIR__ . '/../templates/jokes.html.php';

        $output = ob_get_clean();

        return ['output' => $output, 'title' => $title];

    }

public function edit() {
    if (isset($_POST['joke'])) {

        $joke = $_POST['joke'];
        $joke['jokedate'] = new DateTime();
        $joke['authorId'] = 1;

        $this->jokesTable->save($joke);

        header('location: jokes.php');

    }
    else {

        if (isset($_GET['id'])) {
            $joke = $this->jokesTable->findById($_GET['id']);
        }

        $title = 'Edit joke';
```

```
        ob_start();

        include __DIR__ . '/../templates/editjoke.html.php';

        $output = ob_get_clean();

        return ['output' => $output, 'title' => $title];
    }
}
```

The `return` value of each of the functions is an array that contains the `output` and `title` variables. Now, when one of the methods is called, it will return the output and title strings, which can then be used.

Importantly, because each method returns data in the same format (an array with `output` and `title` keys), no matter which of the methods is called, we'll have an array with two variables.

Until now, we've had each different page using its own file: `index.php`, `jokes.php`, `editjoke.php`, and `deletejoke.php`.

Single Entry Point

With the controller complete, we can now write a single file to handle any page. Importantly, this single file can contain all the code that was previously repeated in each of the files. As a starting point, here's a very crude way of using the new class:

```
<?php
try {
    include __DIR__ . '/../includes/DatabaseConnection.php';
    include __DIR__ . '/../classes/DatabaseTable.php';
    include __DIR__ . '/../controllers/JokeController.php';

    $jokesTable = new DatabaseTable($pdo, 'joke', 'id');
    $authorsTable = new DatabaseTable($pdo, 'author', 'id');
```

```
    $jokeController = new JokeController($jokesTable,
    $authorsTable);

    if (isset($_GET['edit'])) {
        $page = $jokeController->edit();
    } elseif (isset($_GET['delete'])) {
        $page = $jokeController->delete();
    } elseif (isset($_GET['list'])) {
        $page = $jokeController->list();
    } else {
        $page = $jokeController->home();
    }

    $title = $page['title'];
    $output = $page['output'];
} catch (PDOException $e) {
    $title = 'An error has occurred';

    $output = 'Database error: ' . $e->getMessage() . ' in '
      . $e->getFile() . ':' . $e->getLine();
}

include __DIR__ . '/../templates/layout.html.php';
```

You can find this example in OOP-EntryPoint

Save this over the top of index.php in the public directory and visit the home page at http://http://192.168.10.10/. If everything is correct, the page will display as expected.

While you have the public directory open, delete jokes.php, editjoke.php and deletejoke.php. We've moved the relevant code from these files into JokeController, so they're no longer needed.

The new index.php page follows the same structure as each of our controllers. A lot of this code looks familiar, but let's go through the new lines individually.

```
$jokeController = new JokeController($jokesTable,
    $authorsTable);
```

This creates an instance of the JokeController class that we just wrote. When the constructor is called, it's passed the instances of DatabaseTable, $jokesTable, and $authorsTable.

```
if (isset($_GET['edit'])) {
    $page = $jokeController->edit();
}

else if (isset($_GET['delete'])) {
    $page = $jokeController->delete();
}

else if (isset($_GET['list'])) {
        $page = $jokeController->list();
}

else {
    $page = $jokeController->home();
}
```

This if … else if block is the clever part. These if statements examine the $_GET variables to determine which of the methods in the JokeController class is called. Because of the else clause, at least one of these blocks is guaranteed to get executed.

Regardless of how this page is accessed, the $page variable will be created, and will contain two values—the page title, in the title key, and the page contents, stored under the output key.

The final part creates the $title and $output variables for use in the template by reading them out of the newly created $page array.

```
$title = $page['title'];
```

```
$output = $page['output'];
```

To check all this works, open up the home page in your browser at `http://192.168.10.10/`.

Unfortunately, if you click any of the links—for example the **Jokes List** link—you'll see an error.

That's because there are no longer individual pages that represent each *page* of the website. Now, everything is diverted through `index.php`. To access any of the pages on the website, you'll have to type `index.php` followed by a relevant URL variable.

To access the "Joke List" page, you'll have to visit `http://192.168.10.10/index.php?list`.

This is called a **single entry point** or **front controller**.

We'll have to go through and change all links to the old pages to go via `index.php`, but before we do that, let's do some tidying up.

I already called the new `index.php` crude, because it's not very efficient. Every time you want to add a page to the website, you'll need to do two things:

1. add the method in `JokeController`
2. add the relevant `else if` block in `index.php`

You've probably already noticed that the GET variable name maps exactly to the name of the function:

- when `$_GET['edit']` is set, the `edit` function is called
- when `$_GET['list']` is set, the `list` function is called

This seems a bit redundant. PHP allows some cool stuff. For example, you can do this:

```
$function = 'edit';
```

```php
$jokeController->$function();
```

This will evaluate `$function` to `edit` and actually call
`$jokeController->edit()`. We can utilize this feature to read the GET variable
and call the method with that name.

Commonly, a function in a controller is called an **action**. We could use the GET
variable `action` to call the relevant function on the controller.
`index.php?action=edit` would call the edit function, `index.php?action=delete`
would call delete, and so on. The code for this is remarkably simple:

```php
<?php
try {
    include __DIR__ . '/../includes/DatabaseConnection.php';
    include __DIR__ . '/../classes/DatabaseTable.php';
    include __DIR__ . '/../controllers/JokeController.php';

    $jokesTable = new DatabaseTable($pdo, 'joke', 'id');
    $authorsTable = new DatabaseTable($pdo, 'author', 'id');

    $jokeController = new JokeController($jokesTable,
     $authorsTable);

    $action = $_GET['action'] ?? 'home';

    $page = $jokeController->$action();

    $title = $page['title'];
    $output = $page['output'];
} catch (PDOException $e) {
    $title = 'An error has occurred';

    $output = 'Database error: ' . $e->getMessage() . ' in '
      . $e->getFile() . ':' . $e->getLine();
}

include __DIR__ . '/../templates/layout.html.php';
```

The whole `if … else` block that selects the relevant action has been replaced with two lines:

```
$action = $_GET['action'] ?? 'home';
$page = $jokeController->$action();
```

The first line utilizes the confusingly named "null coalescing operator" I introduced in Chapter 6. This reads the GET variable called `action`. If it's set, `action` is read from the GET variable, and if it's not, `$action` is set to "home".

The second line calls the relevant method on the `$jokeController` object.

If you open up your browser and visit `index.php?action=listjokes`, you'll see the list of jokes. If you visit `index.php` without an `action` set, you'll see the home page.

The advantage of this approach is that, to add a new page to the website, all we need to do is add a method to the `JokeController` class and link to `index.php`, supplying the relevant action variable.

Now that the URL structure of the website has changed completely, we'll need to go through each page and update any links, form actions, or redirects.

Firstly, `layout.html.php`:

```
<!doctype html>
<html>
    <head>
        <meta charset="utf-8">
        <link rel="stylesheet" href="jokes.css">
        <title><?=$title?></title>
    </head>
    <body>
        <nav>
            <header>
                <h1>Internet Joke Database</h1>
            </header>
            <ul>
```

```
                <li><a href="index.php">
                Home</a></li>
                <li><a href="index.php?action=list">
                Jokes List</a></li>
                <li><a href="index.php?action=edit">
                Add a new Joke</a></li>
            </ul>
        </nav>

        <main>
            <?=$output?>
        </main>

        <footer>
            &copy; IJDB 2017
        </footer>
    </body>
</html>
```

Now open `jokes.html.php`, change the "Edit" link and form action for deleting:

```
<p><?=$totalJokes?> jokes have been submitted
to the Internet Joke Database.</p>

<?php foreach ($jokes as $joke): ?>
<blockquote>
    <p>
    <?=htmlspecialchars($joke['joketext'],
    ENT_QUOTES, 'UTF-8')?>

 (by <a
↪ href="mailto:<?=htmlspecialchars($joke['email'],
    ENT_QUOTES, 'UTF-8'); ?>">
 <?=htmlspecialchars($joke['name'], ENT_QUOTES, 'UTF-8');
↪ ?></a> on
<?php
$date = new DateTime($joke['jokedate']);
```

```
echo $date->format('jS F Y');
?>)
 <a
↪ href="index.php?action=edit&id=<?=$joke['id']?>">
    Edit</a>
    <form action="index.php?action=delete" method="post">
    <input type="hidden" name="id"
        value="<?=$joke['id']?>">
    <input type="submit" value="Delete">
    </form>
    </p>
</blockquote>
<?php endforeach; ?>
```

Finally, change the two redirects in `JokeController` from `header('location: jokes.php');` to `header('location: index.php?action=list');`.

You can find this example in *OOP-EntryPoint2*

Keeping it DRY

You're nearly done! A large proportion of your PHP code is now neatly organized into methods inside classes, and you can quickly add new pages to the website by simply creating a new method inside `JokeController`. Before we continue, let's quickly remove some of the remaining repeated code.

If you examine `JokeController`, most of the methods perform the same set of steps. The `edit` method contains this code:

```
ob_start();

include __DIR__ . '/../templates/editjoke.html.php';

$output = ob_get_clean();

return ['output' => $output, 'title' => $title];
```

The home method contains this code:

```
ob_start();

include __DIR__ . '/../templates/home.html.php';

$output = ob_get_clean();

return ['output' => $output, 'title' => $title];
```

The list method contains this code:

```
ob_start();

include __DIR__ . '/../templates/jokes.html.php';

$output = ob_get_clean();

return ['output' => $output, 'title' => $title];
```

These blocks of code are all very similar. Some of the lines are identical. As always, whenever you see repeated code like this, it's worth considering how it can be removed.

Rather than having each action include this block of code, it would be simpler to have the action provide a file name—such as home.html.php—and then have it loaded from within index.php.

To make that change, firstly open up index.php and change it to this:

```
<?php
try {
    include __DIR__ . '/../includes/DatabaseConnection.php';
    include __DIR__ . '/../classes/DatabaseTable.php';
    include __DIR__ . '/../controllers/JokeController.php';
```

```
    $jokesTable = new DatabaseTable($pdo, 'joke', 'id');
    $authorsTable = new DatabaseTable($pdo, 'author', 'id');

    $jokeController = new JokeController($jokesTable,
     $authorsTable);

    $action = $_GET['action'] ?? 'home';

    $page = $jokeController->$action();

    $title = $page['title'];

    ob_start();

    include __DIR__ . '/../templates/' . $page['template'];

    $output = ob_get_clean();
} catch (PDOException $e) {
    $title = 'An error has occurred';

    $output = 'Database error: ' . $e->getMessage() . ' in '
     . $e->getFile() . ':' . $e->getLine();
}

include  __DIR__ . '/../templates/layout.html.php';
```

I've moved the three repeated lines from the individual methods into `index.php`. `index.php` now expects the `$page` variable to provide a `template` key. Let's amend each of the controller actions to provide it. The controller actions will no longer provide the `$output` variable, but instead just a filename for `index.php` to include.

The `home` method:

```
public function home() {
    $title = 'Internet Joke Database';

    return ['template' => 'home.html.php', 'title' =>
```

```
        $title];
}
```

The list method:

```
public function list() {
    $result = $this->jokesTable->findAll();

    $jokes = [];
    foreach ($result as $joke) {
        $author = $this->authorsTable->
            findById($joke['authorId']);

        $jokes[] = [
            'id' => $joke['id'],
            'joketext' => $joke['joketext'],
            'jokedate' => $joke['jokedate'],
            'name' => $author['name'],
            'email' => $author['email']
        ];
    }

    $title = 'Joke list';

    $totalJokes = $this->jokesTable->total();

    return ['template' => 'jokes.html.php', '
    title' => $title];
}
```

The edit method:

```
public function edit() {
    if (isset($_POST['joke'])) {

        $joke = $_POST['joke'];
        $joke['jokedate'] = new DateTime();
```

```
        $joke['authorId'] = 1;

        $this->jokesTable->save($joke);

        header('location: index.php?action=list');
    }
    else {

        if (isset($_GET['id'])) {
            $joke = $this->jokesTable->findById($_GET['id']);
        }

        $title = 'Edit joke';

        return ['template' => 'editjoke.html.php',
        'title' => $title];
    }
}
```

Each action now provides the name of a template that gets loaded in `index.php`. We've saved ourselves from needing to repeat the output buffer and `include` lines.

However, if you try the code above, only the home page will work. If you try viewing the list of jokes, you'll get an error:

```
Notice: Undefined variable: totalJokes in
↪ /home/vagrant/Code/Project/templates/jokes.html.php on line 2
```

The reason for this error is that `jokes.html.php` is now being included from `index.php` and `index.php` does not include the variable `$totalJokes`.

We need a way to get the `$totalJokes` and `$jokes` variables into `index.php`.

On first glance, you might think to do it in the `return` statement, the same way that we did with the `title`, `output`, and later `template` variables:

```
return ['template' => 'jokes.html.php',
'title' => $title,
'totalJokes' => $totalJokes,
'jokes' => $jokes];
```

And then recreate the variables in `index.php`:

```
$action = $_GET['action'] ?? 'home';

$page = $jokeController->$action();

$title = $page['title'];

$totalJokes = $page['totalJokes'];

$jokes = $page['jokes'];
ob_start();

include __DIR__ . '/../templates/' . $page['template'];

$output = ob_get_clean();
```

If you try this, the jokes list page will work as expected. However, as soon as you navigate to another page, you'll get errors. For example, the "Edit Joke" page requires a variable called `joke`, and it doesn't provide the variables for `totalJokes` or `jokes`.

A very messy solution would be to have each method in the controller return every single variable that's needed, but leave the array values blank when they're not needed. The edit `return` statement would then end up looking like this:

```
return ['template' => 'jokes.html.php',
'title' => $title,
'totalJokes' => '',
'jokes' => '',
'joke' => $joke];
```

This is obviously not a viable solution. Each time we add a template that requires a variable with a new name, we'd need to amend every single controller method to provide an empty string for that variable and then amend `index.php` to set it!

Template Variables

Instead, we'll solve the problem in the same way we did for the `return` statement. Each method will supply an *array* of variables.

The `list` return statement will now look like this:

```
return ['template' => 'jokes.html.php',
    'title' => $title,
    'variables' => [
        'totalJokes' => $totalJokes,
        'jokes' => $jokes
    ]
];
```

This is called a **multi-dimensional array**: there's an array inside an array. In this case, the `variables` key maps to a second array that contains the keys `totalJokes` and `jokes`.

Although the code is slightly more difficult to read, the advantage of this approach is that each controller method can provide a different array in the `variables` key. The `editJoke` page can use this return statement:

```
return ['template' => 'editjoke.html.php',
    'title' => $title,
    'variables' => [
        'joke' => $joke ?? null
    ]
];
```

In the code above, the joke array key is mapped to $joke ?? null. You were probably expecting to see 'joke' => $joke. However, because the joke variable may or may not have been set by the code above, the joke key is set either to the contents of the joke variable or to null. null is an *empty value.*

Both the list and edit controller actions now consistently return an array with the keys template, title and variables.

We can now use the variables array in index.php. The simplest way to achieve this would be to create a variable called $variables inside index.php, in the same way we did with $title:

```
$title = $page['title'];

$variables = $page['variables'];

ob_start();

include __DIR__ . '/../templates/' . $page['template'];

$output = ob_get_clean();
```

Each template (such as jokes.html.php) now has access to the $variables array, and could read values from it—for example, by replacing this:

```
<p><?=$totalJokes?> jokes have been submitted to
↪ the Internet Joke Database.</p>
```

... with this:

```
<p><?=$variables['totalJokes']?> jokes have been
↪ submitted to the Internet Joke Database.</p>
```

This solution works, but it means opening up and changing every template file. A simpler alternative is to create the variables that are required.

Luckily, PHP provides a method of doing exactly that. The extract function can be used to create variables from an array:

```php
$array ['hello' => 'world'];

extract($array);

echo $hello; // prints "world"
```

A variable is created for any key in the array, and its value is set to the corresponding value. We can use extract to create the relevant template variables in index.php:

```php
$action = $_GET['action'] ?? 'home';

$page = $jokeController->$action();

$title = $page['title'];

if (isset($page['variables'])) {
    extract($page['variables']);
}

ob_start();

include __DIR__ . '/../templates/' . $page['template'];

$output = ob_get_clean();
```

You can find this example in *OOP-EntryPoint3*.

If $page['variables'] is an array that's come from the list method, variables called totalJokes and jokes will be created. If it was created by the edit method, a single variable named joke will be created.

I've surrounded the extract call with if (isset($page['variables'])), because some methods, like the home method, may not need to provide any methods to the template.

Be Careful With Extract

Everything is working perfectly, and we've managed to remove the repeated code from the controller's methods. Unfortunately, we're not quite done yet.

One of the biggest problems with `extract` is that it creates variables in the current scope. Take another look at this block of code:

```php
$action = $_GET['action'] ?? 'home';

$page = $jokeController->$action();

$title = $page['title'];

if (isset($page['variables'])) {
    extract($page['variables']);
}

ob_start();

include __DIR__ . '/../templates/' . $page['template'];
```

What would happen if the array `$page['variables']` contained the keys `page` and `title`? The `$title` and `$page` variables would be overwritten! It's likely the overwritten `$page` variable would not be an array with a key called `template` that contains the name of a template file.

If the return statement from a controller action happened to include a key called `page` in the `variables` array, it would prevent that controller action from loading a template.

It is possible to tell the extract function not to overwrite variables, but then if the template is expecting a variable called `$page`, it's going to be given the wrong information.

A very simple solution to this is moving the code that loads the template into its own function. Amend index.php to this:

```php
<?php
function loadTemplate($templateFileName, $variables = [])
{
    extract($variables);

    ob_start();
    include __DIR__ . '/../templates/' . $templateFileName;

    return ob_get_clean();
}

try {
    include __DIR__ . '/../includes/DatabaseConnection.php';
    include __DIR__ . '/../classes/DatabaseTable.php';
    include __DIR__ . '/../controllers/JokeController.php';

    $jokesTable = new DatabaseTable($pdo, 'joke', 'id');
    $authorsTable = new DatabaseTable($pdo, 'author', 'id');

    $jokeController = new JokeController($jokesTable,
    $authorsTable);

    $action = $_GET['action'] ?? 'home';

    $page = $jokeController->$action();

    $title = $page['title'];

    if (isset($page['variables'])) {
        $output = loadTemplate($page['template'],
            $page['variables']);
    } else {
        $output = loadTemplate($page['template']);
    }
} catch (PDOException $e) {
    $title = 'An error has occurred';

    $output = 'Database error: ' . $e->getMessage() . ' in '
    . $e->getFile() . ':' . $e->getLine();
```

```
}

include __DIR__ . '/../templates/layout.html.php';
```

If the variables array does contain keys called page or title, placing the code for loading a template in its own function (loadTemplate) means the existing variables won't be overwritten, because they don't exist inside the function's scope.

In this chapter, I showed you how to use object-oriented programming to break up the code further and reduce repetition. We also began to add a clearer structure to the controller code. In the next chapter, I'll show you how to make index.php usable with other controllers, so the code above doesn't need to be repeated.

Chapter

9

Creating an Extensible Framework

Now that you're able to write a controller with methods, and call those methods from `index.php`, the next step is to add the rest of the pages for managing the website. Currently, we can add jokes to the database through `index.php` by specifying an `action` URL parameter. However, a real website will need to do considerably more than handle basic database operations for a single table.

The next extension of the website will be allowing users to register as authors and post their own jokes. However, before we do that I'll show you how to write a modern, flexible framework to build upon. By the end of this chapter, you'll have the foundation for building any website, and you'll have a good understanding of the techniques and concepts used by professional PHP developers.

We're not going to add any new features. Instead, I'm going to show you how the code can be organized so that it can be reused on each website you build.

In the last chapter, we ended with this code in `index.php`:

```php
<?php
function loadTemplate($templateFileName, $variables = [])
{
    extract($variables);

    ob_start();
    include __DIR__ . '/../templates/' . $templateFileName;

    return ob_get_clean();
}

try {
    include __DIR__ . '/../includes/DatabaseConnection.php';
    include __DIR__ . '/../classes/DatabaseTable.php';
    include __DIR__ . '/../controllers/JokeController.php';

    $jokesTable = new DatabaseTable($pdo, 'joke', 'id');
    $authorsTable = new DatabaseTable($pdo, 'author', 'id');

    $jokeController = new JokeController($jokesTable,
     $authorsTable);

    $action = $_GET['action'] ?? 'home';

    $page = $jokeController->$action();

    $title = $page['title'];

    if (isset($page['variables'])) {
        $output = loadTemplate($page['template'],
            $page['variables']);
    } else {
        $output = loadTemplate($page['template']);
    }
} catch (PDOException $e) {
    $title = 'An error has occurred';

    $output = 'Database error: ' . $e->getMessage() . ' in '
```

```
      . $e->getFile() . ':' . $e->getLine();
}

include __DIR__ . '/../templates/layout.html.php';
```

This lets us call any of the functions in the `JokeController` class by specifying the `action` URL parameter—for example, by linking to or visiting `index.php?action=list`.

Search Engines

Before we make any structural changes to the code, we need to do a little housekeeping. In PHP, functions are not case sensitive. `list` is treated exactly the same way as `LIST`. Due to case insensitivity, visiting `index.php?action=list` will display the page, but so will `index.php?action=LIST` or `index.php?action=List`. This may seem like a good thing, as people will be able to mistype the URL and still see the correct page. However, this feature can also cause problems for search engines.

Some search engines will see these two URLs as two entirely different pages, even if they display the exact same content. Both `index.php?action=LIST` and `index.php?action=list` will appear in search results. You might think "Great, more of my pages will appear in search results!" But search engines generally dislike "duplicate content", either ranking it lower or ignoring it altogether. Would you prefer one result on the first page or two results potentially much further down in the search pages?

There are several ways to fix this. You can tell search engines to ignore certain pages. Or you can tell them which is the "canonical" (primary) version. But this can be difficult to manage on larger sites, and it's usually simpler to enforce strict URLs. A common way to do this is forcing all URLs to lowercase.

Forcing URLs to lowercase is possible using a simple piece of PHP code, which detects whether or not the user entered a lowercase URL:

```php
<?php

$action = $_GET['action'];

if ($action == strtolower($action)) {
    $jokeController->$action();
} else {
    echo 'Sorry that page does not exist.';
}
```

This code compares `$action` to a lowercase version of `$action`. The `strtolower` function converts any string to lowercase: `LISTJOKES`, `listJokes` or `listjokes` all become `listjokes`. By comparing the original `$action` to the lowercase version, it's possible to work out whether or not someone came to the page using a lowercase value for `$action`. If they didn't, an error is displayed. Visitors and search engines will only see the content on the lowercase version of the URL.

While doing this will prevent duplicate content and protect your search engine ranking, it's not very helpful for users who accidentally mistype the URL. Luckily, we can get the best of both worlds by redirecting non-lowercase pages to their lowercase equivalents.

We've already used the `header` function to redirect people to different pages. We can also use the `header` function to send all uppercase URLs to their lowercase equivalents:

```php
<?php

$action = $_GET['action'];

if ($action == strtolower($action)) {
    $jokeController->$action();
} else {
    header('location: index.php?action=' . strtolower($action));
}
```

Now anyone who visits `index.php?action=LISTJOKES` or
`index.php?action=listJokes` will be redirected to
`index.php?action=listjokes`. However, there's one more thing we need to do.
There are two types of redirection, **temporary** and **permanent**. To tell search
engines not to list the page, you need to tell them the redirection is permanent.

This is done with an "HTTP response code". You've probably come across at least
one of these while browsing the web. The code 404 means "Not found". Each
time a page is sent to the browser, a response code is sent along with it to tell the
browser and search engines how to treat the page. To tell the browser that a
redirect is permanent, you need to send the code 301. PHP has a function called
`http_response_code` that can be used to send the 301 response code along with
the redirect:

```php
<?php
$action = $_GET['action'];

if ($action == strtolower($action)) {
    $jokeController->$action();
} else {
    http_response_code(301);
    header('location: index.php?action=' . strtolower($action));
}
```

HTTP Response Codes

There are many different HTTP response codes you can use. 404 is particularly
useful when you display an error message, as this will stop the page appearing in
search results and prevent the page from going into the browser's history. You don't
generally want "Sorry, the product you requested is no longer available" appearing
in search engines. You can even change the HTTP response code to 404 to get
search engines to unlist pages that are no longer relevant.

A complete list of response codes and their meaning can be found on the W3.org
website[1].

[1.] https://www.w3.org/Protocols/rfc2616/rfc2616-sec10.html

Make Things Generic

In PHP and any other programming language, if you can make a piece of code *generic* and able to cope with different use cases, it's generally considered *better*, because it's more flexible. If you can reuse existing code, it saves you from needing to write similar code repeatedly. This is the approach we took with the `DatabaseTable` class. Rather than writing similar code elsewhere in our application, the `DatabaseTable` class can be used any time we need to interact with the database.

The `index.php` code we already have allows any function to be called in the `JokeController` class by specifying the `action` URL parameter.

Using a single file to handle any controller action is an improvement over having a unique file for each action, because it avoids us repeating code.

The complete `index.php`, including the redirect that we just added, now looks like this:

```php
function loadTemplate($templateFileName, $variables = []) {
    extract($variables);

    ob_start();
    include __DIR__ . '/../templates/' . $templateFileName;

    return ob_get_clean();
}

try {
    include __DIR__ . '/../includes/DatabaseConnection.php';
    include __DIR__ . '/../classes/DatabaseTable.php';
    include __DIR__ .
     '/../classes/controllers/JokeController.php';

    $jokesTable = new DatabaseTable($pdo, 'joke', 'id');
    $authorsTable = new DatabaseTable($pdo, 'author', 'id');

    $jokeController = new JokeController($jokesTable,
     $authorsTable);

    $action = $_GET['action'] ?? 'home';

    if ($action == strtolower($action)) {
        $page = $jokeController->$action();
    }
    else {
        http_response_code(301);
        header('location: index.php?action=' .
         strtolower($action));
    }

    $title = $page['title'];

    if (isset($page['variables'])) {
        $output = loadTemplate($page['template'],
         $page['variables']);
    }
    else {
```

```
            $output = loadTemplate($page['template']);
        }
    }
    catch (PDOException $e) {
        $title = 'An error has occurred';

        $output = 'Database error: ' . $e->getMessage() . ' in '
          . $e->getFile() . ':' . $e->getLine();
    }

    include __DIR__ . '/../templates/layout.html.php';
```

Thinking Ahead: User Registration

The next step for us will be to allow someone to register as a user so they can post a joke. To do this, we'll need a new page on the website. Although it would be possible to keep adding methods to the `JokeController` class, on any nontrivial website this would result in a very large class that contained the code for every single page on the website.

Instead, we'll create a new controller called `RegisterController` with some methods to handle user registration. This helps keep the code manageable, by keeping anything to do with jokes in `JokeController` and any page related to user registration in `RegisterController`.

With the `index.php` above, we'd need to write a new PHP script to utilize `RegisterController`, such as `register.php`, that looked like this:

```
<?php
try {
    include __DIR__ . '/../includes/DatabaseConnection.php';
    include __DIR__ . '/../classes/DatabaseTable.php';
    include __DIR__ . '/../controllers/RegisterController.php';

    $jokesTable = new DatabaseTable($pdo, 'joke', 'id');
    $authorsTable = new DatabaseTable($pdo, 'author', 'id');
```

```
    $registerController = new RegisterController($authorsTable);

    $action = $_GET['action'] ?? 'home';

    if ($action == strtolower($action)) {
        $page = $registerController->$action();
    } else {
        http_response_code(301);
        header('location: index.php?action=' .
         strtolower($action));
    }

    $title = $page['title'];

    if (isset($page['variables'])) {
        $output = loadTemplate($page['template'],
            $page['variables']);
    } else {
        $output = loadTemplate($page['template']);
    }
} catch (PDOException $e) {
    $title = 'An error has occurred';

    $output = 'Database error: ' . $e->getMessage() . ' in '
     . $e->getFile() . ':' . $e->getLine();
}

include __DIR__ . '/../templates/layout.html.php';
```

Most of this code is identical to index.php. The only differences are:

1. include 'JokeController.php'; becomes include
    'RegisterController.php';

2. $jokeController = new JokeController($jokesTable, $authorsTable);
    becomes $registerController = new
    RegisterController($authorsTable);

3. `$jokeController->$action();` becomes `$registerController->$action();`

It would be better if a single `index.php` could work with any controller in the same way it works with any action, avoiding the need for different PHP files for loading each controller. To achieve that, we'd need to make it so that the same `index.php` can be used for any controller.

The third change is very easy to fix, so let's remove that difference first.

The only reason this needs changing is because of the different variable names `$jokesController` and `$registerController`. If the same variable names were used throughout—such as `$controller`—then this change wouldn't be needed. `$controller = new RegisterController($authorsTable);` or `$controller = new JokeController($jokesTable, $authorsTable);` could both work with `$controller->$action();`.

The solution to 1. will be simple to implement. As we saw when loading templates, the `include` statement can be used to include files using a string stored in a variable.

Making this change to include the correct file is fairly simple:

```
$controllerName = ucfirst($_GET['controller']) .
  'Controller';

include __DIR__ . '/../controllers/' . $controllerName .
  '.php';
```

As you already know, variables can be built up from other variables, including `$_GET` variables. Using the same process we used to define `$action`, it's also possible to specify a URL parameter for `controller`, like so: `index.php?controller=jokes&action=listJokes`. We could use this to load `JokesController` and call the action `listJokes`.

To build the class name, I've used `ucfirst` to make the first letter of the controller from the URL uppercase to match the filename. `joke` as supplied in the URL becomes `Joke`. The string `Controller.php` is then appended to give the complete class name.

Using the URL parameter `controller=register` would mean the file `RegisterController.php` is included.

Now the file that contains the controller will be included by specifying the controller name in the URL, so that it's available in `$_GET['controller']`.

That fixes problem 1. and partially fixes problem 3. The new code looks like this:

```
include __DIR__ . '/../controllers/' . $_GET['controller'] .
  '.php';

$jokesTable = new DatabaseTable($pdo, 'joke', 'id');
$authorsTable = new DatabaseTable($pdo, 'author', 'id');

$controller = new RegisterController($authorsTable);

$action = $_GET['action'] ?? 'home';

if ($action == strtolower($action)) {
    $page = $controller->$action();
}
```

For change 2. we need to be able to substitute the line `$controller = new JokeController($jokesTable, $authorsTable);` with a line that creates the relevant controller (for now, either `JokeController` or `RegisterController`).

Just as a variable can be used in place of a method name, a variable can also be used in place of a class name, so it's possible to substitute the class name with a variable from `$_GET`:

```
$controllerObject = new $controllerName($jokesTable,
  $authorsTable);
```

`new $controllerName()` will create an instance of the class name provided in the `$_GET` variable `controller`. Visiting `index.php?controller=joke&action=list`

will now load the controller with the name `JokeController`.

We can also apply the same logic as before to do the following:

- select a default controller ("joke") if no `$_GET['controller']` variable is set:

```
$controllerName = $_GET['controller'] ?? 'joke';
```

- redirect to the lowercase URL if required:

```
if ($action == strtolower($action) &&
$controllerName == strtolower($controllerName)) {

}
else {
    // redirect to lowercase version
}
```

Now we can take the name from `$controllerName` and get the class name by making the first letter uppercase (the `ucfirst` function does this for any string) and then appending the string `Controller`:

```
$className = ucfirst($controllerName) . 'Controller';
```

Finally, include the relevant file and create the controller instance:

```
include __DIR__ . '/../controllers/' . $className . '.php';

$controller = new $className($jokesTable, $authorsTable);
```

The complete block of code looks like this:

```
$action = $_GET['action'] ?? 'home';

$controllerName = $_GET['controller'] ?? 'joke';
```

```
if ($action == strtolower($action) &&
 $controllerName == strtolower($controllerName)) {
    $className = ucfirst($controllerName) . 'Controller';

    include __DIR__ . '/../controllers/' . $className . '.php';

    $controller = new $className($jokesTable, $authorsTable);
    $page = $controller->$action();
}
else {
    http_response_code(301);
    header('location: index.php?controller=' .
    strtolower($controllerName) . '&action=' .
    strtolower($action));
}
```

If we add this to index.php and visit one of the joke pages—via
index.php?controller=joke&action=list, for example—it will work as
intended.

However, you may have spotted a potential problem. When the controller is
created, its constructor is called and passed the $jokesTable and $authorsTable
objects.

What if different controllers require different objects to work? For example, the
RegisterController class will only require $authorsTable.

Dependencies

Different controllers will inevitably require different dependencies. The
JokeController we built in the last chapter requires the $jokesTable and
$authorsTable objects, but not all controllers will require those same objects.

An object that's required by another object is called a **dependency**. For example,
JokeController is *dependent* on the $jokesTable instance, as without it, it
won't work correctly.

To identify a dependency in a piece of code, look for a function call on another object. For example, the `delete` method in the controller depends on the `jokesTable` variable, and that variable must contain a `DatabaseTable` instance. Without a `DatabaseTable` instance, the `delete` method below can't work. It's *dependent* on functionality from another class.

```php
public function delete() {
    $this->jokesTable->delete($_POST['id']);
    header('Location: .');
    exit();
}
```

The method being called `jokesTable->delete()` is in another class. If the `DatabaseTable` class didn't exist, this delete function would fail. We can say that the `JokeController` class is *dependent* on the `DatabaseTable` class. Likewise, we can say that the `DatabaseTable` class has a dependency on the `PDO` class, because it can't function without it.

We're going to add a second controller, `RegisterController`, that deals with allowing new authors to register so they can post jokes.

To begin with, we'll create a single form for registration. When submitted, information will need to be inserted into the `author` table. There's no reason this controller will ever need to interact with the `$jokesTable` object, so a `RegisterController` object would be instantiated like this:

```php
$controller = new RegisterController($authorsTable);
```

Other controllers might need other database tables—for example, a `categories` table for categorizing the jokes or objects that don't even deal with database access, to validate data that's been entered.

We face a problem here. We can use a variable in place of the class name like so:

```php
$controllerName = $_GET['controller'];
```

```
$controller = new $controllerName($authorsTable);
```

But there's no easy way to determine what dependencies the required controller needs.

I'll warn you now, this is the most complicated topic in this book, and something even very experienced developers struggle with! Different people have come up with some potential solutions, and there are many approaches you can take. However, many are considered "bad practice" and should be avoided. I could write a book on this subject alone (it's a large section of my PhD thesis!) so instead of telling you what not to do (creating the objects in the constructor of the controller, singletons or service locators), I'm going to stick with best practices and show you a few options for handling it in the preferred way.

It's a very good idea to pass dependencies into the constructor of classes that need them. As I mentioned in the last chapter, this stops an object being able to exist without having the dependencies set. The problem we have is that different controllers will require different dependencies. The `JokesController` class constructor looks like this:

```
public function __construct(DatabaseTable $jokesTable,
  DatabaseTable $authorsTable) {
    $this->jokesTable = $jokesTable;
    $this->authorsTable = $authorsTable;
}
```

And when we write the code for the `RegisterController` class, the constructor will look like this:

```
public function __construct(DatabaseTable $authorsTable) {
    $this->authorsTable = $authorsTable;
}
```

The `JokesController` class has dependencies on two `DatabaseTable` objects, one

for authors and one for jokes. The `RegisterController` class only has a
dependency on one, `$authorsTable`. If we're trying to automate creation of the
controllers, it presents a problem: if the constructors are different, how can the
objects be automatically created?

One method of fixing this would be to ensure that all controllers have the same
constructor. They all require access to all the possible `DatabaseTable` objects.
This works, but it's messy. It results in controllers with dependencies on
everything that any controller may ever need. One major downside to this
approach is that, when a new database table is added, all the controllers'
constructors must be changed. We could overcome this by passing an array of all
the possible dependencies and picking out the ones we need. This is essentially
something known as a "Service Locator", and it's a common approach, although
it's been widely considered bad practice over the last few years.

The technical term for what we're doing is **dependency injection**. It sounds
complicated, but it's just a fancy term for passing dependencies into constructors.
You've been doing it all along without even knowing!

The simplest way of solving the problem of different constructors needing
different arguments is a series of if statements. This way, each controller can be
created with the correct dependencies:

```php
$action = $_GET['action'] ?? 'home';
$controllerName = $_GET['controller'] ?? 'joke';

if ($controllerName === 'joke') {
 $controller = new JokeController($jokesTable,
↪ $authorsTable);
}
else if ($controllerName === 'register') {
    $controller = new RegisterController($authorsTable);
}

$page = $controller->$action();
```

Now the controller is selected by the variable supplied in $_GET['controller'], and the method defined in `$_GET['action']` is called on the controller object.

This approach is very flexible. It allows us to call any method in any controller by specifying the class name in the `controller` URL variable and method name in the `action` URL variable. Although this adds some flexibility, it also opens up several security issues. Someone can alter the URL and run any method in any class. Depending on what our controllers are doing, this may cause a problem.

Instead, it's more secure, and only a little extra code, to specify a single URL variable that triggers a specific controller action. This single URL variable is called a **route**:

```php
$route = $_GET['route'] ?? 'joke/home'; // If no route
↪ variable is set, use 'home'

if ($route === 'joke/list') {
    include __DIR__ .
     '/../classes/controllers/JokeController.php';
    $controller = new JokeController($jokesTable,
        $authorsTable);
    $page = $controller->list();
}
else if ($route === 'joke/home') {
    include __DIR__ .
     '/../classes/controllers/JokeController.php';
    $controller = new JokeController($jokesTable,
        $authorsTable);
    $page = $controller->home();
}
else if ($route === 'register') {
    include __DIR__ .
     '/../classes/controllers/RegisterController.php';
    $controller = new RegisterController($authorsTable);
    $page = $controller->showForm();
}
```

Although this is slightly more code and we have some repetition, it's considerably more secure. Someone can only instantiate a controller and call a method if it's in this list. In this case, the repetition is preferable to the potential security hole of letting anyone call any method.

I've used `joke/list` and `joke/edit`, with the `joke/` prefix, because each page needs a unique identifier. In future, we may want to create a page that lists or allows editing authors, which can then be stored on the URLs `author/list`, `author/edit`, etc.

The complete `index.php` now looks like this:

```php
<?php
function loadTemplate($templateFileName, $variables = [])
{
    extract($variables);

    ob_start();
    include __DIR__ . '/../templates/' . $templateFileName;

    return ob_get_clean();
}

try {
    include __DIR__ . '/../includes/DatabaseConnection.php';
    include __DIR__ . '/../classes/DatabaseTable.php';

    $jokesTable = new DatabaseTable($pdo, 'joke', 'id');
    $authorsTable = new DatabaseTable($pdo, 'author', 'id');

     //if no route variable is set, use 'joke/home'
    $route = $_GET['route'] ?? 'joke/home';

    if ($route == strtolower($route)) {
        if ($route === 'joke/list') {
            include __DIR__ .
             '/../classes/controllers/JokeController.php';
            $controller = new JokeController($jokesTable,
             $authorsTable);
            $page = $controller->list();
        } elseif ($route === 'joke/home') {
            include __DIR__ .
             '/../classes/controllers/JokeController.php';
            $controller = new JokeController($jokesTable,
             $authorsTable);
            $page = $controller->home();
        } elseif ($route === 'joke/edit') {
            include __DIR__ .
             '/../classes/controllers/JokeController.php';
            $controller = new JokeController($jokesTable,
             $authorsTable);
```

```
                 $page = $controller->edit();
             } elseif ($route === 'joke/delete') {
                 include __DIR__ .
                  '/../classes/controllers/JokeController.php';
                 $controller = new JokeController($jokesTable,
                  $authorsTable);
                 $page = $controller->delete();
             } elseif ($route === 'register') {
                 include __DIR__ .
                  '/../classes/controllers/RegisterController.php';
                 $controller = new RegisterController($authorsTable);
                 $page = $controller->showForm();
             }
         } else {
             http_response_code(301);
             header('location: index.php?route=' . strtolower($route));
         }

         $title = $page['title'];

         if (isset($page['variables'])) {
             $output = loadTemplate($page['template'],
              $page['variables']);
         } else {
             $output = loadTemplate($page['template']);
         }
     } catch (PDOException $e) {
         $title = 'An error has occurred';

         $output = 'Database error: ' . $e->getMessage() . ' in '
           . $e->getFile() . ':' . $e->getLine();
     }

     include __DIR__ . '/../templates/layout.html.php';
```

Note that I've also amended the if statement that checks case to use the new
$route variable.

Ideally, we were looking to be able to use *any* controller without editing `index.php`. But for simplicity's sake, we'll stick with this approach.

Now that the routes have changed, we'll also need to amend `layout.html.php` to use the new routes in the menu:

```
<li><a href="index.php?route=joke/list">Jokes
↪ List</a></li>
<li><a href="index.php?route=joke/edit">Add a
↪ new Joke</a></li>
```

Before we go ahead and change all the links throughout the website, I want to introduce an approach called **URL Rewriting**, which is another reason for using a single *route* variable instead of separate *controller* and *action* variables.

URL Rewriting

A lot of websites are written in PHP, including Facebook and Wikipedia. If you visit one of these sites, you'll see that the URLs don't look like the ones we've been using on the joke website.

The URL for SitePoint's Wikipedia page is `https://en.wikipedia.org/wiki/ SitePoint`, and its Facebook page URL is `https://www.facebook.com/ sitepoint/`.

Using the structure we've looked at so far, you'd probably expect to see something like `https://www.facebook.com/ index.php?controller=page&id=sitepoint` or `https://en.wikipedia.org/ index.php?route=wiki/sitepoint`.

Most PHP websites don't actually show you the PHP filename in the URL. Many years ago, search engines preferred this approach. These days, search engines don't care about URL structureURL structure[2], and friendly URLs are used more for aesthetic reasons.

As most websites use this approach, it's useful to know how to do it.

---

[2] https://www.sitepoint.com/friendly-urls/

URL Rewriting is a tool for forwarding one URL to another. You can configure your web server so that when someone visits `/jokes/list`, it actually runs `index.php?route=jokes/list`, or even when someone visits `contact.php` it instead it runs `index.php?route=contact`.

Importantly, the original URL is still shown in the browser's address bar.

URL Rewriting is a long and complex topic. You can set up all kinds of wonderful and impressive rules. However, almost all modern PHP websites use the same rule: if a file requested doesn't exist, load `index.php`.

In fact, the Homestead Improved box we're using is already set up to do this. Visit `http://192.168.10.10/I-dont-exist.php` or any whimsical filename you can think of and you'll see the website home page rather than an error page.

If you create the file `I-dont-exist.php` and visit the page in the browser, it will be loaded. Otherwise, all requests are sent to `index.php`.

NGINX

If you need to configure an NGINX server for URL rewriting, the guide on the NGINX website is the first place to look for examples[3].

However, for most setups you'll just need the configuration directive:

```
location / {
    try_files $uri $uri/ /index.php;
}
```

For Apache servers, the same can be achieved by creating a file called .htaccess in the public (or, more likely for Apache, public_html or httpdocs) directory with the following contents:

```conf
RewriteEngine on
RewriteCond %{REQUEST_FILENAME} !-f
RewriteCond %{REQUEST_FILENAME} !-d
RewriteRule ^.*$ /index.php [NC,L,QSA]
```

How this works is beyond the scope of this book, but it will have the same effect. If a file doesn't exist, it will load index.php rather than display and error. More information on configuring URL rewriting when using Apache can be found in the SitePoint article "Learn Apache mod_rewrite: 13 Real-world Examples"[4].

You know just enough about URL rewriting to make use of it on the site. Rather than using a $_GET variable to determine the route, you can use the URL that the person used to connect to the website. PHP supplies this information in the variable $_SERVER['REQUEST_URI'].

Open up index.php and replace this:

```
$route = $_GET['route'] ?? 'joke/home';
```

[3.] https://www.nginx.com/blog/creating-nginx-rewrite-rules/
[4.] https://www.sitepoint.com/apache-mod_rewrite-examples/

... with this:

```
$route = ltrim(strtok($_SERVER['REQUEST_URI'], '?'), '/');
```

The `ltrim` function removes the leading `/`. If you visit `http://192.168.10.10/joke/list`, `$_SERVER['REQUEST_URI']` will store the string `/joke/list`. By trimming any leading slashes, we can match the request URI to our existing routes.

Because the `$_SERVER['REQUEST_URI']` contains the complete URL, if the URL contains `$_GET` variables, the entire URL string is included in the variable. We don't want these in our routes.

The following code will return the entire string up to the first question mark, or the entire string if there's no question mark:

```
strtok($_SERVER['REQUEST_URI'], '?')
```

Now, visit `http://192.168.10.10/joke/list` and you'll see the joke list on the prettier URL ... with one problem! One issue with URL rewriting in this manner is that the browser will see the `/` in `joke/list` as a directory separator.

```
<link rel="stylesheet" href="jokes.css">
```

When the browser sees the line above, it will look for `jokes.css` at `http://192.168.10.10/joke/jokes.css`. As that file doesn't exist, the stylesheet won't be applied.

There are two possible fixes:

1. The HTML `<base>` tag. Although it's a viable solution, it introduces a few issues that are not worth covering here.

2. Make all URLs relative to the domain. To do this, just prefix all links with a `/`.

The second option is more work but causes fewer issues. Let's open up `layout.html` and change this:

```
<link rel="stylesheet" href="jokes.css">
```

... to this:

```
<link rel="stylesheet" href="/jokes.css">
```

By prefixing a link in an HTML document with a forward slash /, it tells the browser to look for the file from the top level of the website. If we refresh the page, we'll see the styles now display correctly.

If we just visit `http://192.168.10.10/` without specifying a file name, we'll see an error. That's because we don't have a route set up for an empty string.

In `index.php`, we replace `else if ($route === 'joke/home') {` with `else if ($route === '') {`. If we refresh the home page, it should display as expected.

Finally, let's amend each link on the website to use the new prettier format.

`layout.html.php`:

```
<ul>
    <li><a href="/">Home</a></li>
    <li><a href="/joke/list">Jokes List
    </a></li>
    <li><a href="/joke/edit">Add a new Joke
    </a></li>
</ul>
```

The edit link and delete form action in `jokes.html.php`:

```
<a href="/joke/edit?id=<?=$joke['id']?>">Edit
</a>
```

```
<form action="/joke/delete" method="post">
    <input type="hidden" name="id"
        value="<?=$joke['id']?>">
    <input type="submit" value="Delete">
</form>
```

And finally the two redirects in `JokeController.php`:

```
header('location: /joke/list');
```

You can find this example in *CMS-Controller-Rewrite*.

Now you know why we're making these structural changes before our website has too many pages!

Tidying Up

You've probably noticed that `index.php` is getting a bit long and unwieldy. Before we get into creating `RegisterController.php`, let's tidy up `index.php` a little.

Make it OOP

One of the primary causes of overly complex code is nested `if` statements. With any long piece of code, it's possible to break it up into a single class with a set of functions.

This can be done by identifying unique tasks within the code. Looking at the code, we can see the following distinct tasks:

- instantiating the controller and calling the relevant action based on `$route`
- the `loadTemplate` function
- redirecting to a lowercase version of the URL if required
- loading the relevant template file and setting its variables

Let's take each of these and make it a function inside a class called `EntryPoint`, inside the `classes` directory.

This class will take a single variable, `$route`, representing the route to load. It will then store the route in a class variable so that each function can use it:

```php
<?php
class EntryPoint
{
    private $route;

    public function __construct($route)
    {
        $this->route = $route;
    }
}
```

The next step is checking that the route is the correct case and redirecting to the lowercase version if it's not:

```php
private function checkUrl() {
    if ($this->route !== strtolower($this->route)) {
        http_response_code(301);
        header('location: ' . strtolower($this->route));
    }
}
```

I've amended the logic here slightly so that the `if` statement checks to see if the supplied route is the same as the lowercase version.

This function can be called directly from the constructor:

```php
public function __construct($route) {
    $this->route = $route;
    $this->checkUrl();
}
```

By putting the function call in the controller, this class won't even get constructed if either $controller or $action are not lowercase.

The existing loadTemplate function can be copied directly into the class. I've made it private, as we're going to call it from another method in the same class:

```php
private function loadTemplate($templateFileName,
  $variables = []) {
    extract($variables);

    ob_start();
    include __DIR__ . '/../templates/' . $templateFileName;

    return ob_get_clean();
}
```

There are two parts left: loading/instantiating the controller and handling the $page variable to generate the layout.

Firstly, let's copy/paste the entire if statement that checks the route and move it to its own function called callAction. The task for this method is calling the relevant controller action and returning the $page variable:

```php
private function callAction() {
    include __DIR__ . '/../classes/DatabaseTable.php';
    include __DIR__ . '/../includes/DatabaseConnection.php';

    $jokesTable = new DatabaseTable($pdo, 'joke', 'id');
    $authorsTable = new DatabaseTable($pdo, 'author', 'id');

    if ($this->route === 'joke/list') {
        include __DIR__ .
            '/../classes/controllers/JokeController.php';
        $controller = new JokeController($jokesTable,
            $authorsTable);
        $page = $controller->list();
    }
    else if ($this->route === '') {
```

```
        include __DIR__ .
         '/../classes/controllers/JokeController.php';
        $controller = new JokeController($jokesTable,
         $authorsTable);
        $page = $controller->home();
    }
    else if ($this->route === 'joke/edit') {
        include __DIR__ .
         '/../classes/controllers/JokeController.php';
        $controller = new JokeController($jokesTable,
         $authorsTable);
        $page = $controller->edit();
    }
    else if ($this->route === 'joke/delete') {
        include __DIR__ .
         '/../classes/controllers/JokeController.php';
        $controller = new JokeController($jokesTable,
         $authorsTable);
        $page = $controller->delete();
    }
    else if ($this->route === 'register') {
        include __DIR__ .
         '/../classes/controllers/RegisterController.php';
        $controller = new RegisterController($authorsTable);
        $page = $controller->showForm();
    }

    return $page;
}
```

I've made this function a method private. Once again, we'll only be calling it from within the class.

Because the new `DatabaseTable` lines are the only parts of our code that need the $pdo database connection or `DatabaseTable` class, I've moved the `include` statement for `DatabaseConnection.php` and `DatabaseTable.php` here. In fact, if `DatabaseConnection.php` wasn't included here, the line `$jokesTable = new DatabaseTable($pdo, 'joke', 'id');` would fail, as there's no $pdo variable in this scope.

Finally, we can place the remaining code for loading the relevant template and supplying it variables into a method called run. This will be the only public method in the class:

```php
public function run() {
    $page = $this->callAction();

    $title = $page['title'];

    if (isset($page['variables'])) {
        $output = $this->loadTemplate($page['template'],
          $page['variables']);
    }
    else {
        $output = $this->loadTemplate($page['template']);
    }

    include __DIR__ . '/../templates/layout.html.php';
}
```

There's nothing new here, but we've moved each task into its own method. The callAction method deals entirely with the controllers and returns the $page variable.

Using the new EntryPoint class, index.php can now be rewritten like this:

```php
<?php
try {
    include __DIR__ . '/../classes/EntryPoint.php';

    $route = ltrim(strtok($_SERVER['REQUEST_URI'], '?'), '/');

    $entryPoint = new EntryPoint($route);
    $entryPoint->run();
} catch (PDOException $e) {
    $title = 'An error has occurred';
```

```
    $output = 'Database error: ' . $e->getMessage() . ' in '
     . $e->getFile() . ':' . $e->getLine();

    include __DIR__ . '/../templates/layout.html.php';
}
```

The complete EntryPoint.php looks like this:

```php
<?php
class EntryPoint
{
    private $route;

    public function __construct($route)
    {
        $this->route = $route;
        $this->checkUrl();
    }

    private function checkUrl()
    {
        if ($this->route !== strtolower($this->route)) {
            http_response_code(301);
            header('location: ' . strtolower($this->route));
        }
    }

    private function loadTemplate($templateFileName,
     $variables = [])
    {
        extract($variables);

        ob_start();
        include __DIR__ . '/../templates/' . $templateFileName;

        return ob_get_clean();
    }

    private function callAction()
    {
        include __DIR__ .
         '/../classes/DatabaseTable.php';
        include __DIR__ .
         '/../includes/DatabaseConnection.php';

        $jokesTable = new DatabaseTable($pdo, 'joke', 'id');
        $authorsTable = new DatabaseTable($pdo, 'author', 'id');
```

```php
        if ($this->route === 'joke/list') {
            include __DIR__ .
             '/../classes/controllers/JokeController.php';
            $controller = new JokeController($jokesTable,
             $authorsTable);
            $page = $controller->list();
        } elseif ($this->route === '') {
            include __DIR__ .
             '/../classes/controllers/JokeController.php';
            $controller = new JokeController($jokesTable,
             $authorsTable);
            $page = $controller->home();
        } elseif ($this->route === 'joke/edit') {
            include __DIR__ .
             '/../classes/controllers/JokeController.php';
            $controller = new JokeController($jokesTable,
             $authorsTable);
            $page = $controller->edit();
        } elseif ($this->route === 'joke/delete') {
            include __DIR__ .
             '/../classes/controllers/JokeController.php';
            $controller = new JokeController($jokesTable,
             $authorsTable);
            $page = $controller->delete();
        } elseif ($this->route === 'register') {
            include __DIR__ .
             '/../classes/controllers/RegisterController.php';
            $controller = new RegisterController($authorsTable);
            $page = $controller->showForm();
        }

        return $page;
    }

    public function run()
    {
        $page = $this->callAction();

        $title = $page['title'];
```

```
        if (isset($page['variables'])) {
            $output = $this->loadTemplate($page['template'],
            $page['variables']);
        } else {
            $output = $this->loadTemplate($page['template']);
        }

        include __DIR__ . '/../templates/layout.html.php';
    }
}
```

We just made some very substantial changes. Although none of the code is new, and it doesn't produce any different output, the structure is completely different. Take a look through the completed `EntryPoint.php` to see how it works. Each task is now in its own method, rather than being nested inside a series of if statements.

Our `index.php` and `EntryPoint.php` can now be used to load any controller class, and call any method on it, by specifying the appropriate route.

A controller can be easily added by creating a class in the `controllers` directory and adding the logic for creating the controller and calling the relevant action in the `callAction` method.

As every single page on the website is now going to be loaded using the `EntryPoint` class, it's worth taking some time to make sure it's correct. Before we add another controller, let's consider how code can be reused on a much larger scale than we've looked at until now.

Reusing Code on Different Websites

Now that we've tidied up `index.php`, it's worth considering what we've achieved by doing so. We've broken up the code into more easily manageable chunks, and the code is easier to read. If there's a problem with the redirect check, you know to look in the `checkURL` method. If a template isn't loading correctly, you know to look in the `loadTemplate` method. And if a URL isn't displaying the page it should, you know to look in the `callAction` method.

Even though we haven't finished our *Internet Joke Database* website yet, it's worth thinking about your *next* website. You probably didn't buy this book so you could make a website for people to post jokes. You likely have a real project in mind that you're planning to build using the knowledge you learn from this book.

How much of the code we've written so far can be used without modification on your next website?

We specifically built the `DatabaseTable` class so that it can work with *any* database table. Not only can it work with tables that exist for the joke website, `joke` and `author`, it could work with tables called `customer`, `product` and `order` for a shopping website, or `account` and `message` on a social media website, or indeed any database table on any website.

Generic or Project Specific?

Besides the `DatabaseTable` class, how much of the code we've written so far would be useful on another website? The templates probably wouldn't. Another website would likely have completely different HTML, its forms would have completely different fields, and the website would deal with a different topic.

The controllers would be different. The code in `JokeController` is very specific to the joke website we're building. It's unlikely the code in the controller will be useful without changing it.

However, the code we just wrote in the `EntryPoint` class that loads controllers and template files would be useful on another website. The templates and controllers loaded would be different, but the code to load those files would be the same.

There are two types of code files in any given website:

1. project-specific files containing code that's only relevant to that particular website
2. generic, reusable files containing code that can be used to build any website

The more code we can make *generic*, the bigger the foundation we have to work from when we start a new website. If we can use a lot of code from our previous website on our next website, we'll save ourselves a lot of time.

Rather than having to write code that's similar to the `EntryPoint` and `DatabaseTable` classes for our next website, we could save a lot of time by using the code we already have.

This foundation is called a **framework**—a set of generic code (usually classes) that can be quickly built on to build any website. It doesn't contain any code that's specific to one particular project.

It's important to make a distinction between *framework code* and *project-specific code*. If we can successfully separate them, we can reuse our framework code in every website we build, saving significant upfront development time. If we have framework code mixed with project-specific code, we'll find ourselves writing very similar code for every website we build.

When we first start out, it can be difficult to recognize which parts of the code belong specifically to that project, and which can be used across different projects.

As a rule of thumb, processes are generic but data is specific. For example, *adding a joke to the database* is specific to the joke site, but *adding to the database* is a generic process that's needed on most websites.

In Chapter 8, I showed how to separate out the generic *add to database* process from the project-specific process of *adding a joke*. Anything related to *jokes* is in `JokeController.php`, but all the code related to *adding to the database* is stored in `DatabaseTable.php`.

By identifying the process and separating it from the project-specific data being worked with, we can repeat the same process of *adding to the database* with any data on any website by reusing the `DatabaseTable` class.

The first step to making something *generic* is usually placing it inside a *class*. This helps us break up the problem into smaller parts. Once we've broken the problem up into individual methods, we can then see which are *generic* and which are *project specific*.

A dead giveaway that something is *project specific* is a hardcoded value or variable name that alludes to something for that project only.

Let's apply that to the new `EntryPoint` class. The methods `loadTemplate`, `checkUrl` and `run` don't contain any references to *jokes*, *authors* or anything that's specific the joke website. Indeed, we'll need a way of loading controllers and templates on future websites; they just won't be dealing with jokes and authors.

However, the `callAction` method contains several references to *jokes* and *authors*. If we wanted to reuse this class on a different website—for example, an online shop—we'd need to rewrite the entire method. It won't have controllers or database tables dealing with `jokes` authors; it will have controllers and database tables for `products`, `customers`, and `orders`.

Let's imagine we do have two websites—the joke website and an online shop. We've copy/pasted the file `EntryPoint.php` and changed `callAction` to suit each website. If there's a bug in the `checkUrl` or `run` methods, we'd need to fix the bug in two places, while being careful not to change any code specific to that website.

Instead, if the file contained only the *generic* framework code, we could overwrite the old `EntryPoint.php` with the new one everywhere it's being used, and fix the bug without worrying about undoing changes that were made specifically for one project.

Making `EntryPoint` Generic

The answer, then, is to remove all references to project-specific concepts from otherwise generic classes.

This process is more of an art than a science, and even experienced developers can struggle to work out where to draw the line between generic and project-specific code. However, I'm going to show you a fairly simple step-by-step process that can be used to remove a project-specific method from a class, turning it into a framework class.

1. Identify the method you want to remove.

In this case, it's the `callAction` method:

```php
private function callAction() {
    include __DIR__ . '/../classes/DatabaseTable.php';
    include __DIR__ . '/../includes/DatabaseConnection.php';

    $jokesTable = new DatabaseTable($pdo, 'joke', 'id');
    $authorsTable = new DatabaseTable($pdo, 'author', 'id');

    if ($this->route === 'joke/list') {
        include __DIR__ .
         '/../classes/controllers/JokeController.php';
        $controller = new JokeController($jokesTable,
         $authorsTable);
        $page = $controller->list();
    }
    else if ($this->route === '') {
        include __DIR__ .
         '/../classes/controllers/JokeController.php';
        $controller = new JokeController($jokesTable,
         $authorsTable);
        $page = $controller->home();
    }
    else if ($this->route === 'joke/edit') {
        include __DIR__ .
         '/../classes/controllers/JokeController.php';
        $controller = new JokeController($jokesTable,
         $authorsTable);
        $page = $controller->edit();
    }
    else if ($this->route === 'joke/delete') {
        include __DIR__ .
         '/../classes/controllers/JokeController.php';
        $controller = new JokeController($jokesTable,
         $authorsTable);
        $page = $controller->delete();
    }
    else if ($this->route === 'register') {
        include __DIR__ .
         '/../classes/controllers/RegisterController.php';
        $controller = new RegisterController($authorsTable);
        $page = $controller->showForm();
```

```
    }

    return $page;
}
```

2. Move the method to its own class and make it *public*.

Create a class called IjdbRoutes in classes/IjdbRoutes.php:

```php
<?php
class IjdbRoutes
{
    public function callAction()
    {
        include __DIR__ . '/../classes/DatabaseTable.php';
        include __DIR__ . '/../includes/DatabaseConnection.php';

        $jokesTable = new DatabaseTable($pdo, 'joke', 'id');
        $authorsTable = new DatabaseTable($pdo, 'author', 'id');

        if ($this->route === 'joke/list') {
            include __DIR__ .
             '/../classes/controllers/JokeController.php';
            $controller = new JokeController($jokesTable,
             $authorsTable);
            $page = $controller->list();
        } elseif ($this->route === '') {
            include __DIR__ .
             '/../classes/controllers/JokeController.php';
            $controller = new JokeController($jokesTable,
             $authorsTable);
            $page = $controller->home();
        } elseif ($this->route === 'joke/edit') {
            include __DIR__ .
             '/../classes/controllers/JokeController.php';
            $controller = new JokeController($jokesTable,
             $authorsTable);
            $page = $controller->edit();
```

```
        } elseif ($this->route === 'joke/delete') {
            include __DIR__ .
             '/../classes/controllers/JokeController.php';
            $controller = new JokeController($jokesTable,
             $authorsTable);
            $page = $controller->delete();
        } elseif ($this->route === 'register') {
            include __DIR__ .
             '/../classes/controllers/RegisterController.php';
            $controller = new RegisterController($authorsTable);
            $page = $controller->showForm();
        }

        return $page;
    }
}
```

3. Replace any referenced class variables with arguments.

Replace $this->route with $route and add the $route as arguments for the
method.

```
<?php
class IjdbRoutes
{
    public function callAction($route)
    {
        include __DIR__ . '/../classes/DatabaseTable.php';
        include __DIR__ . '/../includes/DatabaseConnection.php';

        $jokesTable = new DatabaseTable($pdo, 'joke', 'id');
        $authorsTable = new DatabaseTable($pdo, 'author', 'id');

        if ($route === 'joke/list') {
            include __DIR__ .
             '/../classes/controllers/JokeController.php';
            $controller = new JokeController($jokesTable,
             $authorsTable);
```

```
        $page = $controller->list();
    } elseif ($route === '') {
        include __DIR__ .
         '/../classes/controllers/JokeController.php';
        $controller = new JokeController($jokesTable,
         $authorsTable);
        $page = $controller->home();
    } elseif ($route === 'joke/edit') {
        include __DIR__ .
         '/../classes/controllers/JokeController.php';
        $controller = new JokeController($jokesTable,
         $authorsTable);
        $page = $controller->edit();
    } elseif ($route === 'joke/delete') {
        include __DIR__ .
         '/../classes/controllers/JokeController.php';
        $controller = new JokeController($jokesTable,
         $authorsTable);
        $page = $controller->delete();
    } elseif ($route === 'register') {
        include __DIR__ .
         '/../classes/controllers/RegisterController.php';
        $controller = new RegisterController($authorsTable);
        $page = $controller->showForm();
    }

    return $page;
    }
}
```

4. Remove the method from the original class.

Remove callAction from the EntryPoint class.

5. Add a new constructor argument/class variable to the original class.

Add $controllerArguments as a constructor argument/class variable to
EntryPoint:

```php
class EntryPoint {
    private $route;
    private $routes;

    public function __construct($route, $routes) {
        $this->route = $route;
        $this->routes = $routes;
        $this->checkUrl();
    }

// ...
```

We'll use the $routes variable to contain an instance of IjdbRoutes.

6. Pass in an instance of the new class when the original class is created.

In index.php, replace $entryPoint = new EntryPoint($route); with
$entryPoint = new EntryPoint($route, new IjdbRoutes());, and remember
to include the IjdbRoutes.php file in index.php.

The new index.php looks like this:

```php
<?php
try {
    include __DIR__ . '/../classes/EntryPoint.php';
    include __DIR__ . '/../classes/IjdbRoutes.php';

    $route = ltrim(strtok($_SERVER['REQUEST_URI'], '?'), '/');

    $entryPoint = new EntryPoint($route, new IjdbActions());
    $entryPoint->run();
} catch (PDOException $e) {
    $title = 'An error has occurred';

    $output = 'Database error: ' . $e->getMessage() . ' in '
      . $e->getFile() . ':' . $e->getLine();

    include __DIR__ . '/../templates/layout.html.php';
```

```
}
```

7. Change the method call to reference the new object and pass in any required variables.

In `EntryPoint`, change `$page = $this->callAction();` to `$page = $this->routes->callAction($this->route);`.

You can find this code in *CMS-EntryPoint-Framework*

With that complete, we now have a generic `EntryPoint.php`. There are no longer any references to *jokes*, *authors* or anything specific to one particular website.

In future, to create a website for an online shop, we can write the relevant `ShopActions` class with a `callAction` method to handle the arguments for that specific website:

```
class ShopActions {
    public function callAction($route) {
        // load the controller and call the relevant action
        // …

        return $controller->$action();
    }
}
```

By splitting out the framework code from the project-specific code, it's possible to use the same `EntryPoint` class in any project. We can pass it the actions it's going to use when it's constructed. The `index.php` for the shop website would contain this line:

```
$entryPoint = new EntryPoint($controller, $action, new
 ↪ ShopActions());
```

Autoloading and Namespaces

One line of code we're repeating often is the `include` line to include a relevant class each time a class is required.

Any time we use one of the classes we've created, it must be referenced with an `include` statement. This can get tricky to manage, as you need to ensure the class file has been included before you use the class. On top of that, if you accidentally issue the `include` statement twice for the same class, you'll see an error.

Our `IjdbRoutes` class has to include the `DatabaseTable` and controller classes, and `index.php` has to include the `EntryPoint` and `Ijdb` classes.

Some pages may require some classes to be loaded, whereas others may require other classes to be loaded.

A very inefficient but easy-to-organize method of managing loading classes would be to include every single class at the top of the `index.php` file, so that any class that might be needed has already been loaded. Using this method, we'll never have to write an `include` statement for a class outside `index.php`.

A major drawback of this approach is that each time you add a new class to the project, you'll have to open up `index.php` and add the relevant `include` statement. This is time consuming, and will use an unnecessary amount of memory on the server, as all classes would be loaded whether they're needed or not.

I've advised placing classes in their own files throughout this book, as well as naming files to match identically the name of the classes they contain. The class `DatabaseTable` is inside the file `DatabaseTable.php`, `JokeController` is stored in `JokeController.php`, and `EntryPoint` is stored in a file called `EntryPoint.php`.

One of the reasons I've advised structuring files this way is that it's considered good practice. It helps someone reading the code to find the classes that are referenced. If they want to look at the code for `JokeController`, they know to look in `JokeController.php`.

One other advantage of a standardized file structure is that PHP contains a feature called **autoloading**. Autoloading is used to *automatically load* PHP files that store classes. As long as your file names are consistent with the class names, it's easy to write an autoloader to load the relevant PHP file.

Once we've written an autoloader, we'll never need to write an `include` line for a class anywhere in the project.

When we use the statement `new ClassName()`, if the class `ClassName` doesn't exist (because it hasn't been included), PHP can trigger an *autoloader* that can then load the file `ClassName.php`, and the rest of the script will continue as normal without us ever needing to manually write the line `include 'ClassName.php';`.

An **autoloader** is a function that takes a class name as an argument and then includes the file that contains the corresponding class. The function can be as simple as this:

```
function autoloader($className) {
    $file = __DIR__ . '/../classes/' . $className . '.php';
    include $file;
}
```

It would be possible to use this function manually to save a little time:

```
autoloader('DatabaseTable');
autoloader('EntryPoint');
```

This would include both `DatabaseTable.php` and `EntryPoint.php`. However, it's possible to instruct PHP to call this function automatically whenever it can't find a class that's referenced:

```
spl_autoload_register('autoloader');
```

The function `spl_autoload_register` is built into PHP and allows us to tell PHP to call the function with the name we've given if it comes across a class that hasn't yet been included.

The `autoloader` function will be called automatically when a class is used for the first time:

```php
function autoloader($className) {
    $file = __DIR__ . '/../classes/' . $className . '.php';
    include $file;
}

spl_autoload_register('autoloader');

$jokesTable = new DatabaseTable($pdo, 'joke', 'id');
$controller = new EntryPoint($jokesTable);
```

Now files will automatically be included the first time the class stored in them is used. `new DatabaseTable` will trigger the autoloader with `DatabaseTable`, as the `$className` argument and `DatabaseTable.php` will be included.

Case Sensitivity

PHP classes are not case sensitive, but file names usually are. This can cause a problem with autoloaders. The first time a class is used it will be included, and `new DatabaseTable` will load `DatabaseTable.php`. However, `new databasetable` will cause an error, because the filename is case sensitive and `databasetable.php` doesn't exist.

So a problem is caused in a situation like this:

```php
$jokesTable = new DatabaseTable($pdo, 'joke', 'id');
$authorstable = new databasetable($pdo, 'author', 'id');
```

The code above will work as intended, because the first time `DatabaseTable` is loaded with the correct case, the file is successfully included and PHP's case insensitivity allows both objects to be constructed.

However, if we reverse the order of arguments—because the autoloader is triggered with a lowercase name—we'll get an error:

```php
$authorstable = new databasetable($pdo, 'author', 'id');
$jokesTable = new DatabaseTable($pdo, 'joke', 'id');
```

An alternative is to make all file names lowercase and have the autoloader convert the class name to lowercase before loading the file. Although this is a more robust approach and arguably a better technical implementation, it goes against PHP community conventions, and will cause problems if we want to share our code with other people in the future.

Implement an Autoloader

Let's implement an autoloader. To keep things organized, let's create autoload.php and save it in the includes directory:

```php
<?php
function autoloader($className)
{
    $file = __DIR__ . '/../classes/' . $className . '.php';
    include $file;
}

spl_autoload_register('autoloader');
```

Now we can amend index.php to include the autoloader, but remove the include lines that explicitly include EntryPoint.php and IjdbRoutes.php:

```php
<?php
try {
    include __DIR__ . '/../includes/autoload.php';
```

```
    $route = ltrim(strtok($_SERVER['REQUEST_URI'], '?'), '/');

    $entryPoint = new EntryPoint($route, new IjdbRoutes());
    $entryPoint->run();
} catch (PDOException $e) {
    $title = 'An error has occurred';

    $output = 'Database error: ' . $e->getMessage() . ' in '
      . $e->getFile() . ':' . $e->getLine();

    include __DIR__ . '/../templates/layout.html.php';
}
```

We can also remove the include line for `DatabaseTable` from `IjdbRoutes.php`:

```php
<?php
class IjdbRoutes {
    public function callAction($route) {
        include __DIR__ . '/../includes/DatabaseConnection.php';

        $jokesTable = new DatabaseTable($pdo, 'joke', 'id');
        $authorsTable = new DatabaseTable($pdo, 'author', 'id');

        if ($route === 'joke/list') {
```

You can find this code in *CMS-EntryPoint-Autoload*.

Notice that `DatabaseConnection.php` is still included manually, because it doesn't include a class. It sets up the `$pdo` variable, which is used by both `DatabaseTable` objects. Autoloaders can only be used to load classes, and that's one of the reasons it's a good idea to structure as much of our code as possible inside classes.

Redecorating

If we peruse the rest of the code for `include` statements, we'll see that the autoloader works for all classes that are *framework* classes, but doesn't work for `JokeController` or `RegisterController`. The controller is still loaded in `IjdbRoutes.php` on several lines:

```
include __DIR__ .
↳ '/../classes/controllers/JokeController.php';
```

We might try removing this line and having the autoloader load it automatically. If we do, we'll see an error. That error occurs because, when PHP encounters `new JokeController` and triggers the autoloader, it attempts to load `JokeController.php` from the `classes` directory, rather than from the `classes/controllers` directory where the file is actually stored.

Earlier in this chapter, I mentioned the difference between *framework* code—the code you might want to use on every website you build—and project-specific code that exists only for one particular website.

It's a good idea to keep these separated in different directories, so that you can easily copy/paste *framework* files between websites without copying files that are specific to a single project.

Let's name our framework after the title of this book, *Ninja*. Move all the framework code into a directory called `Ninja` inside the classes directory. We should move `EntryPoint.php` and `DatabaseTable.php`, as these are our two *generic* framework files.

Similarly, let's create a new directory inside the classes directory called `Ijdb`. This is where we'll keep all the code that's specific to the joke site and can't be reused on future websites. We'll move `IjdbRoutes.php` into the `Ijdb` directory and move the `controllers` directory inside as well.

While we're moving things around, for consistency, let's give the `Controllers` directory an uppercase *C* and ensure the `Ninja` and `Ijdb` directories all start with an uppercase letter.

When we're finished, `EntryPoint.php` and `DatabaseTable.php` should be located inside `classes/Ninja/`, while `JokeController` should be stored inside `classes/`

Ijdb/Controllers and IjdbRoutes.php inside classes/Ijdb.

Don't try loading the website! As we've moved all the files around, everything is broken!

Because all of our classes are now one level deeper inside the file structure, we'll need to amend any include lines in the files we just moved around.

Firstly, let's open up EntryPoint.php and change this:

```
include   __DIR__ . '/../templates/' . $templateFileName;
```

... to this:

```
include   __DIR__ . '/../../templates/' . $templateFileName;
```

I've added the extra ../ before templates/ so it looks up an additional directory. Now we should change this:

```
include   __DIR__ . '/../templates/layout.html.php';
```

... to this:

```
include   __DIR__ . '/../../templates/layout.html.php';
```

Now, inside IjdbRoutes.php, we'll need to change this:

```
include __DIR__ . '/../includes/DatabaseConnection.php';
```

... to this:

```
include __DIR__ . '/../../includes/DatabaseConnection.php';
```

If we do try loading a page at this point, we'll see some errors. That's because the autoloader is now looking in the wrong place.

To solve this, we could add some logic to the autoloader that looks at the name of the class and loads the file from the correct location, or store an array of class names mapped to file names.

Instead, we're going to use a new tool: namespaces.

Namespaces

Each of our classes has a unique name. However, are they truly unique? If we download some code someone else has written, it may well contain a class named `DatabaseTable` or `EntryPoint`. In a world with thousands of PHP developers, these names aren't unique.

Modern PHP is great: we can find code online that does almost anything we can dream of—creating graphs and charts, turning web pages into PDFs, manipulating images and videos, connecting to Twitter streams, controlling services on a Raspberry Pi. The list is almost endless.

What if we found a great-looking library we wanted to use but it included a class named `DatabaseTable`? This name clash would present a problem. When we run the line `new DatabaseTable`, PHP has to know which class should be used.

One feature that has revolutionized PHP and made it much easier to share code online is **namespaces**.

Before namespaces came along, PHP developers would name their classes with a prefix. For example, we might name our classes `Ninja_EntryPoint`, `Ninja_DatabaseTable` and `Ijdb_JokeController`.

That way, when we wanted to use `SuperLibary_DatabaseTable`, it wouldn't clash with `Ninja_DatabaseTable`, and we could use both `DatabaseTable` classes on the same website.

Namespaces provide a simpler method of solving the same problem. Every class we write can (and should!) be placed within a namespace.

You can think of namespaces a bit like folders on your computer. Inside any given folder on your computer, each file has to have a unique name. For example, our `public` directory can only contain one file named `index.php`, but a different directory could also contain a different file also named `index.php`.

Let's move our framework files into the `Ninja` namespace. At the top of `EntryPoint.php` and `DatabaseTable.php`, add the following code:

```
namespace Ninja;
```

The first few lines of `DatabaseTable.php` now look like this:

```php
<?php
namespace Ninja;

class DatabaseTable {
    private $pdo;
    private $table;

    // ...
```

Now add the namespace `Ijdb` to `IjdbRoutes.php`:

```php
<?php
namespace Ijdb;

class IjdbRoutes {
    public function callAction($route) {
        // ...
```

Before giving the final class (`JokeController`) a namespace, I'll show you how to use the classes now that they have a namespace.

index.php has the code new `EntryPoint` and new `IjdbRoutes`. Now that the classes are inside namespaces, this won't work. We'll need to specify the namespace when instantiating the class by using a backslash (\), followed by the namespace, another backslash, and then the class.

This line:

```
$entryPoint = new EntryPoint($route, new IjdbRoutes());
```

… will become this:

```
$entryPoint = new \Ninja\EntryPoint($routes, new
↪ \Ijdb\IjdbRoutes());
```

Similarly, in `IjdbRoutes.php`, we need to change new `DatabaseTable` to new `\Ninja\DatabaseTable`:

```
$jokesTable = new \Ninja\DatabaseTable($pdo, 'joke', 'id');
$authorsTable = new \Ninja\DatabaseTable($pdo, 'author',
↪ 'id');
```

At this point, we might be inclined to add the namespace `Ijdb` to `JokeController`. We'll be giving `JokeController` a namespace containing `Ijdb`, but we'll give it the namespace `Ijdb\Controllers`.

The backslash (\) in the namespace represents a **sub-namespace**—a namespace within a namespace. This isn't strictly necessary, but it's a good idea to keep related code together. In this case, we'll place all controllers inside the `Ijdb\Controllers` namespace and the `Ijdb/Controllers` directory.

While we're changing the `JokeController.php` file to include the namespace, we'll rename the class (and file) to `Joke`. That way, the class is `\Ijdb\Controllers\Joke` rather than `\Ijdb\Controllers\JokeController`, and the word "Controller" isn't repeated unnecessarily in the full class name.

This parallel between directory structures and namespaces is important. It allows us to write an autoloader than can use both namespaces and class names to locate the file it needs to load.

The combined namespace and class name now represent the folder structure, making it easy to autoload the classes.

This convention is known as **PSR-4** (PSR stands for PHP Standards Recommendations), and it's used by almost all modern PHP projects. Each class should be contained inside a file that directly maps to its namespace and class name. The full class name including namespace should exactly match the directory and file name, including case sensitivity. The PSR-4 standard also provides a few other rules that I won't go into here. To read more about PSR-4, take a look at the PHP-FIG website[5]

Autoloading with PSR-4

By using PSR-4, it's simple to convert a class name in a namespace to a file path. Let's replace `autoload.php` with this PSR-4 version:

```php
<?php
function autoloader($className)
{
    $fileName = str_replace('\\', '/', $className) . '.php';

    $file = __DIR__ . '/../classes/' . $fileName;

    include $file;
}

spl_autoload_register('autoloader');
```

When the autoloader is triggered with a class inside the namespace, it's passed the entire class name including the namespace. For example, when *EntryPoint* is loaded, the autoloader is given the class name `Ninja\EntryPoint`.

---

[5] http://www.php-fig.org/psr/psr-4/.

The line str_replace('\\', '/', $className) . '.php'; replaces
backslashes with forward slashes to represent the file in the file system. Ninja\
EntryPoint becomes Ninja/EntryPoint.php, referencing the file.

With the autoloader in place, we can now remove the include lines from
IjdbRoutes.php, which load JokeController and RegisterController:

```
include __DIR__ .
  '/../classes/controllers/JokeController.php';
```

Then we should change the reference to the controllers to use the full class name:

```
$controller = new \Ijdb\Controllers\Joke($jokesTable,
  $authorsTable);
```

Nearly there! We're close to having the site up and running again using the new
file and namespace structure. However, if we try to load one of the pages, we'll
see this error:

```
Uncaught TypeError: Argument 1 passed to
↪ Ninja\DatabaseTable::__construct() must be an instance of
↪ Ninja\PDO, instance of PDO given
```

To fix it, we can open up DatabaseTable.php and change the type hint in the
constructor from PDO to \PDO. We saw this error because namespaces are *relative*.
If you provide a reference to a class name, in a type hint or following the new
keyword, PHP will look for a class with that name in the current namespace. We
also need to replace DateTime with \DateTime and PDOException with
\PDOException in this file.

Because the DatabaseTable class is inside the Ninja prefix, without the
backslash prefix PHP will to load the class \Ninja\PDO rather than the inbuilt
PHP class PDO.

The PDO class is in something called the **global** namespace—that is, a class that exists at the very top level, effectively not inside a namespace. To reference a class in the global namespace, we must prefix it with a backslash.

Save `DatabaseTable.php` and refresh the page. There's just one more error to fix:

```
Fatal error: Uncaught TypeError: Argument 1 passed to
↪ Ijdb\Controllers\Joke::__construct() must be an instance of
↪ Ijdb\Controllers\DatabaseTable, instance of
↪ Ninja\DatabaseTable given
```

This is the same problem as above. Because there's no namespace specified, PHP looks for a class called `DatabaseTable` in the *current* namespace. As the controller is in the `Ijdb` namespace, PHP will try to load the class `Ijdb\DatabaseTable`.

We could fix this the same way as above—by providing the class name with the namespace (which PHP refers to as a **Fully qualified class name**): `\Ninja\DatabaseTable`. But a neater solution is *importing* the class `DatabaseTable` into the current namespace.

We can do this with the **use** keyword after the namespace declaration:

9-4. CMS-EntryPoint-Namespaces

```php
<?php
namespace Ijdb\Controllers;
use \Ninja\DatabaseTable;

class Joke {
    private $authorsTable;
    // …
```

If we've done everything correctly, we should be able to refresh the website and see everything working once again.

We've made a lot of changes here, but only to the structure of the code. Most of the code is the same as before; we've just moved it around. To recap, we've done the following:

- split our code up into classes, recognizing the code that's specific to the joke website and the code that can be used on any future website

- organized all our classes in either the `Ijdb` directory, for project-specific files, or the `Ninja` directory for our framework files

- given all our classes namespaces

- removed all include statements for classes by implementing a PSR-4 compatible autoloader

A Note on Composer

Most modern PHP applications use a tool called Composer to handle all autoloading. It's also used to quickly and easily download and install third-party libraries. It's beyond the scope of this book, but if you follow the PSR-4 convention, your classes are good to go when you want to start using it, and you can use composer's autoloader as a drop-in replacement for the `autoload.php` we just wrote.

When you do start using Composer, just add this code to your `composer.json` file:

```
{
    "autoload": {
    "psr-4": {
            "Ninja\\": "classes/Ninja",
            "Ijdb\\": "classes/Ijdb"
    }
    }
}
```

For an overview of Composer, take a look at the SitePoint article "Re-Introducing Composer – the Cornerstone of Modern PHP Apps"[6].

[6.] https://www.sitepoint.com/re-introducing-composer/

And the REST

The current iteration of our router uses a very simplistic approach. Each route is a string from the URL that maps to a controller and calls a specific action.

If we continue using this approach, we'll quickly find ourselves repeating logic in the controllers.

Our edit joke form contains the following logic: *if the form is submitted, process the submission, otherwise display the form.*

This logic will be required for any form on the website. Similarly, we can envisage other features in the future requiring similar logic in the controller. For example: *display the page if the user is logged in, otherwise display the login form.*

When the edit joke form is submitted, it uses the POST method. Any other request to pages on the website will use the GET method.

PHP can detect whether the page was requested using GET or POST. The variable `$_SERVER['REQUEST_METHOD']` is created by PHP and will contain either the string GET or the string POST, depending on how the page was requested by the browser.

We can use this to determine if the form was submitted, and call a different controller action if the form was submitted:

```php
else if ($route === 'joke/edit' &&
 $_SERVER['REQUEST_METHOD'] === 'GET') {
    $controller = new \Ijdb\Controllers\Joke($jokesTable,
      $authorsTable);
    $page = $controller->edit();
}
  else if ($route === 'joke/edit' &&
↪ $_SERVER['REQUEST_METHOD'] === 'POST') {
    $controller = new \Ijdb\Controllers\Joke($jokesTable,
      $authorsTable);
    $page = $controller->editSubmit();
```

```
}
```

This approach works, but it's rather long-winded. Instead, we can use nested arrays to create a *data structure* that represents all of the routes in the application:

```
$routes = [
    'joke/edit' => [
        'POST' => [
            'controller' => $jokeController,
            'action' => 'saveEdit'
        ],
        'GET' => [
            'controller' => $jokeController,
            'action' => 'edit'
        ]

    ],
    'home' => [
        'GET' => [
            'controller' => $jokeController,
            'action' => 'home'
        ]
    ]

    // …
```

This may look fairly strange, but this kind of multidimensional data structure is used frequently in programming, so it's a good tool to learn.

Looking at the code for the $routes array, the downside of this approach is obvious: it requires writing out exactly which controller and action to call for every single page on the website. There are ways around this by using wildcards, but I'll leave that as an exercise for the reader.

The $routes variable is a standard array. It's possible to extract the nested arrays. If we wanted to get the controller and action for the POST method for the route joke/edit, we could do it like this:

```
// First read the route
$route = $routes['joke/edit'];

// Now read the value stored in the `POST` key:
$postRoute = $route['POST'];

// Finally, read the controller and action:
$controller = $postRoute['controller'];
$action = $postRoute['action'];
```

We are effectively "digging down" into the array, choosing which branch of the data structure to follow—a bit like the file/folder structure on your computer.

This can also be expressed in a much shorter way by chaining the square brackets for looking up each value in the arrays:

```
$controller = $routes['joke/edit']['POST']['controller'];
$action = $routes['joke/edit']['POST']['action'];
```

By using variables in place of strings, it's possible to substitute the hardcoded values with values from the $_SERVER variables REQUEST_URI and REQUEST_METHOD:

```
$route = $_SERVER['REQUEST_URI'];

$method = $_SERVER['REQUEST_METHOD'];

$controller = $route[$route][$method]['controller'];
$action = $route[$route][$method]['action'];

$controller->$action();
```

This approach of having the same URL perform different actions depending on the request method is loosely known as **Representational State Transfer** (REST).

REST Methods

Although REST typically supports the methods PUT and DELETE along with GET and POST, because web browsers only support GET and POST, PHP developers tend to use POST in place of both PUT and DELETE requests. As such, it's not worth examining the differences in this book.

Some PHP developers have found superficial ways of mimicking PUT and DELETE, but most developers just stick to using POST for writing data and GET for reading.

For more information on REST, see the SitePoint article "Best Practices REST API from Scratch – Introduction"[7].

Let's go ahead and implement a router using the REST approach on our site.

To begin with, change the `callAction` method in the `IjdbRoutes` class to include both the `$routes` array for the jokes website and the code for selecting the relevant route:

```php
<?php
namespace Ijdb;

class IjdbRoutes
{
    public function callAction($route)
    {
        include __DIR__ . '/../../includes/DatabaseConnection.php';

        $jokesTable = new \Ninja\DatabaseTable($pdo, 'joke', 'id');
        $authorsTable = new \Ninja\DatabaseTable($pdo, 'author',
          'id');

        $jokeController = new \Ijdb\Controllers\Joke($jokesTable,
          $authorsTable);

        $routes = [
            'joke/edit' => [
```

```php
                'POST' => [
                    'controller' => $jokeController,
                    'action' => 'saveEdit'
                ],
                'GET' => [
                    'controller' => $jokeController,
                    'action' => 'edit'
                ]

        ],
        'joke/delete' => [
            'POST' => [
                'controller' => $jokeController,
                'action' => 'delete'
            ]
        ],
        'joke/list' => [
            'GET' => [
                'controller' => $jokeController,
                'action' => 'list'
            ]
        ],
        '' => [
            'GET' => [
                'controller' => $jokeController,
                'action' => 'home'
            ]
        ]
    ];

    $method = $_SERVER['REQUEST_METHOD'];

    $controller = $routes[$route][$method]['controller'];
    $action = $routes[$route][$method]['action'];

    return $controller->$action();
    }
}
```

Now split the edit method in Controllers/Joke.php into a method for displaying the form and another for the handling the submission:

```php
public function saveEdit() {
    $joke = $_POST['joke'];
    $joke['jokedate'] = new \DateTime();
    $joke['authorId'] = 1;

    $this->jokesTable->save($joke);

    header('location: /joke/list');
}

public function edit() {
    if (isset($_GET['id'])) {
        $joke = $this->jokesTable->findById($_GET['id']);
    }

    $title = 'Edit joke';

    return ['template' => 'editjoke.html.php',
        'title' => $title,
        'variables' => [
            'joke' => $joke ?? null
        ]
    ];
}
```

Once again, it's worth taking a look at the code for the new IjdbRoutes class. On the next website, we'll need to repeat the logic for selecting the correct controller and calling the action. This logic will be identical on any site we build:

```php
$method = $_SERVER['REQUEST_METHOD'];

$controller = $routes[$route][$method]['controller'];
$action = $routes[$route][$method]['action'];

return $controller->$action();
```

Instead, we'll just use the `IjdbRoute` class to provide the `$routes` array. We'll rename the `callAction` method `getRoutes`, remove the argument, and have it return the array rather than accessing it:

```php
<?php
namespace Ijdb;

class IjdbRoutes
{
    public function getRoutes()
    {
        include __DIR__ . '/../../includes/DatabaseConnection.php';

        $jokesTable = new \Ninja\DatabaseTable($pdo, 'joke', 'id');
        $authorsTable = new \Ninja\DatabaseTable($pdo, 'author',
         'id');

        $jokeController = new \Ijdb\Controllers\Joke($jokesTable,
         $authorsTable);

        $routes = [
            'joke/edit' => [
                'POST' => [
                    'controller' => $jokeController,
                    'action' => 'saveEdit'
                ],
                'GET' => [
                    'controller' => $jokeController,
                    'action' => 'edit'
                ]

            ],
            'joke/delete' => [
                'POST' => [
                    'controller' => $jokeController,
                    'action' => 'delete'
                ]
```

```
        ],
        'joke/list' => [
            'GET' => [
                'controller' => $jokeController,
                'action' => 'list'
            ]
        ],
        '' => [
            'GET' => [
                'controller' => $jokeController,
                'action' => 'home'
            ]
        ]
    ];

    return $routes;
    }
}
```

Now we'll amend `EntryPoint` to use both `$method` and `$route`. We could hard code the `$route` and `$method` variables in the run method by reading from the server here:

```
public function run() {

    $method = $_SERVER['REQUEST_METHOD'];
    $route = $_SERVER['REQUEST_URI'];
    // …
```

The problem with this approach is that it's not very flexible. If we ever want to use the `EntryPoint` class in an application that isn't web based, it won't work, because these server variables won't be set.

Instead, let's create a class variable and amend the constructor to take the method along with the route:

```
class EntryPoint {
    private $route;
    private $method;
    private $routes;

    public function __construct($route, $method, $routes) {
        $this->route = $route;
        $this->routes = $routes;
        $this->method = $method;
        $this->checkUrl();
    }
```

Next, we amend the run method to make use of both class variables:

```
public function run() {

    $routes = $this->routes->getRoutes();

    $controller = $routes[$this->route]
    [$this->method]['controller'];
    $action = $routes[$this->route]
    [$this->method]['action'];

    $page = $controller->$action();

    $title = $page['title'];

    if (isset($page['variables'])) {
        $output = $this->loadTemplate($page['template'],
        $page['variables']);
    }
    else {
        $output = $this->loadTemplate($page['template']);
    }

    include __DIR__ . '/../../templates/layout.html.php';
}
```

Then we supply the method in `index.php`:

```
$entryPoint = new \Ninja\EntryPoint($route,
  $_SERVER['REQUEST_METHOD'], new \Ijdb\IjdbRoutes());
```

You can find this code in *CMS-EntryPoint-Namespaces-Router*.

Avoiding hardcoding like this is a very good habit to get into. The trend in PHP (and software development in general) is towards **test-driven development** (TDD), and hardcoded values like `$_SERVER['REQUEST_METHOD']` make testing difficult. Although TDD is well beyond the scope of this book, I do want to teach you practices that will make your eventual move to TDD as easy as possible.

Enforcing Dependency Structure with Interfaces

In Chapter 8, when we created the `DatabaseTable` class, we wrote the constructor so that it would check the types of its arguments:

```
 public function __construct(PDO $pdo, string $table, string
↪ $primaryKey) {
```

Using this approach, it's impossible to construct an instance of the `DatabaseTable` class without supplying an instance of `PDO` as the first argument.

The `EntryPoint` class has a dependency on `IjdbRoutes`, and it calls the `getRoutes` method on it:

```
$routes = $this->routes->getRoutes();
```

However, what happens if the `$this->routes` variable is not an instance of `IjdbJokes`, or it's an object that doesn't have a `getRoutes` method?

As we did with `DatabaseTable`, we can enforce the types using hints in the constructor:

```php
public function __construct(string $route, string $method,
↳ \Ijdb\IjdbRoutes $routes) {
```

With the type hints in place, it's impossible to construct the `EntryPoint` class without supplying an instance of `IjdbRoutes` as the third argument. But this breaks our flexibility! What happens when we build the online shop and we want to use a class called `\Shop\Routes`? Ideally, we want the flexibility of allowing each website to supply a different set of routes, but we also want the robustness that type checking gives us.

This can be achieved using something called an **interface**. An interface can be used to describe what methods a class should contain, but doesn't contain any actual logic. Classes can then *implement* the interface.

An interface for the routes would look like this:

```php
<?php
namespace Ninja;

interface Routes
{
    public function getRoutes();
}
```

You'll notice that it looks a little like a class. It has a namespace, a name and a method. However, the difference between an interface and a class is that it only contains the method **header** (the first line), and doesn't contain any logic.

Let's save the interface in the `Ninja` directory as `Routes.php`. Like classes, interface files can be loaded by the autoloader.

We can now type hint the *interface* in `EntryPoint`:

```php
public function __construct(string $route, string $method,
↳ \Ninja\Routes $routes) {
```

Currently, this will prevent us from passing an instance of `Ijdb\IjdbRoutes` into `EntryPoint`'s constructor. However, we can make `IjdbRoutes` *implement* the interface:

```php
<?php
namespace Ijdb;

class IjdbRoutes implements \Ninja\Routes {
```

You can find this codd in *CMS-EntryPoint-Interface*.

This has two effects:

1. The class `IjdbRoutes` *must* contain the methods described in the interface. If not, an error is displayed.

2. The `IjdbRoutes` class can now be type hinted using the interface.

Now, when we build the online shop or any other website, we can make a new version of the routes class by implementing the interface:

```php
namespace Shop;
class Routes implements \Ninja\Routes {
    public function getRoutes() {
        // Return routes for the online shop
    }
}
```

Interfaces are very useful for the kind of generic framework we've built. By providing a set of interfaces, each website can provide classes that implement the interfaces, guaranteeing that the framework code and project-specific code fit together.

You can connect your TV to a Blu-ray player, a satellite TV receiver, a games console, or even a computer, because they all use HDMI. The makers of the TV don't know what's going to be connected to it, but anything that follows the HDMI standard will work with the TV. Similarly, anything that uses the `Ninja\`

`Routes` interface will work with the `Ninja` framework.

Interfaces, when used correctly, are a very powerful tool for bridging framework and project-specific code.

Your Own Framework

Writing a framework is a rite of passage for a PHP developer. Everyone does it, and we've just written one! Through this book, I hope I've helped you avoid some of the common traps developers fall into.

In this chapter you learned:

- the difference between framework code and project-specific code
- how to differentiate them by use of directory structures and namespaces
- how to write an autoloader
- the basics of interfaces and REST
- routing and URL rewriting

Although we haven't added any *functionality* in this chapter, the knowledge covered here will put you on a very firm footing when working with modern PHP applications and third-party code from fellow developers.

Chapter

10

Allowing Users to Register Accounts

Now that we've done all the hard work of building an extensible framework, it's time to add some new functionality to the website. We're going to make it so that users can register accounts on the website with a view to letting them post jokes themselves.

You should already have the table for **authors** in the database with some data you added via MySQL Workbench. If you don't, you can execute this query to create the table:

```
CREATE TABLE author (
id INT NOT NULL AUTO_INCREMENT PRIMARY KEY,
name VARCHAR(255),
email VARCHAR(255)
) DEFAULT CHARACTER SET utf8mb4 ENGINE=InnoDB
```

Don't worry about adding any records if you have none. We'll be creating a form that lets us add authors from the website.

The first step is to add another column to the database to store the password that users will use to log in. Let's create another column, either using MySQL Workbench's GUI or running the following query:

```
ALTER TABLE author ADD COLUMN password VARCHAR(255)
```

The column name should be password and the type VARCHAR(255). I know that 255 characters sounds like a very long password, but there's a reason for making the column so large, which we'll get to later.

The first thing that's needed is the controller code. Create the file Register.php in the Ijdb\Controllers directory, then create the class with the following variables, constructor and a method for loading the registration form. For registering users, the only dependency needed is the DatabaseTable object that represents the authors table:

```php
<?php
namespace Ijdb\Controllers;

use \Ninja\DatabaseTable;

class Register
{
    private $authorsTable;

    public function __construct(DatabaseTable $authorsTable)
    {
        $this->authorsTable = $authorsTable;
    }

    public function registrationForm()
    {
```

```
        return ['template' => 'register.html.php',
            'title' => 'Register an account'];
    }

    public function success()
    {
        return ['template' => 'registersuccess.html.php',
            'title' => 'Registration Successful'];
    }
}
```

I've added two actions: one for displaying the form, and one for displaying the *Registration Successful* page.

Here's the template, `register.html.php`, in the `templates` directory:

```
<form action="" method="post">
<label for="email">Your email address</label>
<input name="author[email]" id="email" type="text">

<label for="name">Your name</label>
<input name="author[name]" id="name" type="text">

<label for="password">Password</label>
<input name="author[password]" id="password"
    type="password">

<input type="submit" name="submit"
    value="Register account">
</form>
```

Here's `registersuccess.html.php`:

```
<h2>Registration Successful</h2>

 <p>You are now registered on the Internet Joke
↳ Database</p>
```

And finally, the routes in `IjdbRoutes.php`:

```php
// …
$jokeController = new \Ijdb\Controllers\Joke($jokesTable,
 $authorsTable);
$authorController =
 new \Ijdb\Controllers\Register($authorsTable);

$routes = [
    'author/register' => [
        'GET' => [
            'controller' => $authorController,
            'action' => 'registrationForm'
        ]
    ],
    'author/success' => [
        'GET' => [
            'controller' => $authorController,
            'action' => 'success'
        ]
    ],
    'joke/edit' => [
// …
```

If we visit `http://192.168.10.10/author/register`, we should see the form. To make the form work, we'll need to add the `POST` route in `IjdbRoutes` and the relevant method in the controller.

```php
'author/register' => [
    'GET' => [
        'controller' => $authorController,
        'action' => 'registrationForm'
    ],
    'POST' => [
        'controller' => $authorController,
```

```
        'action' => 'registerUser'
    ]
],
```

Register.php:

```
public function registerUser() {
    $author = $_POST['author'];

    $this->authorsTable->save($author);

    header('Location: /author/success');
}
```

You can find this code in *Registration-Form*.

Once the form is submitted, the router will execute the `registerUser` method and save the new author information by reading from the `$_POST` array.

Check if it works by filling out the form, submitting it and selecting all the records from the `author` table using MySQL Workbench. If you don't see the data for the record you just added, double check all your code and try again.

We have a basic registration form working, but there are some problems with it in its current state. We need some control over what's allowed in the database. There are some rules we probably want to enforce on the data before allowing the record to be inserted:

- All fields should actually contain some data, so no blank email or name.
- The email address should be a real email address. For example, `paul@example.org` is allowed, but `abc123` isn't.
- The email address entered must not already belong to an account.

These validation rules need to be checked before the data is inserted, but also after the form is submitted. If there's a problem with the submission, it's good practice to show the form to the user again so they can fix their mistakes.

Each one of these validation rules needs to be applied in slightly different ways, but with a similar result. We'll use `if` statements for each check and set a boolean variable `$valid` to keep track of whether the data is valid or not. For example, to check that each field has a value inside it, we can use a series of `if` statements that set the `$valid` variable to false if one of the fields is empty:

```php
public function registerUser() {
    $author = $_POST['author'];

    // Assume the data is valid to begin with
    $valid = true;

    // But if any of the fields have been left blank
    // set $valid to false
    if (empty($author['name'])) {
        $valid = false;
    }

    if (empty($author['email'])) {
        $valid = false;
    }

    if (empty($author['password'])) {
        $valid = false;
    }

    // If $valid is still true, no fields were blank
    // and the data can be added
    if ($valid == true) {
        $this->authorsTable->save($author);

        header('Location: /author/success');
    }
    else {
        // If the data is not valid, show the form again
        return ['template' => 'register.html.php',
                'title' => 'Register an account'];
    }
}
```

Using `empty()` Above

I've used `empty($author['name'])` instead of `$author['name'] == ''` here, because this will also catch invalid form submissions without causing an error.

It's possible for someone to submit a POST request without filling in your form! It's likely they might not supply values (an empty string is still a value!) for some of the form fields. It's better to avoid these kinds of errors than potentially alert malicious users to how the site works.

Try it yourself by submitting the form and leaving one or more fields blank. You should see the blank form again rather than the "Registration Successful" message.

If `$valid` has been set to false because one of the fields is empty, then the form is shown again by returning a title and template. If you did try this for yourself, you'll have immediately noticed that whatever you typed into the box has been removed, and there's no indication to the user of what was wrong.

To fix this, let's first create a second array to keep a list of error messages to show to the user:

```php
public function registerUser() {
    $author = $_POST['author'];

    // Assume the data is valid to begin with
    $valid = true;
    $errors = [];

    // But if any of the fields have been left blank
    // set $valid to false
    if (empty($author['name'])) {
        $valid = false;
        $errors[] = 'Name cannot be blank';
    }

    if (empty($author['email'])) {
```

```php
        $valid = false;
        $errors[] = 'Email cannot be blank';
    }

    if (empty($author['password'])) {
        $valid = false;
        $errors[] = 'Password cannot be blank';
    }

    // If $valid is still true, no fields were blank
    //   and the data can be added
    if ($valid == true) {
        $this->authorsTable->save($author);

        header('Location: /author/success');
    }
    else {
        // If the data is not valid, show the form again
        return ['template' => 'register.html.php',
                'title' => 'Register an account'];
    }
}
```

Remember the [ ] = operator for arrays? This will be added to the end of the $errors array, so if the user leaves all three fields blank, all three error messages will be stored in the $errors array. These errors will need to be shown to the user by displaying them in the template.

When we created the joke list page, we supplied the template some variables using the variables key in the returned array. The same thing can be done here with the errors:

```php
// If the data is not valid, show the form again
return ['template' => 'register.html.php',
'title' => 'Register an account',
'variables' => [
    'errors' => $errors
]
```

```
];
```

And now the $errors variable can be used in `register.html.php`:

```php
<?php
if (!empty($errors)) :
    ?>
    <div class="errors">
        <p>Your account could not be created,
         please check the following:</p>
        <ul>
        <?php
            foreach ($errors as $error) :
                ?>
                <li><?= $error ?></li>
                <?php
            endforeach; ?>
        </ul>
    </div>
<?php
endif;
?>
<form action="" method="post">
    <label for="email">Your email address</label>
    <input name="author[email]" id="email" type="text">

    <label for="name">Your name</label>
    <input name="author[name]" id="name" type="text">

    <label for="password">Password</label>
    <input name="author[password]" id="password"
        type="password">

    <input type="submit" name="submit"
        value="Register account">
</form>
```

To make the errors look a bit nicer, add the following to `jokes.css`:

```css
.errors {
    padding: 1em;
    border: 1px solid red;
    background-color: lightyellow;
    color: red;
    margin-bottom: 1em;
    overflow: auto;
}
.errors ul {
    margin-left: 1em;
}
```

If there are any errors now, they'll all be printed in a list at the top of the page before the form, and the user will know what went wrong.

To make things even easier, we'll re-fill the form with the data from `$_POST`.

Firstly, let's supply the `$author` information to the template by amending the `return` value:

```php
return ['template' => 'register.html.php',
'title' => 'Register an account',
'variables' => [
    'errors' => $errors,
    'author' => $author
]
];
```

Now print the values in the form fields if they're set. This is exactly the same approach we took in `editjoke.html.php` to fill the form with the information in the database:

```html
<label for="email">Your email address</label>
<input name="author[email]" id="email" type="text"
```

```
    value="<?=$author['email'] ?? ''?>">

<label for="name">Your name</label>
<input name="author[name]" id="name" type="text"
    value="<?=$author['name'] ?? ''?>">

<label for="password">Password</label>
<input name="author[password]" id="password"
    type="password"
    value="<?=$author['password'] ?? ''?>">

<input type="submit" name="submit" v
    alue="Register account">
```

You can find this code in *Registration-Validation*.

Validating Email Addresses

The validation above will prevent someone from leaving the email address field blank. However, it doesn't guarantee they've entered a valid email address. They can still enter "a" into the field and it will pass the validation.

To ensure they enter a valid email address, we need to do some checking. We could look at each character in the string and look for an "@" symbol, ensuring it's not the first character, and perhaps also look for a "." after the "@" to match "x@x.x". However, this will take quite a few lines of code and will be complex to implement.

As for most common problems, PHP includes a method of validating email addresses that's far more accurate and simpler to use than building your own. There's no need to reinvent the wheel.

To check an email address in PHP, you can use the `filter_var` function like so:

```
$email = 'tom@example.org';

if (filter_var($email, FILTER_VALIDATE_EMAIL) == false) {
```

```
    echo 'Valid  email address';
}
else {
    echo 'Invalid email address';
}
```

The `filter_var` function is provided by PHP and takes two arguments. The first is the string to validate, and the second is the type of data to check against. There are several options, including `FILTER_VALIDATE_URL` and `FILTER_VALIDATE_INT`, for checking whether a given string is a valid URL or integer. The only one we need at this moment is `FILTER_VALIDATE_EMAIL`, which is used to validate email addresses. For a complete list of all the options supported by `filter_var`, see the function's page on the PHP website[1].

Let's implement this check in the `Register` controller:

```
if (empty($author['email'])) {
    $valid = false;
    $errors[] = 'Email cannot be blank';
}
else if (filter_var($author['email']) == false) {
    $valid = false;
    $errors[] = 'Invalid email address';
}
```

You can find this code in *Registration-Validation-Email*.

First, we check whether the email address has been provided, and if it has, whether it's a valid email address using `filter_var`. If both checks pass, the email address is valid and no errors are displayed.

Preventing the Same Person from Registering Twice

There's one other check we need to do on the email address: ensuring the same

---

[1] http://php.net/manual/en/function.filter-var.php

person can't have multiple accounts. Allowing someone to have multiple accounts can cause problems with a website. If they log in, which account do they log in to? If they can see their previous jokes, they'll only see the ones posted by the account they're logged in to, and any information tailored to them will only be displayed on one account.

It's very good practice to prevent the same person from registering twice with the same email address. This can be enforced in the database, but it's more consistent to use PHP to check this. We already have the $authorsTable object for searching for records in the author database table. We can make use of it to check if an email address already exists.

Currently, the class DatabaseTable contains a findById method that allows you to retrieve a record from the table by its ID.

Let's add another method called find that takes two arguments:

■ the column to search in
■ the value to search for

```
$results = $authorsTable->find('email',
  'tom@example.org');
```

Once implemented, the find method will select all the records where the email column is set to tom@example.org using the query SELECT * FROM author WHERE email = 'tom@example.org'.

Because the DatabaseTable class already contains the query function, we can implement the find function in a similar way to the current findyById function:

```
public function findById($value) {
    $query = 'SELECT * FROM ' . $this->table . ' WHERE ' .
    $this->primaryKey . ' = :primaryKey';

    $parameters = [
        'primaryKey' => $value
    ];
```

```php
    $query = $this->query($query, $parameters);

    return $query->fetch();
}

public function find($column, $value) {
    $query = 'SELECT * FROM ' . $this->table . ' WHERE ' .
     $column . ' = :value';

    $parameters = [
        'value' => $value
    ];

    $query = $this->query($query, $parameters);

    return $query->fetchAll();
}
```

There are two differences, but the code is very similar. Instead of searching using the column name from `$this->primaryKey`, the column name is provided by the argument `$column`, and the `return` statement uses `$query->fetchAll()` to return all the records as an array.

The `$query->fetch` function will only return one record. If we're searching any column for any value, it's possible that multiple records may have the same value. The `fetchAll` method is used to return all the matched records. Ideally, we want a generic `find` function that we can use anywhere we'd like to search the database for records that have a value set for a specified column.

Now that the `find` function has been added, we can use it to determine whether an email address already exists in the database:

```php
  if (count($authorsTable->find('email', $author['email']))
  ↪ > 0) {
    $valid = false;
    $errors[] = 'That email address is already registered';
```

```
}
```

The count function can be used to tally the number of records returned by the find method. If it's greater than zero (> 0), there's already a record in the system with the email address being searched for, and you can display an error accordingly.

The only issue with this approach is that it's case sensitive. If the user has already registered with tom@example.org and then re-registers using TOM@EXAMPLE.ORG, these will be seen as different email addresses. In order to correctly determine whether tom@example.org has already signed up, the email address can be stored in the database in lowercase, and searched using the lowercase version. The complete registerUser method now looks like this:

```
public function registerUser() {
    $author = $_POST['author'];

    // Assume the data is valid to begin with
    $valid = true;
    $errors = [];

    // But if any of the fields have been left blank
    // set $valid to false
    if (empty($author['name'])) {
        $valid = false;
        $errors[] = 'Name cannot be blank';
    }

    if (empty($author['email'])) {
        $valid = false;
        $errors[] = 'Email cannot be blank';
    }
    else if (filter_var($author['email'],
      FILTER_VALIDATE_EMAIL) == false) {
        $valid = false;
        $errors[] = 'Invalid email address';
    }
```

```php
    else { // If the email is not blank and valid:
        // convert the email to lowercase
        $author['email'] = strtolower($author['email']);

        // Search for the lowercase version of $author['email']
        if (count($this->authorsTable->
        find('email', $author['email'])) > 0) {
            $valid = false;
            $errors[] = 'That email address is already registered';
        }
    }

    if (empty($author['password'])) {
        $valid = false;
        $errors[] = 'Password cannot be blank';
    }

    // If $valid is still true, no fields were blank
    // and the data can be added
    if ($valid == true) {

        // When submitted, the $author variable now contains a
        // lowercase value for email
        $this->authorsTable->save($author);

        header('Location: /author/success');
    } else {
        // If the data is not valid, show the form again
        return ['template' => 'register.html.php',
        'title' => 'Register an account',
        'variables' => [
            'errors' => $errors,
            'author' => $author
        ]
    ];
    }
}
```

By converting the email address to lowercase, when inserting the data and when searching for it, we can deal with email addresses in a case-insensitive manner.

Email Addresses and Case-sensitivity

Technically, email addresses can be case-sensitive[2]. However, this is discouraged, and for all practical applications it's safe to assume that email addresses are not case sensitive. No major email provider allows case-sensitive email addresses.

The alternative is hoping that users always type in their email address with the same case, which is not a good assumption to make.

Securely Storing Passwords

Now that the validation has been added, it's possible for anyone who enters valid data into the form to sign up and have their information added to the database. Go ahead and add some test users and check that it's working correctly by verifying that the record has been added to the author table.

Using the approach above, if someone types "mypassword123" into the password field, that's what will be stored in the database. We might think that's not a problem, since only we have access to the database, and we're not going misuse the information. But would we really want the developers of every website we use to know our password?

If our website gets hacked, it's then possible for the hacker to see all of our users' passwords, and because people are forgetful, they tend to use the same password for every website they visit.

Someone with access to someone else's email/password combination could, therefore, do quite a bit of damage beyond accessing the account on this one site we just built—such as reading their email or accessing their PayPal account.

A good website developer will help protect their users from this kind of attack. The most common method of achieving this is using a "one way hashing function".

A **hashing function** takes a string like mypassword123 and converts it to an

---

[2.] https://tools.ietf.org/html/rfc5321#page-42

encrypted version of the string, known as a **hash**. For example, `mypassword123`
would be *hashed* and produce a seemingly random string of numbers and letters
such as `9c87baa223f464954940f859bcf2e233`.

To convert a string to a hash, we can use one of several available hashing
functions built into PHP, including `md5` and `sha1`. Using these functions is simple:

```
echo md5('mypassword123');
// prints 9c87baa223f464954940f859bcf2e233
```

This isn't "encryption" in the true sense. There's no way to decrypt that
seemingly random string of letters and numbers back into `mypassword123`.

One method of storing passwords is to store these hashes in the database. When a
user types "mypassword123" into the password field,
`9c87baa223f464954940f859bcf2e233` is stored in the password column in the
database instead of `mypassword123`.

Now, if someone does manage to gain access to the database, all they'll see is a
list of names and hashes. For example:

```
Kevin    9c87baa223f464954940f859bcf2e233
Laura    47bce5c74f589f4867dbd57e9ca9f808
Tom      9c87baa223f464954940f859bcf2e233
Jane     8d6e8d4897a32c5d011a89346477fb07
```

This solves the problem of someone with access to the database being able to read
everyone's password. However, it's not perfect. What do you know about Kevin
and Tom's passwords? Looking at the list you can see that they're the same! If you
can work out Kevin's password, you'll also know Tom's.

And, what's worse, we actually know what the password is, because we already
discovered that `9c87baa223f464954940f859bcf2e233` is the hash for
`mypassword123`. Because people all use the same common passwords, hackers
will generate the hashes for common passwords in order to quickly work out
which users are using them. Once you know that the hash for `password` is

5f4dcc3b5aa765d61d8327deb882cf99, you can query the database for any user who has that hash and you'll know their password is password. Do this for the top 100, 200 or 1000 passwords, and on a large site you'll work out dozens of real email/password combinations.

You'll have heard about the importance of using a secure, not easily guessable password, and this is one of the many reasons why. If your password is uncommon, hackers won't have generated a hash for it, and won't be able to easily work out what your password is!

There are several methods for solving this problem with duplicated hashes, but there's a lot to consider, and making a truly secure password hash is more difficult than it seems. If you want to learn more about the theory for solving this, take a look at the SitePoint article "Password Hashing in PHP"[3].

Luckily for us, PHP includes a very secure way of storing passwords. It's at least as good as any solution developers will come up with, and avoids developers like us needing to fully understand the security problems that can occur. For this reason, it's strongly recommended to use the inbuilt PHP algorithm for hashing passwords rather than to create your own.

Now that you understand the importance and the theory behind password hashing, let's put it into practice.

PHP contains two functions, password_hash and password_verify. For now, we're only interested in password_hash. We'll use password_verify in the next chapter when we're checking to see whether someone entered the correct username and password when logging in.

This is how we can hash a password using the password_hash function:

```
$hash = password_hash($password, PASSWORD_DEFAULT);
```

$password stores the text of the password being hashed, and PASSWORD_DEFAULT is the algorithm to use. It's generally best to leave it up to the PHP developers, as this will choose the best algorithm currently available. (At the time of writing,

---

[3.] https://www.sitepoint.com/password-hashing-in-php/

this is an algorithm known as bcrypt[4], but it may change over time.)

If we run the code above with a password such as "mypassword123" and echo the $hash variable, we'll see something like this:

```
$2y$10$XPtbphrRABcV95GxoeAk.OeI8tPgaypkKicBUhX/YbC9QYSSoowRq
```

I say "something like", because each time you run the function, you'll get a different result. Even if you use "mypassword123" as the password each time, you'll get a different hash as a result. If two people have the same password, different hashes will be stored in the database.

Earlier in the chapter, when we added the password column to the database table, I said to make it 255 characters. This is because hashes can be long, and if the default algorithm changes, they may grow in size.

Let's implement the `password_hash` function in the registration form. It's surprisingly easy:

```
// …
if ($valid == true) {
    // Hash the password before saving it in the database
    $author['password'] = password_hash($author['password'],
     PASSWORD_DEFAULT);

    // When submitted, the $author variable now contains a
    // lowercase value for email and a hashed password
    $this->authorsTable->save($author);

    header('Location: /author/success');
}
// …
```

The `password` value in the $author array is replaced with the hashed version. Now, when the data is saved, the hashed password is stored in the database,

---

[4.] https://www.npmjs.com/package/bcrypt

instead of the value `mypassword123` (or whatever was entered into the form).

Registration Complete

The final version of the `Register` controller looks like this:

```php
<?php
namespace Ijdb\Controllers;

use \Ninja\DatabaseTable;

class Register
{
    private $authorsTable;

    public function __construct(DatabaseTable $authorsTable)
    {
        $this->authorsTable = $authorsTable;
    }

    public function registrationForm()
    {
        return ['template' => 'register.html.php',
            'title' => 'Register an account'];
    }

    public function success()
    {
        return ['template' => 'registersuccess.html.php',
            'title' => 'Registration Successful'];
    }

    public function registerUser()
    {
        $author = $_POST['author'];

        // Assume the data is valid to begin with
        $valid = true;
        $errors = [];

        // But if any of the fields have been left blank
        // set $valid to false
        if (empty($author['name'])) {
            $valid = false;
            $errors[] = 'Name cannot be blank';
```

```
        }

        if (empty($author['email'])) {
            $valid = false;
            $errors[] = 'Email cannot be blank';
        } elseif (filter_var($author['email'],
         FILTER_VALIDATE_EMAIL) == false) {
            $valid = false;
            $errors[] = 'Invalid email address';
        } else { // If the email is not blank and valid:
            // convert the email to lowercase
            $author['email'] = strtolower($author['email']);

            // Search for the lowercase version of $author['email']
            if (count($this->authorsTable->find('email',
             $author['email'])) > 0) {
                $valid = false;
                $errors[] = 'That email address is already
registered';
            }
        }

        if (empty($author['password'])) {
            $valid = false;
            $errors[] = 'Password cannot be blank';
        }

        // If $valid is still true, no fields were blank
        // and the data can be added
        if ($valid == true) {
            // Hash the password before saving it in the database
            $author['password'] =
password_hash($author['password'],
             PASSWORD_DEFAULT);

            // When submitted, the $author variable now contains a
            // lowercase value for email and a hashed password
            $this->authorsTable->save($author);

            header('Location: /author/success');
```

```
        } else {
            // If the data is not valid, show the form again
            return ['template' => 'register.html.php',
                'title' => 'Register an account',
                'variables' => [
                    'errors' => $errors,
                    'author' => $author
                ]
            ];
        }
    }
}
```

In this chapter, I showed you how to add a new controller to the website, allow users to sign up for accounts, validate the data that's entered into a form, and how to store passwords securely.

In the next chapter, we'll build a login form, using a tool called *sessions* to track whether a user is logged in or not.

Chapter **11**

Cookies, Sessions, and Access Control

In the last chapter, I showed you how users can register accounts on the website. Now it's time to make those accounts functional, so that users can *log in* to the website. The process is familiar to web users: they enter a username and password, and get access to content that's unique to their account.

Although a familiar process from the perspective of someone using the website, for a developer, building a website that allows *logging in* can seem daunting at first.

By its nature, HTTP is **stateless**. You connect to a website, the server gives you a file. As you've already seen, you can send data from the browser to the server using GET variables and HTML forms. However, the information is provided to a single page, and is only available when the browser provides GET (or POST) variables.

For a login system, the user will need to send their username and password to the server once, and then maintain a "logged-in" state on every subsequent page request.

Although this information could be sent via URL parameters or HTML forms, it would need to be provided to each page. From a user's point of view, entering their username and password each time they visit a different page is time consuming and inefficient.

Two technologies, *cookies* and *sessions*, can be used to store information about a particular user between pages.

Cookies and sessions are two of those mysterious technologies that are almost always made out to be more intimidating and complex than they really are. In this chapter, I'll debunk those myths by explaining in simple language what they are, how they work, and what they can do for you. I'll also provide practical examples to demonstrate each.

Finally, we'll use these new tools to give our newly registered users the ability to navigate around the website and post jokes associated with their account.

Cookies

Most computer programs these days preserve some form of **state**, whether it be the position of the application window, or the names of the last five files you worked with. The values are usually stored in a small file on your system so they can be read back the next time the program is run. When web developers took web design to the next level, and moved from static pages to complete, interactive online applications, there was a need for similar functionality in web browsers. And thus, cookies were born.

A **cookie** is a name–value pair, an array of sorts, associated with a given website, and stored on the computer that runs the client (browser). Once a cookie is set by a website, all future page requests to that same site will send the information stored in the cookie back to the website until it **expires** (or becomes out of date). Other websites are unable to access the cookies set by your site, and vice versa. So, contrary to popular belief, they're a relatively safe place to store personal information. Cookies in and of themselves are incapable of compromising a user's privacy.

The life cycle of a PHP-generated cookie is as follows:

1. First, a web browser requests a URL that corresponds to a PHP script. Within that script is a call to the `setcookie` function that's built into PHP.

2. The page produced by the PHP script is sent back to the browser, along with an HTTP `set-cookie` header that contains the name (for example, `mycookie`) and the value of the cookie to be set.

3. When it receives this HTTP header, the browser creates and stores the specified value as a cookie named `mycookie`.

4. Subsequent page requests to that website contain an HTTP `cookie` header that sends the name–value pair (`mycookie=value`) to the script requested.

5. Upon receipt of a page request with a `cookie` header, PHP automatically creates an entry in the `$_COOKIE` array with the name of the cookie (`$_COOKIE['mycookie']`) and its value.

In other words, the PHP `setcookie` function lets us set a variable that will automatically be set by subsequent page requests from the same browser. Each browser (or website visitor) can have a different value set in the same cookie.

Before we examine an actual example, let's take a close look at the `setcookie` function[1]:

```
bool setcookie ( string $name [, string $value = "" [,
  int $expire = 0 [, string $path = "" [,
  string $domain = "" [, bool $secure = false [,
  bool $httponly = false ]]]]]] )
```

[1.] http://php.net/manual/en/function.setcookie.php

Square Brackets

The square brackets ([...]) indicate arguments of the function that are optional. You can omit these arguments and some defaults will be set by PHP automatically.

Like the `header` function we saw in <u>Chapter 4</u>, the `setcookie` function adds HTTP headers to the page, and thus *must be called before any of the actual page content is sent*. Any attempt to call `setcookie` after page content has been sent to the browser will produce a PHP error message. Typically, therefore, we'll use these functions in our controller script before any actual output is sent (by an included PHP template, for example).

The only required parameter for this function is the `name` parameter, which specifies the name of the cookie. Calling `setcookie` with only the name parameter will actually delete the cookie that's stored on the browser, if it exists. The value parameter allows you to create a new cookie, or modify the value stored in an existing one.

By default, cookies will remain stored by the browser, and thus will continue to be sent with page requests until the browser is closed by the user. If you want the cookie to persist beyond the current browser session, you must set the `expiryTime` parameter to specify the number of seconds from January 1, 1970 to the time at which you want the cookie to be deleted automatically. Although that sounds arbitrary, this is a very common time format known as a **unix timestamp**, and PHP has inbuilt functions for calculating this so you don't need to do it yourself.

The current time in this format can be obtained using the PHP `time` function. Thus, a cookie could be set to expire in one hour, for example, by setting `expiryTime` to `time() + 3600`. To delete a cookie that has a preset expiry time, change this expiry time to represent a point in the past (such as one year ago: `time() - 3600 * 24 * 365`). Here are two examples showing these techniques in practice:

```
// Set a cookie to expire in 1 year
setcookie('mycookie', 'somevalue',
  time() + 3600 * 24 * 365);
```

```
// Delete it
setcookie('mycookie', '',
  time() - 3600 * 24 * 365);
```

 UNIX Timestamps

Unix timestamps will change in the future. In the year 2038, they'll suffer a similar problem to the Y2K bug, because the data type used to store them can't store a high enough number to count the seconds after January 19, 2038.

This may seem a long way off at the moment, but it's worth keeping in mind. To make a cookie persistent, we must set an expiration date. We might be inclined to make this a date very far in the future so that it effectively never expires—perhaps the current date + 20 years.

Doing this calculation will break if our script executes after January 19, 2018, because the expiration date will be after 2038 and the cookie will not be set. Selecting 10 years' time will break our program in 2028. I recommend we select one year, so that we're safe until 2037—by which time there'll be a proper fix in place.

The path parameter lets us restrict access to the cookie to a given path on our server. For instance, if we set a path of `'/admin/'` for a cookie, only requests for pages in the `admin` directory (and its subdirectories) will include the cookie as part of the request. Note the trailing `/`, which prevents scripts in other directories beginning with `/admin` (such as `/adminfake/`) from accessing the cookie. This is helpful if you're sharing a server with other users, and each user has a web home directory. It allows us to set cookies without exposing our visitors' data to the scripts of other users on our server.

The domain parameter serves a similar purpose: it restricts the cookie's access to a given domain. By default, a cookie will be returned only to the host from which it was originally sent. Large companies, however, commonly have several host names for their web presence (for example, `www.example.com` and `support.example.com`). To create a cookie that's accessible by pages on both servers, we would set the domain parameter to `'.example.com'`. Note the leading `.`, which allows anything ending in `.example.com` to access the cookie. However, cookies are never shared across different domains. Setting the domain parameter to `example2.com` won't make the cookie available on another site.

The secure parameter, when set to 1, indicates that the cookie should be sent only with page requests that happen over a secure (SSL) connection (that is, with a URL that starts with `https://`).

The `httpOnly` parameter, when set to 1, tells the browser to prevent JavaScript code on our site from seeing the cookie that we're setting. Normally, the JavaScript code we include in our site can read the cookies that have been set by the server for the current page. While this can be useful in some cases, it also puts the data stored in our cookies at risk should an attacker figure out a way to inject malicious JavaScript code into our site. This code could then read your users' potentially sensitive cookie data and do unspeakable things with them. If we set `httpOnly` to 1, the cookie we're setting will be sent to our PHP scripts as usual, but will be invisible to JavaScript code running on our site.

While all parameters except `name` are optional, we must specify values for earlier parameters if we want to specify values for later ones. For instance, to call `setcookie` with a domain value, we also need to specify a value for the `expiryTime` parameter. To omit parameters that require a value, we can set string parameters (`value`, `path`, `domain`) to `''` (the empty string) and numerical parameters (`expiryTime`, `secure`) to 0.

Let's now look at an example of cookies in use. Imagine we want to display a special welcome message to people on their first visit to our site. We could use a cookie to count the number of times a user has been to our site before, and only display the message when the cookie hasn't been set. Here's the code:

```php
<?php

if (!isset($_COOKIE['visits'])) {
    $_COOKIE['visits'] = 0;
}
$visits = $_COOKIE['visits'] + 1;
setcookie('visits', $visits, time() + 3600 * 24 * 365);

if ($visits > 1) {
    echo "This is visit number $visits.";
} else {
    // First visit
    echo 'Welcome to our website! Click here for a tour!';
}
```

This code starts by checking if $_COOKIE['visits'] is set. If it isn't, it means the visits cookie has yet to be set in the user's browser. To handle this special case, we set $_COOKIE['visits'] to 0. The rest of our code can then safely assume that $_COOKIE['visits'] contains the number of previous visits the user has made to the site.

Next, to work out the number of *this* visit, we take $_COOKIE['visits'] and add the value 1. This variable, $visits, will be used by our PHP template.

Finally, we use setcookie to set the visits cookie to reflect the new number of visits. We set this cookie to expire in one year's time.

The images below shows what this example looks like the first time a browser visits the page and after the second visit.

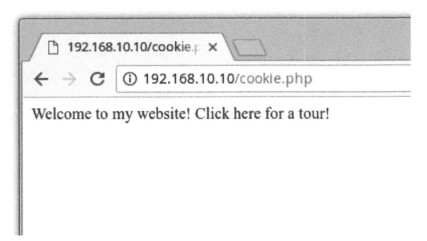

Welcome to my website! Click here for a tour!

11-2. The first visit

This is visit number 2.

11-3. The second visit

Before we go overboard using cookies, we have to be aware that browsers place a limit on the number and size of cookies allowed per website. Some browsers will start deleting old cookies to make room for new ones after we've set 20 cookies from our site. Other browsers will allow up to 50 cookies per site, but will *reject* new cookies beyond this limit. Browsers also enforce a maximum combined size for all cookies from all websites, so an especially cookie-heavy site might cause our own site's cookies to be deleted.

Each time someone visits our website, all of the cookies are sent to the web server. If we store a lot of information in the cookie, it can slow down the responsiveness of the website, because extra data must be transferred with each page view.

Cookies can also be read by anyone who gains access to the computer they're stored on, so cookies are only as secure as the computer being used to view the website.

For these reasons, we should do our best to keep the number and size of the cookies our site creates to a minimum.

PHP Sessions

Because of the limitations I've just described, cookies are inappropriate for storing large amounts of information. If we run an ecommerce website that uses cookies to store items in shopping carts as users make their way through our site, it can be a huge problem. The bigger a customer's order, the more likely it will run afoul of a browser's cookie restrictions.

Sessions were developed in PHP as the solution to this issue. Instead of storing all our (possibly large) data as cookies in our visitor's web browser, sessions let us store the data on our web server. The only value that's stored in the browser is a single cookie containing the user's **session ID**—a long string of letters and numbers that serves to identify that user uniquely for the duration of their visit to our site. It's a variable for which PHP watches on subsequent page requests, and uses to load the stored data that's associated with that session.

Unless configured otherwise, a PHP session automatically sets a cookie in the user's browser that contains the session ID. The browser then sends that cookie, along with every request for a page from our site, so that PHP can determine which of the potentially many current sessions the request belongs to. Using a set of temporary files that are stored on the web server, PHP keeps track of the variables that have been registered in each session, along with their values.

Before you can go ahead and use the spiffy session-management features in PHP, we should ensure that the relevant section of our `php.ini` file has been set up properly. If we're using the Homestead box described in Chapter 1, it's safe to assume this has been done for us. Otherwise, we need to open our `php.ini` file in a text editor and look for the section marked `[Session]`. Beneath it, we'll find around 20 options that begin with the word `session`. Most of them are fine as they are, but there are a few crucial ones we'll want to check:

```
session.save_handler      = files
session.save_path         = "/tmp"
session.use_cookies       = 1
```

 Finding `php.ini`

The `php.ini` configuration applies globally to our PHP scripts, and can be stored on the server in various locations. On the Homestead Improved box we're using, it's located at `/etc/php/7.1/php.ini`. This location may change if you're using a newer version of the virtual machine, and will almost certainly be different on a real web server.

To find out the location of the configuration file that's in use, run this PHP script:

```php
<?php
echo phpinfo();
```

You'll see a line near the top that says "Loaded Configuration File", which is the path to the `php.ini` configuration file that's in use on the website.

`session.save_path` tells PHP where to create the temporary files used to track sessions. It must be set to a directory that exists on the system, or we'll receive ugly error messages when we try to create a session on one of our pages. On macOS and Linux systems, `/tmp` is a popular choice. In Windows, we could use `C:\WINDOWS\TEMP`, or some other directory if you prefer (`D:\PHP\SESSIONS`, for example). With these adjustments made, we restart our web server software to allow the changes to take effect. This directory must be writable by the user that PHP is running as.

We're now ready to start working with PHP sessions. Before we jump into an example, let's quickly look at the most common session management functions in PHP. To tell PHP to look for a session ID, or start a new session if none is found, we simply call `session_start`. If an existing session ID is found when this function is called, PHP restores the variables that belong to that session. Since this function attempts to create a cookie, it must come before any page content is sent to the browser, just as we saw for `setcookie` above:

```
session_start();
```

To create a session variable that will be available on all pages in the site when accessed by the current user, we set a value in the special `$_SESSION` array. For example, the following will store the variable called `password` in the current session. The `$_SESSION` variable will be empty until we've called `session_start()`, so we need to ensure we don't read or write to it before the session has been started.

It's useful to have an understanding of how sessions work behind the scenes. Once we call `session_start()`, it actually creates a cookie with a unique ID to represent each individual user. For example, the first person on the web page may be user 1, the second 2, and so on.

Then, when they visit the next page, their ID is sent back to the website, and when the session is started, all the information stored for that user is retrieved. For example, all the information stored for ID 1 represents user 1, and the information for session ID 2 represents user 2.

This allows sessions to keep track of different information for each user of the website. In practice, IDs aren't simple sequential numbers like 1, 2 or 3. They're complex, difficult to guess strings of seemingly random numbers and letters. If sessions were easy to guess, hackers could easily pretend to be each user of the website by changing the ID stored in their session cookie!

After the session has been started, we can treat the `$_SESSION` variable like a normal array, reading and writing values to it:

```
$_SESSION['password'] = 'mypassword';
```

To remove a variable from the current session, we can use PHP's `unset` function:

```
unset($_SESSION['password']);
```

Finally, if we want to end the current session and delete all registered variables in the process, clear all the stored values and use `session_destroy`:

```
$_SESSION = [];
session_destroy();
```

For more detailed information on these and the other session-management functions in PHP, see the relevant section of the PHP Manual.[2]

Now that we have these basic functions under our belt, let's put them to work in a simple example.

Counting Visits with Sessions

I showed you how to use cookies to track the number of times someone had visited the page, and the same thing can be done with sessions:

[2.] http://www.php.net/session

```php
<?php
session_start();

if (!isset($_SESSION['visits'])) {
    $_SESSION['visits'] = 0;
}
$_SESSION['visits'] = $_SESSION['visits'] + 1;

if ($_SESSION['visits'] > 1) {
    echo 'This is visit number ' . $_SESSION['visits'];
} else {
    // First visit
    echo 'Welcome to my website! Click here for a tour!';
}
```

$_SESSION is used in place of $_COOKIE, and you'll notice the code is a little simpler than the code used for cookies.

For the cookie, we needed to calculate the lifetime and set an expiration time. Sessions are simpler: no expiration time is required, but any data stored in the session is lost when the browser is closed.

Access Control

One of the most common reasons for building a database-driven website is that it allows users to interact with a site from any web browser, anywhere! But in a world where roaming bands of jubilant hackers will fill our site with viruses and pornography, we need to stop and think about the security of our website.

At the very least, we'll want to require username and password authentication before a visitor can post anything to the website. There are two main ways of doing this:

- configure our web server software to require a valid login for the relevant pages
- use PHP to prompt the user and check the login credentials as appropriate

If we have access to our web server's configuration, the first option is often the easiest to set up, but the second is by far the more flexible. With PHP, we can design our own login form, and even embed it into the layout of our site if we wish. PHP also makes it easy to change the credentials required to gain access, or manage a database of authorized users, each with their own credentials and privileges.

In this section, we'll enhance our joke database site to protect sensitive features with username/password-based authentication. In order to control which users can do what, we'll build a sophisticated role-based access control system.

"What does all this have to do with cookies and sessions?" you might wonder. Well, rather than prompting our users for login credentials every time they want to view a confidential page or perform a sensitive action, we can use PHP sessions to hold on to those credentials throughout their visit to our site.

Logging In

In the last chapter, I showed you how users could register accounts on the website and have their password stored securely. The next step is to allow those registered users to log in and post jokes to the website.

Obviously, access control is a feature that will be handy in many different PHP projects and on different pages on the website. Therefore, like our database connection code and `DatabaseTable` class, it makes sense to write as much of our access control code as possible as a shared class, so that we can then reuse it throughout the website and in future projects.

The general process for "logging in" consists of the user supplying an email address and password. If the database contains a matching author, it means the user filled out the login form correctly and we have to log in the user.

But what exactly does "log in the user" mean? There are two approaches to this, both of which involve using PHP sessions:

1. We can log in the user by setting a session variable as a "flag" (for example, `$_SESSION['userid'] = $userId`). On future requests, we can just check if this variable is set and use it to read the ID of the logged-in user.

2. We can store the supplied email address and password in the session, and then on future requests, we can check if these variables are set. If they are, we can check the values in the session against the values in the database.

The first option will give better performance, since the user's credentials are only checked once—when the login form is submitted. The second option offers greater security, since the user's credentials are checked against the database every time a sensitive page is requested.

In general, the more secure option is preferable, since it allows us to remove authors from the site even while they're logged in. Otherwise, once a user is logged in, they'll stay logged in for as long as their PHP session remains active. That's a steep price to pay for a little extra performance.

The theory behind this is simple to implement, but it's made more difficult because the password field in the database doesn't store the password in plain text, as typed by the user. Instead, it stores a hashed password like this:

```
$2y$10$XPtbphrRABcV95GxoeAk.OeI8tPgaypkKicBUhX/YbC9QYSSoowRq
```

There's no way to decrypt the password to do the comparison, but because we used `password_hash` to hash the password, we can use `password_verify` to check it.

`password_verify` takes two arguments: the plain text password to check and the hashed password from the database. It returns true or false depending on whether the password is correct.

To check the password, we'll need the hash password from the database before being able to use it with `password_verify`. Luckily, thanks to the `DatabaseTable` class and the existing `$authorsTable` variable, it's easy for us to look up the hashed password of a user by using their email address:

```
$author = $authorsTable->find('email',
↪ strtolower($_POST['email']));
```

Once the user's information is stored in `$author`, it's possible to check the password using the `password_verify` function, like so:

```
if (!empty($author) &&
  password_verify($_POST['password'],
  $author[0]['password'])) {
    // Login successful
}
else {
    // Passwords don't match, an error occurred
}
```

Note the [0] after `$author`. That's because the `find` function may return more than one record. We need to specifically read the first record returned.

The first condition in the `if` statement checks to see if an author has been retrieved from the database. If one has, the second condition will check that the password entered by the user matches the one in the database.

The order is important here. PHP will run and (&&) conditions left to right, and stop when one evaluates to false. If the order was reversed and the password check was done before `!empty($author)`, an error might occur, because `$author` might not contain an array with a `password` key! By putting the `!empty($author)` check first, we know that something is set in the `password` key for the `$author` array.

 Hashing

You may have thought that we could use this:

```
if (password_hash($_POST['password'],
  PASSWORD_DEFAULT) == $author[0]['password']) { ...
```

However, `password_hash` creates a different hash each time it's called, even if it's called with the same password string! We must use `password_verify` to check the password.

Once the user has entered the email address and password, they can be "logged in" by setting the session variable.

After checking the password was correct using `password_verify`, it's time to write some data to the session. There are various options here. We could just store the user ID or the email address of the person who's been logged in.

However, it's good practice to store both the login name and password in the session and check them both on each page view. That way, if the user is logged in on two different computers and the password is changed, they'll be logged out and required to log back in.

This is a useful security feature for users, since if one of those logged in locations were not really the user, someone having managed to get unauthorized access to their account, the attacker would be logged out as soon as the password was changed. Without storing the password in the session, the attacker could log in once, and as long as the browser was left open, they'd maintain access to the user's account.

One method of achieving this is to store both the email address and password in the session:

```php
$_SESSION['email'] = $_POST['email'];
$_SESSION['password'] = $_POST['password'];
```

Then, on each page view, we'd check the information in the session against the database:

```php
$author = $authorsTable->find('email',
 strtolower($_SESSION['email']))[0];

if (!empty($author) &&
 password_verify($_SESSION['password'],
 $author['password'])) {
    // Display password protected content
}
else {
```

```
    // Display an error message and clear the session
    // logging the user out
}
```

This is theoretically what we want to do. With this approach, if the password is changed in the database, or the author is removed from the database, the user will be logged out.

However, there's an obvious security issue here. Although sessions are stored on the server, if someone did gain access to our web server, they could see the plain text password of any logged-in users, completely forfeiting the benefit of hashing the password in the first place.

To avoid storing the plain text password of the logged-in users in the session, we'll need to adjust the logic slightly.

Instead of storing the plain text password in the session, it's better to store the password hash from the database in the session. If someone is able to read the session data from the server, they'll only see the hash, not the real password!

To store the hash in the session, we can use the following code:

```php
$_SESSION['email'] = $_POST['email'];
$_SESSION['password'] = $author['password'];
```

With the email address and hash stored, we can check the values from the database, and if either the email address or password stored in the database have changed, the user can be logged out.

On each page, we'll need to run this code:

```php
$author = $authorsTable->find('email',
  strtolower($_SESSION['email']));

if (!empty($author) && $author[0]['password'] ===
  $_SESSION['password']) {
```

```
    // Display password protected content
}
else {
    // Display an error message and log the user out
}
```

The code above does three things:

1. It searches the database for the user with the email address from the session, which would have been set when the user submitted the login form.

2. It checks a record has been retrieved from the database. After all, it's possible the user entered an email address that doesn't actually exist in the database.

3. It compares the password in the session to the password that's currently in the database. If it's changed between logging in and viewing this page, the user will be logged out.

As this check will need to be done on every page we want to password protect, let's move it into a class for easy reuse. We'll need two methods for now:

- one that's called when the user tries to log in with an email address and password
- one that's called on each page to check whether the user is logged in or not (with the check that ensures the password hasn't changed in the database)

Since this is something that's going to be useful on any website we build, we'll place it in the `Ninja` framework namespace:

```php
<?php
namespace Ninja;

class Authentication
{
    private $users;
    private $usernameColumn;
    private $passwordColumn;
```

```php
    public function __construct(DatabaseTable $users,
     $usernameColumn, $passwordColumn)
    {
        session_start();
        $this->users = $users;
        $this->usernameColumn = $usernameColumn;
        $this->passwordColumn = $passwordColumn;
    }

    public function login($username, $password)
    {
        $user = $this->users->find($this->usernameColumn,
         strtolower($username));

        if (!empty($user) && password_verify($password,
         $user[0][$this->passwordColumn])) {
            session_regenerate_id();
            $_SESSION['username'] = $username;
            $_SESSION['password'] =
$user[0][$this->passwordColumn];
            return true;
        } else {
            return false;
        }
    }

    public function isLoggedIn()
    {
        if (empty($_SESSION['username'])) {
            return false;
        }

        $user = $this->users->find($this->usernameColumn,
         strtolower($_SESSION['username']));

        if (!empty($user) &&
         $user[0][$this->passwordColumn]
         === $_SESSION['password']) {
            return true;
        } else {
```

```
            return false;
        }
    }
}
```

Let's save this as `Authentication.php` in the `classes/Ninja` directory so it can be used later.

This is mostly the same code I already showed you with a few minor changes. Firstly, take a look at the constructor. There are three variables required for this class:

1. a `DatabaseTable` instance, which is configured for the table that stores user accounts
2. the name of the column that stores the login names
3. the name of the column that stores the password

As this class will be useful on multiple websites, we need to code it so that it can be used in as many situations as possible. Although the column names that store the login names and passwords are `email` and `password` on this website, on another website the login name might be stored under `username` or `customer_login` or any other name you can think of. The same is true for the password.

By making these constructor arguments rather than hardcoding them into the class, it's now possible to use this class on any website, regardless of whether the column names in the database are `email` and `password` or something else.

Each time we want to read the password from the database, the class variables are used. The code is slightly more complex: `$user[0][$this->passwordColumn]` instead of `$user[0]['password']`.

But the added flexibility of being able to use this on websites that have the password stored in a column with a different name heavily outweighs the small additional complexity in this class.

When the `Authentication` class is created, it starts the session. This avoids us needing to manually call session_start on each page. As long as the Authentication class has been instantiated, a session will have been started. When login or isLoggedIn are called, the session must have been started.

Both login and isLoggedIn return true or false, which we can later call to determine whether the user has entered valid credentials or is already logged in.

There's also an initial check in the isLoggedIn method, ensuring there is data in the session. If not, it returns false, as without a session variable username, the user is not logged in.

One final security measure that's worth implementing is changing the session ID after a successful login. Earlier I mentioned that session IDs should not easily be guessable. Otherwise, hackers could pretend to be someone else, an attack commonly known as **session fixation**. All the hacker needs to steal someone else's session is the session ID.

It's good practice to change the session ID after a successful login just in case someone managed to get hold of the session ID before the user logged in. PHP makes this very easy, and the single function session_regenerate_id does this by picking a new random ID for that user.

This can be placed in the if block that runs when the login is successful:

```
if (!empty($author) && password_verify($password,
  $author[0]['password'])) {
    session_regenerate_id();
    $_SESSION['email'] = $email;
    $_SESSION['password'] = $author['password'];
    return true;
}
```

If you follow the logic through, you may have realized that frequently changing the session ID can increase security. In fact, it would be very secure to change the user's session ID on every page load.

However, doing so causes several practical problems. If someone has different pages open in different tabs, or the website uses a technology called Ajax, they effectively get logged out of one tab when they open another! These problems are worse than the minor security benefit of changing the session ID on every page.

Protected Pages

Now that the authentication class is complete, it's time to use it in the website. Before creating a login page, let's secure some of the existing pages so they can't be viewed unless as user is logged in (or the isLoggedIn function returns true).

Currently, we only have the Joke controller. The listJokes method should be visible without logging in, but the facility to add, edit or delete a joke should only be available to users who are logged in.

To achieve this, we'll need to determine whether or not a user is logged in. If they are, the page is displayed as normal. If not, an error message is displayed in its place.

We already have the Authentication class, which allows us to determine whether or not someone is logged in. We could pass the $authentication instance into each controller and add a check to each controller action, like so:

```php
public function edit() {
    if (!$this->authentication->isLoggedIn()) {
    return ['template' => 'error.html',
        'title' => 'You are not authorized to view this page'];
    }
    else {
    // Display the form
    }

    // …
```

We'd also require a relevant error.html.php to display an error message such as "You must be logged in to view this page".

Although this approach will work, it will result in repeated code. Every controller action that should only be available to logged-in users would require repeating this same if statement. As you already know, if you find yourself repeating very similar code in multiple places, it's usually better to move the code so it can be written once and reused.

In this case, a better approach is adjusting the router to perform the login check and either use the requested route or display an error page.

Firstly, let's open up IjdbRoutes.php and add 'login' => true to each of the routes that we want to secure, joke/edit and joke/delete:

```
'joke/edit' => [
    'POST' => [
    'controller' => $jokeController,
    'action' => 'saveEdit'
    ],
    'GET' => [
    'controller' => $jokeController,
    'action' => 'edit'
    ],
    'login' => true

],
'joke/delete' => [
    'POST' => [
    'controller' => $jokeController,
    'action' => 'delete'
    ],
    'login' => true
],
```

Next, we'll add a new method, getAuthentication. This method will return the Authentication object used by this website. By placing this method here, it allows us to configure the Authentication class differently on different websites. This object needs to be used in the EntryPoint class, but we need to avoid constructing it there, as the table and column names will be different on each website we build.

By constructing the object in the IjdbRoutes class, it can be changed for each website we build.

```php
public function getAuthentication() {
    $authorsTable = new \Ninja\DatabaseTable($pdo,
     'author', 'id');
    return new \Ninja\Authentication($authorsTable,
     'email', 'password');
}
```

As the `Authentication` class requires an instance of `DatabaseTable` representing the table that stores the logins, I've copied the line that creates the `$authorsTable` object. This copy/paste approach is not ideal from either a performance or maintainability point of view. It's better to have a single instance representing the `authors` table. To achieve that, move the construction of the `database` table into the constructor and store it in a class variable:

```php
<?php
namespace Ijdb;

class IjdbRoutes implements \Ninja\Routes
{
    private $authorsTable;
    private $jokesTable;
    private $authentication;

    public function __construct()
    {
        include __DIR__ . '/../../includes/DatabaseConnection.php';

        $this->jokesTable = new \Ninja\DatabaseTable($pdo,
         'joke', 'id');
        $this->authorsTable = new \Ninja\DatabaseTable($pdo,
         'author', 'id');
        $this->authentication =
         new \Ninja\Authentication($this->authorsTable,
         'email', 'password');
    }
```

```php
public function getRoutes()
{
    $jokeController =
     new \Ijdb\Controllers\Joke($this->jokesTable,
     $this->authorsTable);
    $authorController = new \Ijdb\Controllers\Register
     ($this->authorsTable);

    $routes = [
    'author/register' => [
    'GET' => [
        'controller' => $authorController,
        'action' => 'registrationForm'
    ],
    'POST' => [
        'controller' => $authorController,
        'action' => 'registerUser'
    ]
    ],
    'author/success' => [
    'GET' => [
        'controller' => $authorController,
        'action' => 'success'
    ]
    ],
    'joke/edit' => [
    'POST' => [
        'controller' => $jokeController,
        'action' => 'saveEdit'
    ],
    'GET' => [
        'controller' => $jokeController,
        'action' => 'edit'
    ],
    'login' => true

    ],
    'joke/delete' => [
    'POST' => [
        'controller' => $jokeController,
```

```
                'action' => 'delete'
        ],
        'login' => true
        ],
        'joke/list' => [
        'GET' => [
            'controller' => $jokeController,
            'action' => 'list'
        ]
        ],
        '' => [
        'GET' => [
            'controller' => $jokeController,
            'action' => 'home'
        ]
        ]
    ];

        return $routes;
    }

    public function getAuthentication()
    {
        return $this->authentication;
    }
}
```

For consistency, I've also made $jokesTable into a class variable. As the
Authentication object might be required by controllers, I've moved that into the
constructor as well. It then gets returned by the getAuthentication method.

Interfaces and Return Types

Before adding an authentication check to EntryPoint, let's add
getAuthentication to the interface Routes:

```
<?php
```

```
namespace Ninja;

interface Routes
{
    public function getRoutes();
    public function getAuthentication();
}
```

With the method `getAuthentication` added to the interface, any class that implements it must have a method called `getAuthentication`. When we add the relevant `ShopRoutes` class for an online shop, it will need to provide an array and an `authentication` object.

Let's improve the interface slightly. The `Routes` interface will ensure that the two methods exist in the class. However, what if `getAuthentication` in the `IjdbRoutes` class were not to return an `Authentication` object? If whatever is calling `getAuthentication` is expecting an `Authentication` object, perhaps to call the `isLoggedIn` method, and an instance of `DatabaseTable` or an array is returned, it will cause an error.

As an extra line of defense, it's possible to type hint a return value. If the method returns something other than the expected type, an error will occur.

Let's amend the interface like so:

```
<?php
namespace Ninja;

interface Routes
{
    public function getRoutes(): array;
    public function getAuthentication(): \Ninja\Authentication;
}
```

I've amended the method headers to include a return type appending : \Ninja\ `Authentication` to the method header. If the method returns anything other than an `Authentication` object, or doesn't return anything at all, PHP will display a meaningful error.

You'll notice I've also hinted the return type for the `getRoutes` method: it must return an array.

Once we've amended the interface, we'll need to amend the `IjdbRoutes` class to match:

```
public function getRoutes(): array {
    $jokeController =
    new \Ijdb\Controllers\Joke($this->jokesTable,
    $this->authorsTable);
    // …
    return $routes;
}

public function getAuthentication(): \Ninja\Authentication {
    return $this->authentication;
}
```

The interface is now very explicit. Anyone who wants to build a website using our `Ninja` framework knows that the `Routes` class they create for that website must include a method called `getRoutes`, which returns an array and a method called `getAuthentication` that returns an `Authentication` object.

An interface like this is very useful if we're writing code we want others to build on. The interface can act as documentation and give other developers instructions to follow. By writing their code to fit our interface, it will work correctly with our class.

PHP programmers share code all the time, and interfaces like this make doing so a lot easier. We can share our `Ninja` framework and another developer knows how to use it by writing classes that implement our interface. Interfaces are a very powerful but under-utilized tool that act as bridge between framework code and project-specific code.

An interface describes some gaps in the framework code that need to be filled by the project-specific code. Each project can then fill those gaps with code that's specific to the individual website being built.

Making Use of the Authentication Class

In `EntryPoint.php`, add a check that looks for the `login` key in the route array. If it's set, and it's set to true, and the user is not logged in, redirect to a login page. Otherwise, display the page as normal:

11-5. Sessions-LoginCheck

```php
if (isset($routes[$this->route]['login']) &&
 isset($routes[$this->route]['login']) &&
  !$authentication->isLoggedIn()) {
    header('location: /login/error');
}
else {
    $controller = $routes[$this->route]
     [$this->method]['controller'];
    $action = $routes[$this->route][$this->method]
     ['action'];
    $page = $controller->$action();

    $title = $page['title'];

    if (isset($page['variables'])) {
    $output = $this->loadTemplate($page['template'],
     $page['variables']);
    }
    else {
    $output = $this->loadTemplate($page['template']);
    }

    include  __DIR__ . '/../../templates/layout.html.php';
}
```

For pages that require users to be logged in, it's important that the controller action is never called. Consider the following code:

```
if (isset($routes[$this->route]['login']) &&
 isset($routes[$this->route]['login']) &&
 !$authentication->isLoggedIn()) {
    header('location: /login/error');
}

$controller = $routes[$this->route][$this->method]
 ['controller'];
$action = $routes[$this->route][$this->method]
 ['action'];
$page = $controller->$action();

// …
```

Without the **else** statement, this would look like it was working. If we visited joke/delete, we'd get redirected to the login page. However, take a look at what's happening here: the redirect is being sent, but then the controller action is called. This would be a huge problem: although we'd be redirected to the login page, the relevant DELETE query would still be sent to the database!

Login Error Message

If we test the code above by trying to add a joke, we should see a page of errors, as we'll have been redirected to /login/error. Let's create a page at that location to display a more meaningful error message.

You should be familiar with the process of adding a page to the website by now. Try adding the error page yourself. If you're not quite sure or want to be consistent with the provided examples, follow these steps:

Firstly, add loginerror.html.php in the templates directory:

```
<h2>You are not logged in</h2>

 <p>You must be logged in to view this page. <a
↪ href="/login">Click here to log in</a> or <a
↪ href="/author/register">Click here to register an
```

```
↳ account</a></p>
```

Now add the controller `Login.php` in the `Ijdb\Controllers` directory:

```php
<?php
namespace Ijdb\Controllers;

class Login
{
    public function error()
    {
        return ['template' => 'loginerror.html.php', 'title'
        => 'You are not logged in'];
    }
}
```

Finally, instantiate the controller and add the route to `IjdbRoutes.php`:

```php
public function getRoutes(): array {
    $jokeController = new \Ijdb\Controllers\Joke
    ($this->jokesTable, $this->authorsTable);
    $authorController = new \Ijdb\Controllers\Register
    ($this->authorsTable);
    $loginController = new \Ijdb\Controllers\Login();

    $routes = [
    'author/register' => [
        'GET' => [
        'controller' => $authorController,
        'action' => 'registrationForm'
        ],
        'POST' => [
        'controller' => $authorController,
        'action' => 'registerUser'
        ]
    ],
    // …
    'login/error' => [
        'GET' => [
        'controller' => $loginController,
        'action' => 'error'
        ]
    ]
    ];
```

If we visit any page where `login` is set to true in the `$routes` array, we'll see the error page. By adding `'login' => true` to a route, we now have a quick and easy method of restricting access to pages, and we don't need to perform this check in every controller action.

Creating a Login Form

Now that the login check is in place and we know that it works, it's time to build a form for logging in. As it stands, there's no way to add or edit a joke, because there's no facility to log in.

We already created the `Login` controller, and we'll need to add two methods—one for displaying the form, and one for handling the submission.

As the login form will need to call the `login` method we created in the `Authentication` class, it will need the `Authentication` class as a constructor argument and class variable:

```php
<?php
namespace Ijdb\Controllers;

class Login
{
    private $authentication;

    public function __construct(\Ninja\Authentication
      $authentication)
    {
        $this->authentication = $authentication;
    }

    public function error()
    {
        return ['template' => 'loginerror.html.php', 'title'
          => 'You are not logged in'];
    }
}
```

Once the constructor has been added, the function to display the form and check the login credentials can be added. Just displaying the form is simple:

```php
public function loginForm() {
    return ['template' => 'login.html.php',
      'title' => 'Log In'];
}
```

Now we can add the template `login.html.php`:

```php
<?php
if (isset($error)):
    echo '<div class="errors">' . $error . '</div>';
endif;
?>
<form method="post" action="">
    <label for="email">Your email address</label>
    <input type="text" id="email" name="email">

    <label for="password">Your password</label>
    <input type="password" id="password" name="password">

    <input type="submit" name="login" value="Log in">
</form>

 <p>Don't have an account? <a
↪ href="/author/register">Click here to register an
↪ account</a></p>
```

You'll notice I've included some PHP code for displaying an error message in case logging in is not successful.

Finally, amend `IjdbRoutes.php` to add the route. We'll also need to provide the login controller with the `$authentication` instance:

```php
public function getRoutes(): array {
    // …
    $loginController = new \Ijdb\Controllers\
    Login($this->authentication);

    $routes = [
    // …
    'login' => [
        'GET' => [
        'controller' => $loginController,
        'action' => 'loginForm'
```

```
        ]
    ],
    // …
    ];
```

If we visit `http://192.168.10.10/login`, we'll see a familiar login form with text boxes for entering our email address and password. As there's no POST route or any logic to process the form, it won't do anything yet.

Let's add the POST action and a simple page for displaying a "Login Successful" message:

`IjdbRoutes.php`:

```
$routes = [
    // …
    'login' => [
    'GET' => [
        'controller' => $loginController,
        'action' => 'loginForm'
    ],
    'POST' => [
        'controller' => $loginController,
        'action' => 'processLogin'
    ]
    ],
    'login/success' => [
    'GET' => [
        'controller' => $loginController,
        'action' => 'success'
    ],
    'login' => true
    ]
```

We've already built the functionality for logging in, and checking whether a user is logged in, in the Authentication class. This is the difficult part of the login process, and we can call the existing login method with data that's been entered on a form by the user. If the `login` method returns true, their details were correct and we can redirect to a page that says "Login successful". Otherwise, show an error.

`Login.php`:

```php
public function processLogin() {
    if ($this->authentication->login($_POST['email'],
     $_POST['password'])) {
    header('location: /login/success');
    }
    else {
    return ['template' => 'login.html.php',
        'title' => 'Log In',
        'variables' => [
        'error' => 'Invalid username/password.'
        ]
    ];
    }
}

public function success() {
    return ['template' => 'loginsuccess.html.php',
     'title' => 'Login Successful'];
}
```

`loginsuccess.html.php`:

```php
<h2>Login Successful</h2>

<p>You are now logged in.</p>
```

You can find this code in *Sessions-LoginForm*.

If you haven't already, create an account using the registration form we created in the previous chapter. Visit `http://192.168.10.10/login` and log in. If you're logged in, you'll be able to add, edit and delete jokes. If you're not logged in, an error message is shown.

 Privacy Pointers

It would be possible to display different messages to the user depending on why their login failed—for example, "Invalid email address" when the email address doesn't exist, and "Invalid password" when the email address is registered but the passwords don't match.

Although this helps the user by letting them see what went wrong, it's a privacy breach. Anyone can type in someone else's email address and see if they're registered on your website based on the error message that's shown.

Logging Out

Let's add a new button to the site layout to allow logging in or logging out. For logged-in users, a "Log out" button should show. For users who aren't logged in, the button should show "Log in".

This change will require editing `layout.html` to add the menu link. However, it will require some logic to display one of the two links.

Currently, `layout.html.php` is just included directly with this line:

```
include __DIR__ . '/../../templates/layout.html.php';
```

For consistency, and to reuse the code we already have, let's use the existing `loadTemplate` function so that we can pass variables to `layout.html`. In this case, we'll create a single variable, `$loggedIn`, which stores whether or not the user is logged in. Replace the `include` line with the following:

```
echo $this->loadTemplate('layout.html.php', ['loggedIn'
↪ =>
$authentication->isLoggedIn(),
    'output' => $output,
    'title' => $title
]);
```

Now, inside `layout.html.php` the variable `loggedIn` will store true or false depending on whether or not the user is logged in.

Open up `layout.html.php` and add the log in/log out links with an `if … else` statement to display the correct link, depending on whether or not the user is logged in:

```
<ul>
    <li><a href="/">Home</a></li>
    <li><a href="/joke/list">Jokes List
    </a></li>
    <li><a href="/joke/edit">Add a new Joke
    </a></li>

    <?php if ($loggedIn): ?>
    <li><a href="/logout">Log out</a>
    </li>
    <?php else: ?>
    <li><a href="/login">Log in</a></li>
    <?php endif; ?>

</ul>
```

Finally, let's create the logout page and route:

Login.php:

```
public function logout() {
    unset($_SESSION);
    return ['template' => 'logout.html.php',
     'title' => 'You have been logged out'];
}
```

`unset($_SESSION);` will remove any data from the current session, logging the user out.

Let's add the route to `IjdbRoutes`:

```
'logout' => [
    'GET' => [
    'controller' => $loginController,
    'action' => 'logout'
    ]
],
```

`logout.html.php`:

```
<h2>Logged out</h2>

<p>You have been logged out</p>
```

You can find this code in *Sessions-Logout*.

Assigning Added Jokes to the Logged-in User

Now that users can register and log in, it's time to make it so that when a joke is posted, it's associated with the user who's logged in. We already have an `authorId` column in the `joke` table. All we need to do is give it a value when the joke is added. The `saveEdit` method in the `Joke` controller currently contains this code:

```
public function saveEdit() {
    $joke = $_POST['joke'];
    $joke['jokedate'] = new \DateTime();
    $joke['authorId'] = 1;

    $this->jokesTable->save($joke);

    header('location: /joke/list');
}
```

At the moment, `authorId` is always set to 1. To get the ID of the logged-in user, we'll need to amend the `Authentication` class slightly to provide a way of retrieving the record for the logged-in user.

In the `Authentication` class, add the following method:

```
public function getUser() {
    if ($this->isLoggedIn()) {
        return $this->users->find($this->usernameColumn,
        strtolower($_SESSION['username']))[0];
    }
    else {
        return false;
    }
}
```

This function checks to see if the user is logged in, and if they are, returns an array that contains the record representing the user who's logged in. As with the `login` and `isLoggedIn` methods, we need `[0]` after the `find` method call to return the first record retrieved.

It's possible just to return the ID of the logged-in user, but later on we might want to know the name or the email address of the user. Returning the entire record gives more flexibility moving forward.

Let's make the `Authentication` class available in the `Joke` controller by adding a use line for `Ninja\Authentication` and adding the class variable and constructor argument:

```
<?php
namespace Ijdb\Controllers;
use \Ninja\DatabaseTable;
use \Ninja\Authentication;

class Joke {
```

```
    private $authorsTable;
    private $jokesTable;

    public function __construct(DatabaseTable $jokesTable,
     DatabaseTable $authorsTable,
     Authentication $authentication) {
    $this->jokesTable = $jokesTable;
    $this->authorsTable = $authorsTable;
    $this->authentication = $authentication;
    }
```

Here's the argument list in IjdbRoutes:

```
 $jokeController = new
↪ \Ijdb\Controllers\Joke($this->jokesTable,
↪ $this->authorsTable, $this->authentication);
```

Once JokesController has access to the authentication class, assigning an author to a joke when it's created is very easy:

```
public function saveEdit() {
    $author = $this->authentication->getUser();

    $joke = $_POST['joke'];
    $joke['jokedate'] = new \DateTime();
    $joke['authorId'] = $author['id'];

    $this->jokesTable->save($joke);

    header('location: /joke/list');
}
```

You can find this code in *Sessions-AuthorId*.

Whenever a joke is added, the author's ID is assigned to the joke in the database.

The currently logged-in user is retrieved from the database and their ID copied to the `authorId` column of the `joke` table.

But there's a concern here. What if `$author` contains `false` because the user isn't logged in? Because the login check already happens in `EntryPoint`, there should be no way for the `saveEdit` method to be called unless someone is logged in.

Go ahead and add a few jokes to the website. You'll need to be logged in, but the jokes should get attributed to you! When you view the list of jokes, the jokes you post will be listed as being posted by you.

You now have a fully functional login system. You can add pages to the website and make them visible only to logged-in users. Your users can register for accounts and log in to the website!

User Permissions

If you've been testing out the login system and have been playing around editing, deleting and adding jokes, you'll have noticed a problem: anyone can delete or edit anyone else's jokes!

For most websites, when someone posts something, they have complete control over it and only they are able to delete it or make changes to it. Imagine how confusing Facebook or Twitter would be if people could edit and delete each other's posts!

Let's add some checks to the site that prevent users from being able to add or edit each other's jokes.

The first thing to do is hide the **edit** and **delete** buttons from the joke list for jokes that don't belong to the logged-in user.

To do this, firstly we'll need to provide the ID of the author along with the name and email in the `$jokes` array in the `list` method:

```
public function list() {
    $result = $this->jokesTable->findAll();
```

```
$jokes = [];
foreach ($result as $joke) {
$author = $this->authorsTable->
findById($joke['authorId']);

$jokes[] = [
    'id' => $joke['id'],
    'joketext' => $joke['joketext'],
    'jokedate' => $joke['jokedate'],
    'name' => $author['name'],
    'email' => $author['email'],
    'authorId' => $author['id']
];

}

// …
```

Then, in the same method, we'll pass the ID of the logged-in user to the template:

```
// …
$totalJokes = $this->jokesTable->total();

$author = $this->authentication->getUser();

return ['template' => 'jokes.html.php',
    'title' => $title,
    'variables' => [
    'totalJokes' => $totalJokes,
    'jokes' => $jokes,
    'userId' => $author['id'] ?? null
    ]
];
```

As the person viewing the page may not be logged in, there may not be an author ID associated with the current user. To account for that, I've used $author['id'] ?? null to set the userId variable in the template to null when no user is logged in.

Finally, in the `jokes.html.php`, add an `if` statement inside the loop that iterates over the jokes. If the currently logged-in user is the user who posted the joke, display the **edit** and **delete** buttons. Otherwise, don't show them:

```
// …
echo $date->format('jS F Y');
?>)

<?php if ($userId == $joke['authorId']): ?>
    <a href="/joke/edit?id=<?=$joke['id']?>">
    Edit</a>
    <form action="/joke/delete" method="post">
    <input type="hidden" name="id"
     value="<?=$joke['id']?>">
    <input type="submit" value="Delete">
    </form>
<?php endif; ?>
    </p>
</blockquote>
<?php endforeach; ?>
```

You can find this code in *Sessions-CheckUser*

The clever part here is the `if` statement. It checks that `$userId`, which stores the ID of the currently logged-in user, is equal to the `authorId` of the joke being printed. If the logged-in user posted the joke, then the **edit** and **delete** buttons are displayed.

Mission Accomplished?

If you test the site at this point, you might think that's done. Users can't edit or delete each other's jokes. However, that's not quite true. Users can't see the **edit** or **delete** buttons for jokes they didn't post, but there's nothing to stop them from visiting the edit page directly.

Try visiting `http://192.168.10.10/joke/edit?id=1` and changing the ID in the

URL. You'll see the edit page for any of the jokes, regardless of whether your account posted them.

To fix this, we need to add a check to this page in the same way we did for the joke list.

Firstly, like the joke list page, we supply the editjoke.html.php template with the ID of the logged-in user:

```php
public function edit() {
    $author = $this->authentication->getUser();

    if (isset($_GET['id'])) {
        $joke = $this->jokesTable->findById($_GET['id']);
    }

    $title = 'Edit joke';

    return ['template' => 'editjoke.html.php',
    'title' => $title,
    'variables' => [
        'joke' => $joke ?? null,
        'userId' => $author['id'] ?? null
    ]
    ];
}
```

Then, in editjoke.html.php, only display the form if the userId matches the joke's authorId:

```php
<?php if ($userId == $joke['authorId']): ?>
<form action="" method="post">
    <input type="hidden" name="joke[id]"
     value="<?=$joke['id'] ?? ''?>">
    <label for="joketext">Type your joke here:
    </label>
    <textarea id="joketext" name="joke[joketext]" rows="3"
     cols="40"><?=$joke['joketext'] ?? ''?>
```

```
    </textarea>
    <input type="submit" name="submit" value="Save">
</form>
<?php else: ?>

<p>You may only edit jokes that you posted.</p>

<?php endif; ?>
```

I've included an error message so that something is displayed in case someone does try to edit a joke they didn't create.

Now the user can't see the edit form for jokes they didn't create. Before celebrating the new security of our site, there's one more thing we need to do.

A sneaky attacker could create an HTML file with a form that posted data to your website. For example, they could create the file editjoke.html:

```
<form action="http://192.168.10.10/joke/edit?id=1"
    method="post">
    <input type="hidden" name="joke[id]" value="1">
    <label for="joketext">Type your joke here:
    </label>
    <textarea id="joketext" name="joke[joketext]" rows="3"
     cols="40"></textarea>
    <input type="submit" name="submit" value="Save">
</form>
```

As long as they were logged in to the website, they could submit this form and regardless of who they were logged in as, edit the joke with the ID 1. We need to add the same check to the method that handles the form submission.

To do this, we need to read the existing joke from the database and check that the ID matches the ID of the existing user:

```
public function saveEdit() {
```

```php
$author = $this->authentication->getUser();

if (isset($_GET['id'])) {
  $joke = $this->jokesTable->findById($_GET['id']);

  if ($joke['authorId'] != $author['id']) {
    return;
  }
}

$joke = $_POST['joke'];
$joke['jokedate'] = new \DateTime();
$joke['authorId'] = $author['id'];

$this->jokesTable->save($joke);

header('location: /joke/list');
}
```

The check here issues the `return` command if the joke's `authorId` column is not the same as the ID of the currently logged-in user. The `return` command will exit the method, and the rest of the code won't run.

The same thing needs to be done in the `delete` method to prevent someone creating a form to delete other people's jokes:

```php
public function delete() {

    $author = $this->authentication->getUser();

    $joke = $this->jokesTable->findById($_POST['id']);

    if ($joke['authorId'] != $author['id']) {
        return;
    }

    $this->jokesTable->delete($_POST['id']);
```

```
    header('location: /joke/list');
}
```

You can find this code in *Sessions-CheckUser-Secured*

That's it! You've secured all the relevant features of the website so that jokes can only be edited or deleted by the person who posted them.

It's very easy to forget that hiding a link is not enough to make something secure. We also need to ensure that people can't find the URL and access the page anyway.

The Sky's the Limit

In this chapter, you learned about the two main methods of creating persistent variables—those variables that continue to exist from page to page in PHP. The first stores the variable in the visitor's browser in the form of a cookie. By default, cookies terminate at the end of the browser session, but by specifying an expiry time, they can be preserved indefinitely. Unfortunately, cookies are fairly unreliable, because you have no way of knowing when the browser might delete your cookies, and because some users occasionally clear their cookies out over concern for their privacy.

Sessions, on the other hand, free you from all the limitations of cookies. They let you store an unlimited number of potentially large variables. Sessions are an essential building block in modern ecommerce applications, as we demonstrated in our simple shopping cart example. They're also a critical component of systems that provide access control, like the one we built for our joke content management system.

At this point, you should be equipped with all the basic skills and concepts you need to build your very own database-driven website. While you may be tempted to skip the challenge of building a complete system for safely accepting public submissions, I encourage you to give it a try. You already have all the skills necessary to build it, and there's no better way to learn than to make a few mistakes of your own. At the very least, set this challenge aside for now and come back to it when you've finished this book.

If you can tackle it with confidence, you may wish to try another challenge. Want to let users rate the jokes on the site? How about letting joke authors make changes to their jokes, but with the backup of requiring an administrator to approve the changes before they go live on the site? The power and complexity of the system is limited only by your imagination.

In the rest of this book, I'll cover more advanced topics that will help optimize our site's performance and solve some complex problems using less code. Oh, and of course we'll explore more exciting features of PHP and MySQL!

In the nex chapter, we'll take a step away from our joke database and have a close-up look at MySQL server maintenance and administration. We'll learn how to make backups of our database (a critical task for any web-based company), how to administer MySQL users and their passwords, and how to log in to a MySQL server if you've forgotten your password.

Chapter **12**

MySQL Administration

At the core of most well-designed, content-driven sites is a relational database. In this book, we've used the MySQL Relational Database Management System (RDBMS) to create our database. MySQL is a popular choice among web developers because it's free, and because MySQL servers are fairly simple to set up. As I demonstrated in Chapter 1, with proper instructions and a pre-configured Vagrant box, getting a MySQL database up and running only takes a couple of minutes.

If all you need is a MySQL server so you can play with a few examples and experiment a little, the initial a process we went through inChapter 1 is likely to be all you'll need. If, on the other hand, you want to set up a database back end to a real live website—perhaps a site your company depends on—there are a few more fundamentals you'll need to learn before you can rely on a MySQL server day in, day out.

First, we'll look at backups. Backing up data that's important to you or your business should be an essential item on any administrator's list of priorities. Because administrators usually have more interesting work to do, though, backup procedures are often arranged once out of necessity and deemed "good enough" for all applications. If, until now, your answer to the question, "Should we back up our databases?" has been, "It's okay; they'll be backed up along with everything else," you really should read on. I'll show you why a generic file-backup solution is inadequate for many MySQL installations, and I'll demonstrate the *right* way to back up and restore a MySQL database.

Next, it's time we looked more closely at how to control access to your MySQL database. I showed you the basics early in this book, but it turns out there are some tricky details that can make your life difficult if you don't understand them. Oh, and I'll show you how to regain control of your MySQL server should you forget your password!

Then we'll turn our attention to performance, and how to keep our SELECT queries running quickly. With the careful application of database indexes (a skill many working PHP developers lack, surprisingly), you can keep your database speedy even as it grows to contain thousands (or even hundreds of thousands) of rows.

Finally, I'll show you how to use a feature of MySQL—foreign keys—to express the structure of your database, and how the tables it contains are related to one another.

As you can see, this chapter's a real mixed bag, but by the end of it you'll understand MySQL a whole lot better!

However, MySQL is a large and complex database with a lot of nuances and advanced features. If you're interested in learning MySQL beyond the fairly simple requirements of a website, I recommend SitePoint's *Jump Start MySQL*[1].

Backing Up MySQL Databases

Like web servers, most MySQL servers are expected to remain online 24 hours a

---

[1.] https://www.sitepoint.com/premium/books/jump-start-mysql

day, seven days a week. This makes backups of MySQL database files problematic. Because the MySQL server uses memory caches and buffers to improve the efficiency of updates to the database files stored on disk, these files may be in an inconsistent state at any given time. Since standard backup procedures involve merely copying system and data files, backups of MySQL data files are unreliable, as there's no guarantee the files that are copied are in a fit state to be used as replacements in the event of a crash.

Furthermore, as many website databases receive new information at all hours of the day, standard backups can provide only periodic snapshots of database data. Any information stored in the database that's changed after the last backup will be lost in the event that the live MySQL data files are destroyed or become unusable. In many situations, such as when a MySQL server is used to track customer orders on an ecommerce site, this is an unacceptable loss.

Facilities exist in MySQL to keep up-to-date backups that are largely unaffected by server activity at the time at which the backups are generated. Unfortunately, they require you to set up a backup scheme specifically for your MySQL data, completely apart from whatever backup measures you've established for the rest of your data. As with any good backup system, however, you'll appreciate it when the time comes to use it.

Database Backups Using MySQL Workbench

The MySQL administration tool we've been using throughout this book, MySQL Workbench, also offers a convenient facility for obtaining a backup of your site's database.

After logging in to the server, the right-hand menu has an option for **Data Export**. This opens a panel that displays all the databases on the server.

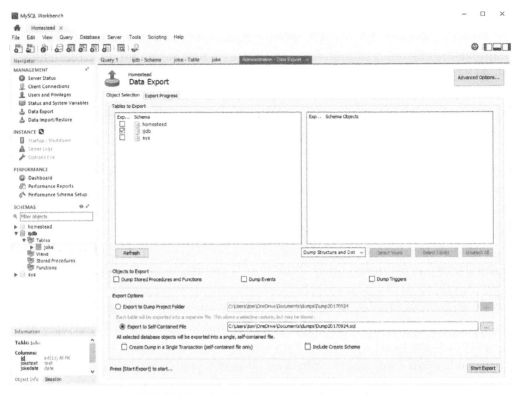

12-1. Click **Data Export** to save a backup of your database

There are two main options: **Export to Dump Project Folder** and **Export to Self-Contained File**. The latter is more useful for us, as it allows us to store the backup in a single file.

Select **Export to Self-Contained File**, pick where you want to store the backup, and press **Start Export**. The default settings are perfect for our needs.

If you open the backup file in a text editor, you'll find it contains a series of SQL `CREATE TABLE` and `INSERT` commands that, if run on a blank database, would reproduce the current contents of your database. Yes, a MySQL database backup is just a series of SQL commands!

To restore your database from a backup file like this one, first make sure your database is empty (right-click on each table and select **Drop Table**). Then just click **Data Import/Restore**. To select the backup file, choose **Import from Self-Contained file**, find your backup file, and select the schema (for the jokes database it's `ijdb`).

In this way, we can use MySQL Workbench to create backups of our databases. MySQL Workbench connects to the MySQL server to perform backups, rather than accessing the MySQL database data files directly. The backup it produces is therefore guaranteed to be a valid copy of the database, instead of merely a point-in-time snapshot of the database files stored on disk, which may be in a state of flux as long as the MySQL server is running.

Database Backups Using `mysqlpump`

MySQL Workbench makes it really easy to obtain a database backup whenever the mood strikes you, but the best backups are automated, and MySQL Workbench is not an automated backup tool.

As you'll already know if you've ever worked with MySQL on Linux, the MySQL database server software comes with a handful of utility programs designed to be run from the command prompt. One of these programs is `mysqlpump`. MySQL Workbench actually uses this tool behind the scenes; it just provides a user-friendly interface.

When run, `mysqlpump` connects to a MySQL server (in much the same way as PHP does) and downloads the complete contents of the database(s) you specify. It then outputs the series of SQL commands required to create a database with those same contents. If you save the output of `mysqlpump` to a file, you'll have yourself the same kind of backup file that MySQL Workbench can generate for you!

You can run `mysqlpump` from your computer if you have MySQL installed. However, the Homestead Improved virtual machine we're using already has the `mysqlpump` tool installed for us.

One of the advantages of using a virtual server such as Homestead Improved is that it acts like a real web server. By learning how to perform a backup on the virtual server, you'll know how to create a backup on a real web server!

For both a real web server and our virtual one, you'll need to log in to the server using a protocol called **Secure Shell** (**SSH** for short). This is a command line protocol that gives you a command prompt on a remote computer. Any commands you run via SSH will be executed on the web server, not on your local PC.

Vagrant includes a shortcut command to do this. Make sure your server is running and you can type `vagrant ssh` to connect to the virtual server via SSH. This is a convenient shorthand, but it's worth understanding what this does behind the scenes so you're familiar with the process on a real server. Connecting to a remote server via SSH is very easy. From the Git Bash command prompt on Windows, or the Terminal/Console on macOS/Linux, type the following:

```
ssh vagrant@127.0.0.1 -p 2222
```

The above command will ask you if you want to trust the server (type `yes`), and when asked for a password, provide `vagrant`.

The `ssh` command can be broken down into three parts: `vagrant` is the username, `127.0.0.1` is the server address and `-p 2222` is the port. For a real web server, the `-p 2222` option will not be necessary, unless you change this in the SSH settings, which is something that's outside the scope of this book. By default, SSH runs on port 22, but Vagrant uses port 2222, which is why we need to specify it when we connect.

Once you've connected to the server via SSH, you can create a database backup with the `mysqlpump` command. The following command (typed all on one line) connects to the MySQL server running on the local machine as user `root` with password `password`, and saves a backup of the `ijdb` database into the file `ijdb.sql`:

```
mysqlpump -u homestead -psecret ijdb > ijdb.sql
```

Let's break this command down to its individual parts:

`mysqlpump` executes the `mysqlpump` application.

`-u homestead` sets the username used to log in to the server. We can specify any user here, including the `ijdb` user we created.

`-psecret` sets the password to `secret`. Note that there's no space between `-p` and the password, `secret`. This is used to specify the password on the command line.

We *could* use only -p, but we'll be prompted for a password. Although more secure, a password prompt is unsuitable for automated backups, as someone has to type in the password each time the database is exported.

ijdb is the name of the schema to export.

The > operator can be used with any command, and is used to redirect the output to a file. Without this, the entire database backup is printed to the screen. For testing purposes, it can be useful to omit this (and the following filename) to check that the output looks correct. There's no point having an automated backup if it's not actually backing up the data we're expecting it to!

ijdb.sql is the name of the file to create. It defaults to the "current working directory", but it can be useful to specify a full path such as /var/backups/ijdb.sql when using automated backups, as the command may not run from a directory you can write to.

To restore this database after a server crash, we could again feed this SQL file to MySQL Workbench. Alternatively, we could use the mysql utility program:

```
mysql -u homestead -psecret ijdb < ijdb.sql
```

This command has the same options as the mysqlpump command. However, in this instance, we're loading a file using the < operator and sending the contents of the file to the mysql program, rather than saving to a file.

But how do we bridge the gap between these snapshots to maintain a database backup that's always up to date?

Incremental Backups Using Binary Logs

As I mentioned, many situations in which MySQL databases are used would make the loss of data—any data—unacceptable. In cases like these, we need a way to bridge the gaps between the backups we made using MySQL Workbench or mysqlpump as recently described.

The solution is to configure the MySQL server to keep a binary log, a record of all

SQL queries that were received by the database, and which modified the contents of the database in some way. This includes INSERT, UPDATE, and DELETE statements (among others), but excludes SELECT statements.

The basic idea of a binary log is that you should be able to restore the contents of the database at the very moment at which a disaster occurs. This restoration involves applying a backup (made using MySQL Workbench or mysqlpump), and then applying the contents of the binary logs that were generated after that backup was made.

You can also edit binary logs to undo mistakes that might have been made. For example, if a co-worker comes to you after accidentally issuing a DROP TABLE command, you can export your binary log to a text file and then edit that file to remove the command. You can then restore the database using your last backup and then running the edited binary log. In this way, you can even preserve database changes that were made *after* the accident. And, as a precaution, you should probably also revoke your co-worker's DROP privileges.

To tell your MySQL server to keep binary logs, you need to edit the server's my.ini (Windows) or my.cnf (macOS or Linux) configuration file. This is a simple text file with a list of options that control some of the finer points of how your MySQL server works. In many cases, MySQL is installed without a configuration file, and simply runs with the default settings. In this situation, you'll need to create a new file and set the appropriate option.

To enable binary logging, you add a log-bin setting to the [mysqld] section of your configuration file. The Homestead Improved virtual machine doesn't have binary logs enabled by default. To enable them, you'll need to connect to the virtual machine via SSH, as described in the previous section, and edit the configuration file.

As you're connected via a command line, you won't be able to open up the configuration file using your normal editor (Sublime Text, Atom or even Notepad) and you'll need to use a command line text editor.

The simplest editor is called **nano**, and the configuration file you'll need to edit is stored at the location /etc/mysql/mysqld.conf.d/mysqld.conf. If you're used to Windows, this file path may look a little strange: there's no drive letter, and there are forward slashes instead of back slashes. Don't worry, this is the way files are referenced on Linux systems.

To open the file in nano, use this command while logged in to the virtual machine with SSH:

```
sudo nano /etc/mysql/mysqld.conf.d/mysqld.conf
```

The sudo prefix will open the file with administrator privileges. After all, you wouldn't want just anyone being able to make changes to the MySQL configuration. If you try the command without sudo, you won't be able to save changes to the file.

With the file open on the screen, you can use the arrow keys to move around. If you're new to command line text editors, it can be a little disconcerting, as there are no scrollbars and your mouse cursor doesn't do anything! Don't worry, we don't have to do much using nano. We'll just uncomment a couple of lines.

The setting we're looking for is called log_bin. This option stores a file path for where we want the binary log to be kept. To find the setting, press Ctrl+W on your keyboard. This issues a "Where" command. (You're probably familiar with Ctrl+F for "Find"; nano uses the term "where" instead.) After pressing Ctrl+W, type log_bin and press **return**. The editor will take you to this line:

```
#log_bin = /var/log/mysql/mysql-bin.log
```

The log-bin setting tells MySQL where to store the binary log files and what name to give them. The default path is fine. The only change needed on this line is to remove the preceding #—which acts as a comment (like // in PHP). Remove the # using the **backspace** or **delete** key so the line reads like this:

```
log_bin = /var/log/mysql/mysql-bin.log
```

We'll also need to uncomment the line above, which is #server-id = 1, again remove the # so it becomes `server-id = 1`. That's all the changes we need to make to the configuration. (If you can't see the line, use `Ctrl+W` again and type `server-id` as you did before for `log_bin`.)

Now save the file by pressing `Ctrl+O`. (That's the letter "o", not a zero. It stands for "output" in nano's terminology). We're nearly done. Press `Ctrl+X` to exit nano and return to the command prompt.

The final step is to restart MySQL so that it reads the updated configuration. To do this, run the following command:

```
sudo systemctl restart mysql.service
```

The `sudo` prefix here is important, as only people with administrator privileges can start and stop services.

 ## Just the Same on a Real Web Server

You've just learned how to enable binary logging and how to change configuration files on a virtual machine, but the process will be the same if you ever need to do this on a real web server.

Now that the binary log is enabled, a new file will be created each time the server flushes its log files. In practice, this occurs whenever the server is restarted.

 ## Where to Store Your Logs

If possible, you should store your binary logs on a hard disk other than the one where your MySQL database files are stored. That way, if a hard disk goes bad, you won't lose both your database and your backups!

From now on, the server will create binary log files. To make sure, check the location you specified, in order to verify that a new log file was created when the server started up. Run the following command:

```
ls /var/log/mysql
```

In the event of a disaster, as long as you have a full backup and the binary log files that were generated after the backup was made, restoring your database should be fairly simple. Set up a new, empty MySQL server, then apply the full backup as described in the previous section. All that's left is to apply the binary logs using the `mysqlbinlog` utility program.

`mysqlbinlog`'s job is to convert the data format of MySQL binary logs into SQL commands that you can run on your database. Say you had two binary log files that you needed to apply after restoring your most recent full backup. You can generate an SQL text file from the two files using `mysqlbinlog`, and then apply that file to your MySQL server just as you would a file generated by `mysqlpump`:

```
mysqlbinlog binlog.000041 binlog.000042 > binlog.sql
mysql -u root -psecret < binlog.sql
```

MySQL Access Control Tips

Homestead Improved

In the case of the Homestead Improved box, the steps in this section have been done for us, and you don't need to make any changes to the user accounts. This section will be beneficial when you want to start working with a real web server.

In Chapter 3, I mentioned that the database called `mysql`, which appears on every MySQL server, is used to keep track of users, their passwords, and what they're allowed to do. In Chapter 4, I showed you how to use MySQL Workbench to create another user account, with access only to your website's database.

The MySQL access control system is fully documented in Chapter 5 of the MySQL Reference Manual[2]. In essence, user access is governed by the contents of five tables in the `mysql` database: `user`, `db`, `host`, `tables_priv` and `columns_priv`. If you plan to edit these tables directly using `INSERT`, `UPDATE` and `DELETE` statements, I suggest you read the relevant section of the MySQL manual first. But for us mere mortals, MySQL Workbench provides all the tools you'll need to

---

[2.] http://dev.mysql.com/doc/refman/5.5/en/privilege-system.html

manage access to your MySQL server.

As a result of the way the access control system in MySQL works, there are some idiosyncrasies you should be aware of if you're going to be responsible for controlling access to a MySQL server.

Host Name Issues

When you create users who can log in to the MySQL server only from the computer on which that server is running (for example, you require them to log in to the server and run the `mysql` command prompt utility from there, or to communicate using server-side scripts like PHP), you may ask yourself what to enter in the **Host** field of MySQL Workbench's **Add a new User** form. Imagine the server is running on `www.example.com`. Should you specify the **Host** as `www.example.com` or `localhost`?

The answer is that neither is reliable enough to handle all connections. In theory, if, when connecting, the user specifies the host name either with the `mysql` command prompt utility program, or with PHP's `PDO` class, that host name will have to match the entry in the access control system. However, as you probably want to avoid forcing your users to specify the host name in a particular way (in fact, users of the `mysql` utility program are likely to want to steer clear of stating the host name at all), it's best to use a workaround.

For users who need the ability to connect from the machine on which the MySQL server is running, it's best to create two user entries in the MySQL access system: one with the actual host name of the machine (`www.example.com`, for example), and the other with `localhost`. Of course, you'll have to grant/revoke all privileges to both user entries individually, but it's the only workaround that you can really rely on.

Another problem commonly faced by MySQL administrators is that user entries whose host names contain wildcards (for example, `%.example.com`) may fail to work. When MySQL's access control system behaves unexpectedly, it's usually due to the way MySQL prioritizes the user entries. In particular, it orders entries so that more specific host names appear first. (For example, `www.example.com` is absolutely specific, `%.example.com` is less specific, and `%` is totally unspecific.)

In a fresh installation, the MySQL access control system contains two root user entries, and two anonymous user entries. (These latter allow connections to be made from the local host using any username. The two entries support connections from `localhost` and the server's actual host name, as described before.) The problem just described occurs when the anonymous user entries take precedence over our new entry, because their host name is more specific.

Let's look at the abridged contents of the user table on `www.example.com`, a fictitious MySQL server, where we've just added a new account for a user named Jess. The rows are sorted in the order in which the MySQL server considers them when it validates a connection:

```
Host                    User       Password
-------------------     --------   -----------------
localhost               root       encrypted value
www.example.com         root       encrypted value
localhost
www.example.com
%.example.com           jess       encrypted value
```

As you can see, since Jess's entry has the least specific host name, it comes last in the list. When Jess attempts to connect from `www.example.com`, the MySQL server matches her connection attempt to one of the anonymous user entries (a blank User value matches anyone). Since a password is unnecessary for these anonymous entries, and presumably Jess enters her password, MySQL rejects the connection attempt. Even if Jess managed to connect without a password, she would be given the very limited privileges that are assigned to anonymous users, as opposed to the privileges assigned to her entry in the access control system.

The solution is either to make your first order of business as a MySQL administrator the deletion of those anonymous user entries (`DELETE FROM mysql.user WHERE User=""`), or to give two more entries to all users who need to connect from `localhost` (that is, entries for `localhost` and the actual host name of the server):

```
Host                    User       Password
```

```
-------------------  --------  ------------------
localhost            root      encrypted value
www.example.com      root      encrypted value
localhost            jess      encrypted value
www.example.com      jess      encrypted value
localhost
www.example.com
%.example.com        jess      encrypted value
```

As it's excessively burdensome to maintain three user entries (and three sets of privileges) for each user, I recommend that you remove the anonymous users, unless you have a particular need for them:

```
Host                 User      Password
-------------------  --------  ------------------
localhost            root      encrypted value
www.example.com      root      encrypted value
%.example.com        jess      encrypted value
```

Locked Out?

Like locking your keys in the car, forgetting your password after you've spent an hour installing and tweaking a new MySQL server can be rather embarrassing! Fortunately, if you have administrator access to the computer on which the MySQL server is running, or if you can log in as the user you set up to run the MySQL server, all is well. The following procedure will let you regain control of the server.

 I'm Assuming You Know How to Log In to the Server

Again, I'm going to go ahead and assume in this section that if you're locked out of your MySQL server, you know how to log in to the server and that you have SSH access.

First, you must shut down the MySQL server by running this command:

```
sudo systemctl stop mysql.service
```

Now that the server's down, you must restart it using the `skip-grant-tables` option. You can do this by adding the option to your MySQL server's `my.cnf` configuration file (see the instructions for setting up such a file in the "Incremental Backups Using Binary Logs" section above):

Under the `[mysqld]` line, add `skip-grant-tables` and save the file:

```
[mysqld]
skip-grant-tables
```

This instructs the MySQL server to allow unrestricted access to anyone. Obviously, you'll want to run the server in this mode as briefly as possible, to avoid the inherent security risks.

Restart the server with this command:

```
sudo systemctl start mysql.service
```

Connect to the MySQL server (using MySQL Workbench or the `mysql` command prompt utility), then change your user's password to a memorable one:

```
UPDATE mysql.user SET Password=PASSWORD("newpassword")
WHERE User="homestead"
```

Finally, disconnect, shut down your MySQL server as above, and remove the `skip-grant-tables` option. Start the server again and you'll be able to connect with the new password.

That's it! (And thankfully, nobody ever has to know what you did.) As for locking your keys in your car, you're on your own there.

Indexes

Just as the index in this book makes it a lot easier to find every mention of a particular topic in its pages, a **database index** can make it much easier for MySQL to find the records you've asked for in a SELECT query. Let me give you an example.

As the Internet Joke Database grows, the joke table might grow to contain thousands or rows, if not hundreds of thousands. Now, let's say PHP asks for the text of a particular joke:

```
SELECT joketext FROM joke WHERE id = 1234
```

In the absence of an index, MySQL must look at the value of the id column in each and every row of the joke table, one by one, until it finds the one with the value 1234. Worse yet, without an index, MySQL has no way of knowing that there is only *one* row with that value, so it must also scan the rest of the table for more matching rows to make sure it gets them all!

Computers are fast, and good at menial labor, but in the web development game, where half seconds count, large tables and complex WHERE clauses can easily combine to create delays of 30 seconds or more!

Fortunately for us, this query will always run quickly, and that's because the id column of the joke table has an index. To see it, open MySQL Workbench, right-click the joke table, and click **Alter table**. At the bottom of the window are some tabs, one of which is **Indexes**. Click on that and you'll see a list of indexes on the table.

12-2. Each of our tables already has a single index

Take a look at the left-hand column and you'll see an index called PRIMARY.

Remember how we defined the id column of the table:

```
CREATE TABLE joke (
    id INT NOT NULL AUTO_INCREMENT PRIMARY KEY,
    joketext TEXT,
    jokedate DATE NOT NULL,
    authorId INT
) DEFAULT CHARACTER SET utf8 ENGINE=InnoDB;
```

In fact, "key" is just a fancy way to say "index" in database parlance, and a primary key is just an index named PRIMARY that requires each value in the table for that particular column to be unique.

What all this boils down to is that every database table we've created so far has an index on its id column. Any WHERE clause that seeks a particular id value will be able to find the record with that value quickly, because it will be able to look it up in the index to know exactly where in the table the relevant record is.

You can confirm this by asking MySQL to *explain* how it performs a particular

SELECT query. To do this, just add the command EXPLAIN at the start of the query:

```
EXPLAIN SELECT joketext FROM joke WHERE id = 1
```

Specifying a Joke ID that Exists

Note that I've specified a joke ID of **1** in this query, which actually exists in my database. Had I used a made-up value like **1234**, MySQL is smart enough to know that this ID doesn't exist in the **joke** table and wouldn't even try to fetch results from the table.

If you run this EXPLAIN query in MySQL Workbench, you'll see something similar to this:

id	select_type	table	partitions	type	possible_keys	key	key_len	ref	rows	filtered	Extra
1	SIMPLE	joke	NULL	const	PRIMARY	PRIMARY	4	const	1	100.00	NULL

12-3. These results confirm that the **SELECT** query will use the PRIMARY index

Now consider this SELECT query, which fetches all jokes by a particular author:

```
SELECT * FROM joke WHERE authorId = 2
```

Ask MySQL to EXPLAIN this SELECT, and you'll see a result like this:

id	select_type	table	partitions	type	possible_keys	key	key_len	ref	rows	filtered	Extra
1	SIMPLE	joke	NULL	ALL	NULL	NULL	NULL	NULL	3	33.33	Using where

12-4. Those NULLs indicate slowness

As you can see, MySQL is unable to find an index to assist with this query, so it's forced to perform a complete scan of the table for results. We can speed up this query by adding an index to the table for the **authorId** column.

But the author Table Has an Index?

Yes, the **id** column of the **author** table has an index by virtue of it being the primary key for that table. This won't help in the case of this query, however, which has no involvement with the **author** table at all.

The **WHERE** clause in this case is looking for a value in the **authorId** field of the **joke** table, which is without an index.

In MySQL Workbench, select the **joke** table, right-click and choose **Alter Table**. On the **Indexes** tab, add a new row under **PRIMARY** by double-clicking the empty cell. Give your index a name (this can be anything, but the column name is often used) and select the type as **INDEX**. We can't use **UNIQUE** here, because that would prevent each author from being able to have more than one joke in the table.

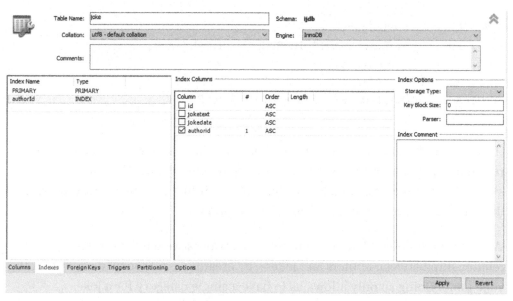

12-5. Creating a new index for the authorId column

Now select the **authorId** column from the middle panel and click **Apply**. Ask MySQL to **EXPLAIN** the **SELECT** query again to confirm that it will use your new **authorId** index this time.

It might be tempting to index each and every column in your database, but I'd advise against it. Not only do indexes require extra disk space, but every time you make a change to the contents of your database (with an **INSERT** or **UPDATE** query, for example), MySQL has to spend time rebuilding all affected indexes!

For this reason, you should usually add the indexes required to keep your website's SELECT queries speedy and no more. As a rule of thumb, you should create an index on any column that you use in a WHERE, GROUP BY, ORDER BY or JOIN ... ON clause.

Multicolumn Indexes

But wait! Not *every* table will have an id column. Consider a table that associates jokes with categories.

We'd need a table for categories, which will have an ID:

```
CREATE TABLE `category` (
    `id` INT NOT NULL AUTO_INCREMENT PRIMARY KEY,
    `name` VARCHAR(255),
    PRIMARY KEY (`id`)
) DEFAULT CHARACTER SET utf8 ENGINE=InnoDB;
```

However, in this instance we'd need what's known as a **many-to-many relationship**. Each joke might fit into more than one category. For example, the joke "Why did the programmer quit his job? He didn't get arrays" fits into both the categories "programming jokes" and "one-liners".

We can't model this relationship in the same way as we have with the relationship between authors and jokes—by creating a categoryId column in the joke table. Doing so only allows us to have a single category for a joke.

Instead, we need to create something called a **join table** or **junction table**, which has two columns, jokeId and categoryId. The joke_category junction table might contain values like this:

```
jokeId | catoryId
     1 |        1
     1 |        2
     2 |        3
```

```
          3 |            1
```

It's all numbers, but assuming category 1 is "one-liners", to find all the jokes in the category we can use this query:

```
SELECT jokeId FROM joke_category WHERE categoryId = 1
```

This would give the following results:

```
jokeId
       1
       3
```

Then we can read the individual jokes from the database by looping over the results and issuing a select query for each of the jokes:

```
SELECT * FROM joke WHERE id = 1;
SELECT * FROM joke WHERE id = 3;
```

The joke_category table doesn't have an obvious primary key. Although we *could* create an id auto increment column, this is far from ideal. We don't want the same record appearing twice. For example:

```
jokeId | catoryId
    1 |         1
    1 |         2
    2 |         3
    3 |         1
    3 |         1
```

Now joke 3 in category 1 appears twice. Any query to select the jokes in category 1 will return joke 3 twice! To prevent that, we can actually create a *multi-column* primary key:

```
CREATE TABLE joke_category (
    jokeId INT NOT NULL,
    categoryId INT NOT NULL,
    PRIMARY KEY (jokeId, categoryId)
) DEFAULT CHARACTER SET utf8 ENGINE=InnoDB;
```

This table's primary key is made up of two columns: `jokeid` and `categoryid`. The image below shows what this index looks like in MySQL Workbench. Because a primary key has to be unique, there's no way for this table to store the same record twice.

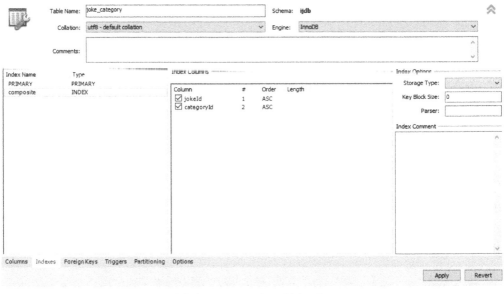

12-6. Indexes can contain multiple columns

A multi-column index like this is called a **composite index**. It's great at speeding up queries that involve both indexed columns, like the one below, which checks if joke ID **3** is in category ID **4**:

```
SELECT * FROM joke_category WHERE jokeid = 3 AND categoryid
↪ = 4
```

A two-column index like this one can also be used as a one-column index on the first column in the list. In this case, that's the `jokeid` field, so this query will also use the index to list the categories that joke ID 1 belongs to:

```
SELECT * FROM joke_category WHERE jokeid = 1
```

Foreign Keys

By now, you should be used to the concept of a column in one table pointing to the `id` column in another table to represent a relationship between the two tables. For example, the `authorId` column in `joke` points to the `id` column in `author` to record which author wrote each joke.

In database design lingo, a column that contains values that match those in another table is called a **foreign key**. That is, we say that `authorId` is a foreign key that references the `id` column in `author`.

Up to this point, we've simply designed tables with foreign key relationships in mind, but these relationships haven't been enforced by MySQL. That is, we've made sure to only store values in `authorId` that correspond to entries in the `author` table. But if we carelessly inserted an `authorId` value without any matches for an author record, MySQL would do nothing to stop us. As far as MySQL is concerned, `authorId` is just a column that contains whole numbers.

MySQL supports a feature called **foreign key constraints**, which you can use to record relationships between tables like this one explicitly and have MySQL enforce them. You can include foreign key constraints in your `CREATE TABLE` commands, or you can add foreign key constraints to existing tables using `ALTER TABLE`:

```
CREATE TABLE joke (
    id INT NOT NULL AUTO_INCREMENT PRIMARY KEY,
    joketext TEXT,
    jokedate DATE NOT NULL,
    authorId INT,
    FOREIGN KEY (authorId) REFERENCES author (id)
```

```
) DEFAULT CHARACTER SET utf8 ENGINE=InnoDB
```

```
ALTER TABLE joke
ADD FOREIGN KEY (authorId) REFERENCES author (id)
```

You can also use MySQL Workbench to create foreign key constraints. First, you must make sure the foreign key column (`authorId` in this case) has an index. MySQL will create this index for you automatically if you use either of these two queries, but MySQL Workbench requires you to do it yourself. Thankfully, we already added an index to `authorId`. Next, on the **Foreign Keys** tab for the `joke` table, double-click in the top row of the **Foreign Key Name** column. A name will be generated for you, and this isn't used by MySQL. It's for your own reference.

Next, we call the key `fk_joke_author` to highlight that we're creating a foreign key between the `joke` and `author` tables. Then select the author table as the referenced table and choose the `authorId` column as the **Column** and `id` column as the **Referenced column**.

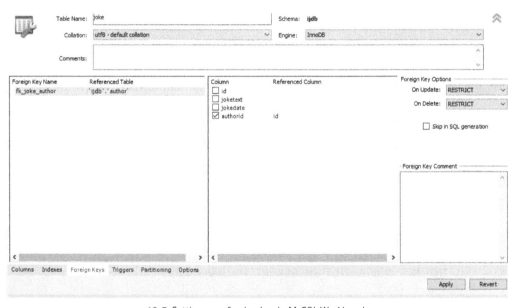

12-7. Setting up a foreign key in MySQL Workbench

With this foreign key constraint in place, MySQL will reject any attempt to insert into joke an authorId value that fails to correspond to an entry in the author table. Furthermore, it will stop you from deleting an entry in the author table unless you first remove any joke records that point to it.

Referential Action

Instead of rejecting attempts to delete or update records that have foreign keys pointing to them (for example, preventing you from deleting authors who still have jokes associated with them), you can perform a **referential action**. This involves configuring a foreign key constraint in MySQL to automatically resolve the conflict.

It can do this either by **cascading** the operation (that is, deleting any jokes associated with the author that you're deleting), or by setting the values of any affected foreign key columns to NULL (setting the authorId of the author's jokes to NULL). That's what the ON RESTRICT and ON UPDATE options for the foreign key constraint in MySQL Workbench are all about.

It can be tempting to use this feature to let MySQL take care of what happens to affected jokes when a user deletes an author or a category. It's certainly easier to select an option in MySQL Workbench than it is to write the PHP code to automatically delete related jokes before removing an author.

The problem with doing this is that it splits the logic of your website into two places: your PHP code and the foreign key constraints. No longer will you be able to see and control everything that happens when you delete a joke by just looking at the PHP controller responsible for doing that job.

For this reason, most experienced PHP developers (myself included) prefer to avoid using referential actions in foreign key constraints. In fact, some developers prefer to avoid using foreign key constraints altogether!

Better Safe than Sorry

Admittedly, this chapter hasn't been the usual nonstop, action–packed codefest to which you may have become accustomed by now. But our concentration on these topics—the backup and restoration of MySQL data, the inner workings of the MySQL access control system, the improvement of query performance with indexes, and the enforcement of the structure of your database with foreign keys—has armed you with the tools you'll need to set up a MySQL database server that will stand the test of time, as well as endure the constant traffic your site will attract.

Chapter **13**

Relationships

As you've worked through the construction of the Internet Joke Database website, you've had opportunities to explore most aspects of Structured Query Language (SQL). From the basic form of a `CREATE TABLE` query to the two syntaxes of `INSERT` queries, you probably know many of these commands by heart now.

In Chapter 5, I showed you how to perform basic `JOIN`s using SQL to fetch data from more than one table at a time. A lot of the time, you'll come across situations where you want to do this—for example, finding information about an author as well as all the jokes they've posted, or finding a category and all the jokes that reside inside it.

SQL `JOIN` is one of many solutions to this problem. Although there are performance advantages to using `JOIN`, unfortunately `JOIN`s don't work well with object-oriented programming. The *relational* approach used by databases is generally incompatible with the nested structure of object-oriented programming. In object-oriented programming, objects are stored in a hierarchical structure. An author **contains**—or, in the correct OOP terminology, **encapsulates**—a list of their jokes, and a category also encapsulates a list of the jokes within the category.

A SELECT query that fetches an author along with all of their jokes can be written like this:

```
SELECT author.name, joke.id, joke.joketext
FROM author
INNER JOIN joke ON joke.authorId = author.id
WHERE authorId = 123
```

Using an object-oriented approach, there are various practical ways of achieving this, which we'll look into shortly. But at a more general level, using OOP, rather than an SQL query, fetching a list of jokes would be expressed like this:

```
// Find the author with the id `123`
$author =  $authors->findById(123);

// Get all the jokes by this author
$jokes = $author->getJokes();

// Print the text of the first joke by that author.
echo $jokes[0]->joketext;
```

Notice that there's no SQL here. The data is coming from the database, but it all happens behind the scenes.

We could fetch all the information by using the SQL query I provided above, but this doesn't work well with the DatabaseTable class we've used so far. It would be very difficult to design the class in such a way that it would account for every possible set of relationships we may want.

So far, we've dealt with the relationship between jokes and authors in a *relational* way. If we wanted to get the information about an author, along with a list of all their jokes, we'd do this:

```
// Find the author with the ID 123
$author = $this->authors->findById(123);

// Now find all the jokes posted by the author with that ID
$jokesByAuthor = $this->jokes->find('authorId',
  $authorId);
```

This runs two separate SELECT queries, and the two DatabaseTable instances are entirely separate.

We used a similar approach when inserting a joke into the database:

```
public function saveEdit() {
    $author = $this->authentication->getUser();

    $joke = $_POST['joke'];
    $joke['jokedate'] = new \DateTime();
    $joke['authorId'] = $author['id'];

    $this->jokesTable->save($joke);

    header('location: /joke/list');
}
```

This code uses the authentication class to fetch the record that stores the currently logged-in user. It then reads the author's id in order to provide it when the joke is added: $joke['authorId'] = $author['id'];.

Whoever writes this code must know about the underlying structure of the database and that the authors and jokes are stored in a *relational* way.

In object-oriented programming, it's preferable to hide the underlying implementation, and the code above would be expressed like this:

```php
public function saveEdit() {
    $author = $this->authentication->getUser();

    $joke = $_POST['joke'];
    $joke['jokedate'] = new \DateTime();

    $author->addJoke($joke);

    header('location: /joke/list');
}
```

Not a lot has changed, so look closely! Firstly, the line `$joke['authorId'] = $author['id'];` has been removed. Secondly, instead of saving the joke to the `$jokesTable` object, it's being passed to the `author` object: `$author->addJoke($joke);`.

What is the advantage of this approach? The person who writes this code doesn't have to know anything about what happens behind the scenes, or how the relationship is modeled in the database—that there's an `authorId` column in the `joke` table.

Instead of modeling the relationships in a relational way, object-oriented programming takes a *hierarchical* approach, using data structures. Just as the routes in the `IjdbRoutes` class is a multi-dimensional array, OOP has multi-dimensional data structures stored within *objects*.

In the example above, the `$author->addJoke($joke)` method call *might* be writing the joke data to a database. Alternatively, it might be saving the data to a file. And that file could be in JSON format, XML format or an Excel spreadsheet. The developer who writes this `saveEdit` method doesn't need to know anything about the underlying storage mechanism—*how* data is being stored—but only that the data *is* being stored somehow, and that it's being stored *inside* the author instance.

In object-oriented programming terminology, this is known as **implementation hiding**, and it has several advantages. Different people can work on different sections of the code. The developer who writes the `saveEdit` doesn't have to be familiar with how addJoke actually works. They only need to know that it *saves data*, and that the data can be retrieved later.

When you use the method $pdo->query, you don't need to know how $pdo actually communicates with the database. You only need to know what the method returns and what arguments it requires. We can imagine what the following lines of code do, knowing *how* each of them works:

```php
$jokes = $author->getJokes();
```

```php
echo $joke->getAuthor()->name;
```

```php
$joke = $_POST['joke'];
$joke['jokedate'] = new \DateTime();

$author->addJoke($joke);
```

In the middle example, as long as you know there's a getAuthor method that you can call on the $joke instance, it doesn't matter how it works. The author name could be hardcoded into the class, or it could go off and fetch it from the database.

This is particularly useful, because the storage system can be changed at any time, and the code above doesn't need to change. The methods getJokes, getAuthor and $joke can be completely rewritten to write to/read from a file, for example, but the code above will still work without any further changes.

If the saveEdit contained the INSERT query with all the relevant database fields, we'd need to rewrite the whole method to change the way the data is stored, and we'd need to do this anywhere data was inserted.

This approach to splitting up the logic is loosely known as **separation of concerns**. The process of *saving a joke* is different from the process of *writing data to the database*. Each of these is a different *concern*. By splitting out the two concerns, you have a lot more flexibility. The `addJoke` method can be called from anywhere without needing to repeat the logic. The way the `addJoke` method works can be completely rewritten to work in a different way, but the code that calls it can remain unchanged.

This added flexibility is incredibly useful for an increasingly popular development methodology called **test-driven development (TDD)**. In TDD, you'd test the code by writing a version of the `DatabaseTable` class that worked as a placeholder for the test, rather than needing a working database containing relevant test data.

Although TDD is beyond the scope of this book, by thinking about separation of concerns, you'll be able to start writing automated tests for your code without making large-scale changes.

A common problem mid-level developers have when first learning about TDD is that they understand the advantages of it, but their code isn't written in such a way that makes it easy to test. By considering separation of concerns earlier on in your programming career, you'll make it easier for yourself moving forward.

For more information on TDD, check out the introductory article "Re-Introducing PHPUnit – Getting Started with TDD in PHP"[1].

Object Relational Mappers

The `DatabaseTable` class we've built step by step so far is a type of library called an **object relational mapper** (or **ORM**). There are a lot of ORM implementations available, such as Doctrine[2], Propelhttp://propelorm.org/ and ReadBeanPHP[3]. These all do essentially the same job as the `DatabaseTable` class we've been building: providing an object-oriented interface for a relational database. They bridge the gap between the relational database's SQL queries and the PHP code we're using for everything else on the website.

Generally, ORMs deal with *Objects*. Using our `DatabaseTable` class to find an

---

[1]. https://www.sitepoint.com/re-introducing-phpunit-getting-started-tdd-php/

[2]. http://www.doctrine-project.org/

[3]. http://redbeanphp.com/index.php

author and print their name, we can use this code:

```
$author = $authors->findById(123);

echo $author['name'];
```

Here, the `$author` variable is an array with keys for each of the columns in the database. Arrays can't contain functions[4], so implementing an `addJoke` method on the `$author` instance isn't possible.

If we want the ability to call methods on the `$author` instance, such as `$author->addJoke($joke)` like above, the `$author` variable needs to be an *object* rather than an array. The first thing we need to do is create the relevant class to represent authors. Firstly, some properties for each of the columns from the database:

```
namespace Ijdb\Entity;

class Author {
    public $id;
    public $name;
    public $email;
    public $password;
}
```

As the properties of an author are unique to the joke website, I've put the class in the `Ijdb` namespace.

A class like this, which is designed to map directly to a record in the database, is commonly known as an **Entity Class**, which is why I've used the name `Entity` in the namespace. We'll have a different entity class for each of the database tables we need to represent. Create the directory `Entity` inside the `Ijdb` folder and save the class inside it with the name `Author.php`.

---

[4] OK, that's a lie. They can contain a special type of function called a **closure**, but doing so has several severe limitations compared to the OOP based approach I'm going to show you instead.

Although the variables don't *need* to be declared here, and what we're doing will work identically whether they are or not, it makes the code easier to read and understand if the variables are included.

There's some repetition here: every time you add a column to the database table, you'll need to add it to this entity class. Because of this, many ORMs provide a method of generating these entity classes from the database schema, or even creating the database table from the object!

I'm not going to show you how to do that, but if you do want to try something similar, you should take a look at the MySQL DESCRIBE query[5] to retrieve a list of columns in a table, or the PHP Reflection library[6] to get a list of properties in a class.

Public Properties

Every time we've created a class variable so far, it's been *private*, so that the data used is only accessible to methods within the class. The advantage of this is that class variables can be easily added, renamed or removed without potentially breaking any of the code that uses the class.

It also prevents developers accidentally breaking the functionality of the class. If the pdo variable were public in the DatabaseTable class, it would be possible to do this:

```
$this->jokesTable->pdo = 1234;
```

Any further call to methods on the DatabaseTable class would break:

```
$this->jokesTable->findById('1243');
```

The findById method would call $this->pdo->query('…'), but because the pdo variable is no longer a PDO instance, it would break!

[5.] https://httpss://dev.mysql.com/doc/refman/5.7/en/getting-information.html
[6.] http://php.net/manual/en/book.reflection.php

In most cases, private properties are strongly preferred over public ones. However, in the case of entity classes, you should use public properties.

The sole purpose of an entity class is to make some data available. It's no good having a class representing an author if you can't even read the author's name!

Nine times out of ten—in fact, ninety-nine times out of a hundred—public properties are the wrong solution to any given problem. However, if the responsibility of the class is to represent a *data structure*, and it's interchangeable with an *array*, then public properties are fine.

Methods in Entity Classes

A *class* is used to store the data about authors instead of an *array*, because the class can contain methods, and we can do things like this:

```
// Find the author with the id 1234
$author = $this->authorsTable->findById('1234');

// Find all the jokes by that author
$author->getJokes();

// Add a new joke and associate it with the author
// represented by $author
$author->addJoke($joke);
```

Let's take a moment to think about what the `getJokes` method might look like. Assuming the `id` property in the `$author` class is set, it would be possible to do this:

```
public function getJokes() {
    return $this->jokesTable->find('authorId',
    $this->id);
}
```

To do this, the author class needs access to the `jokesTable` instance of the

`DatabaseTable` class. Add the `getJokes` method, along with a constructor and class variable to store the reference to the `jokesTable` instance:

```php
<?php
namespace Ijdb\Entity;

class Author
{
    public $id;
    public $name;
    public $email;
    public $password;
    private $jokesTable;

 public function __construct(\Ninja\DatabaseTable
↪ $jokesTable)
    {
        $this->jokesTable = $jokesTable;
    }

    public function getJokes()
    {
        return $this->jokesTable->find('authorId',
        $this->id);
    }
}
```

We're going to amend the `DatabaseTable` class to return an instance of this class instead of an array. But before we do that, let's take a look at how the `Author` class can be used on its own:

```php
$jokesTable = new \Ninja\DatabaseTable($pdo, 'joke', 'id');

$author = new \Ijdb\Entity\Author($jokesTable);

$author->id = 123;

$jokes = $author->getJokes();
```

This would query the database for all the jokes by the author with the ID 123. We can now fetch data that's related to the author, once we have an `Author` instance that represents any given author, by setting the `id` property.

Next, we need the `addJoke` method that takes a joke as an argument, sets the `authorId` property and then inserts it into the database:

```php
public function addJoke($joke) {

    $joke['authorId'] = $this->id;

    $this->jokesTable->save($joke);
}
```

Let's use the new class inside the `Joke` controller's `saveEdit` method to save the jokes using `$author->addJoke($joke)`.

```php
public function saveEdit() {
    $author = $this->authentication->getUser();

    $authorObject = new \Ijdb\Entity\Author
    ($this->jokesTable);

    $authorObject->id = $author['id'];
    $authorObject->name = $author['name'];
    $authorObject->email = $author['email'];
    $authorObject->password = $author['password'];

    $joke = $_POST['joke'];
    $joke['jokedate'] = new \DateTime();

    $authorObject->addJoke($joke);

    header('location: /joke/list');
}
```

You can find this code in *Relationships-Author*.

Using Entity Classes from the DatabaseTable Class

Because the database returns data as an array, I've copied the data from the $author array returned by getUser() to an instance of the newly created Author class.

Both the array $author and the object $authorObject will represent the same author. The only difference is that one is an object and the other is an array.

Most of the lines of code in the method simply copy data from the array to an object. This is obviously inefficient, and the problem can be avoided if we can construct the Author object outside of the saveEdit method and have getUser return the constructed object like so:

```
public function saveEdit() {
    $authorObject = $this->authentication->getUser();

    $joke = $_POST['joke'];
    $joke['jokedate'] = new \DateTime();

    $authorObject->addJoke($joke);

    header('location: /joke/list');
}
```

Currently, an array is created, because the getUser method in the Authentication class calls the findById method in the DatabaseTable class:

```
public function findById($pdo, $table, $primaryKey,
  $value) {
    $query = 'SELECT * FROM ' . $table . ' WHERE ' .
    $primaryKey . ' = :primaryKey';
```

```
    $parameters = [
    'primaryKey' => $value
    ];

    $query = $this->query($query, $parameters);

    return $query->fetch();
}
```

Here, `$query->fetch()` returns an array. Luckily for us, there's also a `fetchObject` method, which returns an instance of a specified class—in our case, `Author`. This will instruct PDO to create an instance of the `Author` class and set the properties on that, rather than returning a simple array.

For example, to have `fetchObject()` return an `Author` object, you can use this code:

```
return $query->fetchObject('Author', [$jokesTable]);
```

There are two arguments here:

1. The name of the class to instantiate.
2. An array of arguments to provide to the constructor when the object is created. Because there's only a single element in the array, `[$jokesTable]` looks a little strange. However, as constructors can have multiple arguments, an array is required so you can provide each constructor argument.

Now, rather than writing `new Author` somewhere in our code, we can have the PDO library create an instance of the `Author` class in place of returning the data as an array.

```
$pdo->query('SELECT * FROM `author` WHERE id = 123');

$author = $query->fetchObject('Author', [$jokesTable]);
```

Because the `Author` class requires the `$jokesTable` class as a constructor argument, this must also be provided as an argument when `fetchObject` is called. However, we can't amend the `DatabaseTable` class to use the `return` line above—firstly, because it doesn't have access to the `$jokesTable` variable, and secondly, because we're using the `DatabaseTable` class to interact with different database tables. When the `findById` method is called, it may be on the `authorsTable` instance, the `jokesTable` instance, or an instance of the `DatabaseTable` class that represents some other database table.

We'll want a different entity class for each table, and they almost certainly won't have the same constructor arguments.

Instead of hardcoding the class name and constructor argument, we can amend the constructor of the `DatabaseTable` class to take two *optional* arguments—the name of the class to create, and any arguments to provide to it:

```
class DatabaseTable {
    private $pdo;
    private $table;
    private $primaryKey;
    private $className;
    private $constructorArgs;

    public function __construct(\PDO $pdo, string $table,
      string $primaryKey, string $className = '\stdClass',
      array $constructorArgs = []) {
    $this->pdo = $pdo;
    $this->table = $table;
    $this->primaryKey = $primaryKey;
    $this->className = $className;
    $this->constructorArgs = $constructorArgs;
    }
```

Notice that I've given *default values* to each of the new arguments. The `stdClass` class is an inbuilt PHP empty class that can be used for simple data storage.

By specifying this as a default value, if no class name is specified, it will use this generic inbuilt one. The advantage this gives us is that we don't need to create a unique entity class for every database table, but only those we want to add methods to!

The `findById` method can now be changed to read the new class variables and use those in place of hardcoded ones in the `fetchObject` method call:

```php
public function findById($value) {
    $query = 'SELECT * FROM `' . $this->table . '` WHERE `' .
     $this->primaryKey . '` = :value';

    $parameters = [
    'value' => $value
    ];

    $query = $this->query($query, $parameters);

    return $query->fetchObject($this->className,
     $this->constructorArgs);
}
```

PDO's `fetchAll` method—which we're using in the `DatabaseTable`'s `find` and `findAll` methods—can also be instructed to return an object by providing `\PDO::FETCH_CLASS` as the first argument, the class name as the second, and the constructor arguments as the third:

```php
 return $result->fetchAll(\PDO::FETCH_CLASS,
↳ $this->className, $this->constructorArgs);
```

Now that we've amended the `DatabaseTable` class, we can change `IjdbRoutes`, where the `DatabaseTable` class is instantiated, and provide the class name and the arguments for the `$authorsTable` instance:

```php
$this->jokesTable = new \Ninja\DatabaseTable($pdo,
 'joke', 'id');
$this->authorsTable = new \Ninja\DatabaseTable($pdo,
 'author', 'id', '\Ijdb\Entity\Author',
```

```
[$this->jokesTable]);
```

Now, when the `$authorsTable` instance is used to retrieve a record, like this:

```
$author = $authorsTable->findById(123);
```

… the `$author` variable will be an instance of the `Author` class, and any methods in the class (such as `addJoke`) will available for us to call.

As we've made a change to the `DatabaseTable` class, this will affect every instance of the class. When jokes are retrieved from the database, an object will also be retrieved. As we haven't specified an entity class for jokes (yet!), they will be an `stdClass` instance.

If you load up the joke list page in your browser, at this point you'll see this error:

```
Fatal error: uncaught Error: cannot use object of type
↳ stdClass as array in
↳ /home/vagrant/Code/Project/classes/Ijdb/Controllers/Joke.php
↳ on line 21
```

We'll fix this later, but first let's get `saveEdit` working. Amend the `saveEdit` method to avoid all the value copying. Change the code from this:

```
public function saveEdit() {
    $author = $this->authentication->getUser();

    $authorObject = new \Ijdb\Entity\Author
    ($this->jokesTable);

    $authorObject->id = $author['id'];
    $authorObject->name = $author['name'];
    $authorObject->email = $author['email'];
    $authorObject->password = $author['password'];
```

```
    $joke = $_POST['joke'];
    $joke['jokedate'] = new \DateTime();

    $authorObject->addJoke($joke);

    header('location: /joke/list');
}
```

... to this:

```
public function saveEdit() {
    $author = $this->authentication->getUser();

    $joke = $_POST['joke'];
    $joke['jokedate'] = new \DateTime();

    $author->addJoke($joke);

    header('location: /joke/list');
}
```

Because getUser now returns an instance of Author with all the properties already set, we can use this instance rather than having to manually create the $authorObject instance and set each property individually.

Before we can test that this works, we'll also need to amend the Authentication class to use an object rather than an array. In the isLoggedIn method, replace this line:

```
if (!empty($user) &&
 $user[0][$this->passwordColumn] ===
 $_SESSION['password']) {
```

... with this:

```
$passwordColumn = $this->passwordColumn;

if (!empty($user) && $user[0]->$passwordColumn
 === $_SESSION['password']) {
```

This code looks complicated! However, let's take a moment to understand what's happening here.

The $user[0] variable now stores an instance of the Author class. The Author class has a property called password. To read this property, you could use this:

```
$user[0]->password
```

However, if you remember back to Chapter 11, you'll recall that the Authentication class has a class variable, which stores the name of the database column that contains the password. It might not be password in every website you build.

Assuming the password column *is* password, once the variables have been evaluated, all we're doing here is replacing $user['password'] with the object variant $user->password. But this is complicated by the fact that we're using a variable for the column name. We really need $user[$this->passwordColumn] to be replaced with $user->$this->passwordColumn.

It's possible to use a variable to access a property on an object using a string, as we do with an array:

```
$columnName = 'password';

// Read value stored under key 'password' from array
$password = $array[$columnName];

// Read value stored under property 'password' from object
$password = $object->$columnName;
```

You might be wondering why I didn't use `$user[0]->$this->passwordColumn`. As PHP evaluates left to right, it would try to look up the contents of the variable `$this` (an object), then try to read a variable with that name. As a variable name can't be an object, PHP will give an error. Instead, I read the value into its own variable, `$passwordColumn`, then used `$user[0]->$passwordColumn`.

 Using Braces

As an alternative to creating a new variable, you can also use braces to tell PHP to evaluate the `$this->passwordColumn` lookup first:

```
$user[0]->{$this->passwordColumn};
```

Do the same with this line in the `login` method:

```
public function login($username, $password) {
    $user = $this->users->find($this->usernameColumn,
     strtolower($username));

    if (!empty($user) && password_verify($password,
     $user[0][$this->passwordColumn])) {
        session_regenerate_id();
        $_SESSION['username'] = $username;
        $_SESSION['password'] =
         $user[0][$this->passwordColumn];
        return true;
    }
    else {
        return false;
    }
}
```

The above code changes to this:

```
public function login($username, $password) {
    $user = $this->users->find($this->usernameColumn,
```

```
    strtolower($username));

    if (!empty($user) && password_verify($password,
    $user[0]->{$this->passwordColumn})) {
        session_regenerate_id();
        $_SESSION['username'] = $username;
        $_SESSION['password'] =
         $user[0]->{$this->passwordColumn};
    return true;
    }
    else {
        return false;
    }
}
```

This code can be found in *Relationships-DatabaseTableEntity*.

After submitting the form, you'll see an error on the list page, but you can check the new `saveEdit` method is working by logging in to the website and adding a joke. When you're redirected to the list page, you'll see an error, but you can check that the joke has been added by viewing the contents of the `joke` table in MySQL Workbench.

Joke Objects

Now we'll fix the joke list page. At the moment it displays an error, thanks to this code in the controller:

```
$author = $this->authorsTable->
findById($joke['authorId']);

$jokes[] = [
    'id' => $joke['id'],
    'joketext' => $joke['joketext'],
    'jokedate' => $joke['jokedate'],
    'name' => $author['name'],
    'email' => $author['email']
```

```
];
```

The error occurs because `$author` and `$joke` are no longer arrays. This is a simple fix: change the syntax that reads from an array to use the object syntax:

```
$author = $this->authorsTable->
findById($joke->authorId);

$jokes[] = [
    'id' => $joke->id,
    'joketext' => $joke->joketext,
    'jokedate' => $joke->jokedate,
    'name' => $author->name,
    'email' => $author->email
];
```

You'll also need to change the method's `return` statement to use the object syntax for the `$author` variable.

```
return ['template' => 'jokes.html.php',
    'title' => $title,
    'variables' => [
    'totalJokes' => $totalJokes,
    'jokes' => $jokes,
    'userId' => $author->id ?? null
    ]
];
```

Now also amend the `delete` method to read the joke's `authorId` from the new object:

```
if ($joke->authorId != $author->id)
```

This code can be found in *Relationships-Objects*.

Although this solution works, now that we're using an object-oriented approach, it can be solved in a much nicer way. Currently, each value from either the `author` or `joke` table is stored under an equivalent key in the `$jokes` array.

The code for generating the `$jokes` array looks like this:

```php
public function list() {
    $result = $this->jokesTable->findAll();

    $jokes = [];
    foreach ($result as $joke) {
        $author = $this->authorsTable->
        findById($joke->authorId);

        $jokes[] = [
            'id' => $joke->id,
            'joketext' => $joke->joketext,
            'jokedate' => $joke->jokedate,
            'name' => $author->name,
            'email' => $author->email
        ];
    }
```

The `$jokes` array is used to provide the template access to each joke and its author.

The process currently looks like this:

- query the database and select all the jokes
- loop over each joke and:
    - select the related author
    - create a new array containing all the information about the joke and the author
- pass this constructed array to the template for display

This is a very long-winded process for something we can make a lot simpler using OOP.

At the moment, we can fetch all the jokes by a specific author using
`$author->getJokes()`. However, we can also model the inverse relationship and
do something like this:

```
echo $joke->getAuthor()->name;
```

This would let us get the author for any given joke, and this code could even be
run from the template.

If the `$this->jokesTable->findAll();` call returned an array of joke *objects*,
each with their own `getAuthor` method, this process of creating an array with
both sets of data would be unnecessary!

Firstly, let's create the `Joke` entity class in `Ijdb/Entity/Joke.php`:

```php
<?php
namespace Ijdb\Entity;

class Joke
{
    public $id;
    public $authorId;
    public $jokedate;
    public $joketext;
    private $authorsTable;

    public function __construct(\Ninja\DatabaseTable
     $authorsTable)
    {
        $this->authorsTable = $authorsTable;
    }

    public function getAuthor()
    {
        return $this->authorsTable->
        findById($this->authorId);
    }
}
```

The Joke class works in the same way as the Author class: it has a constructor that asks for an instance of a DatabaseTable class that contains related data. In this case, it will be passed the DatabaseTable instance, which represents the author database table.

The getAuthor method returns the author for the current joke. If $this->authorId is 5, it will return an Author object that represents the author with the ID 5.

Using the Joke Class

To use the new Joke class, we'll need to update the IjdbRoutes class to provide the authorsTable instance as a constructor argument. The relevant section of code currently looks like this:

```
$this->jokesTable = new \Ninja\DatabaseTable($pdo,
'joke', 'id', '\Ijdb\Entity\Joke',
[$this->authorsTable]);

$this->authorsTable = new \Ninja\DatabaseTable($pdo,
'author', 'id', '\Ijdb\Entity\Author',
[$this->jokesTable]);
```

This will pass the authorsTable instance to the jokesTable instance and the authorsTable instance.

Think about that for a second. It poses a problem that's not immediately obvious.

If the authorsTable instance constructor requires an instance of jokesTable, and the jokesTable constructor requires an authorsTable instance, we have a catch-22: to create the jokesTable instance, you need an existing authorsTable instance. To create the authorsTable instance, you need an existing jokesTable instance. Both instances require the other instance to exist before they do!

If you try the code above, the PDO library will throw an exception—"Cannot call constructor". Although the message isn't very clear, it's because of the problem I just highlighted.

This catch-22 occurs sometimes in object-oriented programming. Luckily, in this case it can be fairly easily solved using something called a *reference*.

References

A **reference** is special type of variable, a bit like a shortcut in Windows, or a symlink in macOS or Linux. A **shortcut** on your computer is a special type of file that doesn't contain any data itself. Instead, it points to another file. When you open the shortcut, it actually opens the file the shortcut is pointing to.

References work in a similar way. Instead of a variable containing a specific value, a it can contain a *reference* to another variable. When you read the value of a variable that stores the reference, it will read the value of the variable being referenced.

To create a reference, you prefix the variable you want to create a reference to with an ampersand (&):

```php
$originalVariable = 1;
$reference = &$originalVariable;
$originalVariable = 2;
echo $reference;
```

The code above will print 2. Without the &, it would print 1! That's because the variable $reference contains a reference to the $originalVariable variable. Whenever the value of $reference is read, it will actually go off and read the value of the variable $originalVariable as it is at that moment in time.

This is important, because it allows us to solve the catch-22 we encountered earlier. By providing references as the constructor arguments for the Joke and Author classes, by the time the authorsTable and jokesTable instances are needed, they'll have been created:

```
$this->jokesTable = new \Ninja\DatabaseTable($pdo,
  'joke', 'id', '\Ijdb\Entity\Joke',
  [&$this->authorsTable]);

$this->authorsTable = new \Ninja\DatabaseTable($pdo,
  'author', 'id', '\Ijdb\Entity\Author',
  [&$this->jokesTable]);
```

Now, when the DatabaseTable class creates a Joke or Author object and has to provide it the authorsTable or jokesTable instance, it will read what's stored in the authorsTable or jokesTable class variables at the time any Author or Joke entity is instantiated.

Simplifying the List Controller Action

The following is now possible inside a controller:

```
$joke = $this->jokesTable->findById(123);

echo $joke->getAuthor()->name;
```

Now that a joke is an *object*, we can pass the whole object into the template and read the author from there.

Remove this code from the list method:

```
$jokes = [];
foreach ($result as $joke) {
    $author = $this->authorsTable->
    findById($joke->authorId);

    $jokes[] = [
    'id' => $joke->id,
    'joketext' => $joke->joketext,
    'jokedate' => $joke->jokedate,
    'name' => $author->name,
```

```
        'email' => $author->email
    ];
}
```

This code was necessary when using arrays, because for each joke, we needed to fetch the information about the joke, and the information about the author of that particular joke, then combine them into a single data structure.

However, now that we're using objects, this ugly copying code is redundant. Once we've removed it, we can also replace this code:

```
$result = $this->jokesTable->findAll();
```

… with this:

```
$jokes = $this->jokesTable->findAll();
```

The DatabaseTable class now provides an array of *objects* rather than arrays. Each Joke object has a method getAuthor, which returns the author of the joke.

Rather than fetching the author in the controller, we can now do it in the template jokes.html.php. Let's update the template to use the new objects rather than the arrays:

```php
 <p><?=$totalJokes?> jokes have been submitted to
↪ the Internet Joke Database.</p>

<?php foreach ($jokes as $joke): ?>
<blockquote>
    <p>
    <?=htmlspecialchars($joke->joketext, ENT_QUOTES,
     'UTF-8')?>

    (by <a href="mailto:<?=htmlspecialchars(
    $joke->getAuthor()->email,
    ENT_QUOTES, 'UTF-8'
); ?>">
    <?=htmlspecialchars(
            $joke->getAuthor()->name,
            ENT_QUOTES,
            'UTF-8'
            ); ?></a> on
<?php
$date = new DateTime($joke->jokedate);

echo $date->format('jS F Y');
?>)

<?php if ($userId == $joke->authorId):
    ?>
    <a href="/joke/edit?id=<?=$joke->id?>">
    Edit</a>
    <form action="/joke/delete" method="post">
        <input type="hidden" name="id"
        value="<?=$joke->id?>">
        <input type="submit" value="Delete">
    </form>
<?php endif; ?>
    </p>
</blockquote>
<?php endforeach; ?>
```

For the fields from the `joke` table, this is fairly simple. We just change the syntax from an array to an object. For example, `$joke['joketext']` becomes `$joke->joketext`.

It's slightly more complicated where we want to read information about each joke's author. Before reading the author's email, we need to fetch the author instance. To read the author's email, we previously used `$joke['email']`, which now becomes `$joke->getAuthor()->email`.

This actually fetches the author from within the template! Previously, when writing the controller, we had to anticipate exactly which variables were needed by the template.

Now, the controller just provides a list of jokes. The template can now read any of the values it needs, including information about the author. If we added a new column in the database—for example, a joke category—we could amend the template to show this value without needing to change the controller.

Tidying Up

Now that we've changed the way the `DatabaseTable` class works, we've broken the "Edit Joke" page. To fix it, open up the template `editjoke.html.php` and replace the array syntax with object syntax for accessing the joke's properties:

```php
<?php if (empty($joke->id) || $userId ==
$joke->authorId):?>
<form action="" method="post">
    <input type="hidden" name="joke[id]"
     value="<?=$joke->id ?? ''?>">
    <label for="joketext">Type your joke here:
    </label>
    <textarea id="joketext" name="joke[joketext]" rows="3"
     cols="40"><?=$joke->joketext ?? ''?>
    </textarea>
    <input type="submit" name="submit" value="Save">
</form>
<?php else:
        ?>

<p>You may only edit jokes that you posted.</p>

<?php endif; ?>
```

We've now got an almost entirely object-oriented website! All the entities have their own class, and we can add any methods we like to each entity class.

Caching

You might have noticed a potential performance problem with the `Joke` entity class. The `getAuthor` method looks like this:

```php
public function getAuthor() {
 return
↳ $this->authorsTable->findById($this->authorId);
}
```

Although this works fine, it's unnecessarily slow. Each time this `getAuthor` method is called, it will send the same query to the database and retrieve the same result. The following code will send three queries to the database:

```
echo $joke->getAuthor()->name;
echo $joke->getAuthor()->email;
echo $joke->getAuthor()->password;
```

Querying the database is considerably slower than just reading a value from a variable. Each time a query is sent to the database, it will slow down the page's speed slightly. Although each query adds only a tiny overhead, if this is done inside a loop on a page, it can cause a noticeable slowdown.

To avoid this problem, you can fetch the author object once, then use the existing instance:

```
$author = $joke->getAuthor();
echo $author->name;
echo $author->name;
echo $author->password;
```

By doing this, we avoid sending three queries to the database, because `getAuthor` is only called once. This method works, but it's rather crude. You have to remember to implement this technique, and on a larger website you'd have to mentally keep track of all the places you'd need to do this.

Instead, it's better to implement a technique called **transparent caching**. The term **caching** refers to storing some data for quicker access later on, and the technique I'm about to show you is called *transparent caching* because the person using the class doesn't even need to know it's happening!

To implement caching, add a property to the `Joke` entity class to store the author between method calls:

```
class Joke {
    // …
    public $joketext;
    private $authorsTable;
    private $author;
```

```
// …
```

Then, in the `getAuthor` method, we can add logic that will do the following:

- check to see if the `author` class variable has a value
- if it's empty, fetch the author from the database and store it in the class variable
- return the value stored in the `author` variable

```
public function getAuthor() {
    if (empty($this->author)) {
 $this->author =
↳ $this->authorsTable->findById($this->authorId);
    }

    return $this->author;
}
```

You can find this code in *Relationships-Cached*.

With this simple `if` statement in place, the database will only be queried the first time the `getAuthor` method is called on any given joke instance.

Now, the following code will only send a single query to the database:

```
echo $joke->getAuthor()->name;
echo $joke->getAuthor()->email;
echo $joke->getAuthor()->password;
```

By solving the potential performance issue inside the class, it no longer matters how it's used externally. There will only ever be a single query for each instance of the class.

Joke Categories

Now that you know how to add relationships between different tables and model them using classes, let's add a new relationship.

At the moment, we have a single list of jokes. As we only have half a dozen jokes on the website, this works fine, but moving forward as more people register for the website and post jokes, the joke list page will keep getting longer!

People viewing the website may want to view a specific type of joke. For example, *programming jokes*, *knock-knock jokes*, *one-liners*, *puns* and so on.

The most obvious way to achieve this is the way we modeled the relationship between jokes and authors: create a `category` table to list the different categories, then create a `categoryId` column in the `joke` table to allow each joke to be placed in a category.

However, a joke may fall into more than one category.

Before modeling the relationship, let's add a new form that allows creating new categories and storing them in the database. It's been a while since we've added a new page to the website, and we've made a few changes since we last did, so I'll go through this in detail.

Firstly, let's create the table to store the categories:

```
CREATE TABLE `ijdb_sample`.`category` (
    `id` INT NOT NULL AUTO_INCREMENT,
    `name` VARCHAR(255) NULL,
    PRIMARY KEY (`id`));
```

Either use the SQL code above or use MySQL Workbench to create the `category` table with two columns: `id` and `name`. `id` is the primary key, so make sure it's `AUTO_INCREMENT`, and type should be `VARCHAR`.

Create a new controller called `Category` in `Ijdb/Controllers/Category.php`. This controller will need access to a `DatabaseTable` instance that allows interacting with the new `category` table.

```php
<?php
namespace Ijdb\Controllers;

class Category
{
    private $categoriesTable;

    public function __construct(\Ninja\DatabaseTable
      $categoriesTable)
    {
        $this->categoriesTable = $categoriesTable;
    }
}
```

Like the controller for jokes, we'll need several actions: `list` to display a list of categories, `delete` to delete a category, `edit` to display the add/edit form, and `saveEdit` to handle the form submission.

Let's add the form first. Create the template `editcategory.html.php`:

```php
<form action="" method="post">
    <input type="hidden"
        name="category[id]"
        value="<?=$category->id ?? ''?>">
    <label for="categoryname">Enter category name:
    </label>
    <input type="text"
        id="categoryname"
        name="category[name]"
        value="<?=$category->
        name ?? ''?>" />
    <input type="submit" name="submit" value="Save">
</form>
```

You can find this code in *Relationships-AddCategory*.

Like `editjoke.html.php`, this template will be used for both the edit and add pages, so we'll pre-fill the text box if the `$category` variable is set.

Add the `edit` method to the new `Category` class:

```php
public function edit() {

    if (isset($_GET['id'])) {
 $category =
↪ $this->categoriesTable->findById($_GET['id']);
    }

    $title = 'Edit Category';

    return ['template' => 'editcategory.html.php',
    'title' => $title,
    'variables' => [
        'category' => $category ?? null
    ]
    ];
}
```

Open up `IjdbRoutes`. The first thing to do here is to create the instance of the `DatabaseTable` class for the `category` table. Like `authorsTable` and `jokesTable`, this can be stored in a class variable and created in the constructor:

```php
class IjdbRoutes implements \Ninja\Routes {
    private $authorsTable;
    private $jokesTable;
    private $categoriesTable;
    private $authentication;

    public function __construct() {
    include __DIR__ . '/../../includes/DatabaseConnection.php';

    $this->jokesTable = new \Ninja\DatabaseTable($pdo,
      'joke', 'id', '\Ijdb\Entity\Joke',
      [&$this->authorsTable]);
```

```
    $this->authorsTable = new \Ninja\DatabaseTable($pdo,
      'author', 'id',
      '\Ijdb\Entity\Author',
      [&$this->jokesTable]);
  $this->categoriesTable = new \Ninja\DatabaseTable($pdo,
↪ 'category', 'id');

    // …
```

Notice that I haven't specified an entity class for the `category` table. Unless we need to add some functionality to it, it can use the `stdClass` class that we set as the default.

Next, create an instance of the `Category` controller and add the route for the edit page. We'll display this on the URL `/category/edit`:

```
                                        13-3. Relationships-AddCategory2

$authorController = new \Ijdb\Controllers\Register
($this->authorsTable);
$loginController = new \Ijdb\Controllers\Login
($this->authentication);
$categoryController = new \Ijdb\Controllers\Category
($this->categoriesTable);

$routes = [
// …
'category/edit' => [
    'POST' => [
    'controller' => $categoryController,
    'action' => 'saveEdit'
    ],
    'GET' => [
    'controller' => $categoryController,
    'action' => 'edit'
    ],
    'login' => true
],
// …
```

If you've followed the steps above, visit `http://192.168.10.10/category/edit` and you should see the form. We've already set up the route, so let's add the `saveEdit` method to add a category to the database when the form is submitted:

```
                                    13-4. Relationships-AddCategory-Save

public function saveEdit() {
    $category = $_POST['category'];

    $this->categoriesTable->save($category);

    header('location: /category/list');
}
```

If you test the form and press **Submit**, you'll see an error message, because we haven't built the list page yet. However, you can check the form is working by selecting all the records from the table in MySQL Workbench.

Once a category has been added, you should even be able to edit it by visiting `http://192.168.10.10/category/edit?id=1`.

At this point, it's worth momentarily stepping back and considering the benefit of the classes and framework we've built. With fairly little effort, we've created a form that allows inserting data into the database, loading a record into it and editing. Think back to Chapter 4, when we were manually writing INSERT and UPDATE queries, and think about how much more code you would have needed to write with that approach!

List Page

We can also add the list page with fairly little code. Firstly, let's create a template, `categories.html.php`, that loops through a list of categories and displays an **edit/ delete** button for each of them:

```
<h2>Categories</h2>

<a href="/category/edit">Add a new category</a>

<?php foreach ($categories as $category): ?>
<blockquote>
    <p>
    <?=htmlspecialchars($category->name,
      ENT_QUOTES, 'UTF-8')?>

    <a
      href="/category/edit?id=<?=$category->id?>">
    Edit</a>
    <form action="/category/delete" method="post">
    <input type="hidden"
        name="id"
        value="<?=$category->id?>">
    <input type="submit" value="Delete">
    </form>
    </p>
```

```
</blockquote>

<?php endforeach; ?>
```

Here's the controller action in `Category.php`:

```
public function list() {
    $categories = $this->categoriesTable->findAll();

    $title = 'Joke Categories';

    return ['template' => 'categories.html.php',
    'title' => $title,
    'variables' => [
        'categories' => $categories
    ]
    ];
}
```

And finally, here's the route in `IjdbRoutes`:

```
'category/list' => [
    'GET' => [
    'controller' => $categoryController,
    'action' => 'list'
    ],
    'login' => true
],
```

You can find this code in *Relationships-ListCategories*.

The **Edit** link from the template already works. Add the route and controller action for the **Delete** button to finish the category management pages:

```
'category/delete' => [
```

```
    'POST' => [
    'controller' => $categoryController,
    'action' => 'delete'
    ],
    'login' => true
],
```

```
public function delete() {
    $this->categoriesTable->delete($_POST['id']);

    header('location: /category/list');
}
```

Example: Relationships-DeleteCategory

Assigning Jokes to Categories

Now that categories can be added to the website, let's add the ability to assign a joke to a category.

As I mentioned previously, the *simplest* approach would be to have a `<select>` box on the add joke page, which sets a `categoryId` column in the `joke` table.

However, this approach is the least flexible. It's possible that a joke will fall into more than one category. Instead, we're going to model this relationship using a **join table**—that is, a table with just two columns.

In our case, the columns will be `jokeId` and `categoryId`.

Let's create the following table using either MySQL Workbench or by running this query:

```
CREATE TABLE `ijdb_sample`.`joke_category` (
    `jokeId` INT NOT NULL,
    `categoryId` INT NOT NULL,
```

```
PRIMARY KEY (`jokeId`, `categoryId`));
```

Note that both the `jokeId` and `categoryId` columns are the primary key. As I explained in Chapter 4, this is to prevent the same joke being added to a category twice.

Before continuing, let's add some categories to the database. Using the form at `http://192.168.10.10/category/edit`, add the categories "programming jokes" and "one-liners".

Currently we have three jokes, each of which falls into the "programming jokes" category:

> How many programmers does it take to screw in a lightbulb? None, it's a hardware problem.

> Why did the programmer quit his job? He didn't get arrays.

> Why was the empty array stuck outside? It didn't have any keys.

Here are some more jokes that fit in the two categories:

> Bugs come in through open Windows. *("programming jokes" and "one-liners" categories)*

> How do functions break up? They stop calling each other. *("programming jokes" only)*

> You don't need any training to be a litter picker, you pick it up on the job. *("one-liners" only)*

> Venison's dear, isn't it? *("one-liners" only)*

> It's tricky being a magician. *("one-liners" only)*

Don't add these just yet. We'll amend the Add Joke page to allow selecting categories and then add the jokes.

Instead of using a `<select>` box, we'll use a series of checkboxes to allow users to select which categories a joke falls into.

As the `Joke` controller will now need to be able to pass a list of categories to the `editjoke.html.php` template, let's amend the controller with a new constructor argument and class variable:

```
class Joke {
    private $authorsTable;
    private $jokesTable;
    private $categoriesTable;
    private $authentication;

    public function __construct(DatabaseTable $jokesTable,
     DatabaseTable $authorsTable,
     DatabaseTable $categoriesTable,
     Authentication $authentication) {
    $this->jokesTable = $jokesTable;
    $this->authorsTable = $authorsTable;
    $this->categoriesTable = $categoriesTable;
    $this->authentication = $authentication;
    }

    // …
```

Aesthetic Choices

For consistency, I've placed the argument before the `Authentication` argument. There's no practical reason for this; it's an entirely aesthetic choice to put all the `DatabaseTable` instances together.

Now we should pass in the `categoriesTable DatabaseTable` instance when the `Joke` controller is instantiated in `IjdbRoutes`:

```
$jokeController = new \Ijdb\Controllers\Joke
($this->jokesTable, $this->authorsTable,
 $this->categoriesTable,
 $this->authentication);
```

In the `edit` method, pass the list of categories to the template:

```php
public function edit() {
    $author = $this->authentication->getUser();
    $categories = $this->categoriesTable->findAll();

    if (isset($_GET['id'])) {
    $joke = $this->jokesTable->findById($_GET['id']);
    }

    $title = 'Edit joke';

    return ['template' => 'editjoke.html.php',
    'title' => $title,
    'variables' => [
        'joke' => $joke ?? null,
        'userId' => $author->id ?? null,
        'categories' => $categories
    ]
    ];
}

}
```

The next step is to set up the list of categories in the `editjoke.html.php` template and create a checkbox for each:

```php
<form action="" method="post">
    <input type="hidden" name="joke[id]"
     value="<?=$joke->id ?? ''?>">
    <label for="joketext">Type your joke here:
    </label>
    <textarea id="joketext" name="joke[joketext]" rows="3"
     cols="40"><?=$joke->joketext ?? ''?>
    </textarea>

    <p>Select categories for this joke:</p>
    <?php foreach ($categories as $category): ?>
```

```
    <input type="checkbox"
        name="category[]"
        value="<?=$category->id?>" />
    <label><?=$category->name?></label>

    <?php endforeach; ?>

    <input type="submit" name="submit" value="Save">
</form>
```

The code here should be familiar by now, but I'll quickly go over the additions I've made.

`<?php foreach ($categories as $category): ?>`: loop over each of the categories.

`<input type="checkbox" name="category[]" value="<?=$category->id?>" />`: this creates a checkbox for each category with the `value` property set to the ID of the category.

`name="category[]"`: by setting the name of the checkbox to `category[]`, an array will be created when the form is submitted. For example, if you checked the checkboxes with the values 1 and 3, the variable `$_POST['category']` would contain an array with the values 1 and 3 (`['1', '3']`).

If you try the code above, the formatting will look strange. Add the following CSS to `jokes.css` to fix it:

```
form p {clear: both;}
 input[type="checkbox"] {float: left; clear: left; width:
↪ auto; margin-right: 10px;}
input[type="checkbox"] + label {clear: right;}
```

You can find this code in *Relationships-JokeCategory*

Now that the categories are listed and selectable on the Add Joke page, we need to change the `saveEdit` method to handle new data from the form submission.

It's important to understand what needs to happen here. When the form is submitted, an array of the IDs of the checked categories will be sent as a $_POST variable. Each category ID and the ID of the new joke will then be written to the joke_category table.

Before we can add records to the joke_category table, we'll need a DatabaseTable instance for it. Add the class variable and create the instance in IjdbRoutes:

```
// …
private $jokeCategoriesTable;

    public function __construct() {
    include __DIR__ . '/../../includes/DatabaseConnection.php';

    $this->jokesTable = new \Ninja\DatabaseTable($pdo,
      'joke', 'id', '\Ijdb\Entity\Joke',
      [&$this->authorsTable]);
    $this->authorsTable = new \Ninja\DatabaseTable($pdo,
      'author', 'id',
      '\Ijdb\Entity\Author',
      [&$this->jokesTable]);
    $this->categoriesTable = new \Ninja\DatabaseTable($pdo,
      'category', 'id');

    $this->jokeCategoriesTable =
      new \Ninja\DatabaseTable($pdo,
      'joke_category', 'categoryId');
    // …
```

We *could* pass the jokeCategoriesTable instance to the Joke controller. However, like we did with the $author->addJoke method, it's better to implement this using an object-oriented approach, where a joke is added to a category using this code:

```
$joke->addCategory($categoryId);
```

To do this, we'll need a `Joke` entity instance in the `saveEdit` method in the `Joke` controller. The code for the updated `saveEdit` method will look like this:

```php
public function saveEdit() {
    $author = $this->authentication->getUser();

    $joke = $_POST['joke'];
    $joke['jokedate'] = new \DateTime();

    $jokeEntity = $author->addJoke($joke);

    foreach ($_POST['category'] as $categoryId) {
    $jokeEntity->addCategory($categoryId);
    }

    header('location: /joke/list');
}
```

The important change to what we have at the moment is the line `$jokeEntity = $author->addJoke($joke);`.

The `addJoke` method, which currently does not have a return value, will need to return a `Joke` entity instance, which represents the joke that has just been added to the database.

As a first thought, a simple approach would be to fetch the joke from the `jokesTable` instance after it's been created, using the following process:

- take the data for the new joke from `$_POST`
- pass it to the `addJoke` method in the `Author` entity class
- retrieve the newly added joke from the database using a `SELECT` query (or the `findById` method)

For example:

```php
public function addJoke($joke) {

    $joke['authorId'] = $this->id;
```

```
    // Store the joke in the database
    $this->jokesTable->save($joke);

    // Fetch the new joke as an object
    return $this->jokesTable->findById($id);
}
```

There are two problems with this:

1. We don't know what the newly created joke's id is.

2. It adds additional overhead. We're actually making two trips to the
    database—once to run an INSERT query to send the data about the new joke,
    and then a SELECT query to fetch that very same information back out of the
    database immediately afterwards! We already have the information in the
    $joke variable, so there's no need to fetch it from the database here.

Although, it would be possible to create the Joke entity instance in the addJoke
method, it makes more sense to place this functionality in the DatabaseTable
class. Whenever save is called, it can return the relevant entity instance. By
placing this logic inside the save method, any time any data is written to any
database table, the save method will return an object representing that newly
added record.

The addJoke method above should be changed to this:

```
public function addJoke($joke) {

    $joke['authorId'] = $this->id;

    return $this->jokesTable->save($joke);
}
```

This will just return the return value of the save method from the DatabaseTable
class. That is, whatever the save method returns to the addJoke method will also

be returned by the `addJoke` method.

Open up the `DatabaseTable` class and find the `save` method:

```php
public function save($record) {
    try {
    if ($record[$this->primaryKey] == '') {
        $record[$this->primaryKey] = null;
    }
    $this->insert($record);
    }
    catch (\PDOException $e) {
    $this->update($record);
    }
}
```

This calls either the `insert` or `update` method. The first thing we need to do here is create an instance of the relevant entity class. For jokes, it will be the `Joke` class; for authors, it will be the `Author` class; and so on.

To create the relevant entity, we can use this code:

```php
$entity = new
↳ $this->className(...$this->constructorArgs);
```

This looks complicated. There are lots of variables, and a brand new operator! It's important to understand what's happening here, so I'll show you how this works.

Let's think about what we want to do for the joke class. To create an instance of the `Joke` entity class, we'd need the following code:

```php
$joke = new \Ijdb\Entity\Joke($authorsTable);
```

The class name, `\Ijdb\Entity\Joke`, is stored in the `$this->className` variable, so the above could be expressed like this:

```
$joke = new $this->className($authorsTable);
```

And this will still work in the same way.

However, each entity class has different arguments and, potentially, a different number of arguments. The Author entity class, for example, requires the $jokesTabe instance. We already have the list of arguments for the entity class in the $this->constructorArgs variable as an array.

The ... operator, known as the **argument unpacking operator** or **splat operator**, allows specifying an array in place of several arguments.

For example, consider this code:

```
$array = [1, 2];

someFunction(...$array);
```

It's the same as this:

```
someFunction(1, 2);
```

In our use case, this code:

```
$entity = new
↪ $this->className(...$this->constructorArgs);
```

... is equivalent to this:

```
$entity = new
↪ $this->className($this->constructorArgs[0],
↪ $this->constructorArgs[1]);
```

Once this code has run, the `$entity` variable will store an object. The type of that object will depend on the class defined in `$this->className`. For the `$jokesTable` instance, it will be an instance of the `Joke` entity class.

This line can be placed inside the `save` method, along with a line to return the newly created entity object:

```php
public function save($record) {
    $entity = new $this->
    className(...$this->constructorArgs);

    try {
    if ($record[$this->primaryKey] == '') {
        $record[$this->primaryKey] = null;
    }
    $this->insert($record);
    }
    catch (\PDOException $e) {
    $this->update($record);
    }

    return $entity;
}
```

With those lines in place, the `save` method will instantiate the relevant, empty, entity class. The next stage is writing the data that was sent to the database to the class. This can be done with a simple `foreach`:

```php
public function save($record) {
    $entity = new $this->
    className(...$this->constructorArgs);

    try {
    if ($record[$this->primaryKey] == '') {
        $record[$this->primaryKey] = null;
    }
    $this->insert($record);
    }
```

```
    catch (\PDOException $e) {
    $this->update($record);
    }

    foreach ($record as $key => $value) {
    if (!empty($value)) {
        $entity->$key = $value;
    }
    }

    return $entity;
}
```

The important line here is `$entity->$key = $value;`. Each time `foreach` iterates, the `$key` variable is set to the column name—for example `joketext`—and the `$value` variable is set to the value being written to that column. By using the `$key` variable after the object access operator (`->`), it will write to the property with the name of the column.

The `if (!empty($value))` check is in place to prevent values that are already set on the entity (such as the primary key) being overwritten with `null`.

```
 $record = ['joketext' => 'Why did the empty array get
↳ stuck outside? It didn\'t have  any keys',
'authorId' => 1,
'jokedate' => '2017-06-22'];

foreach ($record as $key => $value) {
    if (!empty($value)) {
    $joke->$key = $value;
    }
}
```

The code above will have the same result as this:

```
$joke->joketext = 'Why did the empty array get stuck
```

```
↪ outside? It didn\'t have any keys';

$joke->authorId = 1;

$joke->jokedate = '2018-06-22';
```

 ### Converting Arrays to Objects

This approach is a common method of converting an array to an object.

With the `foreach` in place, writing the values to the entity object, the `save` method will return the object with all the values that were passed as an array to the method.

This will work fine for records being updated, as the `$record` variable will include keys for all the columns in the database table.

A newly created record, however, will not have the primary key set. When a joke is added, we pass the `save` method values for the `joketext`, `jokedate` and `authorId` columns, not the `id`. In fact, we couldn't pass the `id` even if we wanted to, as we don't know what it will be before the record has been created in the database.

The `id` primary key is actually created by MySQL inside the database. For `INSERT` queries, we'll need to read the value from the database immediately after the record has been added.

Luckily, the PDO library provides a very simple method of doing this. After an `INSERT` query has been sent to the database, you can call the `lastInsertId` method on the `PDO` instance to read the ID of the last record inserted.

To implement this, let's amend the `insert` method in our `DatabaseTable` class to return the last insert ID:

```
private function insert($fields) {
    $query = 'INSERT INTO `' . $this->table . '` (';
```

```
    foreach ($fields as $key => $value) {
    $query .= '`' . $key . '`,';
    }

    $query = rtrim($query, ',');

    $query .= ') VALUES (';

    foreach ($fields as $key => $value) {
    $query .= ':' . $key . ',';
    }

    $query = rtrim($query, ',');

    $query .= ')';

    $fields = $this->processDates($fields);

    $this->query($query, $fields);

    return $this->pdo->lastInsertId();
}
```

Now, the `save` method can read this value and set the primary key on the created entity object:

```
public function save($record) {
    $entity = new $this->
    className(...$this->constructorArgs);

    try {
    if ($record[$this->primaryKey] == '') {
        $record[$this->primaryKey] = null;
    }

    $insertId = $this->insert($record);

    $entity->{$this->primaryKey} = $insertId;
```

```
    }
    catch (\PDOException $e) {
    $this->update($record);
    }

    foreach ($record as $key => $value) {
    $entity->$key = $value;
    }

    return $entity;
}
```

I've used the shorthand method with braces to set the primary key, but it's the same as this:

```
$insertId = $this->insert($record);

$primaryKey = $this->primaryKey;

$entity->$primaryKey = $insertId;
```

The **save** method is now complete. Any time the **save** method is called, it will return an entity instance representing the record that's just been saved.

Assigning Categories to Jokes

This functionality is required to enable the **joke** controller to assign categories to a joke instance. We can amend the **saveEdit** method in the **Joke** controller to look like this:

```
public function saveEdit() {
    $author = $this->authentication->getUser();

    $joke = $_POST['joke'];
    $joke['jokedate'] = new \DateTime();
```

```
    $jokeEntity = $author->addJoke($joke);

    foreach ($_POST['category'] as $categoryId) {
    $jokeEntity->addCategory($categoryId);
    }

    header('location: /joke/list');
}
```

Now that `$author->addJoke($joke);` returns a `Joke` entity object, we can call methods on an entity representing the record that has just been inserted. In this case, `$jokeEntity->addCategory($categoryId);` can be used to assign a category to the joke that was just added to the database.

Of course, for this to work we'll need to make some changes to the `Joke` entity class.

As the `addCategory` method will write a record to the new `joke_category` table, it will need a reference to the `jokeCategoriesTable DatabaseTable` instance. You know the drill here: add a class variable and constructor argument:

```php
<?php
namespace Ijdb\Entity;

class Joke {
    public $id;
    public $authorId;
    public $jokedate;
    public $joketext;
    private $authorsTable;
    private $author;
    private $jokeCategoriesTable;

    public function __construct(\Ninja\DatabaseTable
      $authorsTable, \Ninja\DatabaseTable
      $jokeCategoriesTable) {
    $this->authorsTable = $authorsTable;
    $this->jokeCategoriesTable = $jokeCategoriesTable;
```

```
    }

    // …
```

Then amend IjdbRoutes to provide the instance as an argument to the constructor of the $jokesTable instance:

```
$this->jokesTable = new \Ninja\DatabaseTable($pdo,
  'joke', 'id', '\Ijdb\Entity\Joke',
  [&$this->authorsTable,
  &$this->jokeCategoriesTable]);
```

By adding &$this->jokeCategoriesTable to the array passed as the fifth argument, each time an instance of \Ijdb\Entity\Joke is created inside the $jokesTable instance, the constructor will be called with the authorsTable and jokeCategoriesTable instances.

Next, add the addCategory method to the Joke entity class:

```
public function addCategory($categoryId) {
    $jokeCat = ['jokeId' => $this->id,
      'categoryId' => $categoryId];

    $this->jokeCategoriesTable->save($jokeCat);
}
```

You can find this code in *Relationships-AssignCategory*

This code is fairly simple. The first line creates an array that represents the record to be added. The jokeId is the id of the joke that we're adding the category to, and the categoryId comes from the argument.

With this code in place, whenever a joke is added to the website it's assigned to the categories that were checked.

Go ahead and add the jokes I supplied earlier, or your own, and verify that the records have been added to the `joke_category` join table by selecting the records from the table in MySQL Workbench.

Displaying Jokes by Category

Now that we have jokes in the database that are assigned to a category, let's add a page that allows selecting jokes by category.

On the Joke List page, let's add a list of categories to allow filtering of the jokes.

The first part is fairly simple: we need a list of categories as links on the Joke List page. This involves two fairly simple steps:

1. Amend the `list` action to pass a list of categories to the template:

```php
public function list() {
    $jokes = $this->jokesTable->findAll();

    $title = 'Joke list';

    $totalJokes = $this->jokesTable->total();

    $author = $this->authentication->getUser();

    return ['template' => 'jokes.html.php',
    'title' => $title,
    'variables' => [
        'totalJokes' => $totalJokes,
        'jokes' => $jokes,
        'userId' => $author->id ?? null,
        'categories' => $this->categoriesTable->findAll()
    ]
    ];
}
```

1. Loop through the categories in the `jokes.html.php` template and create a list with links for each one:

```
<ul class="categories">
    <?php foreach ($categories as $category): ?>
    <li><a href="/joke/list?category=
    <?=$category->id?>">
    <?=$category->name?></a><li>
    <?php endforeach; ?>
</ul>
```

To make it look a little nicer, you can also add a containing div and a div around the list of jokes:

```
<div class="jokelist">

<ul class="categories">
    <?php foreach ($categories as $category): ?>
    <li><a href="/joke/list?category=
    <?=$category->id?>">
    <?=$category->name?></a><li>
    <?php endforeach; ?>
</ul>

<div class="jokes">

 <p><?=$totalJokes?> jokes have been submitted to
↳ the Internet Joke Database.</p>

<?php foreach ($jokes as $joke): ?>
    // …
<?php endforeach; ?>

</div>
```

Then apply the following CSS:

```
.jokelist {display: table;}
 .categories {display: table-cell; width: 20%;
```

```
↳ background-color: #333; padding: 1em; list-style-type: none;}
.categories a {color: white; text-decoration: none;}
.categories li {margin-bottom: 1em;}
.jokelist .jokes {display: table-cell; padding: 1em;}
```

You can find this code in *Relationships-CategoryList*.

That's the list done, but the links currently don't do anything. Each link sets a $_GET variable called `category` to the ID of the category we want to view. If you click on one of the new category links, you'll see the page you visit is /jokes/ list?category=1 or similar.

You've likely already worked out what we need to do now. We need to use the new $_GET variable to display a filtered list of jokes if the `category` variable is set.

If we had done a simpler relationship with a `categoryId` column in the `joke` table, this would be relatively simple. In the `list` controller action, we'd just amend the way in which the $jokes variable was set:

```
if (isset($_GET['category'])) {
    $jokes = $this->jokesTable->find('category',
     $_GET['category']);
}
else {
    $jokes = $this->jokesTable->findAll();
}
```

However, as we have a *many-to-many* relationship, it's not quite so simple. One option is to pass the `jokeCategoriesTable` to the controller and do something like this:

```
if (isset($_GET['category'])) {
    $jokeCategories = $this->jokeCategoriesTable->
    find('categoryId', $_GET['categoryId']);
```

```
    $jokes = [];

    foreach ($jokeCategories as $jokeCategory) {
    $jokes[] = $this->jokesTable->
    findById($jokeCategory->jokeId);
    }
}
else {
    $jokes = $this->jokesTable->findAll();
}
```

In this example, we're getting a list of all the records from the `joke_cagegory` table for the chosen category by its `id`—for example, 4. This gives us a set of records, each with a `categoryId` and a `jokeId`.

In our example, the `categoryId` will always be 4, because we've only selected the records from that category, but each record has a unique `jokeId`. We then loop through all the records and find the relevant record from the `joke` table, adding each `joke` record to the `$jokes` array.

If you want to go ahead and test this approach for yourself, use the code above in the `list` method, create the `jokeCategoriesTable` class variable, constructor argument, and pass the instance into the `Joke` controller from `IjdbRoutes`.

I haven't given you the code for this because it's not a great solution. One of the most difficult parts of programming is placing code in the right place. The logic above is correct. It works, and it was fairly simple to work out. However, it would be better if we could get a list of jokes from a category like this:

```
$category = $this->categoriesTable->
findById($_GET['category']);

$jokes = $category->getJokes();
```

Doing so would allow us to get a list of jokes from a category anywhere in the program, not just the `list` method.

You already know how to achieve this: we did the same thing with
`$joke->getAuthor()`. In principle, this is the same.

We'll need a `Category` entity class that has access to the `jokesTable` instance, the
`jokeCategoriesTable` instance, and has a method called `getJokes`:

```php
<?php
namespace Ijdb\Entity;

use Ninja\DatabaseTable;

class Category
{
    public $id;
    public $name;
    private $jokesTable;
    private $jokeCategoriesTable;

    public function __construct(DatabaseTable $jokesTable,
     DatabaseTable $jokeCategoriesTable)
    {
        $this->jokesTable = $jokesTable;
        $this->jokeCategoriesTable = $jokeCategoriesTable;
    }

    public function getJokes()
    {
        $jokeCategories = $this->jokeCategoriesTable->
        find('categoryId', $this->id);

        $jokes = [];

        foreach ($jokeCategories as $jokeCategory) {
            $joke =  $this->jokesTable->
            findById($jokeCategory->jokeId);
            if ($joke) {
                $jokes[] = $joke;
            }
        }
```

```
        return $jokes;
    }
}
```

Save this in classes/Ijdb/Entity/Category.php. You'll notice the code in the getJokes method is almost the same as the code I showed you earlier. The only differences are that it uses $this->id instead of $_GET['category'] and returns the $jokes array. One minor change I've added is a safety precaution: the if ($joke) check ensures that a joke is only added to the $jokes array if it can be retrieved from the database.

Amend IjdbRoutes to set the categoriesTable instance to use the new Category entity class and provide the two constructor arguments:

```
$this->categoriesTable = new \Ninja\DatabaseTable($pdo,
↪ 'category', 'id', '\Ijdb\Entity\Category',
↪ [&$this->jokesTable,
↪ &$this->jokeCategoriesTable]);
```

Finally, use the new getJokes method to retrieve the jokes in the list controller action:

```
if (isset($_GET['category'])) {
    $category = $this->categoriesTable->
    findById($_GET['category']);
    $jokes = $category->getJokes();
}
else {
    $jokes = $this->jokesTable->findAll();
}
```

You can find this code in *Relationships-CategoryList2*

Using this approach, any time you need a list of jokes that exist in a category, you can find the category and then use $category->getJokes().

If you visit the Joke List page of the website, you'll be able to click on the category links to filter the jokes.

Editing Jokes

We've got most of the functionality for placing jokes in categories, but you'll notice a problem if you try to edit a joke. In fact, there are two problems.

The first, and the most obvious, can be found by editing a joke: try to edit one of the jokes that's already in a category and you'll immediately notice that the boxes aren't checked.

To fix this, we need to amend the code that prints the checkboxes:

```
<p>Select categories for this joke:</p>
<?php foreach ($categories as $category): ?>
<input type="checkbox" name="category[]"
    value="<?=$category->id?>" />
    <label><?=$category->name?></label>
<?php endforeach; ?>
```

To check a checkbox, you add the attribute `checked` to the `input element`:

```
<input type="checkbox" checked name="category[]"
    value="<?=$category->id?>" />
```

This is simple to add with an `if` statement to display `checked` if the joke is inside the category. The difficult part is determining if the joke is inside any given category.

We'll also solve this in an object-oriented way. Let's add a method in the `joke` entity so we can use this:

```
if ($joke->hasCategory($category->id))
```

Add the `hasCategory` method to the `Joke` entity class:

```php
public function hasCategory($categoryId) {
    $jokeCategories = $this->jokeCategoriesTable->
    find('jokeId', $this->id);

    foreach ($jokeCategories as $jokeCategory) {
        if ($jokeCategory->categoryId == $categoryId) {
            return true;
        }
    }
}
```

This works by finding all the categories that are associated with a joke, looping through them and checking to see whether one of those matches a given `$categoryId`.

With that in place, we can use it in the `editjoke.html.php` template:

```php
<p>Select categories for this joke:</p>
<?php foreach ($categories as $category): ?>

<?php if ($joke &&
 $joke->hasCategory($category->id)): ?>
<input type="checkbox" checked name="category[]"
    value="<?=$category->id?>" />
<?php else: ?>
<input type="checkbox" name="category[]"
    value="<?=$category->id?>" />
<?php endif; ?>

<label><?=$category->name?></label>
<?php endforeach; ?>
```

If you go to edit a joke, the relevant category boxes will now be checked, solving the first problem.

The second problem is a little more subtle. If you edit a joke but don't change the categories, everything will appear to work. However, if you uncheck a box, the changes won't be saved!

Try editing one of the jokes and unchecking all the category boxes before pressing **Save**. When you go back to edit the joke, the boxes will still be checked.

The reason for this issue is a common one when dealing with checkboxes in this way. Although we have some logic that says, "If the box is checked, add a record to the `joke_category` table," we don't have anything to remove that record after it's been added and the checkbox has been unticked.

We could use this process:

- loop through every single category
- check to see if the corresponding checkbook box wasn't checked
- if the box wasn't checked and there's a corresponding record, delete the record

We'd need do this check for every category, and it would take a fairly large amount of code to achieve.

Instead, a much simpler approach is to delete all the records from the `joke_category` table that are related to the joke we're editing, then apply the same logic as before: loop through the checked boxes and insert records for each category that was checked.

Admittedly, this isn't entirely efficient. If the joke is edited and the category checkboxes aren't changed, this will cause unnecessary deletion and reinsertion of identical data. However, it's still the simplest approach.

Our `DatabaseTable` class has a `delete` method that allows deleting a record by its primary key. However, our table has two primary keys—`jokeId` and `categoryId`—so we can't use it as it currently is.

Instead, let's add a `deleteWhere` method to the `DatabaseTable` class that works like the existing `find` method:

```
public function deleteWhere($column, $value) {
    $query = 'DELETE FROM ' . $this->table . '
```

```
    WHERE ' . $column . ' = :value';

    $parameters = [
    'value' => $value
    ];

    $query = $this->query($query, $parameters);
}
```

The code here is identical to the `find` method, except that it sends a `DELETE` query to the database rather than a `SELECT` query. For example, `$jokesTable->deleteWhere('authorId', 7)` would delete all the jokes by the author with the `id` of 7.

Add a `clearCategories` method to the `Joke` entity class that removes all the related records from the `jokeCategories` table for a given joke.

```
public function clearCategories() {
    $this->jokeCategoriesTable->deleteWhere('jokeId',
     $this->id);
}
```

When `$joke->clearCategories()` is called, it will remove every record from the `joke_category` table that represents the joke stored in `$joke`. Add this call to the `saveEdit` method in the `Joke` controller:

```
public function saveEdit() {
    $author = $this->authentication->getUser();

    $joke = $_POST['joke'];
    $joke['jokedate'] = new \DateTime();

    $jokeEntity = $author->addJoke($joke);

    $jokeEntity->clearCategories();
```

```
    foreach ($_POST['category'] as $categoryId) {
    $jokeEntity->addCategory($categoryId);
    }

    header('location: /joke/list');
}
```

You can find this code in *Relationships-ChangeCategories*.

Test it for yourself by editing a joke and unchecking some categories, then going back and adding them again. If you've followed the steps here, you'll be able to change the categories as you'd expect.

User Roles

We've now got a fully functional jokes website where users can register, post jokes, edit/delete their own submissions and view jokes by category.

But what happens if someone posts something you want to delete, or you want to fix a spelling mistake in someone else's joke?

At the moment, you can't do that! There's a check in place that only allows authors to edit their own jokes. If someone else posts something, there's currently no way for you to amend it.

The website is also set up so that anyone can add new categories. It would be better if only you (the website owner) were able to do that.

This is a very common problem on websites, and it's generally solved with **access levels**, where different accounts can perform different tasks.

On our website, we would need at minimum the following access levels:

1. **Standard users**: can post new jokes and edit/delete jokes they've posted.

2. **Administrators**: can add/edit/remove categories, post jokes, and edit/delete jokes anyone has posted. They should also be able to turn other users into

administrators.

The simplest way to do this is to have a column in the `author` table that represents the author's access level. A 1 in the column could represent a normal user and, and a 2 could represent an administrator. It would then be easy to add a check on any page to determine whether or not the logged-in user was an administrator:

```
$author = $this->authentication->getUser();

if ($author->accessLevel == 2) {
    // They're an administrator
}
else {
    // Otherwise, they're not
}
```

This method is very simple to understand, and we could even very easily abstract it to `if ($author->isAdmin())` to improve the readability.

This implementation of access levels is fine for small websites with only a few users, or when there's only one administrator.

However, on larger, real-world websites, you often need to give users different levels of access. For example, we may want someone to be able to add categories, but not able to grant other people administrator access, or worse, revoke your administrator privileges so they have complete control of the website!

A more flexible approach is to give each user individual permissions for each action. For example, we could set a user up to be able to edit a category but not add an administrator.

For this website, we've already considered these permissions:

- edit other people's jokes
- delete other people's jokes
- add categories
- edit categories

- remove categories
- edit user access levels

Before we model this in the database, let's think about how we'd check these in the existing code.

Our `Author` entity class could have a method called `hasPermission` that takes a single argument and returns `true` or `false`, depending on whether or not the user has a specific permission.

We could assign numbers to each of the permissions above, so that the following code could be used to check whether they have permission to edit other people's jokes:

```
if ($author->hasPermission(1))
```

2 could represent deleting other users' jokes, 3 could be whether members are allowed to add categories, and so on.

This is roughly what we want to do, but looking at the line of code above, it's really not clear what's happening. If you saw the code `$author->hasPermission(6)`, you'd have to go away and look up what 6 meant.

To make the code much easier to read, each value can be stored inside a **constant**—which, like a variable, is a label given to a value. The difference, however, is that a constant always has the same value. The value is set once at the beginning of the program and can't be changed.

In object-oriented programming, constants are defined in classes like so:

```php
<?php
namespace Ijdb\Entity;

class Author {

    const EDIT_JOKES = 1;
    const DELETE_JOKES = 2;
```

```
const LIST_CATEGORIES = 3;
const EDIT_CATEGORIES = 4;
const REMOVE_CATEGORIES = 5;
const EDIT_USER_ACCESS = 6;
```

 Constant Conventions

By convention, constants are written in uppercase, with words separated by underscores. Although it's possible to use lowercase letters, it's almost universal in every programming language that constants are written like this!

I've defined the constants in the `Author` entity class, since the permissions are related to authors.

We'll also define a method called `hasPermission` in the class:

```php
<?php
namespace Ijdb\Entity;

class Author {

    const EDIT_JOKES = 1;
    const DELETE_JOKES = 2;
    const LIST_CATEGORIES = 3;
    const EDIT_CATEGORIES = 4;
    const REMOVE_CATEGORIES = 5;
    const EDIT_USER_ACCESS = 6;
    // …

    public function hasPermission($permission) {
    // …
    }
}
```

Before we write the code for this method, I'm going to show you how it will be used:

```
$author = $this->authentication->getUser();

if ($author->hasPermission
(\Ijdb\Entity\Author::LIST_CATEGORIES)) {
    // …
}
```

Notice that the constant is prefixed with the namespace and class name, then a
::. The :: operator is used to access constants in a given class.

When accessing a constant, you don't need an instance to be created, as each
instance would have the same value for the constant anyway.

There are two different places we'll need to implement this. The first is page-level
access. As we did with the login check, a check can be done in the router to stop
people even viewing a page if they don't have the correct permissions.

This will need to be done in EntryPoint, but because each website you build
might have a different way of handling these checks, we'll add a new method to
IjdbRoutes called checkPermissions:

```
public function checkPermission($permission): bool {
    $user = $this->authentication->getUser();

    if ($user && $user->hasPermission($permission)) {
    return true;
    } else {
    return false;
    }
}
```

This fetches the current logged-in user and checks to see if they have a specific
permission.

As this is something that will need to be provided by any website you build,
amend the Routes interface to include the checkPermission method:

```php
<?php
namespace Ninja;

interface Routes
{
    public function getRoutes(): array;
    public function getAuthentication(): \Ninja\Authentication;
    public function checkPermission($permission): bool;
}
```

To implement this in the `EntryPointy` class, we'll add an extra entry to the `$routes` array to specify which permissions are required for accessing each page. Let's start with the category permissions:

```php
'category/edit' => [
    'POST' => [
    'controller' => $categoryController,
    'action' => 'saveEdit'
    ],
    'GET' => [
    'controller' => $categoryController,
    'action' => 'edit'
    ],
    'login' => true,
    'permissions' => \Ijdb\Entity\Author::EDIT_CATEGORIES
],
'category/delete' => [
    'POST' => [
    'controller' => $categoryController,
    'action' => 'delete'
    ],
    'login' => true,
    'permissions' => \Ijdb\Entity\Author::REMOVE_CATEGORIES
],
'category/list' => [
    'GET' => [
    'controller' => $categoryController,
    'action' => 'list'
```

```
    ],
    'login' => true,
    'permissions' => \Ijdb\Entity\Author::LIST_CATEGORIES
  ],
```

I've added the relevant permission requirements to each page using an extra key in the array. This only defines an extra value in the array. We'll need to have the EntryPoint class call the checkPermission method that we just added to determine whether the logged-in user is allowed to view the page.

The process here is fairly straightforward. When you visit a page—for example, /category/edit—the EntryPoint class will read the value stored in the permissions key for that route, then call the new checkPermission method to determine whether the user who is logged in and viewing the page has that permission.

This will work in the same way as the login check:

```
if (isset($routes[$this->route]['login']) &&
  !$authentication->isLoggedIn()) {
    header('location: /login/error');
}
  else if (isset($routes[$this->route]['permissions'])
↪ &&
  !$this->routes->checkPermission
  ($$routes[$this->route]['permissions'])) {
    header('location: /login/error');
}
else {
// …
```

Firstly, the login check is performed, then the permissions check. If the route contains a permissions key, the value stored under that key—for example, \Ijdb\Entity\Author::REMOVE_CATEGORIES—is passed to the checkPermission method, which determines whether the logged-in user has the required permission.

Since we haven't written the code for the `hasPermission` method in the `Author` entity class yet, any permission check will always return false. Go ahead and try viewing the category list by visiting `http://192.168.10.10/category/list`.

You'll see the error page that says "You are not logged in". At this point, you might want to add a new template and route that displays a more accurate error message, but by now you should be very familiar with adding pages, so I'm not going to walk you through it!

You can find this code in *Relationships-PermissionsCheck*.

Creating a Form to Assign Permissions

Before we can implement the `hasPermission` method, the website needs a page that allows assigning permissions to any given user.

We'll need two pages—one that lists all the authors, so we can select the one we want to give permissions to, and a second that contains a form with checkboxes for each permission.

Add the following routes:

```
'author/permissions' => [
    'GET' => [
    'controller' => $authorController,
    'action' => 'permissions'
    ],
    'POST' => [
    'controller' => $authorController,
    'action' => 'savePermissions'
    ],
    'login' => true
],
'author/list' => [
    'GET' => [
    'controller' => $authorController,
    'action' => 'list'
    ],
```

```
    'login' => true
],
```

For now, we only have a login check on here. If we add a permissions check right now, we won't be able to use the form to set the permissions, because your account won't have the required permission to view the page!

Rather than adding a new controller, we'll use the `Register` controller that already exists and is used for handling changes to users' accounts.

Author List

Let's do the list first. Add a method in the `Register` controller called `list` that fetches a list of all the registered users and passes them to the template:

```php
public function list() {
    $authors = $this->authorsTable->findAll();

    return ['template' => 'authorlist.html.php',
    'title' => 'Author List',
    'variables' => [
        'authors' => $authors
    ]
    ];
}
```

And here's the template `authorlist.html.php` for listing the users:

```html
<h2>User List</h2>

<table>
    <thead>
    <th>Name</th>
    <th>Email</th>
    <th>Edit</th>
    </thead>
```

```
    <tbody>
    <?php foreach ($authors as $author): ?>
    <tr>
        <td><?=$author->name;?></td>
        <td><?=$author->email;?></td>
        <td>
 <a
↪ href="/author/permissions?id=<?=$author->id;?>">
        Edit Permissions</a></td>
    </tr>
    <?php endforeach; ?>
    </tbody>
</table>
```

If you visit `http://192.168.10.10/author/list`, you'll see the list of registered authors, each with a link for editing their permissions.

The **Edit Permissions** link goes to the `/author/permissions` page, and passes it the `id` of the author whose permissions we want to change.

Edit Author Permissions

There's nothing on the Edit Permissions page yet, because we haven't created it. It's quite a simple page: it will display a checkbox for each permission in the system, and it will be checked if the author currently has that permission.

The template could look like this:

```
 <input type="checkbox" value="1" <?php if
↪ ($author->hasPermission(EDIT_JOKES)) {
    echo 'checked';
} ?> Edit Jokes
 <input type="checkbox" value="2" <?php if
↪ ($author->hasPermission(DELETE_JOKES)) {
    echo 'checked';
} ?> Delete Jokes
```

```
 <input type="checkbox" value="3" <?php if
↳ ($author->hasPermission(LIST_CATEGORIES)) {
    echo 'checked';
} ?> Add Categories
// etc.
```

This would work, but it requires storing the information about the permissions in two different places—the constants in the `Author` entity class, and the template. We also need to write out all the HTML and PHP for each checkbox.

Like most cases when we find repetition like this, there's a much easier way!

It's actually possible to read information about the variables, methods and constants that are contained inside a class using a tool called **Reflection**.

We can actually get a list of constants, and their values, from the class!

PHP makes this fairly simple. To **reflect** the `Author` entity class and read all its properties, you can use the following code:

```
$reflected = new \ReflectionClass('\Ijdb\Entity\Author');

$constants = $reflected->getConstants();
```

The `$constants` array will contain information about all the constants that are defined within the class. If you use `var_dump` to print out the contents of the `$constants` variable, you'll see an array with the constant names as the key and the constant values as the value:

```
array (size=6)
    'EDIT_JOKES' => int 1
    'DELETE_JOKES' => int 2
    'LIST_CATEGORIES' => int 3
    'EDIT_CATEGORIES' => int 4
    'REMOVE_CATEGORIES' => int 5
    'EDIT_USER_ACCESS' => int 6
```

Reflection

Reflection can be a very powerful tool, and I've only scratched the surface of what you can do. For more information on Reflection, see the PHP manual page[7].

By passing this array to the template, we can actually generate the list of checkboxes for permissions from the constants inside the template.

Add this `permissions` method to the `Register` controller.:

```php
public function permissions() {

    $author = $this->authorsTable->findById($_GET['id']);

    $reflected = new \ReflectionClass('\Ijdb\Entity\Author');
    $constants = $reflected->getConstants();

    return ['template' => 'permissions.html.php',
    'title' => 'Edit Permissions',
    'variables' => [
        'author' => $author,
        'permissions' => $constants
    ]
    ];
}
```

And here's the corresponding template `permissions.html.php`:

```php
<h2>Edit <?=$author->name?>'s
↪ Permissions</h2>

<form action="" method="post">

    <?php foreach ($permissions as $name => $value): ?>
```

---

7. http://php.net/manual/en/book.reflection.php

```
    <div>
    <input name="permissions[]"
        type="checkbox"
        value="<?=$value?>"
        <?php if ($author->hasPermission($value)):
        echo 'checked'; endif; ?> />
    <label><?=$name?>
    </div>
    <?php endforeach; ?>

    <input type="submit" value="Submit" />
</form>
```

Like we did with categories, I've made the checkbox list an array. If you go to edit one of the user's permissions, you'll see a checkbox for each of the constants in the Author class!

This makes future developments a lot easier. Once the constant has been added to the Author entity class, it will automatically appear on the list without us having to manually go and edit the template each time we want to add a new permission to the website.

You can find this code in *Relationships-EditPermissions*

Setting Permissions

The next stage is storing the user's permissions once you press **save**. Each user will have a set of permissions, and there are many different ways to represent this in the database.

We could do it in the same way we did with categories: create a user_permission table with two columns authorId and permission. Then we could write a record for each permission. A user with the id of 4 and the permissions EDIT_JOKES, LIST_CATEGORIES and REMOVE_CATEGORIES would have the following records:

```
authorId | permission
       4 |           1
```

```
    4 |         3
    4 |         5
```

You already know how to implement this. You'll need to create the table, the relevant `DatabaseTable` instance, and write the `savePermissions` method to create a record in the `user_permission` table for each checked box. Finally, the `hasPermission` method in the `Author` entity class would look something like this:

```php
public function hasPermission($permission) {
    $permissions = $this->userPermissionsTable->
    find('authorId', $this->id);

    foreach ($permissions as $permission) {
    if ($permission->permission == $permission) {
        return true;
    }
    }
}
```

Before you implement this, I'm going to show you an alternative approach.

A Different Approach

Imagine if we set up the `author` table with a column for each permission:

```sql
CREATE TABLE `author` (
    `id` INT(11) NOT NULL AUTO_INCREMENT,
    `name` VARCHAR(255) DEFAULT NULL,
    `email` VARCHAR(255) DEFAULT NULL,
    `password` VARCHAR(255) DEFAULT NULL,
    `editJoke` TINYINT(1) NOT NULL DEFAULT 0,
    `deleteJokes` TINYINT(1) NOT NULL DEFAULT 0,
    `addCatgories` TINYINT(1) NOT NULL DEFAULT 0,
    `removeCategories` TINYINT(1) NOT NULL DEFAULT 0,
    `editUserAccess` TINYINT(1) NOT NULL DEFAULT 0,
    PRIMARY KEY (`id`)
```

```
) ENGINE=InnoDB CHARSET=utf8;
```

Each column is TINYINT(1), which means it can store a single bit. It can either be a 1 or 0, and I've set it to default to 0.

We could then set any author's permissions using an UPDATE statement. For the user I mentioned earlier with the id of 4, this could be sent to the database as:

```
UPDATE `author` SET `editJokes` = 1, `listCategories` = 1,
↪ `removeCategories` = 1 WHERE `id` = 4
```

It would be possible to name our checkboxes with the names of the columns and use them in the same way as any other field.

The advantage of this approach is that it's simpler. To find out if a user has a permission, you can just use this:

```
// Can this author edit jokes?
if ($author->editJokes == 1)
```

Or this:

```
// Can this author remove categories?
if ($author->removeCategories == 1)
```

This is a nicer approach than a join table, as the same check using a join table would require querying the database for all the user's permissions, looping through the records, and checking to see whether the permission we're looking for has a corresponding record.

The downside to this approach is that every time we add a permission to the website, we'd need to add a column to the table.

In principle, though, this is a lot simpler. It avoids a database table, and checking whether a user has a permission requires significantly less code and fewer database queries.

Each permission is a simple 1 or 0 in the database.

If you examined a user's record in MySQL Workbench, you might see something like 0 1 0 0 1 0 0 in the permissions columns.

A Crash Course in Binary

This sequence of ones and zeros looks a lot like binary. In fact, every number stored in a database is actually stored as a series of ones and zeros behind the scenes.

If you have an INT column and it stores the number 6 for a particular record, it will actually store the binary value 0110 on the hard disk. Everything stored on a computer is binary!

Each binary number is a bit like a database record. Each one or zero is in a specific column, and that column represents a particular value.

In fact, with normal *decimal* numbers, when you see the value 2395, you know that the 3 (since it's in the third column from the right) represents 300.

The above number can actually be expressed like this:

```
2 x 1000 +
3 x  100 +
9 x   10
5 x    1
```

You're so familiar with this process that it's second nature, and you don't need to think about it. Binary works in the same way. The only differences are that only the digits one and zero are available, and the column numbers are different.

In both binary and decimal, numbers are created right to left. As an extra digit is added, it's added to the left-hand side. To add 300 to 27, you add a 3 to the left.

The same thing is true of binary: digits further to the right have a higher value.

In the case of the binary number 0110, the third column from the right represents 4, and the second column from the right represents 2.

To translate the value of the binary number 0110 into decimal, you can do the same kind of calculation as long as you know the values of each column. In decimal, each column is multiplied by ten each time you move to the left. In binary, each column is multiplied by two.

To work out the total of 0110, we can do the same calculation:

```
0 x 8 +
1 x 4 +
1 x 2 +
0 x 1
```

If you calculate this, you'll get 6. Each column is called a **bit**, and in this example we can describe the 8 bit as not being set (because it's set to zero) and the 4 bit as being *set* (because it's set to one).

See if you can convert the following binary numbers to decimal[8]:

- 1000
- 0020
- 1010

Be Bit-Wise

You're probably wondering why any of this matters and what it has to do with user permissions.

In short, binary has nothing to do with permissions. But neither do if statements or checkboxes. All three are tools we can use to solve the problem of permissions.

What's useful is that you can use PHP (and almost every programming language)

[8.] The answers are 8 (1x8), 2 (1x2) and 10 (1x2 + 1x8).

to inquire whether any given integer has a 1 or 0 set for any of the bits that make up the number.

Bitwise Permissions

Rather than using a different database column to store each one or zero, we could use a single binary number to store those ones and zeros in a single column.

By assigning a column to a *permission*, a binary number can represent which permissions any user has.

EDIT_USER_ACCESS	REMOVE_CATEGORIES	EDIT_CATEGORIES
32	16	8
LIST_CATEGORIES	DELETE_JOKES	EDIT_JOKES
4	2	1

The binary number 000001, which has a 1 in the EDIT_JOKES column, would represent a user with EDIT_JOKES permissions.

111111 would represent a user that had all the permissions, and 011111 would represent a user that had every permission apart from being able to edit the permissions of other users (EDIT_USER_ACCESS).

This process is identical to using multiple columns in a database, each with a one or zero. We're just using a binary number to represent the same data. Rather than one column per bit, we can store multiple bits in a single INT column.

Let's convert the binary numbers to decimal: 000001 becomes 1, 111111 becomes 63 and 011111 becomes 31. We can easily store these numbers as integers in a database!

If someone has the permissions value 63, we know they have all the permissions that are available.

Back to PHP

The difficult part is extracting the individual permissions. What if we want to know whether the user has the EDIT_CATEGORIES permission? On the chart above, I've assigned the 8 bit to mean EDIT_CATEGORIES. If a user has the permissions value 13, it's not clear whether the 8 bit is set.

In a database with multiple columns, we can use SELECT * FROM author WHERE id = 4 AND editCategories = 1 to determine whether the editCategories column is set to 1 for a specific user—in this case, the user with the id of 4.

Most programming languages, including PHP and MySQL, support something called **bitwise** operations. These allow you to inquire whether a specific bit is set in any integer. Using a single permissions column, the query above can be expressed as follows:

```
SELECT * FROM author WHERE id = 4 AND 0 & permissions
```

The clever part here is the part AND 8 & permissions. This uses the bitwise and (&) operator to inquire whether the 8 bit is set in the number stored in the permissions column for that record.

PHP also provides the bitwise and operator. You've already seen that the number 6 is represented as 0110, which means that the bits 4 and 2 are set.

The bitwise & operator can be used to determine whether a bit is set in a specific number, and it's used like this:

```
if (6 & 2) {

}
```

This says, "Is the bit 2 set in the number 6?", and it will evaluate to true. If you wanted to check bit 1, however, it would return false, because the 1 bit is not set in the binary representation of 6 (0110):

```
if (6 & 1) {

}
```

Binary operations like this are actually fairly common in PHP! When you set the error_reporting variable in PHP to E_WARNING | E_NOTICE, what you're doing is setting the bits that represent warnings and notices. PHP will then internally check which bits are set when it encounters an error.

Internally, PHP will do something like this:

```
if (E_NOTICE & ini_get('error_reporting')) {
    display_notice($notice);
}
```

We can apply this to permissions. Imagine the author table had a column called permissions: it's possible to determine whether an author has the permission EDIT_CATEGORIES by using this code:

```
if ($author->permissions & 8) {

}
```

This code has the same problem I mentioned earlier: it's not clear exactly what's happening here to anyone looking at the code. Again, we could represent the bits as constants:

```
const EDIT_JOKES = 1;
const DELETE_JOKES = 2;
const LIST_CATEGORIES = 4;
const EDIT_CATEGORIES = 8;
const REMOVE_CATEGORIES = 16;
const EDIT_USER_ACCESS = 32;
```

And we could write the permissions check like so:

```
// Does the author have the EDIT_CATEGORIES permission?
if ($author->permissions & EDIT_CATEGORIES) {

}

// Does the author have the DELETE_JOKES permission?

if ($author->permissions & DELETE_JOKES) {

}
```

You don't even need to understand the underlying binary to understand what's happening here, and the individual numbers don't even matter!

Storing Bitwise Permissions in the Database

Let's implement this on the website. Amend the `author` table by adding a column called `permissions`, and set it to `INT(64)` so we can store a maximum of 64 different permissions.

Change the constant values in the `Author` entity class as I have above.

We don't need to make any changes to the Edit Permissions form page, but we need to add the `savePermissions` method and have it store the binary permissions in the database.

Before we do that, let's consider what will happen when the form is submitted. If you checked the boxes labeled `EDIT_JOKES` and `REMOVE_CATEGORIES`, the variable `$_POST['permissions']` would be an array containing the numbers 1 and 16 (`[1, 16]`).

We want to convert those to the binary representation, where the 1 bit and 16 bits are set. It sounds difficult but, as you'll see very shortly, it's not!

The number we need to generate is `010001`, where bits 16 and 1 are set. Use your new binary knowledge to calculate the decimal version of this value, and you'll work out that this binary number represents 17.

All we need to do is add the numbers together!

Just to prove the theory, let's imagine that the boxes for EDIT_JOKES, DELETE_JOKES, LIST_CATEGORIES and EDIT_USER_ACCESS are ticked. When the form is submitted, we'd get the array [1, 2, 4, 32].

The binary representation of those permissions is 100111. If you work out what that is in decimal, you'll get 39. Add together the values from the array 1 + 2 + 4 + 32 and you'll also get 39!

All we need to do to store the numbers in the database is add together each element in the $_POST['permissions'] array.

PHP even includes a function called array_sum that can do exactly that.

The savePermissions method in the Register controller can be written like this:

```php
public function savePermissions() {
    $author = [
    'id' => $_GET['id'],
    'permissions' => array_sum($_POST['permissions'] ?? [])
    ];

    $this->authorsTable->save($author);

    header('location: /author/list');
}
```

The line 'permissions' => array_sum($_POST['permissions'] ?? []) is used to add all the values from the $_POST['permissions'] array. However, if no boxes are ticked, $_POST['permissions'] won't be set. The ?? operator is used to provide the array_sum operator with an empty array if there's nothing in the $_POST['permissions'] variable.

That's it! The savePermissions method is converting the checked boxes into a number, and that number's binary representation is how we're modeling the permissions of each user.

Join Table or Bitwise

When using the `join` table approach for categories, to cater for boxes that were unchecked, we specifically had to delete all the records and reinsert them each time the form was submitted. As the `permissions` column is a single number, if no boxes are checked, `array_sum` will return 0 and the 0 will be inserted into the database, avoiding the need to specifically handle unchecked boxes.

The final piece is the `hasPermission` method in the `Author` entity class. Add the `$permission` class variable. Then, to check if a user has a permission, we need a single line of code:

```
                                            13-5. Relationships-BinaryPermissions

public function hasPermission($permission) {
    return $this->permissions & $permission;
}
```

There are several advantages to this approach over a `join` table. The first is performance: we don't need to query the database for the user's permissions. Secondly, this is considerably less code for both saving the form and checking whether the permission is set.

The downsides to this approach are that it can be more difficult to understand if you're not familiar with the bitwise operator. However, bitwise operators are fairly common in PHP. They're used by the `PDO` library and for the various `php.ini` configuration settings such as `error_reporting`, so it's a good idea to have a basic understanding of what they do. The second downside is that you're limited to 64 bits, because that's all a CPU can process. However, if you find yourself needing more, you can group the permissions into different columns, such as `jokePermissions` and `adminPermissions`.

Whether you choose to implement user roles as bitwise, like I have here, or whether you use a `join` table, is up to you. There are pros and cons to each approach. Personally, I prefer the shorter code and fewer database operations, which bitwise operators offer.

Cleaning Up

There's a little tidying up left to do. Firstly, we need to add the permissions to the routes.

Make sure you have granted your user account the permission EDIT_USER_ACCESS before making these changes, or you won't be able to change anyone's permissions!

We already amended the routes for LIST_CATEGORIES, EDIT_CATEGORIES and REMOVE_CATEGORIES.

You can test this works by visiting http://192.168.10.10/category/list and giving and revoking your LIST_CATEGORIES permission.

Let's do the same for EDIT_USER_ACCESS. Set the permissions key in the IjdbRoutes $routes array for the author list and permissions pages:

```
$routes = [
    // …
    'author/permissions' => [
    'GET' => [
        'controller' => $authorController,
        'action' => 'permissions'
    ],
    'POST' => [
        'controller' => $authorController,
        'action' => 'savePermissions'
    ],
    'login' => true,
    'permissions' => \Ijdb\Entity\Author::EDIT_USER_ACCESS
    ],
    'author/list' => [
    'GET' => [
        'controller' => $authorController,
        'action' => 'list'
    ],
```

```
'login' => true,
'permissions' => \Ijdb\Entity\Author::EDIT_USER_ACCESS
],
```

This will prevent anyone who doesn't have the EDIT_USER_ACCESS permission from changing the permissions of other users.

Editing Others' Jokes

The final two permissions are EDIT_JOKES and DELETE_JOKES, which determine whether the logged-in user can edit or delete a joke someone else has posted.

We can't do this with the $routes array, because the check isn't done there. The edit link and delete button are hidden in the template, and there are checks inside the joke controller.

Firstly, let's make the **edit** link and **delete** button appear on the list page for all jokes if you have the EDIT_JOKES or DELETE_JOKES permissions.

The relevant section of jokes.html.php looks like this:

```php
<?php if ($userId == $joke->authorId) {
    ?>
    <a href="/joke/edit?id=<?=$joke->id?>">
    Edit</a>
    <form action="/joke/delete" method="post">
    <input type="hidden" name="id"
        value="<?=$joke->id?>">
    <input type="submit" value="Delete">
    </form>
<?php
} ?>
```

Now that we have different permissions for **edit** and **delete**, we'll need two separate if statements—one for the **delete** button and one for the **edit** link.

However, we can't do this with the $userId alone. Instead of passing in the $userId variable to the template, change the list method in the Joke controller to pass in the entire $author object that represents the logged-in user:

```php
return ['template' => 'jokes.html.php',
    'title' => $title,
    'variables' => [
    'totalJokes' => $totalJokes,
    'jokes' => $jokes,
    'user' => $author, //previously 'userId' =>
    $author->id
    'categories' => $this->categoriesTable->findAll()
    ]
];
```

The check in the template can now be amended so that the button and link are only visible to the person who posted the joke, or someone with the relevant permission:

```php
<?php if ($user): ?>
    <?php if ($user->id == $joke->authorId ||
 $user->hasPermission(\Ijdb\Entity\Author::EDIT_JOKES)):
↪ ?>
    <a href="/joke/edit?id=<?=$joke->id?>">
    Edit</a>
    <?php endif; ?>
    <?php if ($user->id == $joke->authorId ||
    $user->hasPermission(\Ijdb\Entity\Author::DELETE_JOKES)):
     ?>
    <form action="/joke/delete" method="post">
    <input type="hidden" name="id"
        value="<?=$joke->id?>">
    <input type="submit" value="Delete">
    </form>
    <?php endif; ?>
<?php endif; ?>
```

This is a lot more complicated, as there are now three `if` statements. I've added `if ($user)` around the entire block, because the `$user` variable may be empty if no one is logged in.

The following two use a logical `or` to determine whether the person who's viewing the page is the same person who posted the joke, or if they have the relevant permission.

Editing the `jokes.html.php` template makes the buttons appear, but if you have the `EDIT_JOKES` permission and attempt to edit a joke you didn't post, you'll see the error "You may only edit jokes that you posted". That's because we added a specific check in the `editjoke.html.php` template, and the `delete` method in the `Joke` controller.

Change `delete` to include the permissions check:

```php
public function delete() {

    $author = $this->authentication->getUser();

    $joke = $this->jokesTable->findById($_POST['id']);

    if ($joke->authorId != $author->id &&
    !$author->hasPermission(\Ijdb\Entity\Author::DELETE_JOKES))
    {
    return;
    }

    $this->jokesTable->delete($_POST['id']);

    header('location: /joke/list');
}
```

And, like the `list` method, pass the entire `author` object to the template in the `edit` method, and adjust the template to include the permissions check.

`controllers/joke.php`:

```
return ['template' => 'editjoke.html.php',
    'title' => $title,
    'variables' => [
    'joke' => $joke ?? null,
    'user' => $author,
    'categories' => $categories
    ]
];
```

In `editjoke.html.php`, this code:

```
<?php if (empty($joke->id) || $userId ==
↳ $joke->authorId):  ?>
```

... becomes this:

```
<?php if (empty($joke->id) || $user->id ==
↳ $joke->authorId ||
↳ $user->hasPermission(\Ijdb\Entity\Author::EDIT_JOKES)):
↳ ?>
```

That's it! All the permission checks are now in place.

Phew!

In this chapter, I showed you how to think in a more object-oriented way, and how to handle relationships between objects in an OOP way rather than a relational way.

You learned how to represent many-to-many relationships using both `join` tables and bitwise operations.

We added permissions to the existing site, but moving forward, you can think about user permissions as you go and create them while you're writing the original code.

That's it! We have a completely functional and working website that does almost anything we would want for a real-world project. I have a couple of small things left to show you, but we're basically done! There's little else I can teach you.

In the next chapter, I'll show you how to make a few tweaks to the `DatabaseTable` class to allow sorting and limiting, but you already have almost all the tools you need to build a fully functional website.

Chapter **14**

Content Formatting with Regular Expressions

We're almost there! We've designed a database to store jokes, organized them into categories, and tracked their authors. We've learned how to create a web page that displays this library of jokes to site visitors. We've even developed a set of web pages that a site administrator can use to manage the joke library without knowing anything about databases.

In so doing, we've built a site that frees the resident webmaster from continually having to plug new content into tired HTML page templates, and from maintaining an unmanageable mass of HTML files. The HTML is now kept completely separate from the data it displays. If you want to redesign the site, you simply have to make the changes to the HTML contained in the PHP templates that you've constructed. A change to one file (for example, modifying the footer) is immediately reflected in the page layouts of all pages in the site. Only one task still requires knowledge of HTML: **content formatting**.

On any but the simplest of websites, it will be necessary to allow content (in our case, jokes) to include some sort of formatting. In a simple case, this might merely be the ability to break text into paragraphs. Often, however, content providers will expect facilities such as **bold** or *italic* text, hyperlinks, and so on.

As it stands, we've stripped out any formatting from text entered by users using the `htmlspecialchars` function.

If, instead, we just `echo` out the raw content pulled from the database, we can enable administrators to include formatting in the form of HTML code in the joke text:

```php
<?php echo $joke->joketext; ?>
```

Following this simple change, a site administrator could include HTML tags that would have their usual effect on the joke text when inserted into a page.

But is this really what we want? Left unchecked, content providers can do a lot of damage by including HTML code in the content they add to your site's database. Particularly if your system will be enabling nontechnical users to submit content, you'll find that invalid, obsolete, and otherwise inappropriate code will gradually infest the pristine website you set out to build. With one stray tag, a well-meaning user could tear apart the layout of your site.

In this chapter, you'll learn about several PHP functions that you haven't seen before, which are used for finding and replacing patterns of text in your site's content. I'll show you how to use these capabilities to provide a simpler markup language for your users that's better suited to content formatting. By the time we've finished, we'll have completed a content management system that anyone with a web browser can use—no knowledge of HTML required.

Regular Expressions

To implement our own markup language, we'll have to write some PHP code to spot our custom tags in the text of jokes and then replace them with their HTML equivalents. For tackling this sort of task, PHP includes extensive support for regular expressions.

A **regular expression** is a short piece of code that describes a pattern of text that may occur in content like our jokes. We use regular expressions to search for and replace patterns of text. They're available in many programming languages and environments, and are especially prevalent in web development languages like PHP.

The popularity of regular expressions has everything to do with how useful they are, and absolutely nothing to do with how easy they are to use—because they're not at all easy. In fact, to most people who encounter them for the first time, regular expressions look like what might eventuate if you fell asleep with your face on the keyboard.

Here, for example, is a relatively simple (yes, really!) regular expression that will match any string that might be a valid email address:

```
/^[\w\.\-]+@([\w\-]+\.)+[a-z]+$/i
```

Scary, huh? By the end of this section, you'll actually be able to make sense of that.

The language of a regular expression is cryptic enough that, once you master it, you may feel as if you're able to weave magical incantations with the code you write. To begin with, let's start with some very simple regular expressions.

This is a regular expression that searches for the text "PHP" (without the quotes):

```
/PHP/
```

Fairly simple, right? It's the text you want to search for, surrounded by a pair of matching **delimiters**. Traditionally, slashes (/) are used as regular expression delimiters, but another common choice is the hash character (#). You can actually use any character as a delimiter except letters, numbers, or backslashes (\). I'll use slashes for all the regular expressions in this chapter.

 Escaping Delimiters

To include a forward slash as part of a regular expression that uses forward slashes as delimiters, you must escape it with a preceding backslash (\ /); otherwise, it will be interpreted as marking the end of the pattern.

The same goes for other delimiter characters: if you use hash characters as delimiters, you'll need to escape any hashes within the expression with backslashes (\ #).

To use a regular expression, you must be familiar with the regular expression functions available in PHP. `preg_match` is the most basic, and can be used to determine whether or not a regular expression is matched by a particular text string.

Consider this code:

```php
<?php
$text = 'PHP rules!';

if (preg_match('/PHP/', $text)) {
    echo '$text contains the string "PHP".';
} else {
    echo '$text does not contain the string "PHP".';
}
```

In this example, the regular expression finds a match, because the string stored in the variable `$text` contains "PHP". This example will therefore output the message shown below.

$text contains the string "PHP".

14-1. The regular expression finds a match

Use of Single Quotes Above

Notice that the single quotes around the strings in the code prevent PHP from filling in the value of the variable `$text`.

By default, regular expressions are case-sensitive. That is, lowercase characters in the expression only match lowercase characters in the string, and uppercase characters only match uppercase characters. If you want to perform a case-insensitive search instead, you can use a pattern modifier to make the regular expression ignore case.

Pattern modifiers are single-character flags following the ending delimiter of an expression. The modifier for performing a case-insensitive match is `i`. So while `/PHP/` will only match strings that contain "PHP", `/PHP/i` will match strings that contain "PHP", "php", or even "pHp".

Here's an example to illustrate this:

```php
<?php
$text = 'What is Php?';

if (preg_match('/PHP/i', $text)) {
    echo '$text contains the string "PHP".';
} else {
    echo '$text does not contain the string "PHP".';
}
```

Again, as shown below, this outputs the same message, despite the string actually containing "Php".

$text contains the string "PHP".

14-2. No need to be picky ...

Regular expressions are almost a programming language unto themselves. A dazzling variety of characters have a special significance when they appear in a regular expression. Using these special characters, you can describe in great detail the pattern of characters that a PHP function like `preg_match` will search for. To show you what I mean, let's look at a slightly more complex regular expression:

```
/^PH.*/
```

The caret (^) is placed at the beginning of an expression and indicates that the pattern much match the start of the string. The expression above will only match strings that start withPH.

The dot (.) means "any single character". The expression /PH./ would match PHP, PHA, PHx and any other string that started with PH and one more letter.

The asterisk (*) is a modifier for the dot, and it means "zero or more of the preceding character". The expression P* would match PPPPPPP but not PHP.

.* matches *any character* zero or more times.

Therefore, the pattern /^PH.*/ matches not only the string "PH", but "PHP", "PHX", "PHP: Hypertext Preprocessor", and any other string beginning with "PH".

When you first encounter it, regular expression syntax can be downright confusing and difficult to remember, so if you intend to make extensive use of it, a good reference might come in handy. Regular expressions are a complex and extensive mini-language. I'm not going to try to cover it here. Instead, I'll introduce the individual characters as we need them. The PHP Manual includes a very thorough regular expression reference[1],, and interactive tools such as regex101.com[2] are incredibly useful visual learning tools.

String Replacement with Regular Expressions

As you may recall, we're aiming in this chapter to make it easier for non-HTML-savvy users to add formatting to the jokes on our website. For example, if a user

---

[1.] http://php.net/manual/en/reference.pcre.pattern.syntax.php
[2.] https://regex101.com/

puts asterisks around a word in the text of a joke—such as `'Knock *knock*…'`—we'd like to display the joke with HTML emphasis tags around that word: `Knock <em>knock</em>…'`.

We can detect the presence of plain-text formatting such as this in a joke's text using `preg_match` with the regular expression syntax we've just learned. However, what we *need* to do is pinpoint that formatting and *replace* it with appropriate HTML tags. To achieve this, we need to look at another regular expression function offered by PHP: `preg_replace`.

`preg_replace`, like `preg_match`, accepts a regular expression and a string of text, and attempts to match the regular expression in the string. In addition, `preg_replace` takes another string of text and replaces every match of the regular expression with that string.

The syntax for `preg_replace` is as follows:

```
$newString = preg_replace($regExp, $replaceWith,
↳ $oldString);
```

Here, `$regExp` is the regular expression, and `replaceWith` is the string that will replace matches in `$oldString`. The function returns the new string with all the replacements made. In that code, this newly generated string is stored in `$newString`.

We're now ready to build our joke formatting function.

Emphasized Text

We could use a relevant `preg_replace` method everywhere it's required in our templates. However, since this is going to be useful in multiple places, and any website we build, we'll create a class for it and place it in our `Ninja` namespace:

```
namespace Ninja;

class Markdown {
```

```
    private $string;

    public function __construct($markDown) {
    $this->string = $markDown;
    }

    public function toHtml() {
    // convert $this->string to HTML

    return $html;
    }
}
```

The plain-text formatting syntax we'll support is a simplified form of Markdown, created by John Gruber.

> Markdown is a text-to-HTML conversion tool for web writers. Markdown allows you to write using an easy-to-read, easy-to-write plain-text format, then convert it to structurally valid XHTML (or HTML). — the Markdown home page[3]

Since this class will convert Markdown to HTML, it's named `MarkDown`.

This first action is to use the `htmlentities` function to convert any HTML code present in the text into text, by removing any characters that are understood by browsers (`<`, `>`, `&`, `"`). We want to avoid any HTML code appearing in the output, except that which is generated from plain-text formatting.[4]

Let's start with formatting that will create **bold** and *italic* text.

In Markdown, you can emphasize text by surrounding it with a pair of asterisks (`*`), or a pair of underscores (`_`). Obviously, we'll replace any such pair with `<em>`

[3.] http://daringfireball.net/projects/markdown/

[4.] Technically, this breaks one of the features of Markdown: support for inline HTML. "Real" Markdown can contain HTML code, which will be passed through to the browser untouched. The idea is that you can use HTML to produce any formatting that's too complex to create using Markdown's plain-text formatting syntax. Since we don't want to allow this, it might be more accurate to say we'll support Markdown-*style* formatting.

and `</em>` tags.[5]

To achieve this, we'll use two regular expressions: one that handles a pair of asterisks, and one that handles a pair of underscores.

Let's start with the underscores:

```
/_[^_]+_/
```

Breaking this down:

`/`: we choose our usual slash character to begin (and therefore delimit) our regular expression.

`_`: there's nothing special about underscores in regular expressions, so this will simply match an underscore character in the text.

`[^_]`: square brackets are used to match a sequence of one or more characters that are placed between the opening bracket `[` and closing bracket `]`. The caret (`^`), when placed inside square brackets, acts as a logical *not*. The expression `[^_]` will match any character that is not an underscore.

`+`: the plus character indicates one or more characters that match the preceding expression. `[^_]+` can be read as *one or more characters that are not an underscore*.

`_`: the second underscore, which marks the end of the italicized text.

`/`: the end of the regular expression.

In English, the expression `/_[^_]+_/` could be translated as: "Find an underscore, followed by one or more characters that aren't an underscore, and stop at the following underscore."

[5.] You may be more accustomed to using `<b>` and `<i>` tags for bold and italic text. However, I've chosen to respect the most recent HTML standards, which recommend using the more meaningful **strong** and **em** tags, respectively. If bold text doesn't necessarily indicate strong emphasis in your content, and italic text isn't representative of emphasis, you might want to use **b** and **i** instead.

Now, it's easy enough to feed this regular expression to `preg_replace`, but we have a problem:

```
$text = preg_replace('/_[^_]+_/', '<em>emphasized
↪ text</em>', $text);
```

The second argument we pass to `preg_replace` needs to be the text that we want to replace each match with. The problem is, we have no idea what the text that goes between the `<em>` and `</em>` tags should be. It's part of the text that's being matched by our regular expression!

Thankfully, another feature of `preg_replace` comes to our rescue. If you surround a portion of the regular expression with parentheses, you can capture the corresponding portion of the matched text and use it in the replacement string. To do this, you'll use the code $n, where n is 1 for the first parenthesized portion of the regular expression, 2 for the second, and so on, up to 99 for the 99th. Consider this example:

```
$text = 'banana';
$text = preg_replace('/(.*)(nana)/', '$2$1', $text);
echo $text; // outputs 'nanaba'
```

So $1 is replaced with the text matched by the first grouped portion of the regular expression (`(.*)`—zero or more non-newline characters), which is `ba` in this case. $2 is replaced by `nana`, which is the text matched by the second grouped portion of the regular expression (`(nana)`). The replacement string `'$2$1'`, therefore, produces `'nanaba'`.

We can use the same principle to create our emphasized text, adding parentheses to our regular expression:

```
/_([^_]+)_/
```

These parentheses have no effect on how the expression works at all, but they create a group of matched characters that we can reuse in our replacement string:

```
$text = preg_replace('/_([^_]+)_/',
↳ '<em>$1</em>', $text);
```

The pattern to match and replace pairs of asterisks looks much the same, except we need to escape the asterisks with backslashes, since the asterisk character normally has a special meaning in regular expressions:

```
$text = preg_replace('/\*([^\*]+)\*/',
↳ '<em>$1</em>', $text);
```

That takes care of emphasized text, but Markdown also supports creating strong emphasis (<strong> tags) by surrounding text with a pair of *double* asterisks or underscores (**strong emphasis** or __strong emphasis__). Here's the regular expression to match pairs of double underscores:

```
/__(.+?)__/s
```

The double underscores at the start and end are straightforward enough, but what's going on inside the parentheses?

Previously, in our single-underscore pattern, we used [^_]+ to match a series of one or more characters, none of which could be underscores. That works fine when the end of the emphasized text is marked by a single underscore. But when the end is a *double* underscore, we want to allow for the emphasized text to contain single underscores (for example, __text_with_strong_emphasis__). "No underscores allowed," therefore, won't cut it: we must come up with some other way to match the emphasized text.

You might be tempted to use .+ (one or more characters, any kind), giving us a regular expression like this:[6]

[6.] The s pattern modifier at the end of the regular expression ensures that the dot (.) will truly match any character, including newlines.

```
/__(.+)__/s
```

The problem with this pattern is that the + is **greedy**: it will cause this portion of the regular expression to gobble up as many characters as it can. Consider this joke, for example:

```
__Knock-knock.__ Who's there? __Boo.__ Boo who? __Aw, don't
↪ cry about it!__
```

When presented with this text, the regular expression above will see just a single match, beginning with two underscores at the start of the joke and ending with two underscores at the end. The rest of the text in between (including all the other double underscores) will be gobbled up by the greedy .+ as the text to be emphasized!

To fix this problem, we can ask the + to be *non-greedy* by adding a question mark after it. Instead of matching as many characters as possible, .+? will match as few characters as possible while still matching the rest of the pattern, ensuring we'll match each piece of emphasized text (and the double-underscores that surround it) individually. This gets us to our final regular expression:

```
/__(.+?)__/s
```

Using the same technique, we can also come up with a regular expression for double-asterisks. This is how the finished code for applying strong emphasis ends up looking:

```
$text = preg_replace('/__(.+?)__/s',
↪ '<strong>$1</strong>', $text);
$text = preg_replace('/\*\*(.+?)\*\*/s',
↪ '<strong>$1</strong>', $text);
```

One last point: we must avoid converting pairs of single asterisks and underscores into `<em>` and `</em>` tags until after we've converted the pairs of double asterisks and underscores in the text into `<strong>` and `</strong>` tags. Our `toHtml` function, therefore, will apply strong emphasis first, then regular emphasis:

```php
namespace Ninja;

class Markdown {
    private $string;

    public function __construct($markDown) {
    $this->string = $markDown;
    }

    public function toHtml() {
    // convert $this->string to HTML
    $text = htmlspecialchars($this->string, ENT_QUOTES,
     'UTF-8');

    // strong (bold)
    $text = preg_replace('/__(.+?)__/s',
     '<strong>$1</strong>', $text);
    $text = preg_replace('/\*\*(.+?)\*\*/s',
     '<strong>$1</strong>', $text);

    // emphasis (italic)
    $text = preg_replace('/_([^_]+)_/',
     '<em>$1</em>', $text);
    $text = preg_replace('/\*([^\*]+)\*/',
     '<em>$1</em>', $text);

    return $text;
    }
}
```

Paragraphs

While we could choose characters to mark the start and end of paragraphs, just as we did for emphasized text, a simpler approach makes more sense. Since your users will type the content into a form field that allows them to create paragraphs using the **Enter** key, we'll take a single newline to indicate a line break (<br />) and a double newline to indicate a new paragraph (</p><p>).

As I explained earlier, you can represent a newline character in a regular expression as \n. Other whitespace characters you can write this way include a carriage return (\r) and a tab space (\t).

Exactly which characters are inserted into text when the user hits **Enter** depends on the user's operating system. In general, Windows computers represent a line break as a carriage return followed by a newline (\r\n), whereas Mac computers used to represent it as a single carriage return character (\r). These days, Macs and Linux computers use a single newline character (\n) to indicate a new line.[7]

To deal with these different line-break styles, any of which may be submitted by the browser, we must do some conversion:

```
// Convert Windows (\r\n) to Unix (\n)
$text = preg_replace('/\r\n/', "\n", $text);

// Convert Macintosh (\r) to Unix (\n)
$text = preg_replace('/\r/', "\n", $text);
```

[7.] In fact, the type of line breaks used can vary between software programs on the same computer. If you've ever opened a text file in Notepad to see all the line breaks missing, you've experienced the frustration this can cause. Advanced text editors used by programmers usually let you specify the type of line breaks to use when saving a text file.

Avoid Using Double-Quoted String with Regular Expressions

All the regular expressions we've seen so far in this chapter have been expressed as single-quoted PHP strings. The automatic variable substitution provided by PHP strings is sometimes more convenient, but they can cause headaches when used with regular expressions.

Double-quoted PHP strings and regular expressions share a number of special character escape codes. `"\n"` is a PHP string containing a newline character. Likewise, `/\n/` is a regular expression that will match any string containing a newline character. We can represent this regular expression as a single-quoted PHP string (`'/\n/'`) and all is well, because the code `\n` has no special meaning in a single-quoted PHP string.

If we were to use a double-quoted string to represent this regular expression, we'd have to write `"/\\n/"`—with a double-backslash. The double-backslash tells PHP to include an actual backslash in the string, rather than combining it with the `n` that follows it to represent a newline character. This string will therefore generate the desired regular expression, `/\n/`.

Because of the added complexity it introduces, it's best to avoid using double-quoted strings when writing regular expressions. Note, however, that I *have* used double quotes for the replacement strings (`"\n"`) passed as the second parameter to `preg_replace`. In this case, we actually do want to create a string containing a newline character, so a double-quoted string does the job perfectly.

With our line breaks all converted to newline characters, we can convert them to paragraph breaks (when they occur in pairs) and line breaks (when they occur alone):

```
// Paragraphs
$text = '<p>' . preg_replace('/\n\n/',
↪ '</p><p>', $text) . '</p>';

// Line breaks
$text = preg_replace('/\n/', '<br>', $text);
```

Note the addition of `<p>` and `</p>` tags surrounding the joke text. Because our jokes may contain paragraph breaks, we must make sure the joke text is output within the context of a paragraph to begin with.

This code does the trick: the line breaks in the text will now become the natural line- and paragraph-breaks expected by the user, removing the requirement to learn anything new to create this simple formatting.

It turns out, however, that there's a simpler way to achieve the same result in this case: there's no need to use regular expressions at all! PHP's `str_replace` function works a lot like `preg_replace`, except that it only searches for strings instead of regular expression patterns:

```
$newString = str_replace($searchFor, $replaceWith,
➥ $oldString);
```

We can therefore rewrite our line-breaking code as follows:

```
// Convert Windows (\r\n) to Unix (\n)
$text = str_replace("\r\n", "\n", $text);
// Convert Macintosh (\r) to Unix (\n)
$text = str_replace("\r", "\n", $text);

// Paragraphs
$text = '<p>' . str_replace("\n\n",
➥ '</p><p>', $text) . '</p>';
// Line breaks
$text = str_replace("\n", '<br>', $text);
```

`str_replace` is much more efficient than `preg_replace`, because there's no need for it to apply the complex rules that govern regular expressions. Whenever `str_replace` (or `str_ireplace`, if you need a case-insensitive search) can do the job, you should use it instead of `preg_replace`.

Hyperlinks

While supporting the inclusion of hyperlinks in the text of jokes may seem unnecessary, such a feature makes plenty of sense in other applications.

Here's what a hyperlink looks like in Markdown:[8]

```
[linked text](link URL)
```

Simple, right? You put the text of the link in square brackets, and follow it with the URL for the link in parentheses.

As it turns out, you've already learned everything you need to match and replace links like this with HTML links. If you're feeling up to the challenge, you should stop reading right here and try to tackle the problem yourself!

First, we need a regular expression that will match links of this form. The regular expression is as follows:

```
/\[([^\]]+)]\((.+)\)/i
```

This is a rather complicated regular expression. You can see how regular expressions have gained a reputation for being indecipherable!

Squint at it for a little while, and see if you can figure out how it works. Try writing out the expression on egex101.com[9] and it will display the regular expression in its groups with some useful highlighting. You can try typing in various strings to see which match.

Let me break it down for you:

/: as with all our regular expressions, we choose to mark its beginning with a slash.

\[: this matches the opening square bracket ([). Since square brackets have a special meaning in regular expressions, we must escape it with a backslash to have it interpreted literally.

([^\]]+): first of all, this portion of the regular expression is surrounded with

---

8. Markdown also supports a more advanced link syntax where you put the link URL at the end of the document, as a footnote. But we won't be supporting that kind of link in our simplified Markdown implementation.
9. https://regex101.com/

parentheses, so the matching text will be available to us as $1 when we write the replacement string. Inside the parentheses, we're after the linked text. Because the end of the linked text is marked with a closing square bracket (]), we can describe it as one or more characters, none of which is a closing square bracket ([^\]]+).

]\(: this will match the closing square bracket that ends the linked text, followed by the opening parenthesis that signals the start of the link URL. The parenthesis needs to be escaped with a backslash to prevent it from having its usual grouping effect. (The square bracket doesn't need to be escaped with a backslash, because there's no unescaped opening square bracket currently in play.)

(.+): as URLs can contain (almost) any character, anything typed inside the markdown parentheses will be matched by .+ and stored inside the group $2 in the replacement string.

\): this escaped parenthesis matches the closing parenthesis ()) at the end of the link URL.

/i: we mark the end of the regular expression with a slash, followed by the case-insensitivity flag, i.

We can therefore convert links with the following PHP code:

```php
$text = preg_replace(
    '/\[([^\]]+)]\(([-a-z0-9._~:\/?#@!$&\'()*+,;=%]+)\)/i',
    '<a href="$2">$1</a>', $text);
```

As you can see, $1 is used in the replacement string to substitute the captured link text, and $2 is used for the captured URL.

Additionally, because we're expressing our regular expression as a single-quoted PHP string, you have to escape the single quote that appears in the list of acceptable characters with a backslash.

Putting It All Together

Here's how our finished class for converting Markdown to HTML looks:

```php
<?php
namespace Ninja;

class Markdown
{
    private $string;

    public function __construct($markDown)
    {
        $this->string = $markDown;
    }

    public function toHtml()
    {
        // convert $this->string to HTML
        $text = htmlspecialchars($this->string, ENT_QUOTES,
          'UTF-8');

        // strong (bold)
        $text = preg_replace('/__(.+?)__/s',
          '<strong>$1</strong>', $text);
        $text = preg_replace('/\*\*(.+?)\*\*/s',
          '<strong>$1</strong>', $text);

        // emphasis (italic)
        $text = preg_replace('/_([^_]+)_/',
          '<em>$1</em>', $text);
        $text = preg_replace('/\*([^\*]+)\*/',
          '<em>$1</em>', $text);

        // Convert Windows (\r\n) to Unix (\n)
        $text = str_replace("\r\n", "\n",
          $text);
        // Convert Macintosh (\r) to Unix (\n)
        $text = str_replace("\r", "\n",
```

```
    $text);

    // Paragraphs
    $text = '<p>' . str_replace("\n\n",
     '</p><p>', $text) . '</p>';
    // Line breaks
    $text = str_replace("\n", '<br>', $text);

    // [linked text](link URL)
    $text = preg_replace(
'/\[([^\]]+)]\(([-a-z0-9._~:\/?#@!$&\'()*+,;=%]+)\)/i',
'<a href="$2">$1</a>',
    $text
);

    return $text;
    }
}
```

We can then use this class in our template that outputs the joke text, `jokes.html.php`:

```
<div class="jokelist">

<ul class="categories">
    <?php foreach ($categories as $category): ?>
    <li><a href="/joke/list?category=
    <?=$category->id?>"><
    ?=$category->name?></a><li>
    <?php endforeach; ?>
</ul>

<div class="jokes">

 <p><?=$totalJokes?> jokes have been submitted to
↳ the Internet Joke Database.</p>

<?php foreach ($jokes as $joke): ?>
```

```
<blockquote>
    <p>
    <?=htmlspecialchars($joke->joketext,
    ENT_QUOTES, 'UTF-8')?>

    (by <a href="mailto:<?=htmlspecialchars(
    $joke->getAuthor()->email,
    ENT_QUOTES,
        'UTF-8'
); ?>">
        <?=htmlspecialchars(
            $joke->getAuthor()->name,
            ENT_QUOTES,
            'UTF-8'
        ); ?></a> on
<?php
$date = new DateTime($joke->jokedate);

echo $date->format('jS F Y');
?>)

<?php if ($user): ?>
    <?php if ($user->id == $joke->authorId ||
 $user->hasPermission(\Ijdb\Entity\Author::EDIT_JOKES)):
↳ ?>
    <a href="/joke/edit?id=<?=$joke->id?>">
    Edit</a>
    <?php endif; ?>
    <?php if ($user->id == $joke->authorId ||
 $user->hasPermission(\Ijdb\Entity\Author::DELETE_JOKES)):
↳ ?>
    <form action="/joke/delete" method="post">
        <input type="hidden" name="id"
            value="<?=$joke->id?>">
        <input type="submit" value="Delete">
    </form>
    <?php endif; ?>
<?php endif; ?>
    </p>
</blockquote>
```

```
<?php endforeach; ?>

</div>
```

The line we're interested in is this:

```
<?=htmlspecialchars($joke->joketext,
ENT_QUOTES, 'UTF-8')?>
```

However, each joke is already wrapped in a <p> tag. This can be removed:

```
<div class="jokelist">

<ul class="categories">
    <?php foreach($categories as $category): ?>
    <li><a href="/joke/list?category=
    <?=$category->id?>">
    <?=$category->name?></a><li>
    <?php endforeach; ?>
</ul>

<div class="jokes">

 <p><?=$totalJokes?> jokes have been submitted to
↪ the Internet Joke Database.</p>

<?php foreach($jokes as $joke): ?>
<blockquote>
    <!-- Remove the opening tag <p> -->

    <?=htmlspecialchars($joke->joketext,
    ENT_QUOTES, 'UTF-8')?>

    <!--- … -->
<?php endif; ?>
    <!-- Remove the closing tag </p> -->
</blockquote>
```

```
<?php endforeach; ?>

</div>
```

Now, replace the line that shows the joke text with this:

```
<?php
$markdown = new \Ninja\Markdown($joke->joketext);
echo $markdown->toHtml();
?>
```

This will pass the contents of `joketext` to the `markdown` class as a constructor argument and call the `toHtml` method to convert the text to HTML.

This is a lot untidier than the original method, as it requires two lines. As with most things in PHP, there is a way to express this using shorter syntax:

```
<?=(new
↪ \Ninja\Markdown($joke->joketext))->toHtml()?>
```

This code can be found in *Formatting-Markdown*.

With these changes made, take your new plain-text formatting for a spin! Edit a few of your jokes to contain Markdown syntax and verify that the formatting is correctly displayed.

Why Using Markdown is Cool

What's nice about adopting a formatting syntax like Markdown for your own website is that there's often plenty of open-source code out there to help you deal with it.

Your newfound regular expression skills will serve you well in your career as a web developer, but if you want to support Markdown formatting on your site, the easiest way to do it would be to *not* write all the code to handle Markdown formatting yourself!

Commonly used Markdown libraries include ParseDown[10] and cebe/markdown[11].

Sorting, Limiting and Offsets

We've spent a lot of time writing PHP code and, thanks to the `DatabaseTable` class, it's been quite some time since you learned about any new SQL.

However, there's a few final MySQL features I'd like to show you before you get your Ninja title.

Sorting

MySQL supports asking for retrieved records in a specific order. At the moment, the Joke List page displays jokes in the order they were posted. It would be better if it showed the newest first.

A `SELECT` query can contain an `ORDER BY` clause that specifies the column that the data is sorted by.

For our jokes table, `SELECT * FROM `joke` ORDER BY `jokedate`` would order the jokes by the date they were posted. You can also specify a modifier of `ASC` (ascending-counting up) or `DESC` (descending-counting down).

```
SELECT * FROM `joke` ORDER BY `jokedate` DESC
```

---

10. https://github.com/erusev/parsedown
11. https://github.com/cebe/markdown

This query would select all the jokes and order them by date in *descending order*, newest first.

Let's implement this on the website. All our SQL queries are generated by the DatabaseTable class, so we'll need to amend that to include an ORDER BY clause.

At the moment, the findAll method looks like this:

```php
public function findAll() {
    $result = $this->query('SELECT * FROM ' .
    $this->table);

    return $result->fetchAll(\PDO::FETCH_CLASS,
    $this->className, $this->constructorArgs);
}
```

Let's add an optional argument for ORDER BY:

```php
public function findAll($orderBy = null) {

    $query = 'SELECT * FROM ' . $this->table;

    if ($orderBy != null) {
    $query .= ' ORDER BY ' . $orderBy;
    }

    $result = $this->query($query);

    return $result->fetchAll(\PDO::FETCH_CLASS,
    $this->className, $this->constructorArgs);
}
```

The SELECT query is now built up in the same way we built the INSERT and UPDATE queries. When a value for $orderBy is supplied, it's appended to the query along with the ORDER BY clause. By making the argument optional, all of our existing code will still work without modification. We can provide a value for the $orderby argument only where it's needed.

To sort the Joke List page by date descending, amend the `Joke` controller's `list` method to supply the argument to the `findAll` method:

```php
public function list() {

    if (isset($_GET['category'])) {
        $category = $this->categoriesTable->
        findById($_GET['category']);
        $jokes = $category->getJokes();
    }
    else {
        $jokes = $this->jokesTable->findAll('jokedate DESC');
    }

    // …
```

At the moment, the main Joke List page is sorted newest first. However, if you click on one of the categories, they're listed oldest first.

You might consider adding the same optional argument to the `find` method:

```php
public function find($column, $value, $orderBy = null) {
    $query = 'SELECT * FROM ' . $this->table . '
    WHERE ' . $column . ' = :value';

    $parameters = [
    'value' => $value
    ];

    if ($orderBy != null) {
        $query .= ' ORDER BY ' . $orderBy;
    }

    $query = $this->query($query, $parameters);

    return $query->fetchAll(\PDO::FETCH_CLASS,
      $this->className, $this->constructorArgs);
}
```

Although this will be useful, it's not going to solve the problem. The list of jokes is generated in the `Category` entity class:

```php
public function getJokes() {
    $jokeCategories = $this->jokeCategoriesTable->
    find('categoryId', $this->id);

    $jokes = [];

    foreach ($jokeCategories as $jokeCategory) {
        $joke = $this->jokesTable->
        findById($jokeCategory->jokeId);
        if ($joke) {
            $jokes[] = $joke;
        }
    }

    return $jokes;
}
```

Because the `find` method is called on the `DatabaseTable` instance that represents the `joke_category` table, we can't easily sort by date.

There are a few ways to solve this. We could add a `date` column to the `joke_category` table for sorting purposes. We could also use an SQL `JOIN`, but that would be difficult to implement into our OOP `DatabaseTable` class.

Instead, we can do the sort in PHP itself, using the `usort` function. The `usort` function takes two arguments: an array to be sorted, and the name of a function that compares two values.

The example given in the PHP manual[12] is this:

---

12. http://php.net/manual/en/function.usort.php

```php
<?php
function cmp($a, $b)
{
    if ($a == $b) {
        return 0;
    }
    return ($a < $b) ? -1 : 1;
}

$a = [3, 2, 5, 6, 1];

usort($a, "cmp");

foreach ($a as $key => $value) {
    echo "$key: $value\n";
}
```

The code above outputs this:

```
0: 1
1: 2
2: 3
3: 5
4: 6
```

The array has been sorted smallest to largest. The `cmp` function is called with two values from the array, and returns 1 if the first should be placed after the second, and -1 if the first should be placed before the second. The important part is this line:

```
return ($a < $b) ? -1 : 1;
```

The syntax here looks strange if you haven't come across it before. You actually know what's happening here, but you've not seen it expressed in this way. The code here is a shorthand (or ternary) `if` statement, and it's identical in execution to this:

```
if ($a < $b) {
    return -1;
} else {
    return 1;
}
```

The comparison function can take arguments that are objects, and we can build a comparison function into our Category class like so:

```
public function getJokes() {
    $jokeCategories = $this->jokeCategoriesTable->
    find('categoryId', $this->id);

    $jokes = [];

    foreach ($jokeCategories as $jokeCategory) {
    $joke =  $this->jokesTable->
     findById($jokeCategory->jokeId);
    if ($joke) {
        $jokes[] = $joke;
    }
    }

    usort($jokes, [$this, 'sortJokes']);

    return $jokes;
}

private function sortJokes($a, $b) {
    $aDate = new \DateTime($a->jokedate);
    $bDate = new \DateTime($b->jokedate);

 if ($aDate->getTimestamp() == $bDate->getTimestamp())
↪ {
    return 0;
    }
```

```
return $aDate->getTimestamp() >
↳ $bDate->getTimestamp() ? -1 : 1;
}
```

You can find this code in *Formatting-Usort*

There's a lot going on here, so I'll go through it line by line. Firstly, the `$jokes` array is sorted using the `usort` function: `usort($jokes, [$this, 'sortJokes']);`. To call a method in a class, rather than just a function, you can use an array containing the object you want to call the method on (in our case, the same instance, `$this`) and the name of the method to be called (`sortJokes`).

The `sortJokes` method starts by converting the dates from each of the `$a` and `$b` objects into `\DateTime` instances for easier comparison. The `getTimestamp` method returns a Unix timestamp—the number of seconds between the January 1 1970 and the date being represented. Using timestamps allows us to compare the dates as integers.

The `if` statement checks to see if the dates have the same timestamp. If so, it returns 0, indicating that neither should be moved before or after the other in the sorted list.

If the dates are different, either 1 or -1 is returned to sort the dates. Notice I've used `$a > $b`, which will sort the array in the opposite order to the example, and put the larger timestamps (later dates) first.

There's a slight performance overhead in using `usort` instead of `ORDER BY` and having the database perform the sort, but unless you're dealing with thousands of records, the difference between the two will be milliseconds at worst!

Pagination with LIMIT and OFFSET

Now that you know how to sort the records, we can think a little about scalability. You've probably got fewer than a dozen jokes in your database at the moment. What will happen after the website has been online a few months and is starting to get popular? You might get users coming on and posting hundreds of jokes a day.

It won't take long before the Joke List page takes a very long time to load because it's displaying hundreds or thousands of jokes. The performance alone will put users off, but nobody is going to sit and read through a page of two thousand jokes.

A common approach is using **pagination** to display a sensible number—for example, ten jokes per page—and allow clicking a link to move between pages.

Before you continue, add at least 21 jokes to your database so we can test this correctly. Alternatively, for testing purposes, change 10 in the following sections to 2 to display two jokes per page.

What If I Don't Know any Jokes?

Don't worry if you can't think of any jokes. Just add some test data like "joke one", "joke two", "joke three", etc.

Our first task is to display just the first ten jokes. Using SQL, this is incredibly easy. The LIMIT clause can be appended to any SELECT query to restrict the number of records returned:

```
SELECT * FROM `joke` ORDER BY `jokedate DESC` LIMIT 10
```

We'll need to build this into findAll and find methods of the DatabaseTable class as optional parameters, as we did with the $orderBy variable:

```
public function find($column, $value, $orderBy = null,
  $limit = null) {
    $query = 'SELECT * FROM ' . $this->table . '
    WHERE ' . $column . ' = :value';

    $parameters = [
    'value' => $value
    ];
```

```
    if ($orderBy != null) {
        $query .= ' ORDER BY ' . $orderBy;
    }

    if ($limit != null) {
        $query .= ' LIMIT ' . $limit;
    }

    $query = $this->query($query, $parameters);

    return $query->fetchAll(\PDO::FETCH_CLASS,
     $this->className, $this->constructorArgs);
}

public function findAll($orderBy = null, $limit = null) {
    $query = 'SELECT * FROM ' . $this->table;

    if ($orderBy != null) {
        $query .= ' ORDER BY ' . $orderBy;
    }

    if ($limit != null) {
        $query .= ' LIMIT ' . $limit;
    }

    $result = $this->query($query);

    return $result->fetchAll(\PDO::FETCH_CLASS,
     $this->className, $this->constructorArgs);
}
```

Then, to limit to ten jokes, open up the Joke controller class and provide the value 10 for the new $limit argument:

```
$jokes = $this->jokesTable->findAll('jokedate DESC',
↪ 10);
```

Also supply the new limit in the `Category` entity class:

```
$jokeCategories =
↳ $this->jokeCategoriesTable->find('categoryId',
↳ $this->id, null, 10);
```

You'll notice I've supplied `null` for the `$orderBy` argument. Even though the argument is optional, to provide a value for `$limit`, a value for all the earlier arguments must be provided.

With that in place, you'll see only ten jokes on the Joke List page. The problem now is how we'll view the rest of the jokes!

The solution is to have different pages that can be accessed by a `$_GET` variable: `/joke/list?page=1` or `/joke/list?page=2` to select which page to show. Page 1 will show jokes 1–10, page 2 will show jokes 11–20, and so on.

Before doing anything using the `page $_GET` variable, let's create the links in the template. We can easily use a `for` loop to display a set of links to different pages:

```
for ($i = 1; $i <= 10; $i++) {
    echo '<a href="/joke/list?page=' . $i . '">' .
    $i '</a>';
}
```

The problem is, we need to know how many pages there will be. It's actually very easy to work out. If we're displaying ten jokes per page, the number of pages is the number of jokes in the database divided by ten, and then rounded up.

With 21 jokes in the system, `21/10` is `2.1`, and if we round up, it gives `3` pages. PHP's `ceil` function can be used to round up any decimal number.

The template already has access to the `$totalJokes` variable, so we can display the pages at the end of `jokes.html.php`:

```
// …
```

```
<?php endif; ?>
</blockquote>
<?php endforeach; ?>

Select page:

<?php
// Calculate the number of pages
$numPages = ceil($totalJokes/10);

// Display a link for each page
for ($i = 1; $i <= $numPages; $i++):
?>
    <a href="/joke/list?page=<?=$i?>">
    <?=$i?></a>
<?php endfor; ?>

</div>
```

If you click the links, the $_GET variable will be set. It's now just a matter of using it to display different sets of jokes.

The SQL clause OFFSET can be used with LIMIT to do exactly what we want:

```
SELECT * FROM `joke` ORDER BY `jokedate` LIMIT 10 OFFSET 10
```

This query will return 10 jokes, but instead of returning the *first* ten jokes, it will display ten jokes starting from joke 10.

We'll need to turn page numbers into offsets. Page 1, will be OFFSET 0, page 2 will be OFFSET 10, page 3 will be OFFSET 20 and so on. This is a simple calculation: $offset = ($_GET['page']-1)*10.

As we did with limit, let's add OFFSET as an optional argument for the findAll and find methods:

```php
public function findAll($orderBy = null, $limit = null,
 $offset = null) {
    $query = 'SELECT * FROM ' . $this->table;

    if ($orderBy != null) {
        $query .= ' ORDER BY ' . $orderBy;
    }

    if ($limit != null) {
        $query .= ' LIMIT ' . $limit;
    }

    if ($offset != null) {
        $query .= ' OFFSET ' . $offset;
    }

    $result = $this->query($query);

    return $result->fetchAll(\PDO::FETCH_CLASS,
     $this->className, $this->constructorArgs);
}

public function find($column, $value,
  $orderBy = null, $limit = null, $offset = null) {
    $query = 'SELECT * FROM ' . $this->table . '
     WHERE ' . $column . ' = :value';

    $parameters = [
    'value' => $value
    ];

    if ($orderBy != null) {
        $query .= ' ORDER BY ' . $orderBy;
    }

    if ($limit != null) {
        $query .= ' LIMIT ' . $limit;
    }

    if ($offset != null) {
```

```
        $query .= ' OFFSET ' . $offset;
    }

    $query = $this->query($query, $parameters);

    return $query->fetchAll(\PDO::FETCH_CLASS,
     $this->className, $this->constructorArgs);
}
```

Then supply the offset in the `list` method in the `Joke` controller:

```
$page = $_GET['page'] ?? 1;

$offset = ($page-1)*10;

if (isset($_GET['category'])) {
    $category = $this->categoriesTable->
    findById($_GET['category']);
    $jokes = $category->getJokes();
}
else {
    $jokes = $this->jokesTable->findAll('jokedate DESC',
     10, $offset);
}

$title = 'Joke List';

$totalJokes = $this->jokesTable->total();

$author = $this->authentication->getUser();

return ['template' => 'jokes.html.php',
    'title' => $title,
    'variables' => [
        'totalJokes' => $totalJokes,
        'jokes' => $jokes,
        'user' => $author,
        'categories' => $this->categoriesTable->findAll()
```

```
        ]
    ];
}
```

Now, if you click between the different page links, you'll see ten different jokes on each page.

This new pagination doesn't work for the lists within categories, and we'll fix that shortly. But at the moment, the links aren't very user friendly. Let's change the styling of the link that represents the current page.

We can pass the number of the current page to the template:

```
return ['template' => 'jokes.html.php',
    'title' => $title,
    'variables' => [
    'totalJokes' => $totalJokes,
    'jokes' => $jokes,
    'user' => $author,
    'categories' => $this->categoriesTable->findAll(),
    'currentPage' => $page
    ]
];
```

Then add a CSS class to the page link if it's the current page:

```
Select page:

<?php

$numPages = ceil($totalJokes/10);

for ($i = 1; $i <= $numPages; $i++):
    if ($i == $currentPage):
?>
    <a class="currentpage"
```

```
            href="/joke/list?page=<?=$i?>">
            <?=$i?></a>
<?php else: ?>
    <a href="/joke/list?page=<?=$i?>">
    <?=$i?></a>
<?php endif; ?>
<?php endfor; ?>

</div>
```

I've added a CSS class `currentpage` to the link if the link being printed is the current page being viewed. Add some CSS to `jokes.css` to make the link stand out. You could change the color, make it bold, underlined or however you like. I've chosen to surround the number with square brackets:

```
.currentpage:before {
    content: "[";
}
.currentpage:after {
    content: "]";
}
```

You can find this code in *Formatting-Pagination*

Pagination in Categories

We have a small bug in the code at the moment. If you click on one of the categories, it won't supply the correct `offset` value.

To fix this, we can add an `$offset` argument to the `Category` entity's `getJokes` method. While you're there, to improve flexibility you may as well supply `$limit` as an argument as well, instead of hardcoding it in the method:

```
public function getJokes($limit = null, $offset = null) {
    $jokeCategories =
```

```
    $this->jokeCategoriesTable->find('categoryId',
    $this->id, null, $limit, $offset);

    $jokes = [];

    foreach ($jokeCategories as $jokeCategory) {
        $joke =
        $this->jokesTable->findById($jokeCategory->jokeId);
        if ($joke) {
            $jokes[] = $joke;
        }
    }

    usort($jokes, [$this, 'sortJokes']);

    return $jokes;
}
```

Then provide the values when the method is called in the `list` method:

```
if (isset($_GET['category'])) {
    $category =
    $this->categoriesTable->findById($_GET['category']);
    $jokes = $category->getJokes(10, $offset);
}
```

With that done, the pagination will work … kind of. You can manually enter the `$_GET` variables in the URL—for example, `http://192.168.10.10/joke/list?category=1&page=1`. However, the links we created don't work.

There are two problems:

1. The page links don't include the category variable.
2. The number of page links displayed is based on the total number of jokes in the database, not the number of jokes in the selected category.

Let's fix these one at a time. The easiest task is providing the category in the link.

In the `list` method, we'll need to pass the category to the template:

```php
return ['template' => 'jokes.html.php',
    'title' => $title,
    'variables' => [
        'totalJokes' => $totalJokes,
        'jokes' => $jokes,
        'user' => $author,
        'categories' => $this->categoriesTable->findAll(),
        'currentPage' => $page,
        'category' => $_GET['category'] ?? null
        ]
    ];
```

Then amend the links in the template to provide the category variable if required:

```php
Select page:

<?php

$numPages = ceil($totalJokes/10);

for ($i = 1; $i <= $numPages; $i++):
    if ($i == $currentPage):
?>
    <a class="currentpage"
        href="/joke/list?page=<?=$i?>
        <?=!empty($categoryId) ?
        '&category=' . $categoryId : '' ?>">
        <?=$i?></a>
<?php else: ?>
    <a href="/joke/list?page=<?=$i?>
    <?=!empty($categoryId) ?
    '&category=' . $categoryId : '' ?>">
    <?=$i?></a>
<?php endif; ?>
<?php endfor; ?>
```

```
</div>
```

I've used the shorthand `if`, which I displayed earlier to append
`&category=$categoryId` to the link if it's set.

We've fixed the first problem, but the number of page links being displayed is still
calculated based on the number of jokes in the entire table, rather than just a
category.

At the moment, the `total` method in the `DatabaseTable` class returns the total
number of records in a given table. To count a subset of the records, it will need a
`WHERE` clause. We can implement it in the same way as the `find` method:

```
public function total($field = null, $value = null) {
    $sql = 'SELECT COUNT(*) FROM `' . $this->table . '`';
    $parameters = [];

    if (!empty($field)) {
    $sql .= ' WHERE `' . $field . '` = :value';
    $parameters = ['value' => $value];
    }

    $query = $this->query($sql, $parameters);

    $row = $query->fetch();
    return $row[0];
}
```

The `total` method now supports doing something like echo
`$this->jokesTable->total('authorId', 4);`, which would give us the total
number of jokes by the author with the `id` of 4.

We can't do the same to count the number of jokes in a category, as there's no
`categoryId` column in the `joke` table. We need to call the `total` method on the
`jokeCategoriesTable` instance:
`$this->jokeCategoriesTable->total('categoryId', 2);`, which would count

the number of jokes in the category with the id of 2.

Instead of implementing this in the `list` method, let's add a new method to the `Category` entity class that returns the number of jokes in that particular category: `$totalJokes = $category->getNumJokes();`:

```
public function getNumJokes() {
    return $this->jokeCategoriesTable->total('categoryId',
     $this->id);
}
```

This can then be called from the `list` method in the `Joke` controller:

```
public function list() {

    $page = $_GET['page'] ?? 1;

    $offset = ($page-1)*10;

    if (isset($_GET['category'])) {
        $category =
        $this->categoriesTable->findById($_GET['category']);
        $jokes = $category->getJokes(10, $offset);
        $totalJokes = $category->getNumJokes();
    }
    else {
        $jokes = $this->jokesTable->findAll('jokedate DESC',
        10, $offset);
        $totalJokes = $this->jokesTable->total();
    }

    $title = 'Joke List';
    // …
```

You can find this code in *Final-Website*.

Notice that I've moved the original `$totalJokes` variable into the **else** branch of the `if` statement. When a category is selected, `$totalJokes` is the total number of jokes in the selected category. When no category has been chosen, `$totalJokes` stores the total number of jokes in the database.

Achievement Unlocked: Ninja

That's it! You're done, and you get your PHP black belt.

In this chapter, I showed you some additional tools that will be useful when you develop your next website. You have a basic understanding of regular expressions, along with the SQL features of `LIMIT` and `OFFSET`, and you know how to combine them to paginate data sets.

You now have all the tools you need to build a real website. You know how to think about writing code, and you know how to separate out project specific code from the code you can use in future projects. You also have an understanding of the concepts behind PHP frameworks. You can jump into Symfony, Zend or Laravel, and although the code will be different, all the concepts you've learned in this book will be familiar.

What Next?

You have all the tools you need to build a fully functional PHP website and put it live on the web. Go ahead and publish your first website. It's a great feeling!

With programming, there's always more to learn. There are different techniques and approaches you can try out, and a lot of different tools that will help you develop more efficiently and reduce bugs.

You're never "done", you never complete the game. You just keep playing. Each time you learn something new, be it a new tool, a new technique, or even a new language, it will extend what you knew before and you'll wonder how you ever coped without it. Things also change constantly, and it's difficult to keep up. Why do you think we're on the sixth edition of this book? Don't be disappointed: learning is fun, and as long as you don't fall into the trap of thinking you know everything, you'll go a long way.

Now that you've finished this book, you do, however, have more than enough knowledge to work on your own projects, or even get a job as a junior PHP developer!

Before taking the next few steps, I recommend getting at least two or three projects finished to ensure you're comfortable with everything from this book. It won't sink in right away, and as you go forward, you'll find yourself solving different sets of problems. It will take you a few attempts to get everything clear in your mind.

Once you've done that, you can move on to the next few steps. What are those steps?

1. Composer[13]. Composer is a package management tool that's used by almost all PHP projects these days. If you want to use someone else's code in your project, you'll need to know how to use Composer.

2. Take a look at some PHP frameworks to see how other people do things. In 2017, I'd recommend Laravel[14] and Symfony[15] as starting points, but that's likely to change within a few years.

3. PHPUnit[16]. Test-driven development has really taken off in PHP over the last few years, and for good reason. Once you start using TDD, it's difficult to go back. Everything seems so much tidier and easier. Rather than having to load up your website, fill in your form, then check the record was inserted into a database, you can just run a script that does all that for you!

4. Git[17]. Git is a vital tool for software developers. You may have come across the website GitHub, which allows sharing code and collaborating with other developers. To use the site, you'll need to understand git. But at its most basic, it's an incredible tool. No more copy/pasting code after making a change, or commenting out large sections. Just delete it, and git will keep track of any changes you make!

---

13. https://www.sitepoint.com/re-introducing-composer/
14. https://www.sitepoint.com/bootstrapping-laravel-crud-project/
15. https://www.sitepoint.com/building-a-web-app-with-symfony-2-bootstrapping/
16. https://www.sitepoint.com/re-introducing-phpunit-getting-started-tdd-php/
17. https://www.sitepoint.com/git-for-beginners/

With that said, there's little else I need to add. However you proceed from this point, rest assured you're starting out with a solid grounding in the essentials and a good understanding of the tools and techniques used by modern PHP websites. That's more than can be said for many developers working today. Take that advantage and use it.

Most importantly, go out there and write some code!

Appendix A: Using The Sample Code Repository

Each code sample in this book is provided in a GitHub repository at `https://github.com/spbooks/phpmysql6`. Where a set of code for an example is available in the archive, it is either captioned with its name over the code sample itself (for example *PHP-Loops*), or I'll let you know the name of the set of code in the text. You can find the complete sample code on the GitHub repository. In Git's terminology, each set of code is known as a *branch*.

There are two ways to use the sample code.

If you just want to view the code for a specific file in a single example, you can do it easily on GitHub. Choose the example by it's name using the `Branch` dropdown on the main GitHub page. You will then see a list of files and directories for the selected example (In Git's terms, this is a *Branch*) and can click on each file to view the code.

Alternatively, if you would like to easily run the sample code without having to copy and paste files in and out of the web server's `Project` directory you can easily do this. I've provided a tool that allows you to quickly and easily view any of the code samples.

To use the code samples, follow these steps:

1. Make sure your `Project` directory is empty.

2. Using the `git bash` tool you use to boot the virtual machine, make sure you have navigated to the directory you normally run `vagrant up` from then run the following command:

```
git clone https://github.com/spbooks/phpmysql6 Project
```

3. Visit `http://192.168.10.10/samples/`, you'll see a list of all the available samples.

Click on the name of the sample you want to view and the files will be created in the `Project` directory and view the files on the URL `http://192.168.10.10/`.

Some Caveats

Switching Samples

Once on a specific sample, the `Project` directory will contain only code for the sample you are viewing. If you had been working on any files they will be hidden. They have not been deleted!

Each time you switch between samples, any changes you have made will be backed up in their own branch based on the branch you made changes to. By default, you will be on the *master* branch. When you switch to one of the samples, all files you have created in the `Project` folder will be saved into a branch called *master* followed by the date at time the snapshot was taken. For example: *Master_2017-10-01-17.16.52*. You can get your code back by switching to this new branch from the list at `http://192.168.10.10/samples/`.

Sample Database

All the sample code uses the database `ijdb_sample`. This database will be deleted and recreated each time you switch between samples, any changes you make to the `ijdb_sample` database will be lost when you switch between samples. If you are following the book, you should make all your changes to the `ijdb` database.

Appendix B: Linux Troubleshooting

As a Linux user, installing the software is incredibly easy but you'll usually need an extra step to connect to the server once it's running. By default Linux will not allow you to connect to the IP address, you will need to run the following commands as root:

```
sudo ip link set vboxnet0 up sudo ip addr add
↪ 192.168.10.1/24 dev vboxnet0
```

Depending on your distribution you may need to manually load VirtualBox's kernel modules. If later you see a warning about VirtualBox's Kernel modules, run the following commands:

```
sudo modprobe vboxdrv sudo modprobe vboxnetadp sudo modprobe
↪ vboxnetflt
```

This will need to be run each time you reboot your computer. To make the changes permanent refer to your distribution's manual regarding kernel modules.